BETWEEN LANGUAGE AND SILENCE

BETWEEN
LANGUAGE
AND
SILENCE

THE NOVELS OF
VIRGINIA WOOLF

HOWARD HARPER

**LOUISIANA
STATE UNIVERSITY PRESS**
BATON ROUGE & LONDON

Designer: Rod Parker
Typeface: Galliard
Typesetter: Graphic Composition
Printer and binder: Thomson-Shore

Library of Congress Cataloging in Publication Data

Harper, Howard M.
   Between language and silence.

   Bibliography: p.
   1. Woolf, Virginia, 1882–1941—Technique.
I. Title.
PR6045.072Z69   823'.912   81–20779
ISBN 0–8071–0996–7   AACR2
ISBN 0–8071–1012–4 (pbk.)

Excerpts from *The Voyage Out, Night and Day, Jacob's Room, Mrs. Dalloway, To the Lighthouse, The Waves, The Years, Between the Acts,* and *Orlando* by Virginia Woolf are reprinted by permission of Harcourt Brace Jovanovich, Inc.; copyright 1920 by George H. Doran and Company; copyright 1922, 1925, 1927, 1931, 1937, 1941 by Harcourt Brace Jovanovich, Inc.; copyright 1928 by Virginia Woolf; copyright 1948, 1950, 1953, 1955, 1956, 1959, 1965, 1969 by Leonard Woolf.

For world rights, outside the United States and its dependencies, acknowledgment is made to the original publisher, The Hogarth Press Ltd., and to the literary estate of Virginia Woolf.

for Jeanne

Where the story-teller is loyal, eternally and unswervingly loyal to the story, there, in the end, silence will speak. Where the story has been betrayed, silence is but emptiness. But we, the faithful, when we have spoken our last word, will hear the voice of silence.

Isak Dinesen
"The Blank Page"
Last Tales

Isa let her sewing drop. The great hooded chairs had become enormous. And Giles too. And Isa too against the window. The window was all sky without colour. The house had lost its shelter. It was the night before roads were made, or houses. It was the night that dwellers in caves had watched from some high place among rocks.

Then the curtain rose. They spoke.

Virginia Woolf
the last words of the last novel,
Between the Acts

CONTENTS

ACKNOWLEDGMENTS

In later chapters I try to acknowledge in footnotes the most specific influences on my approach to the novels of Virginia Woolf. There are other influences, however, which I wish to acknowledge here.

I owe special thanks to two of my colleagues at Chapel Hill. My thinking about the incarnation of the narrative consciousness owes a great deal to "The Incarnation in *Ulysses*" by H. K. Russell, whose example as a teacher has also been so important to so many of us. Especially in its later phases, the book is indebted to the interest, generosity, and literary sensitivity of Louis D. Rubin, Jr.

I have also learned a great deal from my students in the years that I have been "teaching" Virginia Woolf. Those whose work has helped me most are Ann Moss, Marianne Jordan, Debbie Kirkman, Jill Cloonan, Ron Campbell, Cynthia Bullock, Sherron George, Tom O'Neal, Eric Walker, and especially Rebecca Bullock, Karin Gleiter, and Deborah Swain.

I am grateful to the University of North Carolina at Chapel Hill for a Pogue Leave which gave me a term off to write this book. And I especially wish to thank Joyce Bradshaw for typing the manuscript.

BETWEEN LANGUAGE AND SILENCE

INTRODUCTION

Each of the novels of Virginia Woolf can be seen as the "trace" of a dynamic process which creates and explores a "world." Through those explorations the creative imagination tries to discover and disclose the essence of that world, and to test various adaptations to it. These possibilities are tested against the narrative's intuitions of the way things have to be—the laws which govern its created world. In this process the dreaming *anima* continually offers its reveries to the critical judgment of the rational *animus*,[1] and the creative consciousness struggles toward a fuller, more authentic, more satisfying expression of its inner reality. "Style," in the largest sense, is both the medium and the means, the dimension and the force, of that creation.[2]

In that realm of style the narrative consciousness can bring into being something that has never existed before—and thus can experience the joy of discovery. The author's premeditated plans provide a pretext for such discoveries, and may guide them toward deeper levels of creativity, but should not be confused with the discoveries themselves. Although the journals, notebooks, and letters of Virginia

1 My terminology here is that of Gaston Bachelard, *The Poetics of Reverie*, trans. Daniel Russell (Boston: Beacon Press, 1971). Bachelard's theory, as he acknowledges, elaborates the insights of Jung.
2 This is the thesis of Mark Schorer's landmark essay, "Technique as Discovery," *Hudson Review*, I (1948), 67–87, which has been reprinted in many other places.

Woolf provide interesting comments on many of the technical problems and emotional states that she was conscious of during her writing, they rationalize, rather than describe, the creative experience. The primary record of that experience is the text itself.

The "narrative consciousness" discovers and discloses the created world. Like the "implied author" that Wayne C. Booth finds in every novel,[3] this term refers not to the author's "real" personality, but to the particular persona, or aspect of that personality, that creates this particular work of art. Indeed, this persona may express qualities—such as power and control, for example—which cannot find expression in the "real" personality. And the term "narrative consciousness" also acknowledges the dynamic involvement of the creative imagination in its story. In bringing the work of art to realization, the creative consciousness realizes its own potentialities. The evolution of this consciousness, then, within each book and throughout the *oeuvre*, is what Virginia Woolf's fiction is ultimately "about." That is the real story that the novels tell. In these nine books the narrative consciousness is all that we can really know—and all we need to know.

At the heart of all style, as Yeats has said, is "a continuous indefinable symbolism" through which the creative imagination moves beyond the limits of the known, to explore, and evoke, the "unseen," the unknown. To read the fiction of Virginia Woolf is to become involved in this continual process of discovery and naming, and to experience the evolution of a language. Because the lifework is an organic whole, each stage in the development of its symbolic language is related to every other stage. Each novel is related to every other novel, and, between the moment of origin and the moment of closure of the lifework, each moment arises from every one that has gone before, and leads to every one that follows.

The point of origin is the opening of *The Voyage Out*. This first novel is the archetype for the others, the "first articulation" of mythic themes which the later works will continue to develop. It represents a voyage out of the limitations of the given world in which the creative consciousness feels trapped. Primal images, themes, situations,

3 Wayne C. Booth, *The Rhetoric of Fiction* (Chicago: University of Chicago Press, 1961).

and configurations of characters appear here for the first time, as the narrative searches for the most appropriate forms for its feelings. Here, as in all the books, the opening and closing sequences are especially important because they represent the moments of origin and of culmination for the creative consciousness. And the search for the most appropriate forms and style leads to a pattern of dialectical perspectives in which the narrative expresses its shifting feelings.

The search for meaning is a search in consciousness—or in "awareness," since the creative imagination may be aware of something without being entirely conscious of it. As phenomenology insists, consciousness is inescapably perspectival. It can only be *consciousness of* something, and that implies a perspective, a state of being *intent upon* something, or "intentionality."[4] And as Merleau-Ponty has said, "Perspective is much more than a secret technique for imitating a reality given as such to all men. It is the very realization and invention of a world."[5]

In this process of realizing its world, the narrative consciousness searches for meaning, order, stability. This is also a search for perspective. In traditional novels the "plot" operates within the limits set by convention, but in the plot of intentionality the narrative seeks to transcend conventional limits. The conflicts in the plot of intentionality are always on the frontiers of awareness, language, and style, where the creative imagination struggles with the ineffable. Meaning is not something inherent, or at least self-evident, in the given world; rather, it is something to be discovered, achieved, wrested from the struggle with the protean, phenomenal world. The discovery of transcendent meaning becomes the great mythic theme of this drama of intentionality.

Each of the novels of Virginia Woolf enacts this same dramatic theme. In each book—except *Orlando*, where the drama is more veiled—the pattern is the same. The narrative consciousness moves

4 Following Husserl, *intentionality* is the term which philosophers of phenomenology use to describe the dynamic perspectival quality of consciousness: the fact that it must always be *consciousness of*. The term was first used by Brentano.

5 Maurice Merleau-Ponty, *The Prose of the World*, ed. Claude Lefort, trans. John O'Neill (Evanston: Northwestern University Press, 1973), 53. Schorer said essentially the same thing in "Technique as Discovery."

from feelings of anxiety and entrapment at the beginning to a transcendent moment of freedom and "vision" at the end. The opening situations involve roles, conflicts, and imperatives which are essentially sexual, and which become more subtle, complicated, and generalized as the lifework develops. The final "vision" becomes more and more specifically the vision of the creative artist. And each ending is reflexive, in the sense that it shifts everything that has gone before into a new perspective.

Each of these final perspectives is more comprehensive than the one before: each must encompass a larger field of meaning. And so the lifework moves from the lyric cry of *The Voyage Out* through the epic odysseys of *To the Lighthouse*, and *The Waves* to the almost purely dramatic style of *Between the Acts*. This is the classic pattern defined by Stephen Dedalus in *A Portrait of the Artist as a Young Man*—and it describes the trajectory of the lifework of Joyce himself and most major modern novelists. It moves away from the expression of personal anxieties toward an "impersonality," an openness and detachment in which the narrative can allow its story to emerge in its true shape rather than in conformity to some preconceived plan. It is a pattern familiar in modern art—in the Postimpressionist painters in whom Bloomsbury was so interested, in the later attempts of the Surrealists to release the "pure" expression of their libidinal energies. In the fiction of Virginia Woolf this freedom is achieved through the development of a poetic language. There the creative consciousness can explore new fields of meaning without the restrictions imposed by the rules of conventional language and logic: its only law is its own sense of truth.

As structural linguistics has shown, every language "works" through a process of differentiation. This principle may be illustrated most graphically by the language of cinema, which works by making us aware of the differences between successive frames, rather than the similarities between them. In the dramatization of intentionality in the novel, too, the transitions between "frames" at every structural level evoke the complex meanings of the book. In Beckett's early essay on Proust, he calls such moments "periods of transitions that separate consecutive adaptations"; they "represent the perilous zones in the life of the individual, dangerous, precarious, mysterious and fertile, when for a moment the boredom of living is replaced by the suffering of being."[6] The rhythms of Virginia Woolf's novels reflect a similar movement between the comfortable stasis of successful "adaptation" and the anguish—and excitement—of discovery.

These rhythms are analogous to those of cinematic editing. And there are other ways in which the poetic language and the dramatization of intentionality in these novels can be compared to the language of cinema. The narrative consciousness works like a camera, creating the perspectives which constitute the story. The "camera angles" of the narrative imply certain values and attitudes, as they do in cinema. And various parameters of the narrative style can be seen as analogous to cinematographic "composition" and "tone."

In any medium what makes a story unique is its style, *how* it is told. The novels of Virginia Woolf tend to be less concerned with outward realities than with the phenomenology of perception and expression. Their style at times approaches what has been called, in drama and film, expressionism. And they are cinematic, in the sense in which Luis Buñuel envisioned the cinema: "to express the life of the subconscious, the roots of which penetrate poetry so deeply."

Each of the nine novels represents a further evolution of the same essential search for poetic meaning. The search begins as a voyage out, an effort to escape from the stifling roles decreed by the authority of parents and society. As the search continues, however, the need for escape is overshadowed by more positive motives. By the midpoint of its voyage, the narrative consciousness looks toward a center of transcendent meaning which, though it remains ineffable, nevertheless can be recognized and affirmed. The growth in awareness continues, despite some losses, until the very end. At last, transcendent meaning is discovered in the silence between the acts of the personal and social dramas, and, above all, in the mysterious power of consciousness to conceive such a drama.

6   Samuel Beckett, *Proust* (New York: Grove Press, 1958), 8.

CHAPTER I

THE VOYAGE OUT

In his monumental study of the evolution of myth, Claude Lévi-Strauss found that "in the case of any language, the first articulation is immovable, except within very narrow limits."[1] And within the whole mythic structure, he says, this "first level consists of real but unconscious relations which . . . are able to function without being known or correctly interpreted." Some similar intuition, perhaps, leads most readers of Virginia Woolf into her first novel. If her fiction as a whole constitutes the evolution of a mythic world, then *The Voyage Out* is its Book of Genesis, the first articulation of a language whose later forms are more familiar but also more irregular and complex.

Although readings of the later novels can help to clarify this first one, they can also overclarify it, to the extent that its own immediacy, subtleties, complexities, and contradictions can seem to disappear, and what is left is not the work itself, but ideas of it. While *The Voyage Out* is "immovable" within the lifework as a whole, it also has its own authentic "first level" where the creative consciousness struggles to discover the meanings inherent in its own vision. That struggle takes place in a dynamic present in which, whatever the extent to which its

1 Claude Lévi-Strauss, *The Raw and the Cooked: Introduction to a Science of Mythology*, trans. John and Doreen Weightman (New York: Harper, 1969), I, 24.

6

world may later become "known," the creative vision is shaped by its own immediate imperatives. The arena for that struggle, of course, is style, or technique.

While *The Voyage Out* is traditional and conventional in many ways, those are not its most significant aspects. Rather, they provide a horizon against which new forms can emerge, and some stability for the narrative consciousness as it begins the struggle to constitute itself and its world. This is not a sophisticated, authoritative awareness like the one in command of, say, a late Henry James novel, but an unstable, uncertain consciousness searching for its own identity and authenticity. *The Voyage Out* becomes the drama of that search. And it explores the possibilities of one environment, one philosophy, one character, one relationship after another, in search of fulfillment.

As the "first articulation" of a mythic language, *The Voyage Out* is "immovable" in the final context of the lifework. Within the book itself the opening passage is immovable: the still point from which all explorations and transformations must emanate, the world before the creative consciousness says "Let there be light." A close look at the first five paragraphs can reveal the essence of this "given" world:

As the streets that lead from the Strand to the Embankment are very narrow, it is better not to walk down them arm-in-arm. If you persist, lawyers' clerks will have to make flying leaps into the mud; young lady typists will have to fidget behind you. In the streets of London where beauty goes unregarded, eccentricity must pay the penalty, and it is better not to be very tall, to wear a long blue cloak, or to beat the air with your left hand.

One afternoon in the beginning of October when the traffic was becoming brisk a tall man strode along the edge of the pavement with a lady on his arm. Angry glances struck upon their backs. The small, agitated figures—for in comparison with this couple most people looked small—decorated with fountain pens, and burdened with despatch-boxes, had appointments to keep, and drew a weekly salary, so that there was some reason for the unfriendly stare which was bestowed upon Mr. Ambrose's height and upon Mrs. Ambrose's cloak. But some enchantment had put both man and woman beyond the reach of malice and unpopularity. In his case one might guess from the moving lips that it was thought; and in hers from the eyes fixed stonily straight in front of her at a level above the eyes of most that it was sorrow. It was only by scorning all she met that she kept herself from tears, and the friction of people brushing past her was evidently painful. After watching the traffic on the Embankment for a minute or two with a stoical gaze she twitched her husband's sleeve, and they crossed between the swift discharge of motor cars. When they were safe on the further side, she gently withdrew her arm from his, allowing her mouth at the same time to relax, to tremble; then tears rolled down, and, leaning her elbows on the balustrade, she shielded her face from the curious. Mr. Ambrose attempted consolation; he patted her shoulder; but she showed no signs of admitting him, and feeling it awkward to stand beside a grief that was greater than his, he crossed his arms behind him, and took a turn along the pavement.

The embankment juts out in angles here and there, like pulpits; instead of preachers, however, small boys occupy them, dangling string, dropping pebbles, or launching wads of paper for a cruise. With their sharp eye for eccentricity, they were inclined to think Mr. Ambrose awful; but the quickest witted cried "Bluebeard!" as he passed. In case they should proceed to tease his wife, Mr. Ambrose flourished his stick at them, upon which they decided that he was grotesque merely, and four instead of one cried "Bluebeard!" in chorus.

Although Mrs. Ambrose stood quite still, much longer than is natural, the little boys let her be. Some one is always looking into the river near Waterloo Bridge; a couple will stand there talking for half an hour on a fine afternoon; most people, walking for pleasure, contemplate for three minutes; when, having compared the occasion with other occasions, or made some sentence, they pass on. Sometimes the flats and churches and hotels of Westminster are like the outlines of Constantinople in a mist; sometimes the river is an opulent purple, sometimes mud-coloured, sometimes sparkling blue like the sea. It is always worth while to look down and see what is happening. But this lady looked neither up nor down; the only thing she had seen, since she stood there, was a circular iridescent patch slowly floating past with a straw in the middle of it. The straw and the patch swam again and again behind the tremulous medium of a great welling tear, and the tear rose and fell and dropped into the river. Then there struck upon her ears—

> Lars Porsena of Clusium
> By the nine Gods he swore—

and then more faintly, as if the speaker had passed her on his walk—

> That the Great House of Tarquin
> Should suffer wrong no more.

Yes, she knew she must go back to all that, but at present she must weep. Screening her face she sobbed more steadily than she had yet done, her shoulders rising and falling with great regularity. It was this figure that her husband saw when, having reached the polished Sphinx, having entangled himself with a man selling picture postcards, he turned; the stanza instantly stopped. He came up to her, laid his hand on her shoulder, and said, "Dearest." His voice was supplicating. But she shut her face away from him, as much as to say, "You can't possibly understand."

As he did not leave her, however, she had to wipe her eyes, and to raise them to the level of the factory chimneys on the other bank. She saw also the arches of Waterloo Bridge and the carts moving across them, like the line of animals in a shooting gallery. They were seen blankly, but to see anything was of course to end her weeping and begin to walk.[2]

At first glance this given world seems familiar enough. Nominally (at the level of explicit narrative) it seems to reflect a "real" setting: Westminster, near Waterloo Bridge, on an October afternoon in, perhaps, 1906. But the passage is not "realistic" in emphasis or style. And while it has affinities with the "novel of manners" (the class consciousness, the posture of sophisticated detachment, the rather authoritative tone of the commentary), its social concern seems secondary.

Experientially, in its existential dynamics, the narrative is much less stable: it becomes increasingly subjective, uncertain, and even paranoid. The setting feels confining and threatening: the streets are "narrow," the people "have to" act in certain ways, touch seems almost forbidden, and it is "better not to" do anything which could call attention to oneself. Otherwise, "eccentricity must pay the penalty." The fact that the "penalty" is unspecified makes it even more forbidding, and reinforces the feeling that suffering and punishment are arbitrary, inflicted for nothing more serious than "eccentricity." And because of

2   The text I refer to here is the first edition of *The Voyage Out* (London: Duckworth, 1915), which was later revised by Virginia Woolf for the first American edition (New York: Doran, 1920). Each version has its own special authority, and the problem of choosing between them is like that of choosing between the first edition and the later "New York" edition of an early novel by Henry James. The American edition of *The Voyage Out* is a more polished text which represents its author's final wishes and most complete revisions. But since I am especially interested in the book as the point of origin for the whole lifework, the earlier version, completed in 1913, seems preferable. Later English editions derive from it, later American editions from Doran. In the passages I discuss there are no significant differences between the two editions.

Because of differences in pagination among various editions, I try to cite chapter numbers when that would help the reader to find the passage I am discussing.

the narrative perspective, "beauty" and "eccentricity" become implicitly identified with the narrative consciousness rather than with the stereotypes ("lawyers' clerks," "young lady typists") of the crowd. Later this implicit identification extends to the Ambroses and, by implication, with "you," the reader.

Thus in the vein of the "familiar essay" the narrative invites us to smile at a familiar and amusing scene. But this posture soon gives way to a deeper emotional involvement, expressed in the "angry glances" which "struck" the Ambroses "upon their backs," the "small, agitated figures" of the people in the crowds, the "unfriendly stare," the "malice," the "eyes fixed stonily," the "sorrow," the "scorning," the "friction" that "was evidently painful," and so on. Mr. Ambrose, who will later emerge as the archetypal father, is now recognized as Bluebeard, who secretly kills his wives when they trespass into the room that he has forbidden them. It is all too much, too melodramatic. For although most of this suffering and paranoia is *attributed* by the narrative to Mrs. Ambrose, it is really *experienced* in the larger field of intentionality where the constituting consciousness struggles to find objective correlatives for its own feelings. The truth of the passage, therefore, emerges more from its perspectives and feelings than from its more conscious commentary.

These feelings and perspectives can find expression only in specific people and places. Each character materializes for the first time in a symbolically appropriate setting—almost as if the setting itself brings the character into existence. And this opening scene in the streets of Westminster represents an "immovable" pattern of social activity and personal anxiety which will be repeated in *The Voyage Out*—and in later books too. Westminster is seen from the outside here, and that perspective remains essentially immovable—even in *Mrs. Dalloway* with Clarissa, the major character in the *oeuvre* who is most at home in the social and political force-fields of "Westminster." The Ambroses, of course, are seen largely in contrast to these forces. In but not of Westminster, they must somehow make their way *through* it, and the narrative emphasizes the friction and discomfort of their passage.

The Ambroses set an "immovable" archetypal pattern which will be most fully realized in the Ramsays of *To the Lighthouse*: the father and mother who inhabit a strange world of their own, whose contacts with society appear ambiguous, uncomfortable, embarrassing, and motivated largely by a sense of duty. As they first appear here, the narrative becomes aware of them as a very small child might: it sees the father's height and the mother's cloak, and it speaks of the "enchantment" which has placed them "beyond the reach of malice and unpopularity." Thus it is immediately aware of the distances between the parents and the crowd, and easily names a motive and a reason for those distances. But the man and the woman themselves remain within the more mysterious realm of "enchantment" whose distances may have no names, and may be even more formidable. The relationship of Rachel to the Ambroses—niece to aunt and uncle—reflects that distance (in *To the Lighthouse* the distance is even more dramatic: Lily is only a guest in the home of the Ramsays).

The distances between the Ambroses themselves seem even more momentous than those between them and the crowd. They walk together, but are strangely separate: his lips are moving, chanting the cadences of heroic verse which later novels too will ridicule; Mrs. Ambrose's eyes are "fixed stonily." After a perfunctory attempt to console her, he strides off because he feels "it awkward to stand beside a grief that was greater than his." This first motive attributed to him also foreshadows many instances throughout the lifework where women are suddenly hurt by the bewildering egocentricity of men. Indeed, much of this opening scene focuses on the strange impersonality of Mr. Ambrose. His wife sees him as an overwhelming fate to which she is condemned to return always: "Yes, she knew she must go back to all that"—the words themselves seem to move with the monosyllabic cadence of doom. Even his first name, with its echoes of "rid" and "riddle," may express vague subliminal feelings of distance and enigma. Symbolically, he emerges at last in his pure element at the beginning of Chapter 13, where we see him in his study, "like an idol in an empty church," with his existential space "deeply encircled by books" so that "his visitors generally stopped and addressed him from the outskirts." Throughout *The Voyage Out* the narrative glimpses of Ridley seem ambiguous: his impersonality and disinterest inspire a complicated mixture of awe and ridicule. Yet whatever the perspective, his shape seems larger and more remote than most of the other forms in this created world. He remains, along with several more impressive successors in the later fiction, an idol in an empty church.

Perhaps even more "immovable" than Ridley is his wife, the feminine fate that seems to launch this voyage out, and to preside over most of it. The experiential reality of the opening scene—the generalized feelings of repression, discomfort, alienation, grief, and foreboding—soon becomes assigned to Helen Ambrose by the narrative. Just after she is compelled "to end her weeping and begin to walk," the narrative attributes her mood to her impending separation from her children and from London, to her pity for the poor, and to the rain. But in the light of the book as a whole, these motives seem little more than rationalizations, and we begin to see Helen as a woman chafing against a destiny which will prohibit her from ever becoming anything more than "Mrs. Ambrose." As the story develops we see her in implicit contrast with the other women—the innocent Rachel, the sophisticated Mrs. Dalloway, the spinster "scholar" Miss Allan, the bovine Susan Warrington and her invalid aunt Mrs. Paley, the irrepressible Mrs. Flushing, the sympathetic Mrs. Thornbury, the troubled Evelyn Murgatroyd. Helen comes closer than any of them (except Mrs. Flushing, perhaps, whose aristocratic accent, force, creativity, and independence seem to fascinate the narrative consciousness) to being a whole person—and she doesn't come close enough. She foresees a similar fate for her niece, and eventually must abandon her to it. At last Helen herself must disappear from the book along with Rachel: though she seems to know everything, she can do nothing—because she is no longer in a position to make the determining choices—and at last therefore she *is* nothing, and must vanish into the same darkness as Rachel.

From the moment that Helen is first perceived, the narrative seems preoccupied with this question of control—especially self-control and the potential loss of it: "It was only by scorning all she met that she kept herself from tears." The narrative follows her across the crowded street, then watches with fascination as "she gently withdrew her arm from his, allowing her mouth at the same time to relax, to tremble; then tears rolled down." It imagines that "the only thing she had seen, since she stood there" on the bridge "was a circular iridescent patch floating past" on the river, and even that pathetically limited perspective is blurred "behind the tremulous medium of a great welling tear, and the tear rose and fell and dropped into the river." River and sea become metaphoric in this novel—and throughout Virginia Woolf's fiction—for the chaos which always threatens and must eventually engulf the individual identity. Symbolically, the river of this opening passage becomes associated with the loss of perspective and control, and with the overwhelming libidinal forces which flow in the heart of darkness. Rachel's immersion in them will be fevered and ultimately fatal.

As the book opens, however, the narrative has not yet resigned itself to that necessity. At the beginning of the fifth paragraph it imagines the reassertion of control: "As he did not leave her, however, she had to wipe her eyes, and to raise them. . . ." Thus the man is seen here as an imperative force which cancels the woman's perspective. Yet the essential fatality of that perspective persists. The carts moving across Waterloo Bridge remind Helen of "the line of animals in a shooting gallery. They were seen blankly, but to see anything was of course to end her weeping and begin to walk." The implication is that in order to be able merely to survive within this environment she must cease to register what she sees: she knows that her existence is like that of the line of animals in the shooting gallery, but she must deny that knowledge in order to move at all. Yet the movement is toward the heart of darkness, with all its latent terror of the nameless.

This emphasis on the necessities and ambiguities of perception makes *The Voyage Out* seem startlingly modern at times, despite its obvious debts to Victorian tradition. It is concerned not merely with painting a series of scenes, but with the nature of the process of perception itself—and especially with what Virginia Woolf would later refer to habitually as "the moment": the instantaneous reality produced by the interrelation of various perspectives within that scene itself. In the first five paragraphs of the book there are more than twenty references to the psychodynamics of perception—either to the act of seeing or—what is even more significant, perhaps—the refusal to see or be seen. The first of these explicitly announces a motif so pervasive that it might almost serve as a subtitle: "beauty goes unregarded." From the very beginning a tension is established between vision and its limitations, a tension that will continue to build throughout the book. The apotheosis of vision is reached at the moment of Rachel's death, when all limitations seem to have been transcended and Terence feels "perfect happiness." But in the closing chapters it is the world of limitations, rather than of transcendence, which remains. The depth of the book comes from its creation of these multiple perspectives which can coexist in creative tension, with an outcome which is implicit in them, but which can be fully known only in retrospect. The final meanings of *The Voyage Out* are latent in its opening pages. But so are other possibilities. Not until we reach the very end do we realize the ways in which it has been "immovable" from the beginning.

In the opening paragraphs of the book, as we have seen, the narrative consciousness creates a world whose most significant features seem to be its limitations. In that world the consciousness feels trapped. Then comes the search for alternatives which could remove or transcend those limitations: the narrative embarks on its voyage out of this imprisonment. In its search the creative consciousness must explore its own natural resources, and the novel becomes the record of that exploration. Although the search must end without definitive answers, its final ambiguities encompass a much larger field of awareness.

This awareness, as phenomenology insists, is inescapably perspectival. The consciousness may constitute its world (create it and endow it with meaning) only through a perspective, and, despite its yearning for universality, it can inhabit only one perspective at a time. Some progress toward universality is possible, however, because each successive perspective becomes part of the larger background for the text. One "plot" of *The Voyage Out*, then, is this very complex flow of perspectives. Sometimes, as we have seen in the opening paragraphs of this novel, the truth revealed by the perspective itself does not coincide with the truth asserted by the narrative commentary. In such instances we should, as D. H. Lawrence warned unsuspecting readers of American literature, "Never trust the artist. Trust the tale."[3] Furthermore, we must recognize that, as in music or cinema, each moment becomes fully meaningful only in relation to all other moments. The flow of perspectives within the novel is analogous to the flow of shots within a movie, and the problems of analysis are similar. How may we deal with the tremendously complex realm in which a novel or film is *experienced* without either reducing that reality to a few ideas of it or losing its wholeness in a welter of details? How may we most accurately describe a perspective? What are the most appropriate components of sequence to consider? and to what extent do we deform them by removing them from their larger—and perhaps "organic"— context?

With *The Voyage Out*, the major structural components which the author herself consciously identifies—the twenty-seven chapters—are convenient for analysis because they are nicely related to both the macrostructure of the book as a whole and the microstructure of its immediate existential presence. In each chapter the dynamics seem essentially the same as for the book as a whole: each chapter explores an area of possibilities—an avenue of perspectives—of the larger creative vision, moving always toward the discovery and disclosure of the meanings inherent in the phenomena of its creation. Each begins with a situation latent with significance, and ends when it reaches a situation which the narrative consciousness cannot go beyond—either some final revelation, or an exhaustion, of meaning. Each emerges against the dynamic background of cumulative meaning, a constantly developing horizon.

To illustrate how the search for perspective operates within a chapter of *The Voyage Out*, let us consider once again the "immovable" chapter—the first. We have already looked at the first five paragraphs of the book as the "first articulation" of a "world"; let us now consider how they initiate the flow of perspectives, and how these perspectives constitute a story of their own. Throughout this chapter

3   D. H. Lawrence, *Studies in Classic American Literature* (New York: Viking, 1964), 2.

and every chapter, the constituting consciousness searches for some final unifying perspective that will still be compatible with its knowledge of the "given" world.

The first perspective to be tested is that of the "familiar essay." The narrative opens by smiling at the busyness and instinctive conformity of the crowds in the streets of Westminster. But in a more subtle way the style also mocks itself, and the first paragraph ends in a rhythmic climax of trivial generalizations. The style has undercut and deflated itself, and another narrative perspective becomes necessary.

In the second paragraph the search for such a perspective begins, and the narrative then envisions "a tall man" and "a lady" moving through the crowd of "small, agitated figures." In this paragraph the "you" of the familiar essay has been abandoned; the nominative becomes the impersonal "one." At first the narrative point of view seems to become more objective too, recording an objective reality much as a movie camera might record it. Yet that camera is subtly perspectival—and therefore subjective: it is "tracking" the couple rather than the crowd; it sees the couple in an "up angle" (as "tall"), and in sharper focus than the crowd. The man and woman retain more of their essential mystery, while the crowd, with its fountain pens and dispatch boxes, remains merely emblematic. Other factors which are less obviously visual also contribute to the perspective. For example, the ease with which the narrative assigns motives to the crowd helps to distance the center of consciousness further from that crowd. So does the shallow suggestion that appointments to keep, or weekly salaries, could be valid reasons for hostility. By the end of the second paragraph of the book the center of consciousness is clearly separated from, and implicitly hostile to, the crowd.

The relationship of that center of consciousness to the man and woman is more complex and ambiguous. Although it says flatly that the crowd is "angry" and "unfriendly," it is not so certain of the attitudes of the couple: "one might guess" that his motive is thought, and hers sorrow. But the next sentence, "It was only by scorning all she met that she kept herself from tears," seems to show that the narrative has access to the woman's thoughts—though the conclusion of the sentence withdraws to the greater distance of "evidently." Throughout the paragraph the position of the narrative consciousness remains rather uncertain; we don't know whether this is an "omniscient" narrative—on the one hand, it does generalize about the motives of the crowd and the Ambroses too, while on the other it merely observes and guesses. The center of consciousness seems somewhat closer to the woman than to the man. She is in sharper focus and more in the foreground. After the couple are named, Mrs. Ambrose is always called "she" or "her"; he is referred to once as "her husband" and once as "Mr. Ambrose," in addition to the more familiar personal pronouns. The final sentence of the paragraph seems at first glance to show that the narrative is "privileged"[4] to enter into Mr. Ambrose's feelings. Yet what it discovers there seems disparaging of him—so much so that it seems more compatible with the earlier flippancy of the "omniscient" narrative or with the later revelations of Mr. Ambrose's egocentricity than with what he might feel about himself.

In the third paragraph the conclusion that Mr. Ambrose is "grotesque merely" and various other judgments might seem to indicate omniscience. But the perspective seems more limited than that. It seems to be located closer to Mrs. Ambrose, seeing essentially what she could see and registering what it sees in a way sympathetic to her. In the next paragraph the identification becomes closer still as we are told what "she had seen." At last, in the response to her husband's chanting of poetry, the narrative point of view and hers become one: "Yes, she knew she must go back to all that, but at present she must weep." The narrative consciousness becomes identical with the consciousness of Helen Ambrose.

In "It was this figure that her husband saw," the perspective seems to shift toward the man once again, but the words "her husband" keep it feminine despite the seeming withdrawal. In the boat from the Embankment to the *Euphrosyne* "Mrs. Ambrose" at last becomes "Helen." But the narrative immediately withdraws once more,

---

4 Wayne C. Booth uses the terms *privilege* and *limitation* to describe the penetration of the narration into the thought processes of the character. See *The Rhetoric of Fiction*, 70–75 and *passim*. As he points out, this problem is extremely complex and his own discussion is only introductory.

becoming impersonal enough to speak of the Ambroses as "they," and even to adopt an omniscient stance in the phrase "In the minds of both the passengers."

From this position of greater detachment—analogous, in cinematographic terms, to "zooming out" to a "master shot" which now shows the larger context in which some more intimate action has taken place—the scene shifts to the saloon of the *Euphrosyne*. The narrative discovers Rachel in a setting which is her existential space—and which is far from being a room of her own. "Down in the saloon of her father's ship": the first words describing Rachel and her "room" define—aside from their not entirely inappropriate resonances with temperance melodrama—the direction and limitations of her life. She is, the narrative says, "unnaturally braced to receive" the intrusion of the Ambroses. Such symbolic intrusions into the existential "room" of a character become important in the action of *The Voyage Out;* in the first chapter the most conspicuous example is the later exclusion of Helen and Rachel from this same dining room, and their discovery of a meager space, "cold" and grotesquely furnished, which seems to Rachel "more like a landing than a room." As the narrative first discovers Rachel, her existential space is limited: she is trapped in an existence defined by her father and wholly subordinated to his. And even that pathetic identity is violated as her voyage out begins.

As the narrative brings Rachel into existence, its penetration into her consciousness is immediate and assured—unlike the hesitant groping toward the consciousness of Helen. As the book develops, we become aware that some characters are instantly accessible to the narrative consciousness, and some others never are; these patterns, too, help to constitute the experiential reality of the book, quite apart from—and sometimes contradictory to—the explicit commentary. Ridley, for example, remains inaccessible despite the contempt expressed in various ways for his pedantry; the conscious contempt is undercut by unconscious awe. Rachel is accessible at once because she is innocent—and because she is "given": of all the characters, the one who represents most directly the "present moment" of the creative consciousness.

Entering Rachel's consciousness immediately, the narrative then watches Helen enter that room. Seen from the perspective of her niece she is "romantic and beautiful." But just as it discovers that Helen's "voice was low and seductive," the narrative perspective must shift again. It is almost as if the narrative discovers in that low and seductive voice something that it would rather not listen to, and so it returns to the more stable and assured perspective embodied in Helen herself. It remains there—or at least close to Helen's perspective— through the end of the chapter, except for a momentary glimpse into Rachel's feelings about William Pepper, and a few other moments of slight discontinuity. In general the narrative consciousness, though often unmistakably located within Helen herself, seems to be more generalized, and comfortable, within either Helen or Rachel, or close to them, but distinctly excluded—and aware of its exclusion—from the various male characters throughout this first chapter. Despite the frequent use of "objective" techniques—such as impersonality and the straightforward "recording" of dialogue—the cumulative effect is toward total identification with the feminine point of view.

This sense of exclusion is felt most powerfully in the first chapter when Helen and Rachel, uncomfortable and neglected in the rising tide of reminiscences about Cambridge, walk out on deck in the cold wind, which "became rough and chilly. They looked through a chink in the blind and saw that long cigars were being smoked in the dining-room. . . . The ghost of a roar of laughter came out to them, and was drowned at once in the wind. In the dry yellow-lighted room Mr. Pepper and Mr. Ambrose were oblivious of all tumult; they were in Cambridge, and it was probably about the year 1875." Throughout Virginia Woolf's fiction Cambridge is seen as a transfiguring experience—as indeed it was for her own brother Thoby, her husband Leonard, her good friend E. M. Forster (whose *The Longest Journey* is a hymn to Cambridge), and all the "Apostles." In *Jacob's Room* all the mysteries of that experience become simply, and eloquently, "the light of Cambridge." But what is felt here in *The Voyage Out*—and later, much more explicitly in *A Room of One's Own*—is the chill and darkness of exclusion from Cambridge and everything that "she" confers upon "her sons." While Ambrose and Pepper bask in the warmth of that world (now "dry," with its gold muted to "yellow"), Rachel has her own "words rammed down her throat" in the wind, and Helen is "overcome" by her own skirts. Trapped in their roles as women, they can only spy upon the male world (as they do later, and even more strikingly, in Santa Marina) and strain to overhear its laughter. Its language, lost in the wind, can never be theirs.

Excluded even from these dry memories of Cambridge, the two women find their temporary "landing" which "had nothing of the shut stationary character of a room on shore" and whose rather bizarre decoration is described at some length. This sanctuary, of course, is only temporary, and soon invaded by the males, whose complex games and rituals begin again. Oriented as they are toward the achievement or display of power, these complexities seem both threatening and incomprehensible to the women. Helen, like her descendant Mrs. Ramsay in *To the Lighthouse*, has been cast by fate in the exhausting role of peacemaker, whose cue to perform is the awkward silence. In that role this evening she is neither very interested nor very successful, and the chapter culminates in a contretemps between Rachel and her father on the subject of goats,[5] followed by a long disquisition (mercifully summarized by the narrative) by Pepper on how creatures from the bottom of the sea "would explode if you brought them to the surface, their sides bursting asunder and scattering entrails to the winds when released from pressure, with considerable detail and with such show of knowledge, that Ridley was dis-

---

[5] "Rachel was heard to sigh, 'poor little goats!' 'If it weren't for the goats there'd be no music, my dear; music depends upon goats,' said her father rather sharply." This scene may have some private autobiographical meaning. Quentin Bell, *Virginia Woolf* (New York: Harcourt, 1972), I, 24, relates it to an anecdote to illustrate how Virginia may have earned her nickname of "The Goat": responding to a sudden call of nature in Kensington Gardens, she loudly sang "The Last Rose of Summer" to mask other sounds she was making in the bushes. Willoughby's comment in *The Voyage Out* refers to other goat-music, presumably, but that too seems to have ironic overtones: probably he takes the legend of Pan literally, and certainly very seriously.

With her closest friends, Virginia flaunted her identity as "The Goat." *The Voyage Out*, unlike the later novels, was shared with those friends to some extent before its publication, and seems to contain a number of private jokes. For example, *Euphrosyne* echoes the title of a book of poems privately published in 1905 by some of her male friends. Its verses reflect the rather mannered despair they learned at Cambridge. Their posture of disillusioned silence may be satirized in Hewet's plans for the novel of Silence.

gusted, and begged him to stop." The rather vivid imagery of exploding deep sea creatures has subliminal connections with Rachel herself, who early in the second chapter finds herself suddenly looking into the depths of the sea after seeing her aunt and uncle kiss—and who will, in the hallucinations of her final illness, be lost at sea herself. But here, at the end of the first chapter, the narrative consciousness remains located in Helen:

From all this Helen drew her own conclusions, which were gloomy enough. Pepper was a bore; Rachel was an unlicked girl, no doubt prolific of confidences, the very first of which would be: "You see, I don't get on with my father." Willoughby, as usual, loved his business and built his Empire, and between them all she would be considerably bored. Being a woman of action, however, she rose, and said that for her part she was going to bed. At the door she glanced back instinctively at Rachel, expecting that as two of the same sex they would leave the room together. Rachel rose, looked vaguely into Helen's face and remarked with her slight stammer, "I'm going out to t-t-triumph in the wind."

Mrs. Ambrose's worst suspicions were confirmed; she went down the passage lurching from side to side, and fending off the wall now with her right arm, now with her left; at each lurch she exclaimed emphatically, "Damn!"

What gives this moment its finality? What makes it the end of this avenue of exploration? In a way it represents a return to the paranoia with which the chapter began; Rachel's naïve remark abut goats has produced its inevitable hostile response, the penalty that must be paid by eccentricity. But now the despair is somewhat more specific, and therefore more convincing. Helen's "conclusions" are "gloomy": Pepper, Rachel, Willoughby—all seem to her predictable and boring. The passageway in which she "lurches" and swears, fending off the walls which close in upon her, has become her own way of life—and the dark passage that she now begins to envision for Rachel too. Later Helen becomes explicitly identified as a Fate. Here, however, she simply knows that no woman—and especially one like Rachel—can "t-t-triumph in the wind." And how could Helen tell her what she needs to know? What is at the end of her passage is so unspeakable that it can manifest itself, even to the supposedly omniscient narrative consciousness, only much later (near the end of the fifth chapter) and in the form of a dream—Rachel's nightmare, in which she dreams of walking down a long, narrowing tunnel which at last opens into a "vault" inhabited by a "deformed man." Whose "room" is that?

Thus the first chapter of the exploration of the "world" of *The Voyage Out* ends in the finality of the realization—nominally by Helen Ambrose, but more significantly by the narrative consciousness itself—of the narrowing possibilities of feminine destiny. In the fullness of this realization "Helen" becomes "Mrs. Ambrose" once again. The next chapter will begin its own voyage out of this realization.

The opening perspective of the second chapter is radically different in several ways from the closing perspective of the first chapter: the transition from night to the "soft blue sky" of day, from the ship's rolling (and Helen's "lurching") to calm seas, from the unfamiliar to the known, from uncomfortable apprehension to eager expectancy. All of this seems to suggest that the final perspective of the first chapter need not be final for the story as a whole. Indeed, the narrative consciousness finds the new perspective so attractive that it explicitly wishes "that in future years the entire journey perhaps would be represented by this one scene."

Of course this is a futile hope. The narrative cannot continue in this idyllic mood, but must discover Helen's contempt for her brother-in-law, and must then evoke Mr. Pepper's feelings about women. Breakfast ends in an impasse—so uncomfortable that as everyone walks out on deck the narrative perspective emphasizes a sudden new sense of spaciousness, freedom, freshness, clarity, briskness, exhilaration. The perspective then becomes incarnate in Rachel's awareness as she watches her aunt and uncle:

. . . as they moved off it could be seen from the way in which her sloping cheek turned up to his that she had something private to communicate. They went a few paces and Rachel saw them kiss.

Down she looked into the depth of the sea. While it was slightly disturbed on the surface by the passage of the *Euphrosyne*, beneath it was green and dim, and it grew dimmer and dimmer until the sand at the bottom was only a pale blur. One could scarcely see the black ribs of wrecked ships, or the spiral towers made by the burrowings of great eels, or the smooth green-sided monsters who came by flickering this way and that.

This sudden shift in perspective illustrates an important principle which operates throughout the book—and indeed, throughout the lifework. The explanation for the shift in perspective here must remain in the realm of silence: the discovery that "Rachel saw them kiss" must end one paragraph, and "Down she looked into the depths of the sea" must begin a new one. In this passage each paragraph seems analogous to a cinematic "shot": a continuous perception from a single point of view. A new point of view requires a new paragraph. The narrative consciousness constitutes its story by choosing these points of view. It might, after all, have said specifically why Rachel's field of view must suddenly shift from the kiss to the depths of the sea—but that explanation would then constitute something else, another story, a different reality with its own realm of silence. Thus the limits—and the essence—of the narrative are revealed by the intentionality of the constituting consciousness, and there must always be a reality beyond its reach. Here at the limits of its knowledge where all of its real discoveries must be made, it must choose, in accordance with a kind of literary Uncertainty Principle, which of the basic constituting dimensions to explore—since to describe one is to disturb the others.

To some extent the audience of the work of art can choose a different perspective, with a still different realm of uncertainty and silence. The reader of *The Voyage Out* may become aware that what Rachel sees in the depths exists not in an objective English Channel, but in a strange sexual underworld of the narrative consciousness itself. To that consciousness, as well as to Rachel herself, the ultimate meanings of the images inspired by that kiss can be approached only indirectly. In that realm, more than in what can be expressed explicitly, the questing consciousness discovers the significance of its vision. As the search continues at these frontiers created by what Keats called the "negative capability" of the poet, the silence itself begins to acquire shape and meaning. It exists, of course, at every level of the narrative structure, from the ambiance of the moment in which each word appears, to the largest components of the finished work as a whole. At each of these levels, the silence is loudest in the transitions from one structural entity to the next.

The realm of silence in the art of narrative is like the realm of darkness in cinema. This darkness not only surrounds the picture, but actually interpenetrates it and makes its very existence possible: each new frame can come into existence only after an instant of darkness which the viewer's mind bridges through the perceptual process of "persistence of vision." What we actually become aware of, from one frame to the next, are discontinuities—ways in which each frame differs from the preceding one. But we are more *conscious* of the continuities—what the frames have in common. These transitions exist at every level of the film, from the microstructure of the frames themselves to transitions between shots, scenes, sequences, and so on. Whatever the level, the transitions may vary widely—from "natural" ones which we are scarcely aware of to "hard cuts" which emphasize discontinuity. In the art of narrative, too, there must be transitions at every level, from the microstructure of the individual words to the macrostructure of "parts" and "books." At every structural level, the silence and the darkness increase along with the discontinuity. The novel which would be most meaningful is the one which Terence Hewet wishes to write: the novel of Silence.

The creative consciousness may utilize various techniques to bridge the silence, and certain methods tend to become habitual. The more habitual, the more they mask the threatening darkness and silence of the discontinuities. Throughout the opening of *The Voyage Out* the habitual means for bridging the silence seems to be the passage of time. As the story develops, however, a pattern of transitions through character seems to become predominant; paragraphs and even chapters are linked through relative pronouns. It is almost as if the developing love story enables the narrative consciousness to transcend its sense of temporality—until Rachel's death reveals that love too has been temporary.

The first striking discontinuity between chapters of *The Voyage Out* occurs between Chapters 5 and 6. The words which lead into it are those which describe Rachel's nightmare and its aftermath:

24

She dreamt that she was walking down a long tunnel, which grew so narrow by degrees that she could touch the damp bricks on either side. At length the tunnel opened and became a vault; she found herself trapped in it, bricks meeting her wherever she turned, alone with a little deformed man who squatted on the floor gibbering, with long nails. His face was pitted and like the face of an animal. The wall behind him oozed with damp, which collected into drops and slid down. Still and cold as death she lay, not daring to move, until she broke the agony by tossing herself across the bed, and woke crying "Oh!"

Light showed her the familiar things: her clothes, fallen off the chair; the water jug gleaming white; but the horror did not go at once. She felt herself pursued, so that she got up and actually locked her door. A voice moaned for her; eyes desired her. All night long barbarian men harassed the ship; they came scuffling down the passages, and stopped to snuffle at her door. She could not sleep again.

The image of the narrowing corridor here was foreshadowed at the end of Chapter 1, where it represented the constricting possibilities of Rachel's destiny as a woman. It will recur in the climactic hallucinations of her final illness, when she imagines herself "walking through a tunnel under the Thames, where there were little deformed women sitting in archways, playing cards, while the bricks of which the wall was made oozed with damp, which collected into drops and slid down the wall." The "little deformed man" in the nightmare is almost certainly evoked by Richard Dalloway, whose passionate kiss earlier that afternoon had sent "black waves across her eyes," and who had been very much in her mind as she fell asleep. The transformation of this figure into the "little deformed women" of Rachel's final illness is more mysterious. But the women playing cards seem to represent an ominous multiplication of Nurse McInnis, who is playing solitaire as she sits up with Rachel, and who has seemed "inexplicably sinister" to Rachel's fevered imagination. Rachel had seen her only once before— in the chapel, where the nurse's apparent "demure belief in her own virtue and the virtues of her religion" caused her face to become "printed on Rachel's mind with an impression of keen horror." The nurse seems to represent for Rachel the horror of unquestioning, smug acceptance—and perhaps that is why the nurse and her kind must inhabit the oozing tunnel of the deformed man. That "immovable" figure reappears most memorably in *The Years*, as the leering man with the pockmarked face who exposes himself to little Rose. The brick vault of the *Antigone* theme in that novel also links it subliminally with this traumatic nightmare of *The Voyage Out*. The oozing dampness of the tunnel seems to link Rachel's sexual fears with apprehensions of drowning—suggested by the black waves which overwhelm her after Richard's kiss, and made climactically explicit during her final illness, which she experiences as a drowning. Such an experience is imagined both as terrifying and as a consummation devoutly to be wished; it is near the heart of all the novels—and is the fulfillment which Virginia Woolf herself sought at last.

What gives the nightmare its depth in *The Voyage Out* is not so much its imagery as its aftermath: it dominates Rachel's waking life—not just her consciousness, but her very perceptions. She hears and sees "barbarian men" who lust after her like animals. She is naked, exposed, spied upon: "eyes desired her." Even when she sees "the familiar things" (first, significantly, her clothes), "the horror" of her heart of darkness cannot be dispelled. The men are out there "scuffling down the passages" toward her, and time and time again they "stopped to snuffle at her door." The imagery of her waking imagination overwhelms the images of the nightmare itself. Until Richard's kiss, Rachel's ordeal of initiation had often been awkward or embarrassing. But now the narrative discovers that the ordeal may be more than Rachel can cope with.

Out of that realization—and the silence which engulfs it—Chapter 6 must open:

"That's the tragedy of life—as I always say!" said Mrs. Dalloway. "Beginning things and having to end them. Still, I'm not going to let *this* end, if you're willing." It was the morning, the sea was calm, and the ship once again was anchored not far from another shore.

She was dressed in her long fur cloak, with the veils wound round her head, and once more the rich boxes stood on top of each other so that the scene of a few days back seemed to be repeated.

Mrs. Dalloway's words add ironic implications to the previous scene, and emphasize the vast distances between her world of social convention, in which she seems so dominant and comfortable, and Rachel's long night of anguish. The difficulty of bridging these two worlds is also reflected in the style itself. Chapters 2 through 5 had opened with sentences which strengthened the continuity of the narrative—in 2, 3, and 4 by advancing the time to "next morning," and in 5 by the relative pronoun "she." In 6, however, this transitional sentence is delayed until the end of the opening paragraph. This postponement of continuity serves, as in music or poetry, to emphasize the greater discontinuity—the silence—of this transition.

In the first chapter, after several rather hesitant movements toward the minds of the male characters, the narrative consciousness becomes identified with a perspective which is distant from, and even hostile toward, the male. But it is not satisfied to remain there. It begins to intrude into the minds of several male characters: first, rather easily, into William Pepper, of whom it has been contemptuous from the beginning; then, two chapters later, into Richard Dalloway, to whom it condescends because he is a smug politician; then, two chapters farther on, into Ridley Ambrose. The intrusion into Ridley, however, is probably illusory, since he is said to be thinking about "the unkindness of women"—which seems closer to the narrative's view of him than to an authentic thought of his own. Not until the tenth chapter does the narrative enter fully and seriously into a male consciousness.

It first discovers Terence Hewet near the end of Chapter 8. The dynamics of the perspective are, of course, significant. Helen and Rachel are "'Seeing life' . . . the phrase they used for their habit of strolling through the town after dark"—the narrative's euphemism, in turn, for their voyeurism. In the first chapter we saw them, excluded from the warmth of after-dinner cigars and reminiscences of Cambridge, looking in from the cold, windy deck to the saloon of the *Euphrosyne*. Now, in Chapter 8 they actually hide in the shrubbery in order to spy on the hotel guests. This perspective expresses their psychological distance from the social life there. More importantly, it objectifies the reality of the narrative consciousness itself, which from the very beginning of its story has been compelled to express its feelings of alienation from, and contempt for, the mass of society—and yet, its fascination with that society, and a longing to somehow enter into it without being touched by it. That is the complex existential space in which Hewet must first come into being. Significantly, he emerges into the narrative consciousness as "a young man who until now had kept his back turned to the window. He appeared to be rather stout, and had a thick crop of hair." The back turned to the window shows his resistance to the essentially feminine perception of the narrative here, which then focuses on his physicality—in this context, his maleness. (In contrast, St. John Hirst, whom the narrative discovers for the first time in this scene also, remains hidden behind a curtain, and is perceived only as "legs in the shadow" and a disembodied voice.)

The narrative is able to make its first tentative entries into Hewet's consciousness in Chapter 10. And when, in Chapter 11 he is asked for a "short biographical sketch," he responds in an interesting way:

"I am the son of an English gentleman. I am twenty-seven," Hewet began. "My father was a fox-hunting squire. He died when I was ten in the hunting field. I can remember his body coming home . . . just as I was going down to tea, and noticing that there was jam for tea, and wondering whether I should be allowed—"
"Yes; but keep to the facts," Hirst put in.

After this admonition Hewet returns to "the facts," the conventional data of his "biographical sketch," now shaped—and abridged—by the questions of his audience. Society hears what it wants to hear, and specifies the categories in which the significance of one's life must be contained. Hewet's spontaneous comment has revealed, however, that for him his identity is related in some primary way to his father's death. And his most vivid memory of that death was of his own lack of reaction to it. This traumatic experience, repeated several times in Virginia Woolf's own youth, becomes an "immovable" archetype in her work. It is confronted most directly in *The Years* in Delia Pargiter's response to her mother's death, but evoked more poetically in *To the Lighthouse* and *The Waves* when a central presence suddenly and inexplicably becomes an absence. Here in *The Voyage Out* the issue is not really confronted, only alluded to. Unlike Mrs. Ramsay or Percival, Hewet's father is never a presence.

Yet the comment does seem to link Hewet with Rachel, who, when asked for her "biographical sketch," has just "stated that she was twenty-four years of age, the daughter of a ship-owner, that she had never been properly educated; played the piano, had no brothers or sisters, and lived at Richmond with aunts, her mother being dead." Thus the climactic "fact" of Rachel's life, in her own view, is that her mother is dead. This is made much more explicit in earlier manuscript versions of the novel, and whatever the reasons may be for its suppression in the published version,[6] its implications may be more convincing precisely because they are not insisted upon. Hewet may be drawn to Rachel here because they have both experienced the loss of their parental "role models": Hewet, having lost his father, does not quite know how to be a man; and when he learns that Rachel has lost her mother, he may realize that she does not quite know how to be a woman. Perhaps he mentions his father's death to let her know that she is not so alone as she may feel. In any case, death is somehow important in the relationship of Rachel and Hewet from the beginning.

Hewet's mind is probably most fully revealed in Chapter 18 and it seems to work—or not to work—like most of the "masculine" analytical thinking in the later books. He is trying here to formulate a vision of married life in which both he and Rachel could have an authentic existence: "He tried all sorts of pictures" (in what phenomenologists would call "eidetic reduction"), testing various predicates against the subject to determine its "essence." The chapter closes with the collapse of analysis into emotion, with the analyst "tormented by the desire to be in her presence again." This chapter, devoted entirely to Hewet's consciousness, ends by revealing the inadequacy of abstraction. It also reveals in Hewet a tendency toward the kind of transcendental idealism which reaches its climax in his reaction to Rachel's death. This too becomes an "immovable" archetype: Jacob, Mr. Ram-

6 Excerpts from the earlier manuscript versions are quoted by Jane Novak, *The Razor Edge of Balance: A Study of Virginia Woolf* (Coral Gables: University of Miami Press, 1974), 81.

say, Louis, Giles—all of the highly intelligent, analytical males whose assertions of intellectual control are undercut by emotional realities which are not fully recognized, and which finally prevail.

Most critical readings of *The Voyage Out* have seen Hewet largely as Rachel sees him. But the text itself creates a much more complex reality. As Mitchell A. Leaska has pointed out, there is evidence that Hewet is unduly inhibited, immature, insecure, irresponsible, socially inept—perhaps, even that he is compulsively drawn toward women sexually but unable to acknowledge their real humanity.[7] Significantly, Hewet's limitations are most convincingly revealed in his plans for his fiction—not so much in the "novel of Silence" (which is not just pretentious, but quite out of his reach) as in the "other novel" about the young man obsessed by the idea of becoming a gentleman (its theme is "the general corruption of the soul") who marries Lady Theo Bingham Bingley and becomes a real estate agent in Croydon, or his "Stuart tragedy" (conceived to show, it seems, that people in Stuart times "were exactly the same as we are"). In her innocence Rachel hears all this "with a certain amount of bewilderment," but the narrative, which is less innocent, creates the scene so as to reveal Hewet's innocence as well as hers.

In Chapter 22 we see that he has grown, and that his fiction reflects "the world as it appeared to him now that he and Rachel were going to be married. It was different certainly. The book called *Silence* would not now be the same book that it would have been. . . . the world was different—it had, perhaps, more solidity, more coherence, more importance, greater depth." As Hewet meditates, Rachel plays "a very late Beethoven sonata," finds his insistent questions about the nature of "Women" very distracting, and speaks to him about the inadequacy of words. Did it never occur to him, she asks, that human beings themselves are "nothing but patches of light?" Throughout this scene too, although we may respect Hewet's seriousness, we must feel that Rachel's view is larger, more poetic. Both seek the ineffable, and if that can be expressed, as Ruskin suggested, only in "the con-

7 Mitchell A. Leaska, "Virginia Woolf's *The Voyage Out*: Character Deduction and the Function of Ambiguity," *Virginia Woolf Quarterly*, I (Winter, 1973), 18–41.

dition of music," then Rachel's intuitive approach seems preferable to Hewet's rather dogged determination to define "Women."

Although her "biographical sketch" asserts that she has lived with "aunts" in Richmond, this alleged past has no reality in Rachel's consciousness as we see it now: a stream of perceptions of the present and apprehensions about the future. But her life now comes immediately under the influence—indeed, the domination—of another "aunt." Helen Ambrose, as we saw in the first chapter, perceives Rachel as damned—to a fate that Helen herself understands all too well. At the end of Chapter 19 she realizes that Rachel "was in love, and she pitied her profoundly." And after their visit to the primitive village, she realizes that "Rachel had passed beyond her guardianship." The narrative seems to admire Helen for her prescience—but not for her passivity. A much more dynamic female personality is Mrs. Flushing, an aristocrat always on the move, always in command of the situation: she makes things happen. She is also an amateur painter, and her theory of art is uncomplicated and dynamic: "I see things movin'." Yet the narrative tends to paint her as a grotesque. With her shrill opinions ("I hate Shakespeare!") and her total admiration of her husband, she denies her femininity too stridently even for the taste of the essentially feminist consciousness which perceives her.

The book as a whole seems to explore various modes of awareness, in search of one—or of a synthesis, perhaps—that will be ultimately satisfying. But despite the complexities of the search and of the field of awareness, what the narrative finally discovers here—and in the later books as well—is an "immovable" essential duality. Whatever the names we may give to its polarities—intellect and intuition, objectivity and subjectivity, fact and vision, masculine and feminine—we recognize that the work itself arises from the tensions between them.

These tensions become evident in the discontinuities of the transitional passages in which the narrative must confront its own dialectic. As we have seen, the openings and closings of chapters in *The Voyage Out* take on a special importance: the opening passage constitutes the entrance into an avenue of meaning; the closing passage defines the limits of that avenue. It seems significant, therefore, that in each of the closing passages of the first nine chapters of the book the narrative consciousness is incarnate in the awarenesses of female characters. In the endings of the next four chapters a rather weak male consciousness interacts with a rather strong female consciousness. In the next five endings the consciousness is male. Then, after the chapter which ends with Helen and Rachel accepting the invitation to go on the expedition, the next five chapters end in an awareness which is *shared* by male and female characters. The twenty-fifth chapter, in which Rachel dies, ends with a kind of collective consciousness (the perceiving awareness is called *they*). The penultimate chapter ends in a rather undeveloped female awareness (that of Evelyn M.), and the last ends in an almost disembodied male awareness (that of St. John Hirst).

Thus in its psychological voyage out, the questing narrative consciousness begins with a "feminine" perspective. Gradually it becomes able to accept the emergence of a male consciousness, and to test the interactions of that consciousness with the female. This new "masculine" awareness seems authentic and promising enough so that the central part of the book explores avenues which lead to final perspectives within such a consciousness. This, in turn, seems to make possible a series of explorations toward final perspectives in which the male and female modes do not just interact, but actually merge into a larger awareness. But that merging is then revealed to be illusory, enervating, perhaps even insane. It leads, symbolically, to Rachel's death, which must then be seen from the perspective of an impersonal, triumphant *they*. What remains, in the last two chapters, are the modes of awareness which can survive in such a world. Rachel is dead. Hewet and Helen—and even Ridley—have vanished, and in the closing moments a disinterested Hirst watches the familiar patterns begin to flow once more in the public rooms of the hotel.

These stages or phases in the development of psychological perspective in *The Voyage Out* can be seen only in retrospect, of course. To identify them is to rationalize what the narrative consciousness "learns" in the dynamic process of creation. They represent a trace, a fossil structure of what had been, experientially, open and contingent. For the dynamic meanings, then, we must return to the text, where the narrative discovers its own significance—not in the general out-comes that may already be "known" to the creative consciousness, but in that domain of *style* where the narrative's feelings must find their expression. That is the realm of intentionality.

In the first phase of the drama of intentionality in *The Voyage Out* the narrative remains within an essentially "feminine" perspective. In the second phase the creative consciousness ventures into a new world. As Chapter 10 opens we learn that Helen has given Rachel a room— an existential space—of her own, "a fortress as well as a sanctuary ... an enchanted place" in which her belated development can be sheltered. Helen knows what she is doing: "Rooms, she knew, became more like worlds than rooms at the age of twenty-four." Also opened, at least tentatively, is a new masculine world as well. But the main emphasis is on Rachel, and her internal conflict becomes defined in very highly symbolic ways. This second phase concludes with Chapter 13, in which a series of symbolic actions leads to the climactic ques-tion, "What is it to be in love?" which sets the course for the rest of the voyage. This symbolism should not be too narrowly defined. But its broader meanings are clear enough, especially in the context of the symbolic language of the lifework as a whole.

Chapter 13 begins with Rachel's invasion of Ridley's "room," his study, sanctuary of the "masculine" world of the intellect. When she leaves, she is "lost in wonder at her uncle, and his books, and his neglect of dances, and his queer, utterly inexplicable, but apparently satisfactory view of life." His existential space is "more and more deeply encircled by books." His chair is surrounded by stacks of ref-erence books, and the walls of his study are lined with an overwhelm-ing array of classics—which for her are vaguely familiar names, but for him are living realities. And while the narrative seems critical of his detachment and isolation, it also seems to share Rachel's awe and bewilderment. It sees those books as she does—as alien, mysterious, overwhelming: the wisdom of the ages, arranged in an incompre-hensible pattern, in an inaccessible library. Yet she feels compelled to enter it.

From Ridley's study Rachel wanders away from the villa, down to a dry riverbed. "On the bank grew those trees which Helen had said it was worth the voyage out merely to see." In Rachel's head everything "went surging round"—a "tumultuous background from which the present moment, with its opportunity for doing exactly as she liked, sprung more wonderfully vivid even than the night before." The dry riverbed represents her existential space at this moment. Her experience of "the night before" had left her feeling, the morning after the dance, "like a fish at the bottom of the sea," and now, at the dry riverbed, she is entering, unknowingly, a receptivity that will be irreversible. At the end of the chapter she will ask a question that cannot be withdrawn; it will, in effect, release the flood in which she must finally drown.

Because of the echo of the book's title, the comment that the trees on the bank are "worth the voyage out" seems to emphasize their symbolic significance, which becomes fully apparent only very much later—when it can be seen in the perspective of the *oeuvre*. Within *The Voyage Out*, however, the meaning of the magnolia trees here in Chapter 13 may be amplified by a passage in Chapter 15, where magnolias also provide a background for a significant perception, Helen's view of Hirst at the end of that chapter: "She looked at him against the background of flowering magnolia. . . . she had been noticing the patches of shade and the shape of the leaves, and the way the great white flowers sat in the midst of the green. She had noticed it half-consciously, nevertheless the pattern had become part of their talk." The dynamics of the perspective in this passage are interesting. "From her position she saw his head in front of the dark pyramid of a magnolia-tree." This then leads to the observation that Helen's "own figure possessed the sublimity of a woman's of the early world, spinning the thread of fate"—a further amplification of the prescience which has been attributed to her from the beginning. Thus in Chapter 15 the magnolia trees become more closely associated with fate—and with the fatality which Helen seems at times to perceive in Rachel.

But here in Chapter 13 Rachel does not notice the rich magnolia blossoms, for "she walked without seeing. The night was encroaching upon the day." This encroachment provides the "tumultuous background" for the ecstasy of "the present moment." Then, in this state, she might have walked until she had lost all knowledge of her way, had it not been for the interruption of a tree, which, although it did not grow across her path, stopped her as effectively as if the branches had struck her in the face. It was an ordinary tree, but to her it appeared so strange that it might have been the only tree in the world. Dark was the trunk in the middle, and the branches sprang here and there, leaving jagged intervals of light between them as distinctly as if it had but that second risen from the ground. Having seen a sight that would last her for a lifetime, and for a lifetime would preserve that second, the tree once more sank into the ordinary ranks of trees, and she was able to seat herself in its shade. . . .

This strange experience is the first of several similar symbolic "moments" in the lifework—most notably, Neville's encounter with the "immitigable tree" in *The Waves*, an experience which reverberates throughout his soliloquies as "death among the apple trees."[8] Perhaps this tree in *The Voyage Out* has some symbolic connection with the one which Lily realizes she must move to the center of her painting in Part I of *To the Lighthouse*, or with the one which Orlando's poem, rewritten continually through the centuries, celebrates, or with the one which shelters Miss La Trobe and her inspiration in *Between the Acts*. Although there may be traces of more traditional symbolic meanings (the tree of life, of knowledge, the heaven-tree, the cross) in these passages, they all express moments of sudden transfixion, when the narrative is overwhelmed by a revelation which remains beyond the power of conventional expression. In such moments the imagery tends toward an emphasis on light and darkness—as if the darkness penetrates the "luminous halo" of consciousness and gives it shape and pattern.

8 The autobiographical origin of the "immitigable tree" is revealed in "A Sketch of the Past":

Some people called Valpy had been staying at St. Ives, and had left. We were waiting at dinner one night, when somehow I overheard my father or my mother say that Mr. Valpy had killed himself. The next thing I remember is being in the garden at night and walking on the path by the apple tree. It seemed to me that the apple tree was connected with the horror of Mr. Valpy's suicide. I could not pass it. I stood there looking at the grey-green creases of the bark—it was a moonlit night—in a trance of horror. I seemed to be dragged down, hopelessly, into some pit of absolute despair from which I could not escape. My body seemed paralysed. (*Moments of Being*, ed. Jeanne Schulkind, New York: Harcourt, 1976, p. 71.)

Rachel's encounter with the tree in Chapter 13 literally brings her down to earth and enables her to find her place ("she was able to seat herself") in her "world" of the moment. Her psychological state is revealed by the perspective, whose camera angles express the narrative's feelings: she finds herself "looking up" at the mountains and the sky, and then she "looked down" on her books, to find that the grass is "tickling the smooth brown cover of Gibbon, while the mottled blue Balzac lay naked in the sun." With her place in nature settled, and the relationship of these particular books to that nature defined also, she is able to read. In Gibbon it seems that she has discovered "the book of the world turned back to the very first page." Thus the act of constituting that world becomes essentially a literary act—as it is throughout the lifework, which closes with the narrative imagining Miss La Trobe imagining "the first words." Now in Chapter 13 of the first novel, Rachel, Hirst, and Hewet are enveloped in a "haze of wonder." This, like the "golden haze" which surrounds Minta after her engagement in *To the Lighthouse*, is a sexual aura. But it is also a literary radiance. Both books and life are subsumed in the famous "luminous halo which surrounds us from the beginning of consciousness to the end." From that luminosity both life and books are made incarnate, and to it both return. In the present passage this imagery culminates in the comment that Rachel's mind "dwelt on them [Hirst and Hewet] with a kind of physical pleasure such as is caused by the contemplation of bright things hanging in the sun. From them all life seemed to radiate; the very words of books were steeped in radiance."

In the dawning awareness of her own fascination with love, Rachel is once more brought to earth and forced to confront the "most persistent" of her thoughts. No longer in control of her perceptions, but "looking blankly in front of her," she observes for some time—without consciously registering— "a great yellow butterfly, which was opening and closing its wings very slowly on a little flat stone." Throughout the *oeuvre* moths and butterflies are associated with the primal, irresistible—and often, self-destructive—instincts. Rachel's perception of the butterfly evokes the momentous question which brings the second phase of the drama of intentionality to a close: "'What is it to be in love?' she demanded, after a long silence;

each word as it came into being seemed to shove itself out into an unknown sea. Hypnotised by the wings of the butterfly, and awed by the discovery of a terrible possibility in life, she sat for some time longer. When the butterfly flew away, she rose, and with her two books beneath her arm returned home again, much as a soldier prepared for battle." Words themselves, the vessels launched into the sea of chaos here, are identified as the vehicles for the voyage out. The "unknown sea" is always frightening, and Rachel is as "awed" at this moment as Lily is in *To the Lighthouse*, where her painting becomes the vehicle for another voyage out. For Rachel, love is perceived as "a terrible possibility"—the equivalent of Mrs. Ramsay's recognition, in Minta's "golden haze," that the love between man and woman bears within it the seeds of death. Rachel is "hypnotised" by the butterfly, awed by her own recognition of the same irresistible instinct which moves the butterfly's wings. That recognition reduces her to immobility once again, and when she rises at last, it is "as a soldier prepared for battle." The narrative consciousness seems to know—though it must not express that knowledge directly—that the answer to Rachel's momentous question will be fatal. But, driven by the same relentless instincts which move the butterfly's wings, it must search out that destiny to the very end.

The possibility of reversing that decision remains open throughout the next phase of the drama. But the penetration of the heart of darkness turns out to be irreversible, and elicits the fourth phase, with its attendant loss of control—for the narrative as well as for Rachel. This is the most frightening aspect of the "terrible possibility" which Rachel—and more importantly, the narrative consciousness—recognizes in the spasmodic movements of the butterfly. Earlier, Rachel's susceptibility to it is shown dramatically in her relationship with Richard Dalloway. Led to think of him condescendingly because of the attitudes of her father and Helen, she is unprepared to be stirred by his rich, deep voice and his overwhelming physical presence. When he suddenly kisses her passionately, her consciousness can only drown in "black waves."

In Chapter ii the narrative creates another such moment, approaching it more cautiously than in the scene with Richard. At first the experience is given to Susan Warrington, who seems, like the Susan of *The Waves*, to typify an earthiness which the narrative can't imagine for its more central characters. (St. John Hirst, in whose consciousness the book ends, is horrified to think of "the female breast" and of Arthur Venning's "having to get into bed with" Susan.) In Chapter ii the narrative speaks of Susan's growing awareness of "the excitement of intimacy, which seemed not only to lay bare something in her, but in the trees and the sky, and the progress of his [Arthur's] speech which seemed inevitable was positively painful to her, for no human being had ever come so close to her before." Some aspects of the "terrible possibility" are evident enough in the words themselves: *excitement of intimacy, lay bare, inevitable, painful*. Less obvious are the implications of the visual perspective, which reveals that Susan is now looking *up*, that she feels dwarfed by the enormity of what is happening to her, being inflicted upon her; she is helpless; Arthur's speech *seemed inevitable*—she can't stop it. It changes her whole perspective, cancels out her habitual modes of consciousness. She feels exposed, threatened, helpless, frightened—and by words alone. "She was struck motionless as his speech went on, and her heart gave great separate leaps at the last words." As in Rachel's experience with Richard ("She fell back in her chair, with tremendous beats of the heart, each of which sent black waves across her eyes") the male presence is physiologically devastating: the girl is literally *stricken*.

In such passages the narrative, which is capable of some subtlety elsewhere, seems deaf to its own overtones of melodrama. Furthermore, it has not earned the "privilege" of entering Susan's consciousness like this; its earlier view of her has been too shallow to justify this sudden revelation. In another, deeper, sense, however, the passage is true—precisely because it *is* a violation of Susan's privacy. Under the laws which govern the world of *The Voyage Out*, this is what love does to a girl—exposes her. And when Arthur actually embraces Susan at last, the narrative must withdraw into greater impersonality: "He seized her in his arms; again and again they clasped each other, murmuring inarticulately." The increasing—and incongruous—impersonality of the scene has made it suddenly grotesque, and the perspective now becomes unacceptable even to the narrative consciousness, which must try to discover some more satisfactory view of the scene. It begins to recover control with some dialogue, rendered with some sophistication and with enough observed "background" to make it more comfortable. The most threatening moments of passion have been dissipated, and the narrative is able once more to enter Susan's awareness.

But the stability of the perspective can't be maintained, and the next transformation is extraordinary:

They lay in each other's arms and had no notion that they were observed. Yet two figures suddenly appeared among the trees above them.

"Here's shade," began Hewet, when Rachel suddenly stopped dead. They saw a man and woman lying on the ground beneath them, rolling slightly this way and that as the embrace tightened and slackened. The man then sat upright and the woman, who now appeared to be Susan Warrington, lay back upon the ground, with her eyes shut and an absorbed look upon her face, as though she were not altogether conscious. Nor could you tell from her expression whether she was happy, or had suffered something. When Arthur again turned to her, butting her as a lamb butts a ewe, Hewet and Rachel retreated without a word. Hewet felt uncomfortably shy.

"I don't like that," said Rachel after a moment.

"I can remember not liking it either," said Hewet.

The loss of control in this passage is not confined to the characters themselves. The narrative no sooner imagines the couple in each other's arms than it must imagine their discovery. And it is a shocking discovery by "two figures"—impersonal, not even recognized immediately, though they are the central couple of the book. The camera angle places Susan and Arthur in a position inferior and vulnerable to their discoverers. Since the latter are "among the trees" they may acquire, through subliminal associations of that imagery, connotations of the "immitigable," and of fatality. The discovered lovers, who "lay in each other's arms," seem rather helpless, and the words "had no notion" seem to imply that conscious thought could have prevented this moment.

Since the lovers have let themselves go, however, they have lost the stability, the order, of conscious thought—which must now move to the consciousness of the discoverers. There it becomes more formal

and distanced ("they saw. . . . Nor could you tell . . .") than our familiarity with Rachel and Hewet might seem to justify. But that
greater distance has its own justification: this sudden disclosure of a
couple in the throes of love is paralyzing for Rachel (who "suddenly
stopped dead") and embarrassing for Hewet. So great is the shock
that Susan and Arthur are first recognized only as "a man and a
woman," and more importantly, as helpless, "rolling slightly this way
and that as the embrace tightened and slackened." Then Susan is recognized, but her status is uncertain: perhaps she is "not altogether
conscious"—a state into which the experience, and even the imagined
experience, of sex forces one after another of Virginia Woolf's
women. Indeed, the narrative consciousness itself cannot tell whether
Susan is "happy, or had suffered something"—but the context shows
that the latter possibility is favored. The image of the lamb butting
the ewe seems too bizarre even for this context—even though the
name *Rachel* means *ewe*, and the scene may be intended as a symbolic
foreshadowing of her fate. Fortunately for Susan's virginity, the ag-
gressor is a lamb rather than a ram—that would be too much for the
narrative to contemplate. As it is, the scene is enough to compel the
observers to retreat "without a word"; its central meaning is beyond
the realm of language. Yet the words which Rachel and Hewet speak
surround and define that center. She says, simply, "I don't like that."
That? What the narrative feels—degradation, impersonality, helplessness, uncertainty, suffering—and the unspoken causes of those feelings. Hewet's reply is interesting too. One obvious implication is that
he feels that he has overcome his original "not liking"—with the secondary implication that sexual love is not entirely natural, but an acquired taste. And the idea of *memory* here links this scene with that of
Rachel's final illness, when she experiences her struggle for life as a
struggle to remember something which she can never quite call into
her consciousness (it is vaguely associated with Hewet, and specifically with the lines he has read to her from *Comus*). In that struggle
the growing yearning for peace becomes a yearning for forgetfulness
and, ultimately, death.

The third phase ends with Hewet's "exultation" at the end of
Chapter 18: "We'd be free together. We'd share everything together.

No happiness would be like ours. No lives would compare with ours." He too is stricken ("he dropped to the ground") and "tormented" just as Rachel had been at the end of the previous phase. His words here foreshadow those he speaks, or thinks that he speaks—he is no longer able to tell the difference—at Rachel's deathbed. In both situations he is really talking to himself; in both, Rachel exists for him as an *idea*. And the real meaning of the "exultant" hope that "We'd share everything together" is discovered in the heart of darkness itself, where he and Rachel lose their separate identities and lapse into an echolalic unity.

Before this journey into darkness, however, there is a transitional chapter in which the narrative consciousness seems to retreat from, or at least try to postpone, the fate which it has imagined for Rachel. In Chapter 19 she wanders through various corridors and rooms (symbolic, as we have seen, of existential spaces, of modes of existence) in the hotel. First, she is invited into the room of Evelyn M., where she discovers that Evelyn "did not want advice; she wanted intimacy." But Rachel finds that frightening, and in her flight from Evelyn "She did not think which way she was going." She is trapped in a corridor which ends at a window, and the view is the one that Evelyn had described earlier: "They kill hens down there. . . . They cut their heads off with a knife—disgusting!" Disgusting, yes, but irresistible: "The blood and ugly wriggling fascinated Rachel"—so much so that the scene suddenly returns involuntarily to overwhelm her during her last illness—at the moment when Hewet kisses her. The scene becomes, in Rachel's imagination, emblematic of profound sexual hostility and aggression and is imprinted at a time when she feels trapped in the restrictive passage of her destiny, which she realizes is very close to that of Evelyn M.: to be at the mercy of "love."

Rachel is then rescued from this window, this view of the world, by Miss Allan, the literary spinster, and invited to her room. There Rachel is given a taste of ginger (which she spits out), offered a taste of Miss Allan's twenty-six-year-old unopened bottle of creme-dementhe (which she declines), and obliged to watch as the "massive homely figure" repairs her severe hair style and changes her dress. Although she is seen with some sympathy, Miss Allan, writing her silly literary history ("I'm glad there aren't many more ages. I'm still in the middle of the eighteenth century"), seems the avatar of a destiny even less attractive than Evelyn's.

As they are returning to the public rooms, they encounter the deaf invalid Mrs. Paley, whose wheelchair blocks their way.

Rachel suddenly said something inarticulate, and disappeared down the corridor. This misunderstanding, which involved a complete block in the passage, seemed to her unbearable. She walked quickly and blindly in the opposite direction, and found herself at the end of a *cul de sac*. There was a window. . . . She had now reached one of those eminences, the result of some crisis, from which the world is finally displayed in its true proportions. . . . Meanwhile the steady beat of her own pulse represented the hot current of feeling that ran down beneath; beating, struggling, fretting. For the time, her own body was the source of all the life in the world, which tried to burst forth here—there. . . . She was no longer able to see the world as a town laid out beneath her. It was covered instead by a haze of feverish red mist. . . . Thinking was no escape. Physical movement was the only refuge, in and out of rooms, in and out of people's minds, seeking she knew not what.

By this time the situation seems almost familiar: the feeling of sudden helplessness, the blocked passage, the dead end with its window and compulsory view, the feverish haze. But now Rachel's world has become almost explicitly identified as the incarnation of her emotions, whereas before it had been her social world that had seemed to define her. Now, from the perspective of that social world, she has "disappeared." She can no longer pretend to maintain a detachment from her world; she realizes that her being is *in* that world, has no meaning apart from it, and indeed, creates and constitutes it. Graphically, the passage renders what Merleau-Ponty would call the "body-subject." Rachel's new perspective enables—and compels—her to see everything with "startling intensity," culminating in her perception of "a massive green tree . . . as if it were a moving force held at rest." It is then that she gives her assent, with "eagerness," to the journey into the heart of darkness: "Of course I'm coming. So are you, Helen."

Helen's response to this is strangely fatalistic. The narrative says that Rachel's

emotional state and her confusion would have made her an easy prey if Helen had wished to argue or had wished to draw confidences. But instead of talking she fell into a profound silence. . . . Her sense of safety was shaken, as if beneath twigs and dead leaves she had seen the movement of a snake. It seemed to her that a moment's respite was allowed, a moment's make-believe, and then again the profound and reasonless law asserted itself, moulding them all to its liking, making and destroying.

She looked at Rachel. . . . She was in love, and she pitied her profoundly.

Thus the moment of respite closes, and the relentless movement toward the inevitable begins once again. It might almost be a moment from a Hardy novel: aware of other possible outcomes, the narrative can't really believe in them in the face of the destructive, "profound and reasonless law" which the narrative still *knows* is at the heart of its created world.

The fourth phase begins with the journey up the river into a more primitive region, into a territory first seen through English eyes by "Elizabethan voyagers" (in the novels of Virginia Woolf, and especially in her essays, the Elizabethans are seen as celebrating all the values that the Victorians repressed; the contrast is seen most vividly in *Orlando*, where it is exaggerated for comic effect). As the journey continues it becomes increasingly symbolic, almost a series of mythic tableaux. Like the six disembodied voices in *The Waves*, the voyagers here are three men and three women. The river itself was first visible from the Pisgah perspective achieved in the ascent of Monte Rosa, and during the journey the river and surrounding jungle are described in language reminiscent of Conrad's *Heart of Darkness*. Hewet reads aloud from Whitman's *Leaves of Grass* (from the "Calamus" series about love and death and the phallic mysteries), but the words "flickered and went out" in the vastness and the silence. When the six voyagers first disembark, "Terence saw that the time had come as it was fated to come, but although he realised this he was completely calm and master of himself." Beyond the explicit acknowledgment of "fate" here the anxiety about "calm" and self-control very nearly becomes explicit too. Later, in the very heart of darkness, Hewet and Rachel will discover that calm and self-control are no longer possible. A rather blatant hint of that fall is announced to the lovers: " 'Good-bye. Beware of snakes,' Hirst replied. He settled himself still more comfortably under the shade of the fallen tree and Helen's figure." Nevertheless, Rachel and Hewet enter the undersea world of their fated passion, and into a profound and disturbing unity in which their language itself degenerates into a series of sounds and echoes (the sounds are his, the echoes hers, of course). When he and Rachel rejoin the group, Hewet is aware of a new relationship to that group. It is felt in the narrative perspective, which reveals here—as it will throughout the *oeuvre*—that lovers are diminished in their new "world": "Here were the Flushings talking, talking, somewhere high up in the air above him, and he and Rachel had dropped to the bottom of the world together." Language itself loses its accustomed meanings: "Every word sounded quite distinctly in Terence's ears; but what were they saying, and who were they talking to, and who were they, these fantastic people, detached somewhere high up in the air?" Hirst, too, discovers a new truth in the heart of darkness: "God's undoubtedly mad."

As the narrative begins to explore this heart of darkness, it does so largely from an "objective" point of view; it intrudes more into Hewet's mind than Rachel's. But as the exploration continues, the narrative returns more and more to Rachel. Chapter 21 opens with Mr. Flushing telling the others about Mackenzie, "the famous explorer" who (like Kurtz in *Heart of Darkness*) had died "almost within reach of civilization," after penetrating "farther inland than any one's been yet." The other listeners attend to this exemplum "obediently," but "The eyes of Rachel saw nothing." She can no longer even distinguish individual trees, but sees only massive shapes of foliage. (As we might infer from her earlier encounter with the "immitigable tree," this is a fatal sign.) Now "love" returns, and to Rachel "the whole world was unreal." Her echolalia returns too, and she drifts out of control in her stream of consciousness: "almost as if it were the blood singing in·her veins, or the water of the stream running over stones, Rachel became conscious of a new feeling within her. She wondered for a moment what it was, and then said to herself, with a little surprise at recognizing in her own person so famous a thing: 'This is happiness, I suppose.' And aloud to Terence she spoke, 'This is happiness.'" The feeling of Rachel here is rather like that of the dying Henry James, who "is said to have told a friend that as he collapsed he heard a voice exclaiming: "So here it is at last, the distinguished thing!'"[9] The "happiness" of which Rachel speaks (and it is now Hewet's turn to echo) is deeply ironic, and, subliminally, it connects this scene with the ending of Chapter 18 (where Hewet is stricken by his love for Rachel) and later with Rachel's deathbed (where this idealistic "happiness" finds its ultimate fulfillment). Here in Chapter 21 "love" has gone so far that the stream of consciousness becomes an uncontrollable flood:

Voices crying behind them never reached through the waters in which they were now sunk. The repetition of Hewet's name in short, dissevered syllables was to them the crack of a dry branch or the laughter of a bird. The grasses and breezes sounding and murmuring all round them, they never noticed that the swishing of the grasses grew louder and louder, and did not cease with the lapse of the breeze. A hand dropped abrupt as iron on Rachel's shoulder; it might have been a bolt from heaven; she fell beneath it, and the grass whipped across her eyes and filled her mouth and ears. Through the waving stems she saw a figure, large and shapeless against the sky. Helen was upon her. Rolled this way and that, now seeing only forests of green, and now the high blue heaven, she was speechless and almost without sense. At last she lay still, all the grasses shaken round her and before her by her panting. Over her loomed two great heads, the heads of a man and woman, of Terence and Helen.

Both were flushed, both laughing, and the lips were moving; they came together and kissed in the air above her. Broken fragments of speech came down to her on the ground. She thought she heard them speak of love and then of marriage. Raising herself and sitting up, she too realised Helen's soft body, the strong and hospitable arms, and happiness swelling and breaking in one vast wave. When this fell away, and the grasses once more lay low, and the sky became horizontal, and the earth rolled out flat on each side, and the trees stood upright, she was the first to perceive a little row of human figures standing patiently in the distance. For the moment she could not remember who they were.

The imagery of drowning has now become dominant. From Rachel's experience in this first novel to the legend of the Lady in the lily pool in the last, the sexual feelings of women in the fiction of Virginia Woolf are often associated with drowning. In *The Voyage Out* that

9   F. W. Dupee, *Henry James* (New York: William Sloane, 1951), 288–89.

experience for Rachel begins with Richard's kiss: her consciousness drowns in black waves, and her dreams that night turn to nightmares about tunnels oozing with damp, where deformed men lurk. And Rachel will experience her own death as a drowning and, in a sense which remains veiled to her, as an escape from sexual fears.

What might save Rachel from drowning? *Voices*, but they cannot reach her through the flood of sexual feeling. They might restore order by giving feelings a *name*, and by the *repetition* of familiar patterns. But all that Rachel is aware of now are *grasses and breezes*, signs of instability and chaos. The grass *filled her mouth and ears*, depriving her of her customary ability to communicate with the outward world. And through the chaotic grass the *figure* of Helen now materializes *large and shapeless against the sky*, having grown enormous, totally dominant, and expanded far beyond its familiar definition in Rachel's mind. The *figure* is recognized as Helen, but also as *woman*, an archetype. Terence too becomes archetypal, and is perceived, along with the woman, as looming over the scene. Even their kiss becomes strangely impersonal and symbolic: *the lips were moving; they came together and kissed in the air above her*. The announcement of love and marriage arises from overtones of helplessness and doom.

The narrative "knows," of course, that the *voices* here are those of the two other couples. And at some level of awareness, Rachel and Hewet know that too. The voices are not calling, or shouting, but *crying*—a word with rich connotations: a hint of the chase and of animal cries, perhaps, as well as associations with pain, weeping, pleading, public outcries, and so on. The narrative mentions the sounds of the voices, then the louder swishing of the grasses, but insists that Rachel and Hewet do not register what they hear, but transform it into something else. (The narrative's relation to Hewet here may seem problematic: to what extent is he a part of the *they* which is applied to him and Rachel? or does *they* reflect the way she feels? The context makes the latter possibility seem more likely, but the uncertainty remains—and heightens the feeling of anxiety in the passage as a whole.) Rachel herself may no longer have a distinct identity here, but may have been swept under, into a *them*, a collective object of whatever random verb may next emerge in this bewildering stream of experience. Hewet's very name is lost to her (and perhaps to him as well).

The narrative envisions Rachel's fall here primarily as a loss of control, and experiences it through one perceptual shock after another. The perceptions in this passage become much more immediate, much less obviously organized by the narrative intelligence, than elsewhere in the book. The "camera" loses its stability, and tumbles wildly and unpredictably. Rachel feels stricken, diminished, helpless. Her fiancé and her aunt loom above her as enormous archetypes, *man and woman*. The words *Helen was upon her* mark the narrative's discovery of Rachel's destiny as a woman: in the flushes, the laughter, the moving lips which join in a kiss *above her* the narrative recognizes Rachel's fate. And so it says not that Rachel touched Helen's body, but that she *realised* it. She has, in a sense, become Helen. And that realization evokes the *wave*: in Virginia Woolf's symbolic language the wave signifies the miraculous richness of personal experience as it emerges from the vast sea of undifferentiated existence, reaches its transcendent crest, then lapses into that sea once more. And while this *happiness swelling and breaking in one vast wave* is such a crest, this moment of transcendence is more ambiguous than the narrative has yet discovered, for beneath that crest the undercurrent of defeat and death is powerful, and will finally prevail. The motif of happiness is always climactic in this double sense, from its first emergence in the echolalia of the entry into the heart of darkness to its fullest cresting in Rachel's death. (And it too becomes an "immovable" irony throughout the lifework.) In the present scene its ecstasy, as always, is *temporary*: as it *fell away*, the habitual perspectives return once again—sky, earth, and trees (all crucial symbols too) resume their customary orientation. But Rachel's dissociation is now extreme, as the *human figures* and *the distance* indicate. The *wave* has swept her far from her familiar moorings. A final aspect of the loss of control here is the loss of memory. This too will become prominent in Rachel's final illness, where her growing fascination with the underwater world is opposed by her desire to remember something. Memory is mooring.

In the whole drama of narrative perspective in *The Voyage Out*, this scene emerges as the most suddenly violent and distressing—

largely because it is so unexpected. Rachel's death is also distressing, of course, but it moves with an inevitability which the narrative consciousness has always recognized, and at last, in exhaustion, accepts. Richard's kiss is traumatic too, but less frightening, and because her subsequent nightmare and its aftermath could be attributed to that same source, the entire experience could be brought within the realm of rational understanding. But Hewet does not represent such an obvious sexual threat; in fact the narrative says that the engagement arouses in Rachel a *new feeling*, which she classifies as *happiness*. Why, then, should it destroy her stability? and more unexpectedly, the narrative's own stability? The answers remain concealed in the surrounding darkness, and the questions themselves are never directly asked.

This scene in which the narrative perspective undergoes its most violent and radical disorientation is followed by the entry of the travelers into "the village which was the goal of their journey." It is as if, according to the psychodynamic laws which govern the narrative, the discovery of this other way of life is the result of this profound disorientation. The village of "soft instinctive people," Edenic and eternal, moves Rachel and Hewet to forget their self-consciousness, but moves Helen, with her fateful insight, to "presentiments of disaster" and the realization that "Rachel had passed beyond her guardianship." Chapter 21 ends in darkness, which "poured down profusely," like that later darkness of "Time Passes" in *To the Lighthouse*, and with similar results, now veiled, but eventually lethal.

"The darkness fell, but rose again": in the transition to the next chapter the narrative consciousness reveals, though it will not fully acknowledge, that darkness is dominant. Rachel and Terence move in a strange trancelike existence, "forced," "driven," "left alone" by unnamed imperatives which they never really question. "The book called *Silence*" gains "solidity . . . coherence . . . importance . . . depth," Terence feels. He and Rachel become mentally much more intimate, but that only increases their dissatisfaction. In a passage which anticipates Denis de Rougemont's *Love in the Western World*, the narrative says that "The hopelessness of their situation overcame them both. They were impotent; they could never love each other sufficiently to overcome all these barriers, and they could never be satisfied with less."

Chapter 22 closes with a perspective which amplifies that feeling perfectly. Rachel and Terence "stood together in front of the looking-
glass," and they are "chilled" to find that "instead of being vast and
indivisible they were really very small and separate, the size of the
glass leaving a large space for the reflection of other things." That is
what being "in love" does to the personality—turns it into a chimeri-
cal reflection, diminished and apart even from the "other" person it
loves, in a universe of larger and more real "things."

In Chapter 23 Rachel and Terence are considered by society to be
"incapacitated from the business of life" by their engagement, and are
further isolated. Rachel begins to turn toward Hirst at times because
he "took her outside this little world of love and emotion." Although
the narrative does not recognize this explicitly, Hirst represents a
chance of life for Rachel, a chance to escape her fate in "this little
world of love and emotion." At the end of the chapter, Rachel chooses
to leave Helen and to go with Terence—another sign of her resigna-
tion to her fate, since Helen has been her protector and guardian. But
now Rachel is drifting beyond her help. The chapter ends with Hirst
giving the couple his blessing, which leaves them feeling "peaceful
and friendly"; nevertheless, his action also leaves them to their fate.
For Rachel, of course, that fate will be death, and in Chapter 23 there
are several intrusions of death which seem inexplicable except in retrospect, when they are validated as prophecy. Hirst mentions news
from home of a parlour maid who has committed suicide; a man
called Sinclair is threatening suicide if Evelyn M. rejects him; Helen
announces that the human race is more interested in death than in
anything else. Another curious anecdote in this chapter deals with the
expulsion of a prostitute from the hotel; the proximity of this story to
those involving death, and especially suicide, also contributes to an
atmosphere in which sex and death become more intimately associated—and in which Rachel's death too seems to evolve.

Chapter 24, the final one in the fourth phase, begins with Rachel
and Terence returning to the hotel, to find that "nothing has
changed"—as if everything in their "little world of love and emotion"
had taken place outside of the flow of time. Rachel's perspective now
allows her to see the "process" of living, and to move on to an epi-

any, a vision of meaning, of ultimate unity, of transcendent love which is "not the love of man for woman." Alternative feminine destinies pass in review: Miss Allan, with her shallow survey of literature from Beowulf to Browning now complete within its allotted 70,000 words; Evelyn M., with her plans for good works and meetings in Bloomsbury; Mrs. Eliot, in her enslavement to her husband; Susan Warrington, whose future will be defined by the children she will bear (and significantly, such a future is not envisioned for Rachel); and Mrs. Thornbury, who gives tea to Rachel and Terence in the garden and recalls that she had typhoid on her own honeymoon—another not-so-subtle foreshadowing of Rachel's fate, and another warning of the potentially lethal aspect of marriage. As the chapter—and this fourth phase of the drama of narrative perspective—ends, Mrs. Thornbury does not want Rachel and Terence to go. But of course they must; their fates have been decided by their voyage into the heart of darkness.

The final phase of the drama of perspective begins with Chapter 25, in which Rachel's fatal illness runs its course. The chapter opens with the feeling of overwhelming heat, "so hot that the breaking of waves on the shore sounded like the repeated sigh of some exhausted creature." (This image will reach its fullest expression in the "great beast stamping" its message of death on the shore in *The Waves*.) Rachel and Terence search for a book "that would withstand the power of the sun. Many books had been tried and then let fall, and now Terence was reading Milton aloud, because he said the words of Milton had substance and shape, so that it was not necessary to understand what he was saying." As the chapter opens, the perceptions of the wasteland and the feeling of exhaustion are generalized, not yet associated with any single character. Rather, they are the feelings of the narrative consciousness itself, enervated, somehow aware of the inevitable lapse of its story into the undifferentiated sea of possibilities from which it first emerged, but still searching for some way to postpone that fate. Perhaps memory could provide such a way; perhaps the ordering of the past could oppose the chaos of the present. (This is not, of course, Proust's "involuntary memory" which can suddenly rise to overwhelm the present moment.) The narrative seeks an appropriate literary paradigm in the lyric from *Comus*.[10] And it embodies the search in Terence and Rachel. But not even literature, the ultimate form of memory, is efficacious now: Rachel finds that the words "sounded strange; they meant different things from what they usually meant. Rachel at any rate could not keep her attention fixed upon them, but went off upon curious trains of thought suggested by words such as *curb* and *Locrine* and *Brute*, which brought unpleasant sights before her eyes, independently of their meaning. Owing to the heat and the dancing air the garden too looked strange—the trees were either too near or too far, and her head almost certainly ached."

Here she feels the first symptoms of her fatal illness. It manifests itself as a terrifying shift in perspective, and it is linguistic: Milton's words, supposedly solid, reliable cultural artifacts, suddenly lose their stable reference, and allow all kinds of "unpleasant" images to flood the imagination; even the most basic visual perceptions suddenly no longer match the expected patterns.

Throughout Rachel's illness the narrative emphasizes her fevered experience of distorted perspectives. She struggles to bring them back within "normal" limits. She struggles to remember. The narrative stresses the energy and effort of her concentration. But as the final penetration into her consciousness reveals, her energy is not unlimited:

On this day indeed Rachel was conscious of what went on round her. She had come to the surface of the dark, sticky pool, and a wave seemed to bear her up and down with it; she had ceased to have any will of her own; she lay floating on the top of the wave conscious of some pain, but chiefly of weakness. The wave was replaced by the side of a mountain. Her body became a drift of melting snow, above which her knees rose in huge peaked mountains

10 Harvena Richter, *Virginia Woolf: The Inward Voyage* (Princeton: Princeton University Press, 1970), 95–96, 123–25, discusses many of the implications of the allusions to *Comus*. She concludes that Sabrina is the "myth-twin" of Rachel, and that she "saves" the virginal Rachel from her impending marriage to Terence just as she had released the virginal Lady from the spell of Comus in Milton's poem. At the end, "Sabrina, the water spirit, a lovely death-wish, has come for her." Avrom Fleishman, *Virginia Woolf* (Baltimore: Johns Hopkins University Press, 1975), 20, offers a different interpretation: "the famous song points the irony of Rachel's demise: like the lady of the masque, she has been a virgin wooed by a river, but instead of being aided by a divine force she goes down to her death."

of bare bone. It was true that she saw Helen and saw her room, but everything had become very pale and semi-transparent. Sometimes she could see through the wall in front of her. Sometimes when Helen went away she seemed to go so far that Rachel's eyes could hardly follow her. The room also had an odd power of expanding, and though she pushed her voice out as far as possible until sometimes it became a bird and flew away, she thought it doubtful whether it ever reached the person she was talking to. There were immense intervals or chasms, for things still had the power to appear visibly before her, between one moment and the next; it sometimes took an hour for Helen to raise her arm, pausing long between each jerky movement, and pour out medicine. Helen's form stooping to raise her in bed appeared of gigantic size, and came down upon her like the ceiling falling. But for long spaces of time she would merely lie conscious of her body floating to the top of her bed and her mind driven to some remote corner of her body, or escaped and gone flitting round the room. All sights were something of an effort, but the sight of Terence was the greatest effort, because he forced her to join mind to body in the desire to remember something. She did not wish to remember; it troubled her when people tried to disturb her loneliness; she wished to be alone. She wished for nothing else in the world.

"On this day indeed": it is the day of Rachel's death. The narrative knows that, but can disclose that knowledge only indirectly, through implication and imagery. It imagines Rachel's exhausted consciousness drifting in both space and time, out of control, and now too tired to care, between the ultimate antinomies: a visible, moving surface and a beckoning, fathomless depth; a reassuring solidity and a seductive melting; a familiar room and an expansion into infinity; the effort of concentration and of relating to other people and the ecstasy of forgetting and lapsing into a final unconsciousness. Rachel remains aware of the distortions of her perspectives, but ceases to struggle toward any goal or even to maintain her identity. The narrative too lets itself go, and the paragraph culminates in the ecstasy of the desire for unconsciousness, forgetting, melting into the infinite. It is a consummation.

Now the narrative shifts to the consciousness of Terence, where it remains—except for momentary glimpses into the minds of St. John Hirst and Ridley Ambrose, and for a few moments of attempted objectivity—through the time of Rachel's death a few pages later. Significantly, that death must be perceived through the consciousness of Terence:

The light being dim, it was impossible to see any change in her face. An immense feeling of peace came over Terence, so that he had no wish to move or to speak. The terrible torture and unreality of the last days were over, and he had come out now into perfect certainty and peace. His mind began to work naturally again and with great ease. The longer he sat there the more profoundly was he conscious of the peace invading every corner of his soul. Once he held his breath and listened acutely; she was still breathing; he went on thinking for some time; they seemed to be thinking together; he seemed to be Rachel as well as himself; and then he listened again; no, she had ceased to breathe. So much the better—this was death. It was nothing; it was to cease to breathe. It was happiness, it was perfect happiness. They had now what they had always wanted to have, the union which had been impossible while they lived. Unconscious whether he thought the words or spoke them aloud, he said, "No two people have ever been so happy as we have been. No one has ever loved as we have loved."

It seemed to him that their complete union and happiness filled the room with rings eddying more and more widely. He had no wish in the world left unfulfilled. They possessed what could never be taken from them.

This, then, is the fulfillment of that earlier moment in the jungle, when Rachel and Terence had echoed each other's words, "This is happiness."[11] In death Rachel seems to have achieved eternal life in the mind of Terence, beyond the ravages and limitations of physical existence. But the narrative recognizes that this immortality is an illusion too, and outside Rachel's room Terence realizes that "here was a world in which he would never see Rachel again." The chapter ends with what will become a familiar scene in the lifework: the bereaved man, holding out his empty arms, repeating the name of his lost lady.

In Terence's perception of Rachel's death the narrative reaches the climax of the lovers' quest for transcendence. The pathology of

11 Terence's "unconscious" words, "No two people have ever been so happy as we have been," foreshadow the last words that Virginia Woolf ever wrote, which close her suicide note to her husband: "I don't think two people could have been happier than we have been. V." Thus these words, from the very beginning of the lifework, are recognized as originating in the unconscious, and are associated with the dramatization of death.

such quests has been described by Denis de Rougemont in his brilliant study of the Tristan-Iseult legend:

The love of Tristan and Iseult was the anguish of being *two*; and its culmination was a headlong fall into the limitless bosom of Night, there where individual shapes, faces, and destinies all vanish: "Iseult is no more, Tristan no more, and no name can any longer part us!" The other has to cease to be the other, and therefore, to cease to be altogether. . . . But married love is the end of anguish, the acceptance of a limited being whom I love because he or she is a summons to be created, and that in order to witness our alliance this being turns with me towards day.[12]

Rachel and Terence do not love each other—not in the sense of the "married love" of which de Rougemont speaks. Rather, each is "in love" with the idea of love; each is the romantic lover savoring and trying to intensify his own narcissistic feeling. The narrative could not envision Rachel and Terence turning towards day. They belong instead, together and apart, to the night and the silence. So when Rachel dies, Terence must also vanish into that dark silence; his despairing cry, "Rachel, Rachel!" must be, symbolically, his own epitaph too. He is neither seen nor heard again, through the two remaining chapters.

These last two chapters return to the perspectives from which the lovers had taken their voyage out. These perspectives, incarnate in Miss Allan, Mrs. Thornbury, Mr. and Mrs. Flushing, Mrs. Paley, Evelyn Murgatroyd, Arthur Venning, and at times even in a sort of collective consciousness of the English colony in Santa Marina, emerge against an implied background of much more exciting and interesting incarnations. The narrative relies rather heavily on such implied contrasts for dramatic irony, and uses even nature itself rather melodra-

---

12 *Love in the Western World*, trans. Montgomery Belgion (Rev. ed.; New York: Fawcett, 1966), 324. Avrom Fleishman discusses the allusions to Wagner's *Tristan und Isolde*, and says that "It might be possible to equate Rachel's or Clarissa's responses with the criticism that Denis de Rougemont makes of the legend's correlation of love and death. . . . But it will turn out that love and death are, at least for Rachel, simultaneously achieved, and her rapture in the jungle may be seen as her moment of *ascesis*. . . . Woolf manages to scorn the *Liebestod* motif and affirm it, too" (pp. 15–16). The novel itself, however, explores the motif with enough complexity to make terms like *scorn* and *affirm* seem too simplistic.

matically: the waves are "restrained," a thunderstorm comes to regenerate the wasteland, and so on.

The final perspective of *The Voyage Out* becomes incarnate in St. John Hirst. The other residents of the hotel try tentatively to question him about Rachel's death and Terence's reaction.

But St. John made no reply. He lay back in his chair, half-seeing the others, half-hearing what they said. He was terribly tired, and the light and warmth, the movements of the hands, and the soft communicative voices soothed him; they gave him a strange sense of quiet and relief. As he sat there, motionless, this feeling of relief became a feeling of profound happiness. Without any sense of disloyalty to Terence and Rachel he ceased to think about either of them. The movements and the voices seemed to draw together from different parts of the room, and to combine themselves into a pattern before his eyes; he was content to sit silently watching the pattern build itself up, looking at what he hardly saw.

The narrative calls Hirst by his Christian name now (the creation in the gospel of John is not of the world, but the Word). He has entered into a transcendent state which he, like Rachel and Terence before him, identifies as "happiness." But his ecstasy is different from theirs. The public room of the hotel, filled with people and movement and voices, becomes *his* room, the existential space in which he has his being. It is filled with silence—not the dark void into which Rachel and Terence have vanished, but the quiet of warmth and light and "soft communicative voices" whose words need not be heard or understood. It is enough that they are human voices, and that he is aware of them. And so St. John, the prototype of the artist, finds contentment in contemplating the aesthetic structure of the life around him, "watching the pattern build itself up, looking at what he hardly saw."

The pattern continues to develop, and the final paragraph of the book reveals that the pattern itself has now been subsumed within St. John's consciousness: "All these voices sounded gratefully in St. John's ears as he lay half asleep, and yet vividly conscious of everything around him. Across his eyes passed a procession of objects, black and indistinct, the figures of people picking up their books, their cards, their balls of wool, their work-baskets, and passing him one after another on their way to bed." Voices, objects, people—all the phenomena of the created world achieve their epiphany in the creative imagination, "vividly conscious." This sudden and final visionary moment, the largest and fullest perspective possible for the narrative consciousness, becomes the archetypal conclusion for every one of the nine novels of Virginia Woolf. As *The Voyage Out* ends, everyone but St. John is off to bed. That is not the destination, or the destiny, of Virginia Woolf's abstracted artists. Their creation is the word.

As the "first articulation" of a symbolic language, *The Voyage Out* discloses mythic patterns which remain essentially "immovable" throughout the *oeuvre*, even though later works will elaborate and modify them. Each of the novels represents a psychological voyage out of a familiar but oppressive reality toward a realm that is unknown and exciting, and which seems to promise wholeness. The narrative consciousness struggles to transcend the limited roles ordained by the family and society. Although the struggle involves sexual conflict, the final transcendence can be achieved only in a detached, distanced, almost asexual identity which can comprehend experience without drowning in it. This personality can emerge only after all passion is spent. In *The Voyage Out* it is essentially an observer, but in the later works it becomes more and more closely identified with the role of the creative artist—painter, writer, dramatist. The most perilous and fruitful moments in the voyage are always the moments of discontinuity and transition, from one adaptation to another. These transitions and adaptations are achieved through perspective: the narrative cannot really control events, but only choose how to view them.

CHAPTER II

NIGHT AND DAY

The final perspective of *The Voyage Out* had a very high price: the young woman at the heart of the book had to die to make that serenity possible. The second novel, *Night and Day*, explores variations of that same basic story which might allow it to turn out differently. Again it all begins in the heart of London. Again the month is October. Again a young woman embarks upon a voyage out.

But the circumstances of Katharine Hilbery are less severe than those of Rachel Vinrace. Katharine has not lost her mother (that circumstance is assigned to Mary Datchet in *Night and Day*), and she is under no immediate compulsion to begin her journey. She lives in "an extremely nice house" in prestigious Cheyne Walk, Chelsea. She is physically beautiful and socially adept. Her life is much more comfortable than that of the average young woman of her time. But there is a hollowness at the core of her existence, and a longing for meaning which becomes more insistent as the story goes on.

Although the book is primarily her story, the narrative enters the minds of many other characters in its search for the meaning of its "world." It identifies mainly with the younger people of that world. Katharine is twenty-seven years old. Ralph Denham, the man she eventually falls in love with, is twenty-nine. Mary Datchet, the young woman who loves Ralph but must see him fall in love with Katharine, is twenty-five. William Rodney, to whom Katharine becomes engaged early in the story, is thirty-five—though he is the most adolescent character in the book. Cassandra Otway, Katharine's country cousin with whom William later falls in love, is twenty-two. The fact that the narrative specifies the exact ages of so many of the characters is a sign of its concerns with the conflict between generations, and with the problems of growing into maturity in a society in which many people must remain dependent into middle age and beyond. And for women, opportunities for independence are very severely limited. The book considers feminism as a possible answer to this problem—and finds it not very satisfying: Mary Datchet eventually leaves her job with the suffrage movement to work with the Society for the Education of Democracy.

The narrative is also "privileged" to enter the minds of the older generation, where it finds that older people are not necessarily grown up either. Mr. Hilbery (another portrait of Leslie Stephen) remains a spoiled child, although his male authority must remain unchallenged in this "given" world. But his wife is finally more than a match for him. She is "well advanced in the sixties," and her eccentricities are regarded with amused tolerance. But as the story goes on, we can begin to see them as part of her strategy for coping with her social world. At the end she rounds up and reconciles all of the conflicting parties, and does it so deftly that they think they are indulging her—whereas she is actually manipulating them. Thus the resolution to their conflicts is not so much achieved by the young people themselves as it is imposed on them, or at least created for them, by Mrs. Hilbery. And so the young people remain dependent to the end—and beyond.

In its search for the meaning of this second voyage out, the narrative consciousness maintains more distance from its story, and maintains it more consistently, than in the first. Although it enters the minds of many different characters, it never gets lost in them—as it did, for example, in the mind of Rachel at crucial moments in *The Voyage Out*. Throughout, it is concerned with social commentary and criticism. The tone verges on the satirical as the book begins, and it remains rather skeptical even though it grows more serious. The story opens, however, very much in the style of the traditional novel of manners.

It was a Sunday evening in October, and in common with many other young ladies of her class, Katharine Hilbery was pouring out tea. Perhaps a fifth part of her mind was thus occupied, and the remaining parts leapt over the little barrier of day which interposed between Monday morning and this rather subdued moment, and played with the things one does voluntarily and normally in the daylight. But although she was silent, she was evidently mistress of a situation which was familiar enough to her, and inclined to let it take its way for the six hundredth time, perhaps, without bringing into play any of her unoccupied faculties. A single glance was enough to show that Mrs. Hilbery was so rich in the gifts which make tea-parties of elderly distinguished people successful, that she scarcely needed any help from her daughter, provided that the tiresome business of teacups and bread and butter was discharged for her.

Considering that the little party had been seated round the tea-table for less than twenty minutes, the animation observable on their faces, and the amount of sound they were producing collectively, were very creditable to the hostess. It suddenly came into Katharine's mind that if some one opened the door at this moment he would think that they were enjoying themselves; he would think, 'What an extremely nice house to come into!' and instinctively she laughed, and said something to increase the noise, for the credit of the house presumably, since she herself had not been feeling exhilarated. At the very same moment, rather to her amusement, the door was flung open, and a young man entered the room. Katharine, as she shook hands with him, asked him, in her own mind, 'Now, do you think we're enjoying ourselves enormously?' . . . 'Mr. Denham, mother,' she said aloud, for she saw that her mother had forgotten his name.

The fact was perceptible to Mr. Denham also, and increased the awkwardness which inevitably attends the entrance of a stranger into a room full of people much at their ease, and all launched upon sentences. At the same time, it seemed to Mr. Denham as if a thousand softly padded doors had closed between him and the street outside. A fine mist, the etherealized essence of the fog, hung visibly in the wide and rather empty space of the drawing-room, all silver where the candles were grouped on the tea-table, and ruddy again in the firelight. With the omnibuses and cabs still running in his head, and his body still tingling with his quick walk along the streets and in and out of traffic and foot-passengers, this drawing-room seemed very remote and still; and the faces of the elderly people were mellowed, at some distance from each other, and had a bloom on them owing to the fact that the air in the drawing-room was thickened by blue grains of mist. Mr. Denham had come in as Mr. Fortescue, the eminent novelist, reached the middle of a very long sentence. He kept this suspended while the new-comer sat down, and Mrs. Hilbery deftly joined the severed parts by leaning towards him and remarking:

'Now, what would you do if you were married to an engineer, and had to live in Manchester, Mr. Denham?'

'Surely she could learn Persian,' broke in a thin, elderly gentleman. 'Is there no retired schoolmaster, or man of letters in Manchester with whom she could read Persian?'

'A cousin of ours has married and gone to live in Manchester,' Katharine explained. Mr. Denham muttered something, which was indeed all that was required of him, and the novelist went on where he had left off. Privately, Mr. Denham cursed himself very sharply for having exchanged the freedom of the street for this sophisticated drawing-room, where, among other disagreeables, he certainly would not appear at his best. He glanced round him, and saw that, save for Katharine, they were all over forty, the only consolation being that Mr. Fortescue was a considerable celebrity, so that tomorrow one might be glad to have met him.[1]

The stance of the narrative in this opening passage is omniscient: it is in a position to know everything about this world and the people in it. As in a master shot or establishing shot in cinema, it locates the characters and their milieu. In the first sentence it generalizes about Katharine's "class" and the activities of the "young ladies" in it. Then come further generalizations about the activities of her mind. The narrative doesn't really show that mind in operation; rather, it asserts that a "fifth part" of that mind is "occupied" with the tea ceremony, and that the other four fifths "played" with other things. By now the perspective of the narrative is essentially congruent with Katharine's perspective, and the allusion to the fractional parts of her mind may reveal her preoccupation with what the narrative will refer to as "mathematics." Toward the end of the first paragraph, the commentary approximates the tone of Katharine's own thoughts, but still sum-

1 The text I refer to here is the first English edition of *Night and Day* (London: Duckworth, 1919).

marizes and evaluates them rather than rendering them directly. The congruence between the commentary and Katharine's thoughts is reinforced in the second paragraph.

The third paragraph begins, also in the realm of generality, with a transition from Katharine's mind to Ralph's. The narrative penetrates somewhat more deeply into his thoughts than it had into hers, and the sentence about the "fine mists" comes close to the immediacy of his perceptions. But the next sentence withdraws to a greater distance with its commentary about what is "running in his head" and the assertion that his body is "still tingling." By the end of the paragraph the stance is omniscient once again, referring to Ralph as "the newcomer."

Throughout this first chapter, which describes Ralph's visit to the Hilberys, the camera lens of the narrative sees the scene from the perspective of either Katharine or Ralph, or from a somewhat more distanced view which is still compatible with one of those perspectives. The chapter establishes, then, a world in which these two young people are central. It is a world of considerable discomfort. Ralph is aware that he doesn't belong there; he feels trapped; he knows that "he certainly would not appear at his best." Katharine senses his nervousness and detects what she interprets as hostility, and this leads to her "rather malicious determination not to help this young man" in his ordeal. Consequently, the hostility which she imagines she then manages to provoke, and "He was amused and gratified to find that he had the power to annoy his oblivious, supercilious hostess, if he could not impress her; though he would have preferred to impress her." She, in turn, "wished to annoy him, to waft him away from her on some light current of ridicule or satire, as she was wont to do with these intermittent young men of her father's." As the ordeal escalates, so does Ralph's desire to escape—but so does Mrs. Hilbery's repertoire of hospitality,

and at one time it seemed to the young man that he would be hypnotized into doing what she pretended to want him to do, for he could not suppose that she attached any value whatever to his presence. Katharine, however, made an opportunity for him to leave, and for that he was grateful to her, as one young person is grateful for the understanding of another.

Thus the chapter ends, in an unexpected alliance between the two young people and a gesture which enables one of them to become, for the moment at least, free.

The world of this opening chapter is a social world, and the tone and focus of the narrative are those of the traditional novel of manners. But the essence of this world—like every world in the lifework—is psychological. Tension, self-consciousness, hostility, the longing to escape: these are the realities which dominate the "given" world of *Night and Day*, and which the narrative consciousness tries to find a way out of. Katharine is trapped in her social role as dutiful daughter: serving tea to elderly ladies and famous novelists, helping her mother with the amorphous biography of the family poet, shielding her father from the inconveniences of life in the quotidian. She needs to be released from the demands of her parents, yet these demands give structure and definition to her life. And her heritage is valuable to her. Ralph envies her for it and for her self-assurance, and is very conscious of the limitations of his own family. All of this shows the narrative's own ambivalence toward the values of the Hilberys and the Denhams. And the narrative also sees the "given" world from a different perspective than that of the opening of *The Voyage Out*.

Night and Day consists of thirty-four chapters. The story is told in chronological order, from "a Sunday evening in October," sometime "in these first years of the twentieth century," to "a June night" in the summer of the following year. But the sense of time is rather vague throughout the book. The occasional references to the months or the seasons of the year serve more as mileposts in the chronology than as integral parts of the development of the story, as they would, for example, in the novels of D. H. Lawrence.

The dynamics of place seem somewhat more important. The Hilberys live in Chelsea. Ralph Denham and his family live in "a threadbare, well-worn house" in Highgate. Mary Datchet lives in "rather large" rooms just off the Strand, and works in an office in Russell Square, Bloomsbury. William Rodney lives in a suite of small rooms in an eighteenth-century house in the City of London. In Chapters 15 through 19 the action shifts to the country near Lincoln, first to Disham, where Mary's father is a rector, then to Stogdon House, the home of Katharine's cousins the Otways. Each of these places has its own ambiance, usually more implied than explicitly stated, but still rather fully realized and shown, in subtle ways, as nurturing and influencing the characters. Movements from one of these environments to another are important, both as causes and as symptoms of changes in the psychodynamics of the characters and their story.

What is that story about? Apparently, it is about the hopes for marriage of the characters, especially Katharine Hilbery. Why this should be interesting—or extended to over five hundred pages—is puzzling to many readers today. And in a sense *Night and Day* is an historical novel—about the twilight of an era which ended suddenly in 1914. Perhaps the unreality of Katharine's engagements to William Rodney and then to Ralph Denham is part of what the book is about: the range of authentic identities available to her is very painfully limited. At the age of twenty-seven, she is trapped in the role of tea pourer, research assistant, and dutiful daughter to the Hilberys. Her only realistic hope for escape is marriage. Her domineering father is the editor of the *Critical Review*. Katharine's private vice is, of all things, "mathematics," because "in her mind mathematics were directly opposed to literature." She hides her work from everyone, but not so completely that it fails to provide some moments of unintended fun. For instance, her mother finds some of it:

'A plus B minus C equals $x\,y\,z$. It's so dreadfully ugly, Katharine. That's what I feel—so dreadfully ugly.'

It is as if the mother had discovered a book of pornography. And indeed, as this and other excerpts reveal, the narrative consciousness hasn't the faintest idea of what "mathematics" might be about: it is an unknown realm, an arcane language which, in this naïve view, has none of the ambiguities or uncertainties of literary language. Although Katharine is alleged to know "mathematics," to her it means nothing more than the negation of literature.

Katharine, we learn in Chapter 26, should be seen in contrast with her cousin Cassandra. They "seemed to assemble between them a great range of qualities which are never found united in one person and seldom in half a dozen people. Where Katharine was simple, Cassandra was complex; where Katharine was solid and direct, Cassandra was vague and evasive. In short, they represented very well the manly and womanly side of the feminine nature." Emerging from a description of how the cousins are generally perceived by society, this passage does not necessarily represent the whole truth of how they are seen by the narrative consciousness itself. But it is a significant aspect of that truth. Part of Katharine's rebellion is directed against the socially accepted—and imposed—norms of "femininity." That is why she is so deeply moved by Mary Datchet, a young woman who makes almost no compromises with the truth. And partly because of that, perhaps, Mary loses the man she loves to Katharine. Aware of "having lost what is best,"[2] Mary withdraws into her work and becomes a kind of mother confessor for the lovers.

Cassandra represents an opposite destiny: the woman who adopts a role of "femininity" which subordinates her dignity, intellect, and even her identity to the whims of her man. Katharine's own personality evolves toward a mature identity somewhere between those two extremes—or so the narrative consciousness wishes to believe. She can never really let herself go, but must, instead, struggle constantly for "mastery" of every situation. That requires a control of perspective and perception, and leads to a self-consciousness which becomes, at times, pathological. Here, for example, is the beginning of Chapter 32:

Nobody asked Katharine any questions next day. If cross-examined she might have said that nobody spoke to her. She worked a little, wrote a little, ordered the dinner, and sat, for longer than she knew, with her head on her hand piercing whatever lay before her, whether it was a letter or a dictionary, as if it were a film upon the deep prospects that revealed themselves to her kindling and brooding eyes. She rose once, and going to the bookcase, took out her father's Greek dictionary and spread the sacred pages of symbols and fig-

2 This expression is reminiscent of one in Forster's *The Longest Journey* (1907). Ricky, Forster's autobiographical character, shrinks away from sex with Agnes, who had been passionately in love with Gerald. When she "bent down to touch him with her lips," Ricky "started, and cried passionately, 'Never forget that your greatest thing is over.'" He reminds her of this again and again, whenever she seems too aggressive. Agnes, the narrative says with perfect seriousness, "had the sense of something abnormal."

ures [her "mathematics," which she hides in the dictionary, safe, apparently, from her father] before her. She smoothed the sheets with a mixture of affectionate amusement and hope. Would other eyes look on them with her one day? The thought, long intolerable, was now just bearable.

She was quite unaware of the anxiety with which her movements were watched and her expression scanned. Cassandra was careful not to be caught looking at her. . . .

The paranoia of this passage encompasses not just Katharine but the narrative itself, and is one of the central realities of *Night and Day*. The preoccupation here with being interrogated, cross-examined, watched, and of seeing through surfaces to the inner realities of things, the expressions of anxiety—all of this is disproportionate to any discernible cause (other than the obsessions of the narrative consciousness itself.) And the other major characters seem to suffer from the same self-consciousness. It is a governing principle of their "world."

The narrative searches for a way out of that world. Here as in *The Voyage Out*, each chapter constitutes an avenue of that search. And most of these avenues lead toward dead ends, in which the dominant feelings are of entrapment, helplessness, inferiority, dissatisfaction, alienation, disappointment, diminishment, surprise, compulsion, injustice, discomfort, puzzlement, desperation, exposure, escapism, absence, intrusion, misunderstanding, evasion, inexpressiveness, surrender, hollowness, ambivalence. The cumulative effect is depressing: so much sensitivity, so much awareness, comes to so very little in the end.

Five of the first six chapters of the book end in perspectives which are attributed to males. Then comes a series of five chapters which end in female perspectives. After that the pattern becomes more complicated, but the female perspective remains dominant throughout the book, even though it is balanced increasingly by perspectives which are more objective (*i.e.*, distanced from both male and female characters). Two chapters (25 and 34) end in perspectives which seem to be shared by Ralph and Katharine, and in which the name given to the perceiving consciousness is simply "they." Especially prominent in the "male" endings in the book are feelings of self-con-

sciousness, defeat, and diminishment. The "female" endings emphasize feelings of puzzlement, desperation, and being forced. If there is
an overall pattern in the way in which the narrative consciousness
enters the story, it is the growth of a more distanced, impersonal point
of view which moves beyond the limitations of the individual characters. Such a point of view is present from the very beginning, however, and the narrative's quest for incarnation in the individual characters does not go very deep. Although the narrative is, more often
than not, at least vaguely associated with the perspective of one of the
characters, it is careful not to lose itself in their feelings. Although
Katharine is certainly the central figure of *Night and Day*, the narrative consciousness doesn't identify itself only with her point of view.
Scenes where Mary and Katharine are together are often described
through Mary's perspective; scenes with Katharine and Ralph are
often viewed through his. Thus, even though the narrative is theoretically "omniscient," it doesn't always know what Katharine is thinking or feeling. She remains somewhat opaque and mysterious.

The other young people are less interesting. William Rodney is
more a caricature than a character, and the reader may resent Katharine's choice for him of her country cousin—except that Cassandra herself may be silly enough to deserve him. A number of critics have felt
that the plot creaks in this series of pledged and broken betrothals.
And even though it all may be intended as satire, that doesn't make it
much more interesting.

The characters exist more as intellectual identities than as physical
beings. Here is the first physical description of Ralph Denham in the
book: "a bony young man with his face slightly reddened by the wind,
and his hair not altogether smooth"—Ralph as seen by Katharine.
Now Katharine is seen through the eyes of Ralph:

Katharine . . . had a likeness to each of her parents, and these elements were
rather oddly blended. She had the quick, impulsive movements of her
mother, the lips parting often to speak, and closing again; and the dark oval
eyes of her father brimming with light upon a basis of sadness, or, since she
was too young to have acquired a sorrowful point of view, one might say that
the basis was not sadness so much as a spirit given to contemplation and self-

control. Judging by her hair, her colouring, and the shape of her features, she was striking, if not actually beautiful. Decision and composure stamped her, a combination of qualities that produced a very marked character, and one that was not calculated to put a young man, who scarcely knew her, at his ease. For the rest, she was tall; her dress was of some quiet colour, with old yellow-tinted lace for ornament, to which the spark of an ancient jewel gave its one red gleam. Denham noticed that, although silent, she kept sufficient control of the situation to answer immediately her mother appealed to her for help, and yet it was obvious to him that she attended only with the surface of her mind.

Although the narrative allegedly describes Ralph's view of Katharine here, this isn't a very convincing description of the way in which such a man—except, perhaps, a geneticist—would perceive a beautiful young woman for the first time: as an odd blend of certain qualities of her parents. (It is probably very close, however, to Virginia Woolf's perception of herself.) The passage expresses, instead, certain obsessions of the narrative consciousness: the concern with the chances of escape from the imperatives of one's genetic heritage, the yearning for composure and control in social situations, the wish to be thought of as interesting, the need to be valued for qualities which are other than physical. In Katharine, then, the narrative tries to create such a personality, and to imagine how she might seem to a suitable male. All of the aspects, possibilities, and configurations of character and action in the book turn around this male-female axis.

The situation of the central female character is much less extreme than it had been in *The Voyage Out*, where the creative consciousness found that love can be lethal. Rachel's first encounter with sexual desire made her drown in black waves of sensation. And her entry into the heart of darkness with Terence infected her with a fever that was finally fatal. But Katharine still has her mother and her home in London, and is not forced to experience a Santa Marina. Her environment is comforting. Sexual desire never makes an appearance—unless it is suitably disguised as smoke or flame. Instead the focus is on engagements to be married, books to be written, and other social issues. Deviations from the social norms are ridiculed, more or less gently as the transgressions deserve, as in the novel of manners. Yet the satire doesn't have a great deal of conviction either; the book has no very strong center of belief.

The opening chapter, as we have seen, defines a "given" world which the narrative consciousness sees the need to transform or to escape from. In fact, this given world extends far beyond the first chapter: it includes not only Katharine's entrapment in pouring tea and exhibiting the family's "things" but also Ralph's in the demands of his career and of his family in Highgate, Katharine's in the never-finished biography of the poet, Mary's in her feminism, William Rodney's in his studies of Elizabethan metaphor and his playwriting.

A woman can transform or escape from her given world through her choice of a marriage partner. In the view of the narrative consciousness here, at least, this is almost the only meaningful choice that she can make. Mary Datchet's work with the suffrage movement might seem at first to offer another choice, but the narrative reveals that her work is less important to her than her love for Ralph. She refuses his proposal of marriage only because she knows that he really loves Katharine. Although Mary's work is alleged to be important, it has very little reality in the narrative consciousness, which remains preoccupied with other things. And for that matter, the work of Ralph Denham and of William Rodney has even less reality: although the narrative does enter their minds, and is as comfortable in Ralph's as in the mind of any other character, it almost never finds them thinking about their work. On the contrary, their mental realities reflect the concerns of the narrative consciousness itself, which have very little to do with work. What Ralph and William represent are reflections of these concerns rather than autonomous realities.

There is also a mechanical quality in the plot itself and in the configuration of characters which works against their reality as independent entities. The discovery that William Rodney loves Cassandra, for example, comes as a surprise, and is believable primarily as an illustration of the narrative's need to get him out of the way. That need itself has been evident almost from the first view of him. But the narrative does not show the development of their attraction; it merely reveals it as an accomplished fact, and the reader is left to imagine the rationale for it. Are William and Cassandra simply so shallow and conventional that they find each other by default?

But the "testing" of the three main characters, their adaptations to the given world and their attempts to transform it—all of this is believable, at least at the symbolic level. The crucial quality to be tested is reflected in the pervasive emphasis on Katharine's composure, on her ability to stand up against various social trials, on her ability, above all, not to lose control. Control, composure, decision: these are her essential traits, which both Ralph and William notice again and again—and which the narrative itself constantly emphasizes. The ending of the book represents a resolution of that conflict. Whether or not that resolution works—or rather, how it works—may be the most complex question we can ask about *Night and Day*.

The penultimate chapter of *Night and Day* ends in a break between Katharine and her father. When she tells him that she and Ralph are engaged, "he never looked at his daughter, and strode out of the room, leaving in the minds of the women a sense, half of awe, half of amusement, at the extravagant, inconsiderate, uncivilized male, outraged somehow and gone bellowing to his lair with a roar which still somehow reverberates in the most polished of drawing-rooms. Then Katharine, looking at the shut door, looked down again, to hide her tears." Mr. Hilbery's refusal to look at "his daughter" (the term itself shows his possessiveness) signals the end of the special, intimate, unspoken communication between them—and, therefore, the beginning of a new phase of their relationship. The "room" here, as in all of Virginia Woolf's novels, represents a space in consciousness—here, as in most cases, a feminine space. And the fact that Mr. Hilbery has left it also signals the end of his role as the dominant male in that space. The narrative here is quite specific in its listing of the faults of the "male"; the implied contrast between such behavior and the norms of civilization is also obvious. The "shut door" represents the closing of a phase in Katharine's life as well as the end of the special communication between her and her father. She is now ready to "hide her tears," and thus to refuse to allow this possessive, unreasonable man to continue to have the same kind of power over her. Freed from his tyranny, she is now ready to enter a new realm of understanding and experience.

"The lamps were lit": the first words of the final chapter imply the reconciliation of the domains of night and day, the illumination of this new realm of knowledge—the realm of poetry, really, where such reconciliations can take place. In the final chapter the poetic symbols and motifs echo those of *The Voyage Out* and anticipate those of the later novels. *Night and Day*, which has been for the most part a rather dispassionate and even satirical comedy of manners, now moves into that realm of transcendence where all of Virginia Woolf's novels end.

The illumination at the beginning of the chapter suggests the famous "luminous halo" mentioned in the essay "Modern Fiction." The "lustre" of the lamps is reflected throughout the room, in its furnishings, in the wine, and especially in Katharine's eyes. It even civilizes Mr. Hilbery to the extent that "with a sign he listened to the music" which compensates, in its way, for the absence of Katharine. He has contemplated "the closed door for some seconds unwaveringly"—like the door which he had shut between himself and "his daughter" earlier, this one is an emblem of his new relationship with her, a relationship which is saddening for both of them but which is necessary if she is to become a woman. The lamps and the music seem to help him to realize and accept this.

Katharine and Ralph together enter a realm beyond words where they experience a mysterious unity. Their experience here is very much like that of Rachel and Terence in *The Voyage Out*, who found themselves repeating each other's words, or even speaking to each other without any words at all, or any awareness of which of them had spoken. The loss of identity and stability had been frightening to Rachel; she became disoriented and aware of drowning in a chaotic sea of emotion. This is a pervasive feeling throughout the *oeuvre*, and is exemplified most strikingly in Rhoda in *The Waves*, but also in a number of other characters threatened by ontological insecurity. In Katharine and Ralph, however, the narrative consciousness seems to find a relationship which need not be so threatening.

Still, it does have its pathological elements. As Katharine and Ralph leave the house, she tells him "how she had waited, fidgeted, thought he was never coming, listened for the sound of doors, half expected to see him again under the lamp-post, looking at the house." Ralph's lurking by the lamppost and spying on the house is reminiscent of several voyeuristic scenes in *The Voyage Out*, and may also be related, psychologically, to the traumatic encounter of little Rose Pargiter with the exhibitionist who lurks by the lamppost in *The Years* (an incident which was remembered, apparently, from Virginia Woolf's own childhood). Throughout *Night and Day*, as in the first novel, there are many passages in which sexuality appears through overhearing, spying, and other contexts which emphasize the distance of the personalities involved and the intellectualization of sexual feeling.

After Katharine tells Ralph of her waiting, fidgeting, listening, expectation, "They turned and looked at the serene front with its gold-rimmed windows, to him the shrine of so much adoration." This alludes indirectly, once again, to his watching by the lamppost. Katharine is a saint to be worshipped from afar, and her house is a "shrine," a "serene front with its gold-rimmed windows." The narrative implies that this is only a facade; certainly it has rendered scenes within the house itself which contradict this serenity. But again the house is something to be looked at and believed in, an object for this feeling of "adoration." And so Ralph "would not resign his belief."

Now the lovers embark upon a magical journey. Neither of them could tell how "they came to find themselves walking down a street with many lamps, corners radiant with light, and a steady succession of motor-omnibuses plying both ways along it," nor explain why they suddenly board one of them and "mount to the very front seat" on the top deck. Such voyages come to have a mystical significance in the novels of Virginia Woolf—most notably, perhaps, in *Mrs. Dalloway*, where Clarissa explains her "transcendental theory" of immortality to Peter Walsh as they ride an omnibus, and where Elizabeth, many years later, rides through the Strand, symbolically choosing the values of her mother over those of Miss Kilman. The voyage on the omnibus in the final chapter of *Night and Day* reenacts an earlier journey, at the end of the sixth chapter, in which Katharine and Ralph have boarded an omnibus in Tottenham Court Road. Katharine had said it was "like

Venice," but had then suddenly debarked, leaving Ralph bound for the Temple alone. She will not leave him now. They move through vistas of light and darkness, to a perspective in which "they saw the spires of the city churches pale and flat against the sky." The sky in the novels of Virginia Woolf usually suggests a larger unity—as, for example, in *Jacob's Room* when the sunset unites both London and Piraeus, or when the sky over Cambridge is also the sky over Scarborough. Here in *Night and Day* the sky provides a background against which the city churches appear "flat and pale"—an indication that the narrative consciousness is entering into a larger realm of time and space. The lovers are said to feel "in the forefront of some triumphal car, spectators of a pageant enacted for them, masters of life." But when they leave the omnibus, "this exaltation left them."

The perspective now becomes more personal. The illumination is more sharply focused, first on Ralph: Katharine sees "his face isolated in the little circle of light." She looks also at the sky, and is comforted to know that it is "the same everywhere": "she was now secure of all that this lofty blue and its steadfast lights meant to her; reality, was it, figures, love, truth?" This feeling of unity and wholeness is then expressed in a symbol which is important throughout the *oeuvre*: "she held in her hands for one brief moment the globe which we spend our lives in trying to shape, round, whole, and entire from the confusion of chaos." The globe, too, is created by perspective, not just perceived by it. Human perspective is what creates order and wholeness, and what defends those perceptions against the threats of chaos.

When Ralph tells Katharine that he wishes to see Mary Datchet, she first sees this as a threat to her new feeling of unity, but then realizes that she must allow him the freedom "to do what appeared to be necessary if he, too, were to hold his globe for a moment round, whole, and entire." But then she is overcome for a moment by "melancholy," which "obscured at least a section of her clear vision. The globe swam before her as if obscured by tears." Similar sudden blurrings of vision by tears occur elsewhere in the novels—for example, in the next book, *Jacob's Room*, which opens with Betty Flanders' blurred perception of the bay. But here in *Night and Day* the narrative consciousness maintains such a distance from its characters that it must explain why "The globe swam before her." In the opening scene with Betty Flanders the narrative renders the vision itself; it doesn't explain it.

The next paragraph of *Night and Day* deals with the mystical sense of unity which has been growing between the lovers: " 'I regret nothing,' said Ralph firmly. She leant towards him almost as if she could thus see what he saw. She thought how obscure he still was to her, save only that more and more constantly he appeared to her a fire burning through its smoke, a source of life." Ralph's comment shows that he has understood implicitly Katharine's misgivings about his seeing Mary. Katharine's gesture emphasizes the struggle toward unity of perception and perspective. Again, however, the narrative maintains a certain distance from her consciousness, speculating on the meaning of her gestures, summarizing—rather then rendering—her thoughts. The imagery of fire and smoke is also made somewhat more explicit here, defined as "a source of life" rather than left in the realm of mystery. The meditation on the fire is continued for two more short paragraphs. Ralph's words make the flame more splendid in Katharine's view. Her enticing him to "say more" is described in almost explicitly sexual terms, and his growing speech continues the sexual metaphor:

'Why nothing?' she asked hurriedly, in order that he might say more and so make more splendid, more red, more darkly intertwined with smoke this flame rushing upwards.

'What are you thinking of, Katharine?' he asked suspiciously, noticing her tone of dreaminess and the inapt words.

'I was thinking of you—yes, I swear it. Always of you, but you take such strange shapes in my mind. You've destroyed my loneliness. Am I to tell you how I see you? No, tell me—tell me from the beginning.'

Beginning with spasmodic words, he went on to speak more and more fluently, more and more passionately, feeling her leaning towards him, listening with wonder like a child, with gratitude, like a woman. She interrupted him gravely now and then.

Her major "reproof," it seems, has to do with his watching the house from the lamppost. She seems fascinated and excited by his voyeuristic interest in her house, but gets no reply to her question. Instead, "he capped her reproof" by referring to her own state of shock when she "stood in Kingsway looking at the traffic until she forgot."

"'But it was then I first knew I loved you!' she exclaimed." In other words, the proof of sexual love is the sudden, total obliviousness to one's surroundings. Now it is Katharine's turn to confess, to "say more," and

> he persuaded her into a broken statement, beautiful to him, charged with extreme excitement as she spoke of the dark red fire, and the smoke twined round it, making him feel that he had stepped over the threshold into the faintly lit vastness of another mind, stirring with shapes, so large, so dim, unveiling themselves only in flashes, and moving away again into the darkness, engulfed by it. They had walked by this time to the street in which Mary lived. . . . they could pace slowly without interruption . . . raising their hands now and then to draw something upon the vast blue curtain of the sky.

Here the fact that the "statement" is "broken" makes it "beautiful" to Ralph. He has "persuaded" Katharine to lose her composure and control. The "extreme excitement" arises from the attempt to speak of the "dark red fire" and the "smoke" with all that they imply, and from the feeling of the entry at last "into the faintly lit vastness of another mind"—the ultimate transcendence, to escape from one's own mind into the dim "vastness of another." The dimness and shadows are important: they contrast with, and enhance, the "lustre" of the civilizing illumination. And they are much more dangerous and exciting. In love, one is ultimately "engulfed by" the darkness, which is irresistible, illuminated in "flashes" by the "dark red fire" of sexual passion. The consciousness is lured into that darkness. This process later becomes symbolized in the lifework by the image of the moths. Here in *Night and Day* the same feeling is expressed in the image, which haunts Ralph in Chapter 28, of birds crashing into the lighthouse.

The sky in this passage functions, as we noted earlier, as an emblem of unity. And so it is that the lovers "lapsed gently into silence, travelling the dark paths of thought side by side towards something discerned in the distance which gradually possessed them both. They were victors, masters of life, but at the same time absorbed in the flame, giving their life to increase its brightness, to testify to their faith. Thus they had walked, perhaps, two or three times up and down Mary Datchet's street before the recurrence of a light burning behind a thin, yellow blind caused them to stop without exactly knowing why they did so. It burnt itself into their minds." The description of the lovers as "absorbed in the flame, giving their life to increase its brightness" confirms their status as ur-moths, at least.

Mary's light is related to, but also very different from, the sexual flame which draws Katharine and Ralph into the vastness. Hers is the light of purposeful endeavor, of dedication to an ideal. It is like Mr. Ramsay's light in *To the Lighthouse*, but treated without the irony which comments on his efforts to march through the alphabet of human knowledge. Because Katharine instinctively understands and honors Mary's light, she suddenly sees it through tears (the narrative maintains a certain distance from the emotion, however, by naming or identifying it: "the light swam like an ocean of gold behind her tears"). "It signalled to her across the dark street; it was a sign of triumph shining there for ever, not to be extinguished this side of the grave." A woman need not be lured by the "dark red fire" into the terrifying vastness, but may instead create an illumination of her own—and an inspiration for others. Confronted with this kind of idealism, Ralph too is reduced to tears and "unable to speak." Compared to the brilliant but transitory sexual "fire," Mary's light is universal and eternal. And so the lovers "stood for some moments, looking at the illuminated blinds, an expression to them both of something impersonal and serene in the spirit of the woman within, working out her plans far into the night—her plans for the good of a world that none of them were ever to know." Again the narrative consciousness maintains some distance between itself and its story by telling rather than showing the emotions it imagines for the characters, and this omniscient stance also enhances the psychological distance from its subject. The narrative can approach serenity in the contemplation of Mary's idealism, an alternative destiny for a consciousness apprehensive of the dark fire of sexual love.

This intuition of an alternative destiny leads Ralph to an epiphany, "a vision of an orderly world." Katharine shares in his effort, and

Together they groped in this difficult region, where the unfinished, the un-fulfilled, the unwritten, the unreturned, came together in their ghostly way and were the semblance of the complete and the satisfactory. The future emerged more splendid than ever from this construction of the present. Books were to be written, and since books must be written in rooms, and rooms must have hangings, and outside the windows there must be land, and an horizon to that land, and trees perhaps, and a hill, they sketched a habitation for themselves upon the outline of great offices in the Strand and continued to make an account of the future upon the omnibus which took them towards Chelsea; and still, for both of them, it swam miraculously in the golden light of a large steady lamp.

"Books were to be written": this is the future which the narrative imagines for these lovers. The books themselves are not imaginable: they are as vague as Ralph's "dissertation" and Katharine's "mathematics." Against this hypothetical future, the present reality emerges in the chain of adjectives: *difficult, unfinished, unfulfilled, unreturned, ghostly*. The hypothetical future may attempt to rationalize the long dissertation which is *Night and Day* itself: a baroque elaboration of themes which are essentially simple but also so awesome that the narrative can't really confront or explore them. The whole passage consists, of course, of assertions and abstractions, summarizing what Ralph and Katharine are thinking rather than rendering those thoughts in their immediacy. The fact that the future "still, for both of them, swam miraculously in the golden light of a large steady lamp" is an indication of its purely intellectual nature: this is the steady, comforting illumination of impersonal intellect rather than the uncertain, scorching flame of emotional involvement.

The voyage back to Chelsea is made once again on an omnibus, that favorite vehicle for epiphanies in Virginia Woolf. And an interesting effect is that "A few lights in bedroom windows burnt but were extinguished one by one as the omnibus passed them." The narrative must consign these bedrooms to darkness and to silence now—just as it will have to look away from the bedrooms near the end of *Jacob's Room* as Jacob himself enters the realm of death and eternity. The passing of the omnibus extinguishes these last lights of sexual passion: that is, the narrative turns away from that passion, releases it finally into the darkness.

Now Katharine is aware, as she and Ralph "dismounted and walked down to the river,"

that they had entered the enchanted region. She might speak to him, but with that strange tremor in his voice, those eyes blindly adoring, whom did he answer? What woman did he see? And where was she walking, and who was her companion? Moments, fragments, a second of vision, and then the flying waters, the winds dissipating and dissolving; then, too, the recollection from chaos, the return of security, the earth firm, superb and brilliant in the sun. From the heart of his darkness he spoke his thanksgiving; from a region as far, as hidden, she answered him. On a June night the nightingales sing, they answer each other across the plain; they are heard under the window among the trees in the garden. Pausing, they looked down into the river which bore its dark tide of waters, endlessly moving, beneath them. They turned and found themselves opposite the house. Quietly they surveyed the friendly place, burning its lamps either in expectation of them or because Rodney was still there talking to Cassandra. Katharine pushed the door half open and stood upon the threshold. The light lay in soft golden grains upon the deep obscurity of the hushed and sleeping household. For a moment they waited, and then loosed their hands. 'Good night,' he breathed. 'Good night,' she murmured back to him.

This final passage of the book takes Katharine and Ralph to the culmination of their relationship. Dismounting from the omnibus, they turn away from the direction of transcendence, and the descent to the river brings them into an "enchanted"—and dangerous—region. The setting is like that of the opening passage of *The Voyage Out* in which Helen Ambrose gazes down into this same river: a tear falls then and blends with an iridescent patch on the surface of the inexorably flowing river. A similar feeling seems to be implied here in *Night and Day*: Katharine too is on the threshold of her journey. But the narrative will not contemplate the river now, with its relentless "dark tide of waters, endlessly moving, beneath them." This is the flood which, as in *The Voyage Out* and in Conrad's famous novella, lures the consciousness always toward the heart of darkness. Ralph and Katharine are already said to be there: "From the heart of his darkness he spoke his thanksgiving; from a region as far, as hidden, she answered him." But the heart of darkness is named, rather than created, by the narrative. It does not dare, as it had in *The Voyage Out*, to enter into that realm. There it could experience dissolution, or the sudden loss of identity: "What woman did he see?" It is the realm of winds and waters and chaos.

And so the lovers turn away together from the river (the emblem of the voyage out into chaos and dissolution) toward the house, which gives structure to their awareness, which encloses and shelters them, and which is "opposite" to the relentless flow toward the heart of darkness. It is a "friendly place"; its light is the steady glow of the "lamps" of knowledge and of civilization, rather than the exciting but uncontrollable and perhaps even lethal flames of sexuality. Its light is "soft" and "golden" and gives definition to "the deep obscurity of the hushed and sleeping household." And it illuminates the parting of the lovers. They say good night to each other, and in doing so they oppose the absolute dominion of the night and of the heart of darkness.

The length of *Night and Day*—the longest of the novels of Virginia Woolf—may reflect the nature of the story itself, especially the fact that the narrative consciousness doesn't know how to bring it to an end. The narrative tests various actions and feelings against its own inner standards of truth, and is unable to discover an authentic answer to the problems of its young people—an answer, that is, which comes from within the young people themselves rather than from the social world outside.

The book begins by exploring the given situations of Katharine and Ralph. Then the more general question of control—or the limits of control—is examined (Chapters 10–12). The next phase of the exploration turns toward another character, Mary (Chapters 13–15, 18–21) and another environment, the country (Chapters 15–19) in the search for an adaptation which could be both authentic and satisfying. Mary's renunciation of sexual love in Chapter 20 is the crucial act in this phase. It enables her to achieve a certain freedom which the remaining lovers cannot have. Yet the narrative consciousness isn't really interested in such a destiny, and it returns—like moths to a flame, or birds to the lighthouse—to the irresistible attractions of love.

In its return to the story of the lovers (primarily to Katharine and Ralph, because William and Cassandra are too limited and flawed) the narrative now examines the possibilities of expression as a means of control of one's experience. At times, indeed, expression becomes experience. After Mary's renunciation of sexual love, she begins to write. Then William Rodney, rebelling against his domination by Katharine, writes to Cassandra. But writing is shown to be more neurotic than other forms of expression. Ralph's poetry, which he values as "the only thing worth doing," he destroys because it isn't good enough. Katharine's sheets of equations and her dissections of circles and squares serve similar personal needs. So does Mrs. Hilbery's biography of her father, the poet whose portrait watches over the social ceremonies of the household and communicates mysteriously with Katharine. In her mother Katharine can see a woman whose destiny is dominated by her father even after his death; the visit to Stratford, however, seems to free Mrs. Hilbery. Her husband is the editor, the ultimate figure of authority for all these writers—until his wife takes command at the end. Even so, in choosing Ralph over William, Katharine unconsciously confirms her father's judgment: as she tells Mary, "My father always says that he's the most remarkable of the young men who write for him."

The most striking instance, perhaps, of the symbolism of writing as a sublimation of sexual experience appears in Chapter 33. Ralph is directed vaguely to Katharine's room by Mrs. Hilbery. Her gesture "had a dignity that Ralph never forgot"—a sure sign of transcendence, as is his "mounting" through the house. The house itself is no longer seen as a facade (the typical view of it throughout most of the book). Now, for the first time, Ralph enters Katharine's room, her psychological space. He finds her "standing with some white papers in her hand, which slowly fluttered to the ground when she saw her visitor." These are her "mathematics." In a grotesque parody of the sexual essence of the scene, "he took them in his hands and, giving her by a sudden impulse his own unfinished dissertation, with its mystical conclusion, they read each other's compositions in silence." For Katharine "The moment of exposure had been exquisitely painful—the light shed startlingly vivid." And for Ralph, her examination of his "dissertation" is equally painful: he "nearly tore the page from her hand in shame and despair when he saw her actually contemplating the idiotic symbol of his most confused and emotional moments." He is aware that the symbol he has drawn, a dot encircled by flames, on his unfinished essay is an expression of his feeling for Katharine. But she interprets it in a more general way: "'Yes, the world looks something like that to me, too.'" This fills him with "profound joy," and he and Katharine lapse into silence, each contemplating the future with "silent adoration."

Both Ralph's "dissertation" and Katharine's "mathematics" are unfinished, and both are euphemistic translations of a more basic language which neither Katharine nor Ralph can speak aloud. They can only read it. Their relentless poeticizing of their own unacknowledged feelings is, from a certain standpoint, merely silly. But it also expresses an important truth. The emphasis throughout the scene on hiding, blushing, defenselessness, trembling, pain, exposure, shame, staring, muteness, and so on creates a powerful psychological reality even though the scene is far from being realistic. And the qualities of Katharine's room which the narrative notices are also revealing: the large windows full of light, the bare table, the long looking glass. In this space, illumination and reflection are everything. It is a purely mental realm, made of ideas and visions, a space where a man and a woman can only "read each other's compositions in silence." They are in love with the idea of being in love, and their feeling can find physical expression only in writing.

Other forms of expression seem more satisfying. In Chapter 22 Katharine herself reaches the status of editor: she finally gets William to confess his love for Cassandra. In the next chapter she "exulted" when Ralph confesses his feelings for her, and he himself is enabled to feel "mastery." In Kew Gardens, in Chapter 25, she enables him to see that "It was in her loneliness that Katharine was unreserved." And Chapter 27, which begins with the visit of the two couples to the zoo, ends with Katharine and Ralph in a deeper intimacy, having entered a silent realm of "looking at" and "showing" which is beyond words. Katharine's power of expression reaches its peak in Chapter 29, in which she puts both Mrs. Milvain and William firmly in their places regarding the William-Cassandra "scandal."

Yet the problem of being "in love" remains—and especially the problem of recognizing and coming to terms with that state in one-self. For Ralph this moment arrives in Chapter 28, with traumatic effects of "physical ruin and disaster. He trembled; he was white; he felt exhausted." The word *love* occurs to him with "a sense of revelation," and "with something like dismay." Instinctively he runs "to find Mary Datchet," and later becomes obsessed with the "odd image . . . of a lighthouse besieged by the flying bodies of lost birds." To be "in love" is to be out of control, lost, even lured into death.

For Katharine the problem is more complicated. Without the presence of her mother (who has gone to the oracle at Stratford) she feels "blankness and desolation," and becomes disoriented. Like Ralph, she must rush to the one who has renounced—and thus transcended—the sexual struggle, and "she let Mary direct her movements for her." At the end of Chapter 31, "biting her lips to control herself, she opened the door upon Ralph Denham," and in a "flood" of feelings, "she let herself sink within his arms and confessed her love." The narrative's use of words related to drowning is revealing here. But explicit recognition does not come until Chapter 33, when Mrs. Hilbery returns with flowers from Shakespeare's tomb and "could not help exclaiming: 'But, Katharine, you *are* in love! at which Katharine flushed, looked startled, as if she had said something that she ought not to have said, and shook her head." This must then be followed by Mrs. Hilbery's memory of her own voyage out, described in terms which recall Rachel's from the previous novel and which anticipate Mrs. Ramsay's in *To the Lighthouse* (who, as she was stepping ashore from a small boat, had suddenly agreed to marry Mr. Ramsay). Then "love" becomes, for Katharine, no longer something to be ashamed of, but "a soothing word when uttered by another, a riveting together of the shattered fragments of the world." For Katharine, then, being "in love" must be not just authorized, but even recognized, by her mother. And it must be done under literary auspices: "From Shakespeare's tomb!" Mrs. Hilbery exclaims, as she drops her "mass" of flowers on the floor of Katharine's room, "with a gesture that seemed to indicate an act of dedication." This scene emerges in implied contrast to the final one of Chapter 32, where Mr. Hilbery, after losing his temper, had said "let us try to behave like civilized beings. Let us read

Sir Walter Scott." But he reads Scott—as Scott must be read in Virginia Woolf—with a "note of hollowness." The contrast here will be repeated in *To the Lighthouse*, where Mr. Ramsay is moved to tears by Scott while his wife reads Shakespeare's sonnets.

Katharine can't discover on her own what it means to be "in love." Instead her mother must tell her. In *The Voyage Out* Rachel eventually passed beyond the protection of her surrogate mother Helen Ambrose, and entered the heart of darkness with Terence. In *Night and Day* the narrative can't imagine Katharine's discovery of sex, but can only allude to it vaguely in an ambiguous metaphor: "she let herself sink within his arms and confessed her love." The implications of drowning and of confession dimly echo the much more vivid—and fatal—experiences of Rachel. In *Night and Day* the narrative looks away from that experience. Its last vie of Katharine is on the threshold of her house in Chelsea, suspended forever between innocence and experience, light and darkness, intellect and feeling, control and chaos—between all of the conflicting, but complementary, aspects of the narrative's world.

The problem of control is never resolved in *Night and Day*. It isn't even confronted with the depth and intensity that it had been in *The Voyage Out*. But it is explored in a more distanced, indirect, objective way. A number of forces threaten the autonomy of the young people in *Night and Day*. Of all of these, the family is the central and most powerful controlling force, shaping the personalities and destinies of individuals through the creation of feelings—love, gratitude, guilt. To some degree this is seen as genetically determined—as in the passage in which Katharine is described for the first time. But genetics can also be used as a psychological weapon—as when Mrs. Hilbery tries to bring her daughter into line by comparing her behavior with that of "Uncle Judge Peter," who used to rehearse his sentences of death in the bathroom. The almost absolute power of the parents, the tyranny of the father, and perhaps even more importantly, the subtleties of the mother, have shaped Katharine's character in such a way that she is "impotent," we learn in Chapter 9, to express her anger. This sense of helplessness leads her to feel that marriage with William, of whom her mother approves, is "inevitable"—and therefore, to consent to it.

The other young people must also struggle for control of their feelings. Mary, a very self-disciplined person, forgets to guard her feelings as she contemplates the Ulysses of the Elgin Marbles, and then suddenly realizes that she is "in love" with Ralph. He is proud of his self-control, but when he suddenly catches sight of Katharine in the street, his knees tremble. And so it goes. The young people of *Night and Day* are constantly at the mercy of their feelings—above all, the feelings of love. Perhaps the crucial revelation in the book comes when Katharine realizes, in Chapter 24, that "The only truth which she could discover was the truth of what she herself felt." The discovery confirms her isolation and encourages her pessimism. But her loneliness, ironically, becomes her "most expansive feeling," as Ralph recognizes. It is what draws them together.

Various means of regaining and ensuring the control of feelings are explored. Mary chooses to renounce being "in love," and Katharine herself chooses, throughout most of the book, to resist it. Habit is another means of controlling the environment for most of the characters. And Katharine has her "dream world" (Chapter 11) where her "feelings were liberated from the constraint which the real world puts upon them." The ability to manage social situations also seems satisfying: after her renunciation of love, Mary becomes much more outspoken and adept with her committees; Katharine too begins to take more control of her social circumstances.

The control of such situations requires expression, and in a larger sense is expression. We have already noted the emphasis on writing, and even reading, as a means of control. But beyond that, beyond the reach of conventional writing, there is another realm where truth manifests itself in ways which transcend the powers and uses of ordinary language. That is the realm of poetry, of a language which does not merely reflect some known reality, but which actually discovers what had not been known before. The writing of poetry, Ralph says, is the only thing worth doing. But he can't do it.

In the closing chapter of *Night and Day*, as we have seen, the language has a poetic dimension which transcends the world of manners and morals within which most of the action has been confined. But the essence of the story moves in that direction. In that final chapter, and in some other moments, the language of the book shares some of the images and symbols which constitute the larger mythic language of the lifework of Virginia Woolf. The final moment of poetic transcendence is never wholly convincing in any of these novels, and in *Night and Day* especially we may question whether the narrative has earned the right to claim its "vision of order." Nevertheless, the longing for that vision, and the fear of paying the price for it—these are unmistakenly there, and at the heart of what the book is about. To see that is to begin to see that *Night and Day*, the longest and, yes, dullest of the novels, has its own authentic, necessary, and even interesting place in the *oeuvre*.

CHAPTER III

JACOB'S ROOM

After the rather conventional *Night and Day*, the lifework turns again toward the frontiers of literary form. The next novel explores those frontiers. As its title implies, *Jacob's Room* creates the story of its central character largely through indirection, by creating "room" for his existence, and a series of perspectives in which he can be discovered. But the story also dramatizes the narrative consciousness itself. "Jacob's room" is a space created in that consciousness. As that space is explored, however, the mystery of Jacob himself deepens, until at the end the narrative can see only what Jacob's mother and Richard Bonamy see: "a pair of Jacob's old shoes."

Of the nine novels of Virginia Woolf, *Jacob's Room* is the one which has the most noticeable narrator. In *Orlando* there is an implied narrator who sometimes discusses the difficulties of "the biographer" and occasionally interrupts with such tongue-in-cheek comments as "But let other pens treat of sex and sexuality; we quit such odious subjects as soon as we can." And *The Waves* turns out to be the story of Bernard, who rises in the final chapter to become the dominant and unifying voice of the six soliloquists at the beginning, and to subsume the impersonal voice of the interludes as well. In *Jacob's Room*, however, a voice of commentary interrupts the descriptive story from time to time, and eventually goes so far as to announce its own identity ("I") and even its sex (female—already implicit in such early comments as "who shall deny . . . that in these respects every woman is nicer than any man?").

Like the other novels *Jacob's Room* reflects the struggle of the narrative consciousness to bring its story into being. As the process continues, the narrative imagines various personalities, and creates a world of phenomena around them. Yet it also withdraws from them and that world toward a realm of commentary—and eventually to the posture of commentator. But that turns out to be frustrating also, the position of a consciousness removed from the story itself, uncertain of the events which it imagines, yet compelled to comment on them. And so the narrative returns, eventually, to a purely symbolic world in which overt commentary no longer has a part, and in which phenomena speak for themselves.

The opening passage of the book reveals a "given" world of loneliness, pain, bewilderment:

"So of course," wrote Betty Flanders, pressing her heels rather deeper in the sand, "there was nothing for it but to leave."

Slowly welling from the point of her gold nib, pale blue ink dissolved the full stop; for there her pen stuck; her eyes fixed, and tears slowly filled them. The entire bay quivered; the lighthouse wobbled; and she had the illusion that the mast of Mr. Connor's little yacht was bending like a wax candle in the sun. She winked quickly. Accidents were awful things. She winked again. The mast was straight; the waves were regular; the lighthouse was upright; but the blot had spread.

" . . . nothing for it but to leave," she read.[1]

The narrative easily enters the mind and feelings of Betty Flanders, but soon turns out to be separate from, and superior to, her consciousness. She is writing a letter, and the pen stops at the end of her first sentence—which is the first sentence of the book too: "there was nothing for it but to leave." The pale blue ink continues to flow from

1 My quotations throughout this chapter are from the first English edition of *Jacob's Room* (London: Hogarth, 1922). In the passages I quote there are no significant differences among the various editions.

the pen point, blotting her letter; tears fill her eyes, distorting her view of the bay and the lighthouse. The sudden awareness of the need "to leave," then the need to write about that awareness, then the blurring of the writing—and the vision—by some new surge of overwhelming feeling, unexpected, incapacitating, inexpressible: latent in the first few sentences of *Jacob's Room* are the major themes of the book, and of many of the other books as well. Betty's situation here dramatizes the situation of the narrative itself, in its need to leave "Jacob" and to elegize him, but its inability to do so. In this sense the opening scene is a parable about writing and seeing.

The narrative consciousness soon withdraws somewhat from Betty's feelings: it says that she ignores the "full stop" she has written, but the narrative itself doesn't ignore it. Then it withdraws further into generalization: "Such were Betty Flanders' letters to Captain Barfoot—many-paged, tear stained." Now there are overtones of faintly amused superiority. This growing detachment is shown by the easy shift from Cornwall to Scarborough and the assertion that Betty's tears "made Mrs. Jarvis, the rector's wife, think at church . . . that marriage is a fortress and widows stray solitary in the open fields. . . ." The condescension toward Betty is extended to, and confirmed by, the banal clichés attributed to "the rector's wife." This rather patronizing attitude toward such stereotypical figures as sentimental widows and conventional rectors' wives is typical of the narrative in *Jacob's Room*—and, in fact, throughout the *oeuvre*, though it declines in the later works.

Betty's sentimentality momentarily dissolves her perspective in this opening scene. But the narrative consciousness itself seems determined not to give way to such emotion, or even to share in it. And so it soon withdraws from this first brief glimpse of the world through her mind. It comments, indirectly, on her sentimentality by disclosing sentimentality in another character. It enters the consciousness of "the rector's wife," and immediately names her "Mrs. Jarvis." This will be a book in which people, places, and phenomena are *named*, to an extent unprecedented in *The Voyage Out* or *Night and Day*, as if these names could somehow define Jacob's "room." By grounding itself in names, the narrative tries to resist its own sentimentality.[2] But that in itself may be a sentimental gesture.

The cause of Betty's emotion in this opening scene remains undefined. She is writing from Cornwall to her friend Captain Barfoot in Scarborough, explaining that "there was nothing for it but to leave," and thinking that "Accidents were awful things." The immediate occasion, probably, is in Cornwall—possibly "the gunpowder explosion in which poor Mr. Curnow had lost his eye" which she mentions to her boys a little later; at any rate it has necessitated a change in lodgings. "Accidents" may remind her of her husband's death. But the cause of that death remains unspecified too—as will the cause of Jacob's death: we know only that he will not "come back" from the war. The unspoken, the unknown, remains troubling in a way that the known fact does not. This absence of visible links between causes and effects emerges as a law of the world of *Jacob's Room*, where things just happen.

After imagining the thoughts of Betty Flanders and Mrs. Jarvis, the narrative next enters the mind of Charles Steele, the painter who is trying to place Betty in his landscape. Here, as in the other novels, the artist's mind is more accessible, less forbidding, than the thoughts of the more conventionally "masculine" characters. Mr. Steele's function here, it would seem, is to point to little Jacob rather than to ruminate about art. Still, his distraction and frustration, and the ways in which his art and his feelings become confused, are appropriate to many of the book's themes.

At last, in the seventh section of the first chapter,[3] the narrative

2 A famous passage in *A Farewell to Arms* illustrates the dilemma: "there were many words that you could not stand to hear and finally only the names of places had dignity. Certain numbers were the same way and certain dates and these with the names of the places were all you could say and have them mean anything. Abstract words such as glory, honor, courage, or hallow were obscene beside the concrete names of villages, the numbers of roads, the names of rivers, the numbers of regiments and the dates." (Chapter XXVII)

3 Interesting patterns, almost musical in their rhythmic arrangement and in their effects, are involved in the distributions of chapters and sections in *Jacob's Room*. There are fourteen chapters altogether. All except the final one, which serves as an epilogue or coda, are constituted by a number of sections. Chapter beginnings are indicated in the

begins to follow little Jacob, whom it has discovered atop a large rock. After several tentative glimpses into his awareness, it follows him toward a "large black woman" on the sand, and discovers that "The waves came around her. She was a rock. She was covered with the seaweed which pops when it is pressed. He was lost." Here the narrative is fully incarnate in his consciousness. And as it turns out, this is as deep as the narrative ever penetrates into that "room." As Jacob grows older and his personality becomes more "masculine," the narrative finds it more difficult to enter his consciousness—or even to see him from the outside. Its view of his "room" becomes more and more restricted. At last it loses him entirely in the war.

Little Jacob emerges, then, from a world of feelings which the narrative assigns at first to Betty Flanders. The narrative tries to escape from this given situation—from the loneliness, pain, bewilderment, the sudden, helpless blurring of perception and of the world itself. It is a woman's world. The virile male, Seabrook, is dead. The substitute father, Captain Barfoot, is absent. The adult male in this opening scene is the artist, Charles Steele. But he is scarcely more effective in

---

English edition by Roman numerals, section beginnings by an extra line of spacing. Each of the first two chapters consists of twelve sections. The next two chapters modulate this basic number, the third going one above it, the fourth one below. Then, after a chapter with six sections, there is a series of three in which the number of sections steadily diminishes from the basic twelve (11, 10, 9), then a series of three in which each contains ten sections. The last three chapters consists of nineteen, fourteen, and one section.

Some of the extra lines of spacing were omitted in typesetting the American edition, so that the corresponding divisions between sections were lost. For the convenience of readers who may wish to correct their American editions, I list the opening words of these lost sections:

Chapter and Section Number, Opening Words

2/8 Wednesday was Captain Barfoot's day.

3/10 "Let's go round to Simeon's room," said Jacob

5/11 "Next August, remember, Jacob," said Mrs. Durrant

6/6 Mrs. Durrant, sleepless as usual, scored a mark

7/9 "Are you fond of music?" said Mrs. Durrant.

11/4 Then here is another scrap of conversation

11/6 Edward Cruttendon, Jinny Carslake, and Jacob Flanders

12/7 "How very English!" Sandra laughed when the waiter told them

(Section numbers are not printed in any edition; I give them only for convenience.)

controlling it than Betty Flanders is: his subject moves, the ambient light changes, and the artist himself vanishes from the scene. The other males in this opening scene are children. Archer's call to his brother Jacob "had an extraordinary sadness. Pure from all body, pure from all passion, going out into the world, solitary, unanswered, breaking against rocks—so it sounded." Archer's cry, "Ja—cob!" is the cry of the narrative itself, and it is echoed in Bonamy's last call, answered only by falling leaves.

The reality of the opening of *Jacob's Room* is that of the lonely woman, writing a description of her plight. The narrative does not explain how all this came about. Perhaps there is no explanation. In the world of *Jacob's Room* the operation of cause and effect is not always clear. Sometimes things just happen, and reason is overwhelmed. The consciousness is suddenly disoriented; it sees its world through tears. That is the feeling of the opening scene of the book, the feeling from which the narrative consciousness tries always to escape.

The first chapter closes with Jacob said to be "profoundly unconscious," and with the narrative describing the efforts of the crab to escape from the "child's bucket," failing, and "trying again and again." The significance of this final perception isn't clear—and perhaps that ambiguity *is* its significance. The narrative consciousness can discover no meaning in the perception, except that apparent futility of the crab's compulsive circling and its continually frustrated efforts to escape. But as the book develops, other latent possibilities may be identified. Capturing the crab and leaving it in the bucket, Jacob does what will be done to him by some inscrutable and irresistible power, in whose view he is as significant as the crab is to him. And the narrative consciousness itself toys with Jacob and then abandons him. Or perhaps the narrative is more like the crab, continually circling, trying and failing to get outside of "Jacob's room," the limitations of his existence. In any case, the image seems enigmatic: because of its position at the end of the chapter and because of the narrative's focus upon it, the crab seems important—but the reasons for that emphasis remain obscure.

Each segment of the book represents a stage in the search for a way out of the "given" situation, and an aspect of the search for meaning. The most visible segments, of course, are the chapters. Despite the often playful tone of the narrative, the chapters invariably end in revelations of the obscurity of human life. Here, crudely paraphrased, are the "messages" of these endings: Cause and effect seem opaque; the crucial events in human life seem almost accidental. Light glimmers briefly in the eternity of darkness; sound echoes briefly in the vast space of silence. Partings predominate over reunions, leavetakings over arrivals. Human understanding is too little and too late. Violence is the latent reality of human history, always threatening to explode. The fascination that we feel for others is compelling in its power but frustrating in its impossibility of fulfillment. The human "problem," with its conflicting pulls of love and reason, is insoluble. Every person is essentially alone, and apart. Human perceptions are unstable and inadequate. Illusions are inevitable, but also transitory. All human achievements and artifacts are absorbed by the relentless, indifferent processes of nature. Philosophical questioning is futile. History is insignificant, except as a confirmation of despair. Human beings, their cultures, and their experiences are separated by vast distances. The signs with which life confronts us are incomprehensible. The meanings of a single human life, or of the debris which is its legacy to us, are incomprehensible too.

These, then, are the "revelations" in which the chapters culminate. They are evoked quietly and subtly, and none in itself seems unduly distressing. But as a cumulative whole they constitute a cry of despair—all the more convincing, perhaps, because each epiphany seems understated. The book's final revelation, of course, is that "Jacob's room" is empty. Its emptiness is evoked and emphasized by the wealth of facts and names with which the narrative surrounds it.

The narrative consciousness in *Jacob's Room* has no fixed or stable relationship to the characters in its story. This uncertainty in the narrative point of view adds to the feeling of enigma and frustration, and is apparent from the beginning of the book. The narrative enters the minds of more than two dozen characters. But it seldom penetrates their thoughts very deeply. It is very much aware of the difficulty of truly knowing the thoughts of Jacob. Time after time it expresses its doubt about its own insight into him: "Was it to reserve this gift from the past that the young man came to the window . . . ?" "whether this is the right interpretation of Jacob's gloom . . . it is impossible to say," "Jacob, no doubt, thought something in this fashion. . . ." The narrative never expresses such disclaimers for its descriptions of the thoughts of the other characters—who are, of course, primarily reflectors for Jacob. More than half of them are entered by the narrative on no more than one page of the book, and its views of all of them tend to be shallow. In addition to Jacob himself, only eight characters are entered on as many as three different pages: Betty Flanders, Mrs. Jarvis, Mrs. Durrant, Clara Durrant, Fanny Elmer, Richard Bonamy, Sandra Wentworth Williams, and Evan Williams. The treatment of these characters is generally condescending, except perhaps for the Durrants, whom the narrative seems to admire. The characters tend to be defined by their limitations, and primarily by limitations of their awareness. They all see less than the narrative sees in the scenes which define them—and "Jacob's room."

As late as the thirteenth section of Chapter 12, the narrative still reports what Jacob "thought." But this represents a much greater distance from his consciousness than the technique in this scene in which he discovers that "Nanny" is a rock. This kind of intimacy—a rendering of the immediacy of his consciousness—is possible only when Jacob is a child. As he grows older the narrative becomes excluded from his inner nature and from certain aspects of his experience—from Cambridge, from his bedroom, from his masculine intellectual life. His story increasingly becomes one of surfaces, of appearances. The narrative sometimes jokes about this. Beneath the joking, however, the sense of exclusion remains, and grows more frustrating as the story develops. The perspective hovers around Jacob, but is less and less able to become incarnate in him, to become *his* perspective. Instead it grows more conscious of its own "ten years' seniority and a difference of sex."

This sense of "seniority" involves more than chronology. The increasing distance between Jacob and the narrative becomes apparent in the third chapter, at Cambridge. Somewhat in awe of "the light of

Cambridge," the narrative is rather envious of Jacob's experiences there. The sketch of "old Miss Umphelby" of Newnham, the women's college, hopelessly overshadowed by Erasmus Cowan, her counterpart at Trinity, is one of the most poignant moments in the chapter. In the fourth chapter the perspective becomes somewhat more distant and essentially reversed: it begins with Jacob's view of the Scilly Isles and ends with the view of him by the Durrants and their friends. In the fifth chapter the narrative begins to relinquish Jacob to the influence of Bonamy, whose interest in him seems vaguely homosexual and who encourages his tendencies toward snobbery—exemplified in Jacob's devastating, but unprinted, attack on a bowdlerized edition of Wycherley, edited by poor Professor Bulteel of Leeds. In succeeding chapters the narrative watches Jacob recede into still other distances: classical Greek, commercial sex, London society, the British Museum. In all of these aspects his innocence is greater than the narrative's, and his story is rendered with increasing dramatic irony. In the tenth chapter the narrative seems to discover a stable perspective on Jacob in Fanny Elmer, who falls in love with him. But this too becomes ironic. He leaves her for his grand tour, first to Paris and Versailles along with some artists, then to Greece—at first alone, then in the company of Sandra Wentworth Williams and, at times, her husband Evan. Then come the thirteenth chapter, in which Jacob's acquaintances pass in review and Jacob himself vanishes, and the final chapter, an epilogue, really, in which he has become a ghost.

The narrative's "difference of sex" gives it a special perspective. At King's College Chapel "a dog destroys the service completely. So do these women," Jacob thinks—or is said to think, for the narrative point of view is already distinct from his, already speculating about what may be going on in his mysterious masculine mind. Jacob recedes into the distances of his masculine world. His work, probably in a law office, goes entirely unobserved. His sexual desires are regarded with despair: "The problem is insoluble." He finds polite society boring, but "Women like it," he tells Timmy. "Alas, women lie!" he thinks, when Fanny Elmer reads *Tom Jones* just to please him, "But not Clara Durrant," whom he idealizes. "Jacob's letters are so like him," Mrs. Jarvis tells his mother—who is well aware that they tell her nothing about him. None of these women in Jacob's room knows him very well—including the one who is telling his story.

The war is the ultimate male domain. Its imminence is suggested quietly in Chapter 12 (*e.g.*, "The battleships ray out over the North Sea") as a kind of counterpoint to polite conversation. Yet the narrative is so removed from it that Jacob simply disappears into it. At the end of Chapter 13 the narrative imagines a feminine response to the ominous new sounds of war: "'The guns?' said Betty Flanders, half asleep, getting out of bed and going to the window. . . . 'Not at this distance,' she thought. 'It is the sea.'" Betty, in Scarborough, may be hearing the guns of Flanders (whose "distance" is greater than anyone could have guessed) or of naval battles, or the sound of the sea. To her—and to the narrative—they are all the same (like "the great beast stamping" in *The Waves*): incomprehensible, but ominous. In retrospect, it is the stroke of doom, the announcement of the death of Jacob—and of everything he represents. It closes his story, and opens out into a much more complex—and fallen—world. "'Life is wicked— life is detestable,' cried Rose Shaw. The strange thing about life is that though the nature of it must have been apparent to every one for hundreds of years, no one has left any adequate account of it. The streets of London have their map; but our passions are uncharted." An "adequate account," presumably, is what *Jacob's Room* aspires to. Yet the implication is that "our passions" must always defeat such an account. Instead, they create "chasms in the continuity of our ways. Yet we keep straight on." And as if to illustrate this, the narrative reverts once again to Rose's argument. A man called Jimmy had refused to marry a woman called Helen. But after speculating about how Rose's story may have developed, the narrative says that "For my own part, I find it exceedingly difficult to interpret songs without words. And now Jimmy feeds crows in Flanders and Helen visits hospitals. Oh, life is damnable, life is wicked, as Rose Shaw said. The lamps of London uphold the dark as upon the points of burning bayonets." Rose's parable, if that is what it is, has moved the narrative to reveal its own personal bias and skepticism. It ends the story of Jimmy and Helen abruptly, almost savagely. "Jimmy feeds the crows in Flanders": his fate and the word *Flanders* suggest, subliminally, Jacob's fate as well. And Rose's indignation at Jimmy's abandonment of Helen also links his story with that of Jacob, who turns away from several of the women in his life. Perhaps there is also the suggestion that if Jimmy and Jacob had not turned away, their stories could have ended differently.

In the transition here from the fifth to the sixth section of Chapter 8, the narrative moves from the realm of statement to that of symbol once again—another chasm in continuity. In what way could "The lamps of London uphold the dark"? The *burning bayonets* enhance the sense of a surrounding, enveloping, eventually overwhelming darkness. Throughout this sixth section the narrative expands its description of the lights of London (a counterpoint to the "light of Cambridge" which pervades the third chapter). But these momentary scenes are only "rude illustrations, pictures in a book whose pages we turn over and over as if we should at last find what we look for. Every face, every shop, bedroom window, public-house, and dark square is a picture feverishly turned—in search of what? It is the same with books. What do we seek through millions of pages? Still hopefully turning the pages—oh, here is Jacob's room."

Here the narrative consciousness reveals its own torment more openly than anywhere else in the book. Books themselves, it knows, are artifacts in which we search for the essence of our own feelings. Books, then, are also lamps upholding the vast darkness. Thus the belated discovery of "Jacob's room" takes place in a context of deep irony, and must be interpreted in that context.

What the narrative sees in "Jacob's room" here is Jacob reading the newspaper. But it is Jacob's world view, not that of the great *Globe* itself, that creates this reality. Jacob looks "severe." And the narrative says that "He was certainly thinking about Home Rule in Ireland—a very difficult matter." But we know better: we know he has seen Florinda in the street "upon another man's arm" and that his illusion of her fidelity to him has been shattered. And so this scene too becomes another in the long series of "rude illustrations" which try, and fail, to tell Jacob's story. And yet they ultimately succeed, because they convey not only the conscious but also the unconscious aspects of human awareness; in their descriptions of the light they uphold the darkness.

In its search for incarnation, the narrative consciousness explores various places as well as various characters. The book opens in Cornwall. The exact location is unspecified, but like its counterparts in *To the Lighthouse* (nominally the Isles of Skye) and *The Waves* (unnamed), it derives from the St. Ives in which Virginia Woolf spent the summers of her childhood, the familiar seaside setting in which, as in "A Sketch of the Past," consciousness begins. The story begins on the shore, and in the eighth section of the first chapter the narrative consciousness ascends, with Mrs. Flanders and her sons, to a panoramic view of the bay, and the discovery that "The lighthouse was lit. 'Come along,' said Betty Flanders." Here, as in *To the Lighthouse*, the sequence of words links the discovery of the light with the mother's sheltering love. In this love little Jacob, like the youngest Ramsays of the later book, can sleep "profoundly unconscious" and can kick away the sheep's jaw (a vaguely sinister emblem of death, like the boar's skull which Mrs. Ramsay softens with her shawl). On the whole, the handling of the Cornwall setting in *Jacob's Room* seems archetypal—*the* bay, *the* lighthouse, *the* rock, etc. And the Cornish coast here seems relatively uninhabited compared with that of *To the Lighthouse*, where the Ramsays' home is so full of noisy life.

The second chapter is set in Scarborough. Mrs. Flanders has "a house on the outskirts" at the foot of a hill which had been the site of a Roman fortress, and which affords a "magnificent view" of the town. Here, as at the seashore, Jacob is not the central presence, and the setting isn't very fully realized. Of the vista from the fortress, the narrative says that "The entire gamut of the view's changes should have been known to" Mrs. Flanders, and then goes into a description of it which might have come from a tourists' brochure, and concludes with the question "And now, what's the next thing to see in Scarborough?" Butterflies, perhaps—at least these are what the narrative seems to "see" most vividly. Why is Scarborough the setting for Jacob's youth? The emphasis on the Roman fortress there may suggest the inevitability of warfare throughout human history. (Indeed, the novel modifies the actual history of Scarborough: on the hill above the town the Romans built signal stations; the castle itself was built in the twelfth century.) A couple of other facts not directly alluded to in *Jacob's Room* also seem relevant to the theme of war: the last land bridge joined England to the Continent—in fact, to Flanders—here; German warships shelled Scarborough during the war, further damaging the castle.[4]

Geographically, the setting of *Jacob's Room* moves from the southwest coast of England in the first chapter to the northeast coast in the second, establishing vague boundaries for Jacob's "room" and preparing for its eventual center, in London. From Scarborough it moves toward London, to Cambridge, in the third chapter. Then after a holiday in the far southwest (the Scilly Isles) it moves to what seems to be a stable center in the fifth chapter. Throughout the central chapters of the book "Jacob's Room" *is* London. There are occasional sections which are set in Scarborough, and a section describing a hunting trip to Essex. (In the first four chapters, each chapter as a whole had had the same setting.) Then beginning in Chapter 11, there is Jacob's grand tour to France and Greece, in which whole series of sections are set away from London, but even these series emphasize the centrality of London. Beginning with the final section of Chapter 12, however, the setting becomes much more unstable: whereas each previous section had been set in a single location, now the perspective begins to wander all over Europe and the Near East—a subliminal signal that chaos is imminent. When the narrative finally returns to the heart of Jacob's room (in the single section of Chapter 14) there is no one there.

The modulation of setting is only one aspect of the dynamics of form which constitute the world of *Jacob's Room*. Rhythms analogous

4 Scarborough is not a place that Virginia Woolf knew intimately. It is not indexed in Bell's biography, and I have seen no evidence that she ever stayed there. The description of the moor above the town could apply as well to the moor above St. Ives and to Trencrom Hill, with its old fort and its panoramic view of St. Ives Bay to the north and St. Michael's Mount to the south; as a girl she walked on Trencrom with her father (Bell, I, 34). Perhaps Scarborough is imagined as Jacob's birthplace because of its hidden connection with Flanders and its associations with the Romans and the war. Betty Flanders hears the guns there; Virginia Woolf herself heard them on the hill above Asham, her house in Sussex (Bell, II, 53).

to those of cinematic shots, scenes, and sequences shape the flow of paragraphs, sections, and chapters in the narrative. The relative durations of these elements, their contrapuntal relationships to each other, their contrasting and complementary tones—modulation of all of these characteristics creates a narrative of great subtlety and complexity. As in contrapuntal music, the modulation of these parameters reaches always toward a dominant unity, and its power arises from the growing expectation—and postponement—of that unity. The style moves between nervousness and stability, chaos and order, cynicism and lyricism, through a very broad range of psychological space.

The final, brief chapter of *Jacob's Room* serves as a kind of epilogue; the "story" itself is resolved in Chapter 13. As that thirteenth chapter opens Jacob is back in London, not in his rooms, but in Hyde Park, sitting in a rented chair and talking with Bonamy. Rather like the "Wandering Rocks" episode of *Ulysses*, the thirteenth chapter of *Jacob's Room* provides momentary glimpses of various lives which are related to each other in very complex and obscure ways, and also related, of course, to Jacob's life. In a sense, these characters constitute the boundaries of "Jacob's room": Bonamy, his closest friend (*bon ami*), a homosexual, who walks away "in a rage" when he realizes that Jacob is in love with a woman; Clara Durrant ("of all women, Jacob honoured her most"); Julia Eliot, a prototype for Mrs. Ramsay; Florinda, a prostitute; Sandra, an older woman with whom Jacob is now in love and whose "long, flowing letter" he reads; "poor Fanny Elmer," hopelessly in love with Jacob; Timmy Durrant, Clara's brother and Jacob's friend from the university; the Reverend Mr. Andrew Floyd, Mrs. Flanders' former suitor, who gave Jacob the works of Byron; Mrs. Pascoe, whose garden overlooks the sea in the Scilly Isles, where Jacob and Timmy had sailed; and at last Betty Flanders, awakened by the sound of guns—or is it the sea? (like the "great beast stamping" in *The Waves*)—heralding Jacob's death. For each of these persons Jacob himself is a different person. Taken together these relationships define his existential space. Significantly, the first and last persons in this series, Bonamy and Mrs. Flanders, are the only ones present in the final chapter. That is the only chapter to be set exclusively in Jacob's room—as if the narrative were now able for the first time to settle in that space, only to find it irrevocably empty. Perhaps the narrative can settle there only because it is empty, or because it is now *perceived* to be empty.

On one level, Jacob is just another personage among all the rest— speaking with Bonamy, drawing designs in the dust in the park, grumbling at the ticket collector, walking away, seen momentarily by Clara Durrant and then vanishing forever ("She saw Jacob. . . . But she saw no one"). On another level he becomes mythic—"like a British admiral, exclaimed Bonamy"; "Clara only wondered . . . why Jacob had never come"; Julia Eliot, after passing the statue of Achilles, feels that "the present seems like an elegy for past youth and past summers" and she thinks not of Jacob specifically, but of "people passing tragically to destruction"; Florinda thinks of her latest lover, "He's like Jacob"; Sandra thinks of Jacob as Alceste, Moliere's misanthrope; in the British Museum Fanny Elmer, discovering "the battered Ulysses . . . got a fresh shock of Jacob's presence." And at last Clara sees him—and sees no one. Like Ulysses confronting the Cyclops, he becomes a Noman. But unlike Homer's Ulysses—and Joyce's—his role as Noman is not just a disguise. His enemies are not susceptible to his wiles. He turns out to be not Ulysses, but Achilles.

Jacob vanishes in the twelfth section of Chapter 13. As this section ends, in the red light of sunset all the faces under the arch of the London opera house look alike, the narrative says, and it is drawn toward "the steaming bedrooms near by," but chooses not to look into them, for "one must follow; one must not block the way." Here, as in the opening of *The Voyage Out*, one must follow the crowd; one must not be eccentric. The twilight, here assigned to London, in the next section expands to encompass Jacob's experiential world, from its western boundary in the Scilly Isles to its eastern frontier in Greece (though he did travel to Constantinople with the Wentworth Williamses). At the mythic level this is the twilight of a civilization, in which individual identities must vanish into the darkness of the collective fate. Instinctively the narrative consciousness turns toward the bedrooms, but its sense of social responsibility prevails.

The penultimate section of Chapter 13 opens on the western edge of Jacob's experiential room, the Scilly Isles. Now the narrative becomes preoccupied with lost explorers and vanished civilizations, abandoned works and exhausted resources, the relentless imperatives of nature, the inevitability of death: "Clara's moors were fine enough. The Phoenicians slept under their piled grey rocks; the chimneys of the old mines pointed starkly; early moths blurred the heather-bells; cartwheels could be heard grinding on the road far beneath; and the suck and sighing of the waves sounded gently, persistently, for ever."

The opening sentence of the section alludes sardonically to the exchange preceding Clara's final glimpse of Jacob:

"A shame to spend such a night in the theatre!" said Mrs. Durrant, seeing all the windows of the coachmakers in Long Acre ablaze.

"Think of your moors!" said Mr. Wortley to Clara.

"Ah! But Clara likes this better," Mrs. Durrant laughed.

"I don't know—really," said Clara, looking at the blazing windows. She started.

She saw Jacob.

"Who?" asked Mrs. Durrant sharply, leaning forward.

But she saw no one.

Clara doesn't prefer the moors; she prefers Jacob. But the moors themselves are indifferent to the human presence. Chapter II had culminated in a meditation about the moor above Scarborough: "The moonlight destroyed nothing. The moor accepted everything." Clara's moors have accepted the Phoenician skeletons, Betty's the Roman. The earth will have room for Jacob too. Like so many of the transitions in *Jacob's Room*, "Clara's moors were fine enough" announces—and necessitates—a radical shift in perspective.

The next paragraph begins with a return to the present, but then it too lapses into the perspective of eternity. The narrative shifts to a view of the Parthenon, bathed, like the London Opera House of the previous section, in the red light of sunset. The focus, however, is now on "the Greek women," said to be "as jolly as sand-martins in the heat." As in the view of London, the emphasis here is on collective, rather than individual behavior. But this too is extinguished as "the ships in the Piraeus fired their guns." This sound reverberates and echoes "among the channels of the islands." Then "Darkness drops like a knife over Greece." The reverberations of the images themselves are more subtle. This darkness which has "dropped" on Greece will envelop England as well, and as suddenly. The Parthenon, the greatest temple of classical Greece, is also the classic monument to the destructiveness of gunpowder. And surviving both man's wildest dreams of transcendence and his most monumental acts of destruction are these chattering women, untroubled by idealism or the need for power.

Now comes the final section of Chapter 13:

"The guns?" said Betty Flanders, half asleep, getting out of bed and going to the window, which was decorated with a fringe of dark leaves.·

"Not at this distance," she thought. "It is the sea."

Again, far away, she heard the dull sound, as if nocturnal women were beating great carpets. There was Morty lost, and Seabrook dead; her sons fighting for their country. But were the chickens safe? Was that some one moving downstairs? Rebecca with the toothache? No. The nocturnal women were beating great carpets. Her hens shifted slightly on their perches.

The guns, of course, link this section with the previous one. But these are more ominous: they announce not the official time of sunset in the port of Piraeus, but the universal night of the Great War. And the image may also imply the darkness of modern, as opposed to classical, Greece. In any case, the darkness falls for everyone. Betty has not yet acknowledged it, even though it "decorated" her "window," her perception of the world. Although at the deepest level she is aware of the guns, she attributes the sound to the sea. Here, and throughout the lifework, the sea represents the vastness of undifferentiated energy to which each life must return. This death of the separate existence is both alluring and frightening. Imaging it as the sea, the narrative consciousness can dramatize it more fully and effectively. Even the sound of the waves crashing on the shore, because it has become too obviously a sign of death, must be further euphemized as the sound of "nocturnal women beating great carpets." In Betty's subconscious the narrative can discover and objectify the limitations of an entire culture: "her sons fighting for their country. But were the hens safe?" The sequence itself says it: the sons are not safe, but Betty—and English culture as a whole—refuses to ask that question directly. Instead, a fanciful rationalization ("Rebecca with the toothache?") is rejected in favor of an even more fanciful one ("The nocturnal women were beating great carpets"). Yet even the hens are uneasy; something, they seem to sense, is wrong with their world.

The ending of Chapter 13 concludes the story: Jacob has vanished into the darkness in which the guns are heard. Chapter 14 is an epilogue; it provides a reflexive and retrospective comment on the story. Unlike the other chapters, it consists of only one section. It opens with Bonamy standing in the middle of Jacob's room. "Did he think he would come back?" he muses. All the answer that the narrative can think of is to say that "The eighteenth century has its distinction," and then to reiterate a passage from its earlier essay (from the third section of Chapter 5) on the "distinction" of eighteenth-century houses.

"Distinction," the narrative had said in the earlier context, "was one of the words to use naturally" in speaking of Jacob. In Chapter 14, then, the word echoes ironically: the "distinction" of the houses remains, but that of Jacob himself does not. What remains instead is the debris of his life: a bill for a hunting crop, the letters from Sandra, notes from Mrs. Durrant and Lady Rocksbier—these are now his "distinctions," all that remains of his identity, all that distinguishes him from the chaos that has come again.

And so the formulaic description of the eighteenth-century houses reverberates in the essential emptiness of Jacob's room. The point of the words is their pointlessness, their irrelevance. Jacob's room, full of his possessions, becomes even more achingly empty. This isn't the eighteenth century. The rooms, with their high ceilings, their "shapely" proportions, their elegance, their "distinction," belong to that time. But Jacob's time is our own. If he had thought he would come back, he was deeply mistaken. The war he had accepted so unthinkingly was not an eighteenth-century affair like the misadventure in the American colonies; this was profoundly different, the first modern world war, on a scale unprecedented in human history. Could Jacob have known that? Bonamy's comment seems to imply that he should have.

Jacob's life itself had been, in a sense, an eighteenth-century room. Reason, order, proportion, privilege, moderation, tradition, comfort: these were the values he was taught at Cambridge, and which he seems to have believed in. But these values no longer fit the new realities of the twentieth century, where eighteenth-century rooms can be inhabited only by ghosts. Thus the bill for the hunting crop is ironic. The sport itself is now anachronistic, and Bonamy's comment that the bill "seems to have been paid" has a broader meaning than he knows: Jacob has paid the price for his naïve belief in traditional values.

The reference to "Sandra's letters" reinforces this suggestion of Jacob's naïveté. The letters themselves are not quoted; Bonamy is too much the gentleman to read them. But the narrative implies that they are typical of their genre: letters written by the middle-aged married woman who has no intention of leaving her rich and influential husband for the latest in a series of younger lovers (Jacob's gift to her of a volume of Donne had taken its place on her shelf where there were "ten or twelve little volumes already"). Other associations echo here too. "Ah an English boy on tour," Sandra had thought when she first saw him, and, sizing him up in the museum, she "got Jacob's head exactly on a level with the head of the Hermes of Praxiteles. The comparison was all in his favour." Thus Sandra is revealed as a rather predatory connoisseur of English "boys." But the reference to Hermes, messenger of the gods and escort of the dead to Hades, broadens the mythic dimensions of Jacob's destiny and foreshadows it in an appropriately ambiguous way. Another passage, slightly later— and also vague until it is seen in retrospect, shows Sandra thinking of "kisses on lips that are to die." Now, in Chapter 14, "Sandra's letters" confirm that latent *Morituri te salutamus* quality of Jacob's devotion to her.

Mrs. Durrant, the mother of Timmy (Jacob's best friend at Cambridge) and Clara (the girl he "honoured" most), was the first to call Jacob "distinguished looking" and has been fond of him since they first met. This invitation from her shows that she has been trying to keep in touch with him. One of the most poignant aspects of *Jacob's Room* is the undiscovered love between him and Clara Durrant. Her name seems fitting: Jacob "honours" her clarity at the same time that he remains blind to her love for him.

The Countess of Rocksbier (another ominous name) is related to Jacob's mother, fond of him, and able to sponsor him, to some extent, in society. The fact that she too has sent him another invitation emphasizes the suddenness of his departure and death.

The next paragraph repeats the two final sentences of section six of Chapter 3, which described Jacob's room at Trinity, in Neville's Court. Whereas his room in London had been of the eighteenth century, this one, like Cambridge itself, is a product of the Renaissance. What is most important now, however, is its emptiness. Whereas the room in Cambridge in Chapter 3 had been vacant because Jacob was "dining in Hall," his room in London is now irrevocably vacant.

As if to try to recall that presence to this room, Bonamy crosses to the window. What he sees outside is a montage of what Jacob himself had seen from that same window. Then "A harsh and unhappy voice cried something unintelligible." The news cried out now in the London streets is unintelligible because it is unprecedented in human history. But it is a cry in another sense, as if Jacob himself were crying out from some world beyond (like Achilles in the underworld), trying to tell his story, to explain the significance of his experience.

Unable to hear that message or to get into touch with Jacob's presence, Bonamy calls out "Jacob! Jacob!" This, we may recall, was Archer's cry as he searched for Jacob at the beginning. It is also the archetypal cry of bereavement in Virginia Woolf's lifework, from the "Rachel! Rachel!" of *The Voyage Out* to the "Rose! Rose!" of *The Years*. There is, of course, no answer, only the overwhelming silence.

Now Betty Flanders bursts open the bedroom door. That was the door, the narrative playfully told us in Chapter 8, behind which "the obscene thing" was to be found; the mother's letter—and the narrative itself—would do better to remain in the sitting room rather than to intrude upon Jacob and Florinda. But now the obscene thing seems rather different, and the mother herself emerges from the forbidden realm with a pair of Jacob's old shoes. "What am I to do with these, Mr. Bonamy?" she asks. It is a poignant question.

Of all the things that Jacob had left behind, these old shoes may be the most haunting. More than any of his other possessions, they have been shaped by his unique physical presence. And in a way they are the ultimate symbol of *Jacob's Room* itself. The book begins as the story of a little boy like countless others, but through continual increments of details, none of which is unique in itself, it eventually differentiates him from all other human beings. But his identity becomes final only with his death. The significance of his choices—and of his avoidance of choices—also becomes irrevocable only with his death.

Perhaps the image also implies that Jacob's life has been thrown away. In one moment so irrational and obscure that the narrative itself never sees it, the war suddenly destroys what the story had been nurturing so carefully for so long. The shock is traumatic, and final.

The narrative consciousness survives Jacob himself, but only, in a sense, by rejecting him. It certainly rejects his naïve faith in progress, perfectibility, justice, the power of reason, and so on. The "light of Cambridge" which had shone for him even after he had "come down" seems lost in the vast darkness in which the other Edwardian illusions vanished. And while the narrative seems to share Jacob's reverence for that light, the narrative discovers the darkness sooner than he does. But the narrative can't really cope with what, at the deepest level, it knows. In the chapter on Cambridge, the narrative is already aware that "there will be no form in the world unless Jacob makes one for himself."

Jacob Flanders:[5] the last name seems almost to imply a genetic

5   Lytton Strachey wrote to Virginia Woolf that he could "see something of Thoby in Jacob." Undoubtedly the book does owe a great deal to her feelings for her older brother, Julian Thoby Stephen, who died of typhoid in 1906. The final section of the third chapter may be a memorial to him: "'Julian the Apostate. . . .' Which of them said that and the other words murmured round it? . . . if you talk of a light, of Cambridge burning, it's not languages only. It's Julian the Apostate." The name of the Apostate Emperor would have been a natural nickname for Julian Thoby Stephen. Unlike Leonard Woolf, Saxon Sydney-Turner, Lytton Strachey, and Maynard Keynes, Thoby was not elected to the Apostles.

A prototype closer to the "facts" of Jacob's life is Rupert Brooke. Like Jacob, he was educated at Rugby and Kings College, Cambridge; they both "went up to Cambridge in October, 1906." (Thoby went to school at Clifton College, Bristol, and up to Trinity College, Cambridge, in 1899.) In 1911 Virginia deepened her acquaintance with Brooke and the "Neo-Pagans," his circle of friends. She even swam naked with him in the Granta, and was disappointed that her friends weren't more shocked, says Bell (I, 173). In 1915 Brooke died of blood poisoning on the Greek island of Skiros. He left

determination of his death in Flanders' fields, where so many died for so little. And his life story unfolds against the always understated background of his time. Now and then the narrative casually mentions some detail of that background, such as the impersonal "voice" in Whitehall that comments so reassuringly on foreign affairs—but whose cool rationalizations merely mask, temporarily, the irrational violence of what it is commenting on. Despite the subdued voices of Whitehall and of all the Edwardian institutions, despite the subdued quality of the narrative itself, the destructive forces finally overwhelm the story—precisely because this *is* the authentic story of its historical era, of a culture resolutely blind and deaf to the violence seething within it.

The real origins of human events remain mysterious throughout the book. Conventional principles of causality are challenged from the very first sentence. "So of course there was nothing for it but to leave": this opening line, from Betty's letter to Captain Barfoot, is never subsequently explained: the first word of the book is a connective that doesn't connect. And the need "to leave" in this opening passage is no clearer than the need for Jacob to leave at the end. The book doesn't clarify his life; it only makes it more mysterious. For example, Chapter 2, which describes his youth, concludes with a section consisting of a single sentence: "Jacob Flanders, therefore, went up to Cambridge in October, 1906." The word "therefore" could refer to anything or everything which precedes it. Thus the transitions between elements of the narrative create discontinuity as well as conti-

---

behind a collection of sonnets, one of which made him immortal among Englishmen:

If I should die, think only this of me:
That there's some corner of a foreign field
That is for ever England. . . .

For *TLS* Virginia Woolf reviewed *The Collected Poems of Rupert Brooke* (August 8, 1918) and Walter de la Mare, *Rupert Brooke and the Intellectual Imagination* (December 11, 1919). Her idea for "a new form for a new novel," which became *Jacob's Room*, is mentioned in her diary for January 26, 1920, according to Bell (II, 72–73). The reviews in *TLS* are reprinted in *Books and Portraits: Some Further Selections from the Literary and Biographical Writings of Virginia Woolf*, ed. Mary Lyon (London: Hogarth, 1977), 85–89, 90–92. The first review ends with the question "what would he have been, what would he have done?" This expresses the general feeling of both essays, and of *Jacob's Room* too.

nuity. The effect is always to challenge the fundamental principles that structure the text itself.

The narrative searches conscientiously for the essence of Jacob. It tries to imagine his childhood, his education at Cambridge, his travels, his friends, his love affairs, his tastes, his life. . . . But its insight is limited. Time after time it hovers on the verge of some revelation, only to withdraw to some more distant, or perhaps more conventional, perspective. Various reasons are offered for these withdrawals: propriety, uncertainty, sexual differences, the conventions of fiction itself. Amusing as these disclaimers are, they eventually become depressing as the conviction grows that Jacob cannot be known. And at last his death seals that conviction.

Despite the narrative's limitations, however, and despite its skeptical and even satirical views of Jacob, a mythic "room" still emerges. In retrospect, one of the most striking characteristics is a negative one: the absence of a father, or of any mature male. Throughout Jacob's experience, such a figure is either absent (his own father, Seabrook, is dead) or seen as badly flawed or maimed. Years after Jacob's mother had refused the marriage proposal of the red-haired Andrew Floyd (whom she had enticed into giving Latin lessons to her "boys"), the kitten he had given to her son John "is now a very old cat," and Betty "smiled, thinking how she had had him gelded, and how she did not like red hair in men." Although the Reverend Mr. Floyd escapes the literal fate of "poor old Topaz," the one which the narrative imagines for him isn't much more appealing, and is summarized in a sentence: "next day he received a silver salver and went— first to Sheffield, where he met a Miss Wimbush,[6] who was on a visit to her uncle, then to Hackney—then to Maresfield House, of which he became the principal, and, finally, becoming editor of a well-known series of Ecclesiastical Biographies, he retired to Hampstead with his wife and daughter, and is often to be seen feeding the ducks on Leg of Mutton Road."

After Scarborough, Cambridge offers various surrogate fathers, from Professor Plumer and his dreadful Sunday luncheons for under-

6 Perhaps Miss Wimbush here is related to the Wimbushes of Aldous Huxley's first novel, *Crome Yellow* (1921), caricatures of Ottoline and Philip Morrell.

graduates at "Waverly" to Professor Erasmus Cowan and his intonations of Virgil. And there is Bonamy, whose fatherly concern for Jacob isn't incompatible with an unrequited homosexual desire. And finally there is Evan Williams, who adopts him, in a sense, as a son—and lover—for his wife Sandra. Presumably, Jacob learns from each of these "fathers." But in the aftermath of his life there is no evidence that he has grown very far beyond the roles that he was taught at Cambridge.

The form of the narrative itself reflects the quest for stability, order, and knowledge. The quest finally fails. "Jacob's room" finally becomes not just an empty, but an alien, space. The narrative consciousness does not belong there, and Jacob's life and death remain inexplicable: his essence remains beyond the conscious knowledge of the narrative, which can only view him from an increasing distance, and without much sympathy. Born into a woman's world, Jacob moves beyond that world in various ways as he grows older, and eventually disappears from it—to die in a wholly male domain. As he becomes more "masculine," the narrative consciousness grows more aware of its own essential femininity, until at last the story can be told only through an asexual, impersonal style in which feeling is suppressed. The narrative does not follow Jacob into the final darkness. How could it? It can only show that the darkness is there. It has always been aware of that darkness, but has been resisting that knowledge, refusing to become fully conscious of it. That resistance frustrates the narrative's quest for meaning. But it also creates the tension which is the essence of *Jacob's Room*.

CHAPTER IV

MRS. DALLOWAY

Jacob's Room ends with the discovery that the existential space of its central character is now empty. The next novel represents a voyage out from such a view, an effort to discover meaning in the role of "Mrs. Dalloway." Clarissa Dalloway and her husband Richard had suddenly appeared in the third chapter of Virginia Woolf's first novel, dominated the action for three chapters, and then debarked from the *Euphrosyne* at an unnamed port of call. Now, as *Jacob's Room* was being finished, they were beginning to appear again in some short stories.[1] One of these, "Mrs. Dalloway in Bond Street," published in *The Dial* in July, 1923, evolved into the opening sequence of *Mrs. Dalloway*.

There is no reference to any of the events of *The Voyage Out* in

1 "Mrs. Dalloway in Bond Street" appeared in *The Dial*, LXXV (July 1923), 20–27. It is much fuller and more specific in its references to persons and places than the corresponding section of the novel. For a more detailed discussion of this and of the genesis of *Mrs. Dalloway*, see my essay "Mrs. Woolf and Mrs. Dalloway" in *The Classic British Novel* (Athens: University of Georgia Press, 1972), 220–39. Some aspects of my present essay, especially the discussion of characters, echo that earlier one.

Other stories involving the Dalloways include "The New Dress," first published in *Forum*, LXXVII (May, 1927), 704–11, and "The Man Who Loved His Kind," "Together and Apart," and "A Summing Up," all published posthumously in *A Haunted House and Other Short Stories* (1944). Another story, "The Introduction," was published more recently in *Mrs.Dalloway's Party*, ed. Stella McNichol (London: Hogarth, 1973), 37–43, a volume which reprints the other stories also.

the later novel, where the Dalloways themselves, especially Richard, seem rather different. "Pompous and sentimental," Helen Ambrose had called him. Jane Austen put him to sleep, and he loudly opposed women's rights. But he was also sexually attractive to Rachel, and when he suddenly kissed her, she was overwhelmed in "black waves." None of this seems very appropriate for the Richard of *Mrs. Dalloway*, although he is somewhat sentimental and does not, so far as we know, read Jane Austen. His wife in *The Voyage Out* had dressed pretentiously, talked in clichés, and written condescendingly about the other passengers. But her energy, vitality, and her caring for Rachel seemed important too. The differences in Clarissa between the two books arise more from the differences in their perspectives than from differences in Clarissa's personality. In *Mrs. Dalloway* the narrative discovers much greater depth in her.

There are also links between the second and third novels and *Mrs. Dalloway*. Mrs. Hilbery of *Night and Day* and Clara Durrant and her mother of *Jacob's Room* are guests at Clarissa's party. Although these are not important characters, the reflexive connections suggest that *Mrs. Dalloway* is not an entirely independent entity, and perhaps even that it may synthesize what the creative consciousness has discovered so far. Yet is also tries to advance the frontiers of the lifework. In choosing to return to this character from the first novel and to explore her reality more deeply, the creative consciousness turns in an important new direction.

Mrs. Dalloway said she would buy the flowers herself.

For Lucy had her work cut out for her. The doors would be taken off their hinges; Rumpelmayer's men were coming. And then, thought Clarissa Dalloway, what a morning—fresh as if issued to children on a beach.

What a lark! What a plunge! For so it had always seemed to her when, with a little squeak of the hinges, which she could hear now, she had burst open the French windows and plunged at Bourton into the open air. How fresh, how calm, stiller than this of course, the air was in the early morning; like the flap of a wave; the kiss of a wave; chill and sharp and yet (for a girl of eighteen as she then was) solemn, feeling as she did, standing there at the open window, that something awful was about to happen; looking at the flowers, at the trees with the smoke winding off them and the rooks rising, falling; standing and looking until Peter Walsh said, "Musing among the vegetables?"—was that it?—"I prefer men to cauliflowers"—was that it? He must have said it at breakfast one morning when she had gone out on to the terrace—Peter Walsh. He would be back from India one of these days, June or July, she forgot which, for his letters were awfully dull; it was his sayings one remembered; his eyes, his pocket-knife, his smile, his grumpiness and, when millions of things had utterly vanished—how strange it was!—a few sayings like this about cabbages.

She stiffened a little on the kerb, waiting for Durtnall's van to pass. A charming woman, Scrope Purvis thought her. . . .[2]

Thus *Mrs. Dalloway* opens—into the world of Clarissa's consciousness. In the single sentence of the opening paragraph, the narrative perceives her objectively as "Mrs. Dalloway" and summarizes what she "said." In the next sentences, however, the style becomes more recog-

---

2 My quotations throughout this chapter are from the first English edition. In the present quotation the American edition adds a comma after *her* in the third sentence of the third paragraph.

There is one significant difference in the apparent structure of the two editions. The American edition consists of eight sections, separated by an additional line space in the text. In the original Hogarth edition there are twelve sections, also separated by space breaks. For the convenience of readers who may wish to correct their American editions, I list these breaks below:

Paragraph opening	Page in Harvest paperback ed.
"'Poor old woman,' said Rezia Warren Smith."	125
"It was precisely twelve o'clock; twelve by Big Ben. . . ."	142
"One of the triumphs of civilization, Peter Walsh thought."	229
"'But where is Clarissa?' said Peter."	284

In some respects the American edition seems preferable; most of the textual changes from the English edition are improvements, and most seem designed to clarify meanings or to correct mistakes. Nevertheless, the textual divisions in the Hogarth edition seem preferable. The four divisions missing in the American text mark important turning points in the novel: (1) from the view of the old street singer through the eyes of Peter Walsh to the view of her by Rezia, *i.e.*, from an inflated mythologization to a simple human view—and also from the story of the Dalloways to that of the Warren Smiths, (2) at the symbolically important moment of noon, when the actions of Clarissa and the Warren Smiths are linked in the same sentence for the first and only time in the book, (3) as Rezia drifts into a drugged sleep after her husband's suicide and Peter hears the ambulance bell which tolls, presumably, for Septimus, and thinks of the "triumphs of civilization—which, ironically, have just claimed another victim, and (4) as Clarissa returns from her vivid reexperiencing of Septimus' suicide—and from the temptation toward her own—to her party and her role as "Mrs. Dalloway."

nizably like what she must be thinking, and in the fourth sentence the narrative acknowledges that with "thought Clarissa Dalloway."

In retrospect, however, even the opening sentence could be seen as a rendering of her consciousness: she could think of herself in the social role of "Mrs. Dalloway," announcing her plans to her household staff. The flowers are also significant. Ordinarily, Lucy, Clarissa's maid, would be sent for them, but Lucy is busy preparing for the party that night. So Clarissa will walk to the florist's shop herself (the depth and delicacy of her feeling for Lucy are confirmed soon after she returns, in the scene in which Lucy offers to help her mend her dress). Then too, it is a beautiful morning, and the walk from Westminster through St. James's Park to Bond Street will be pleasant. Flowers are important in another way too: Richard brings her roses during the afternoon, intending to tell her that he loves her. At the last moment he finds that too awkward, but the roses tell her for him, and during the party the only flowers she notices are "the roses which Richard had given her." The book begins, then, with this simple promise to "buy the flowers herself." Her voyage out to Bond Street keeps that promise. But the promise is fulfilled far beyond its literal meaning. The love which motivates her here multiplies itself throughout her world, and returns to bless her in manifold and mysterious ways.

As her story continues, Clarissa's ambivalence about her role as "Mrs. Dalloway" is revealed more fully. She wishes both to escape from that role and to enter into it more fully. She feels both sheltered and anonymous, useful and trivial, committed and deluded. Her sense of being trapped in the role becomes explicit later in the opening section, as she reaches Bond Street: "She had the oddest sense of being herself invisible; unseen; unknown; there being no more marrying, no more having of children now, but only this astonishing and rather solemn progress with the rest of them, up Bond Street, this being Mrs. Dalloway; not even Clarissa any more; this being Mrs. Richard Dalloway."

The opening passage also shows that, despite her declarations of faith and her acceptance of responsibility, Clarissa looks for the meaning of her life primarily in the past. She is now in her early fifties. But when she thinks of this June morning, in the present, she must also think of summer mornings at Bourton, her family's home in the country, when she was eighteen. She hears now, more than thirty years later, the squeak of the hinges of the French doors there. In contrast, the doors of her home in Westminster are to be removed today—presumably to open up the interior spaces for her party. In the symbology of Virginia Woolf, as we have seen in the earlier books, this signals an expansion of consciousness. The party fulfills that promise too.

Peter Walsh, the young man who had been in love with her then, is the man she must think of now. His "sayings" are more memorable to her now than anything Richard has ever said to her. But Peter's "sayings" never really mature: "I prefer men to cauliflowers," which Clarissa translates as a saying about "cabbages," is repeated at her party, where it becomes "he did not like cabbages; he preferred human beings." And Clarissa seems comforted by her husband's inability to say any but superficial things to her; Peter was threatening because he always said too much. Yet, after thirty years, it is still Peter who dominates her imagination—which lives not in the London of her present, but in the Bourton of her late adolescence. It was there that she had refused Peter and accepted Richard. And it was there that she experienced "the most exquisite moment of her whole life," a kiss on the lips by Sally Seton.

Now, many years later, Bourton remains a mysterious world which in some ways Clarissa, despite her obsession with it, does not wish to think about. There is one striking passage, for example, in which Peter thinks about Clarissa's skepticism:

her notion being that the Gods, who never lost a chance of hurting, thwarting and spoiling human lives, were seriously put out if, all the same, you behaved like a lady. That phase came directly after Sylvia's death—that horrible affair. To see your own sister killed by a falling tree (all Justin Parry's fault—all his carelessness) before your very eyes, a girl too on the verge of life, the most gifted of them, Clarissa always said, was enough to turn one bitter. Later . . . she evolved his atheist's religion of doing good for the sake of goodness.

It seems strange that Clarissa herself never thinks of Sylvia's death, even though she does think of her father several times during this day. What she had said about it to Peter must have led to his feeling that it was all her father's fault, and that she later came to believe that "no one was to blame." Did she really believe that? or did she repress her earlier feeling? Her comment that Sylvia was "the most gifted of them" may imply that to be gifted is to be doomed—and could help to explain Clarissa's own reluctance to appear to be different. Unconsciously, she—and the narrative—might feel somehow that Sylvia's fate is that of the "gifted girl," and even that the father may be implicated in that fate.[3]

While we can only speculate about Clarissa's complicated feelings about her father and about her sister's death, we can see more clearly the repressive nature of Bourton. "Sally it was who made her feel, for the first time, how sheltered the life at Bourton was," Clarissa thinks— Sally, who read William Morris, sat up all night talking. smoked cigars, rode a bicycle around the parapets of the terrace, forgot her bath sponge and ran naked down a corridor—for which she was summoned into the commanding presence of Helena Parry. The household had been governed by Aunt Helena (a more elderly Helen Ambrose?), aided by such stalwarts as the "grim old housemaid, Ellen Atkins," entertained by such guests as "old Joseph Breitkopf singing Brahms without any voice," and presided over by the figure whom Peter remembers as "that querulous, weak-kneed old man, Clarissa's father, Justin Parry" (a geriatric evolution of Ridley Ambrose and Mr. Hilbery).

Conspicuously absent from all of this is the mother. Until Mrs.

3   If there is an autobiographical parallel for the death of Sylvia, it is the death of Stella, the half-sister whom Virginia loved very much. Her death is reflected more clearly in Prue's death in *To the Lighthouse*. If Virginia felt that her father was in any way responsible for Stella's death, she might have felt that Stella married to escape from his domination and demands. When Stella died of peritonitis a few months later, the fact that she was pregnant may have reinforced Virginia's feeling about the death of her mother: that the demands of the male were ultimately lethal.

Death is important in the genesis of *Mrs. Dalloway*. The death, perhaps by suicide, of Kitty Maxse, the prototype for Clarissa, in October, 1922, probably stimulated a search for the deeper significance of her life (see Bell, II, 87). Kitty Maxse, née Lushington, became engaged under the jackmanii at Talland House in St. Ives (Bell, I, 33); thus she may also be a prototype for Minta Doyle of *To the Lighthouse*. The possibility of suicide must have suggested depths in Kitty that had not been seen before, and may have aroused some guilt because of that. Her death must have made the earlier portrait of Clarissa in *The Voyage Out* seem shallow, or at least unfinished.

Hilbery mentions her at Clarissa's party, she exists only by implication and indirection and, in one strange moment in Clarissa's mind during Peter's visit: then Clarissa becomes both "a child, throwing bread to the ducks, between her parents, and at the same time a grown woman coming to her parents who stood by the lake," holding out her life for their inspection. What has she made of their gift of life? she wonders—another sign of the pall of guilt which hangs over her. Old Mrs. Hilbery, of course, is a more elderly version of the mother in *Night and Day*. It is she who mentions Clarissa's mother for the only time in *Mrs. Dalloway*:

"Dear Clarissa!" exclaimed Mrs. Hilbery. She looked to-night, she said, so like her mother as she first saw her walking in a garden in a grey hat.
    And really Clarissa's eyes filled with tears. Her mother, walking in a garden! But alas, she must go.

The image of the mother in the garden is more fully developed in the next novel, *To the Lighthouse*, in which Mrs. Ramsay becomes identified with the garden, especially in the mind of her son James. The edenic quality of the garden is implied here in *Mrs. Dalloway* too, where the memory of the mother walking in the garden "in a grey hat" might almost belong to the dreamlike "Time Passes" part of *To the Lighthouse* ("They had the moth in them—Mrs. Ramsay's things. . . . There was the old grey cloak she wore gardening [Mrs. McNab fingered it]"). It all begins, of course in *The Voyage Out*, where the central fact of Rachel's life is that her mother is dead. And it continues through the devastating death of Mrs. Rose Pargiter in *The Years*, the disappearance of the loving mother into the grey world of nonbeing, with traumatic effects on the daughters who remain. In *Mrs. Dalloway* this crucial experience is repressed by Clarissa, and perhaps suppressed by the narrative consciousness itself, but it is still there. It may be more important than either Clarissa or the narrative recognize, especially in her troubled relationship with her daughter Elizabeth.
    From the beginning Clarissa's excitement tends toward expression in imagery of the sea and the wind. This too has been familiar from *The Voyage Out*, and Clarissa's anxieties, as well as her excitement, will take linguistic shapes very similar to Rachel's. In more ex-

treme and bizarre forms, they will express the madness of Septimus Warren Smith.

Although the narrative has become identical with Clarissa's consciousness by the third paragraph of the book, it does not stay there, but shifts in the fourth paragraph to the mind of Scrope Purvis, her next-door neighbor, to place her in another perspective. He thinks about her for two sentences, then vanishes, never to reappear in the book. In the next paragraph the narrative is incarnate in Clarissa once again.

The shifts from one mind to another are often more subtle than this—to the extent that it is sometimes difficult to identify precisely the point where the narrative leaves one mind and enters another. For example, the narrative is clearly within Clarissa's mind when she enters the florist's, but then there is this passage:

There were flowers: delphiniums, sweet peas, bunches of lilac; and carnations, masses of carnations. There were roses; there were irises. Ah yes—so she breathed in the earthy garden sweet smell as she stood talking to Miss Pym who owed her help, and thought her kind, for kind she had been years ago; very kind, but she looked older, this year, turning her head from side to side among the irises and roses and nodding tufts of lilac with her eyes half closed, snuffing in, after the street uproar, the delicious scent, the exquisite coolness. And then, opening her eyes, how fresh, like frilled linen clean from a laundry laid in wicker trays, the roses looked. . . .

Somewhere in this passage the perception is probably Miss Pym's. She thinks that Clarissa is kind and was "very kind" "years ago" (perhaps when Miss Pym especially needed that kindness), but now she looks much older. But much of the passage could also reflect Clarissa's consciousness of Miss Pym's feelings about her, or even what she hopes that Miss Pym might feel. Where does Clarissa's train of thought end, and where does it begin again? Or does the narrative float between the two women, rendering the ambiance of their feeling for each other? Clarissa's identity depends upon her differentiation from the world around her, but her extraordinary sensitivity to that world tends to dissolve that differentiation.

Except for brief glimpses into the mind of Scrope Purvis and the feelings of Miss Pym, the entire opening section of *Mrs. Dalloway* renders the consciousness of Clarissa. It discloses her feelings about Bourton, Peter Walsh, London, the war, Lady Bexborough, the month of June, Hugh Whitbread, marriage, freedom, memory and immortality, manipulating other people, the mystery of identity, Bond Street, gloves, her daughter and her dog, Miss Kilman the religious fanatic, the flowers. True to her opening promise, she gets the flowers herself. By the end of the first section the narrative has discovered her essence, which will be elaborated, but not really changed or transformed, by the rest of the book.

In a number of places in the book the narrative consciousness hovers, as it does in the passage we have just seen with Clarissa and Miss Pym, between the minds of the characters. At other times it withdraws into a more impersonal perspective which is not identified with any of the characters, but observes their actions, speculates on their motives, sometimes even pauses for lectures on the meaning of it all. The most conspicuous of these is the discourse on the "goddesses" of Sir William Bradshaw, Proportion and Conversion. Except for these occasional interruptions, *Mrs. Dalloway* represents the luminous halo of consciousness itself. The transitions from one mind to another, and from individual minds to a larger cultural awareness, enhance the feeling that human consciousness transcends the limitations of individual minds. The significance of an individual human life, Clarissa once told Peter, is "completed" by other people, and even by places. That, she sensed, is the secret of immortality, the perpetuation of human meaning beyond the limitations of individual lives. Significantly, the narrative discovers this "theory" of Clarissa's immediately following the suicide of Septimus Warren Smith. Perhaps the theory helps to explain her extraordinary empathy for this young man whom she has never met, and her intuition for the meaning of his death.

The first two digressions of the narrative consciousness, into the minds of Scrope Purvis and Miss Pym, about thirteen pages apart, mark the boundaries of its first extended incarnation in the mind of Clarissa. Neither Mr. Purvis nor Miss Pym appears elsewhere in the book. Neither represents a real alternative incarnation for the narrative. Instead, these minds serve as reflectors for Clarissa. In that sense, the entry of the narrative consciousness into these characters is only nominal and momentary. They come into existence only to express feelings which the narrative consciousness cannot assign to Clarissa herself. It makes no real effort to discover the inner realities of these characters.

The next sustained incarnation of the narrative consciousness is also in the mind of Clarissa. Whereas the first one described her voyage out into Bond Street, this second passage evokes her introspection and her memories. It ends with her "assembling that diamond shape, that single person," her social identity, as mistress of her present household. There are two more sustained evocations of Clarissa's consciousness. The third passage comes shortly after the evocation of Richard's thoughts as he returns to his wife, bearing flowers. And the final passage, of course, is the one in which Clarissa retires to the little room from her party, contemplates Septimus' death and her own, and chooses to return to her guests.

Although our admiration for Clarissa's consciousness probably grows throughout the novel, her mind and her feelings do have their limitations. For instance, in the first section she thinks that the drunks on doorsteps "can't be dealt with, she felt positive, by Acts of Parliament for that very reason: they love life." Such an assertion is believable only as a revelation of Clarissa's insensitivity to the reality of these people. And this is characteristic of a more general insensitivity to various aspects of the lower class by the other middle-class characters—and the narrative itself. Such people tend to be seen less as individuals than as symbols (for instance, the old street singer with her timeless song), and the narrative typically attempts to remove them to some mythic distance.

As the title implies, Clarissa is the central character. She is the subject—and object—of the final "vision": "For there she was." The book begins in her consciousness, and the plot creates her "room" as the preceding book had created Jacob's. And as in *Jacob's Room*, the narrative is attracted toward, yet distant from, rather awed by, and somewhat critical of, the central character. It explores the periphery rather than the heart of her social world, and during the climactic party the perspective shifts from one overawed outsider to another:

Lucy, the devoted lady's maid; Mrs. Walker, the cook; Peter Walsh, the suitor rejected long ago and now a refugee even from the colonial service; Ellie Henderson, the elderly cousin invited only at the last minute and from a sense of duty; Sally Seton, whom Clarissa had been in love with in their youth, but who lives in *nouveau riche* exile in Manchester. Even when the narrative is incarnate in Clarissa herself during her party, it focuses on her feelings of alienation from her own milieu.

After its first two sustained explorations of Clarissa's mind, the narrative consciousness looks elsewhere for the meaning of this complex "world." It first turns to Peter Walsh, in whose mind it is eventually sustained for slightly longer altogether than in the mind of Clarissa herself. Yet the authenticity of its incarnation in Peter sometimes seems questionable. For example, the narrative is nominally within the mind of Peter when the sound of Big Ben, announcing eleven thirty, penetrates the reverie in which he is reliving his recent meeting with Clarissa:

wondering whether by calling at that hour he had annoyed her; overcome with shame suddenly at having been a fool; wept; been emotional; told her everything, as usual, as usual.

As a cloud crosses the sun, silence falls on London; and falls on the mind. Effort ceases. Time flaps on the mast. There we stop; there we stand. Rigid, the skeleton of habit alone upholds the human frame. Where there is nothing, Peter Walsh said to himself; feeling hollowed out, utterly empty within. Clarissa refused me, he thought. He stood there thinking, Clarissa refused me.

Ah, said St. Margaret's, like a hostess who comes into her drawing room on the very stroke of the hour and finds her guests there already. I am not late. No, it is precisely half-past eleven, she says. Yet, though she is perfectly right, her voice, being the voice of the hostess, is reluctant to inflict its individuality. Some grief for the past holds it back; some concern for the present. It is half-past eleven, she says, and the sound of St. Margaret's glides into the recesses of the heart and buries itself in ring after ring of sound, like something alive which wants to confide itself, to disperse itself, to be, with a tremor of delight, at rest—like Clarissa herself, thought Peter Walsh, coming downstairs on the stroke of the hour in white. It is Clarissa herself, he thought, with a deep emotion, and an extraordinarily clear, yet puzzling, recollection of her, as if this bell had come into the room years ago, where they sat at some moment of great intimacy, and had gone from one to the other and had left, like a bee with honey, laden with the moment. But what room? What moment? And why had he been so profoundly happy when the clock was striking? Then, as the sound of St. Margaret's languished, he thought, She has been ill, and the sound expressed languor and suffering. It was her heart, he remembered; and the sudden loudness of the final stroke tolled for death that surprised in the midst of life, Clarissa falling where she stood, in her drawing-room. No! No! he cried. She is not dead! I am not old, he cried, and marched up Whitehall, as if there rolled down to him, vigorous, unending, his future.[4]

In this passage the narrative moves between an immersion in Peter's thoughts and a more impersonal perspective in which it comments, almost in the style of a familiar essay, on the nature of its created world. Its penetrations into Peter's mind here are not as deep as its previous immersions in Clarissa's. The repetition of "he thought" indicates a certain distance between the narrative consciousness and the mind of Peter. The meditation on the silence of the mind begins as an essay ("As a cloud crosses the sun . . . "), then is assigned to Peter. The lovely lyrical meditation on St. Margaret's emerges as a reply to his "thinking, Clarissa refused me." Eventually that reply too is assigned to Peter's mind ("thought Peter Walsh"), but the narrative's comment on the nature of his awareness ("he thought, with a deep emotion . . . ") shows that the narrative is not fully immersed in that awareness. Just before this quoted passage he had been aware of the sound of Big Ben, but not, perhaps, of the "leaden circles" which the narrative mentioned in parenthesis. Is the identification now of "St. Margaret's" his, or is he aware of it only as "this bell"? Such questions can't be answered with certainty. What the narrative does here is to hover over Peter Walsh much as it had hovered over Jacob in the previous novel, now seeming to enter his mind, now seeming to withdraw to some safer distance to generalize on what it may have seen there, now returning, as it does at the end of the quoted passage, to a fuller immersion in that individual reality. The pattern of these immersions and withdrawals, then, constitutes the reality of *Mrs. Dalloway* as a whole.

4 For "coming downstairs" the American edition has "coming down the stairs."

As this quoted passage shows, time is an important theme of this novel. The motif of time serves to define both individual characters and the larger reality in which they interact. Throughout *Mrs. Dalloway* Big Ben announces the time, "First a warning, musical, then the hour irrevocable. The leaden circles dissolved in the air." The motif expresses the ambivalence of the narrative consciousness toward time. It both anticipates the hours (*The Hours* was an early working title for the book) as a promise of meaning and dreads them as an announcement of mortality. Clarissa is in love with the promise, but aware also of her mortality, and this dual awareness is at the heart of her "transcendental theory" of immortality—the survival of meaning beyond the limitations of an individual life. St. Margaret's, Clarissa's clock, represents an experiential sense of time, in which "the moment" expands as it is filled with human meaning.

Inevitably, then, the voice of St. Margaret's breaks, "like the spray of an exhausted wave, upon the body of Miss Kilman" the religious fanatic. And for Septimus, in his deepening madness, time is only a dead, dry word which splits its husk. He composes "an immortal ode to Time," to the dead, and becomes more and more like the leaden, authoritative voice of Big Ben. And there is one other voice of time in *Mrs. Dalloway*: "the clocks of Harley Street nibbled at the June day, counselled submission, upheld authority, and pointed out in chorus the supreme advantages of a sense of proportion. . . ." This, of course, is the voice of the Establishment, and of such characters as the smug but harmless Hugh Whitbread and the smug but very destructive Sir William Bradshaw.

Although the narrative is located within the mind of Peter Walsh for more of *Mrs. Dalloway* than it is within any other character, its immersion in him is not as deep as it is in Clarissa. Even when it is nominally located in Peter's mind, the narrative often withdraws into commentary. For example, it names "three great emotions" that it finds there, rather than rendering these emotions themselves. Peter exists primarily as a reflector to illuminate Clarissa's past. Aspects of his own life which are alleged to be important (his dismissal from Oxford, his work as a civil servant, his passionate involvement with the wife of a British major there) have almost no reality in his thoughts, which at times are merely silly: "For he had a turn for mechanics; had invented a plow in his district, had ordered wheel-barrows from England, but the coolies wouldn't use them. . . ." The reality of such passages is not that of the person Peter Walsh is alleged to be, but of a Bloomsbury intellectual trying to imagine such a person.

The emphasis given to the perspective of Peter Walsh seems out of proportion to his importance as a character in Clarissa's story. Like the other characters, of course, he is a "reflector" of a certain aspect of Clarissa. But in her mind, he looms larger than Richard. It is natural that she should be thinking of Peter more than she usually does: he is returning to London after a long absence. But that alone does not explain his stature in her imagination. Her view of him is retrospective, inseparable from that "white dawn in the country" when the pages of her own life were still unwritten. But life with him would have been impossible for her. With him "everything had to be shared, everything gone into. And it was intolerable," so she chose Richard instead, and Peter's "whole life had been a failure. It made her angry still." She seems to imply that with her his life would not have been a "failure." Yet she could not give him what he needed. Her anger reflects a certain sense of helplessness—which may extend beyond Clarissa to the narrative consciousness itself: the main characters it creates all seem to feel trapped (except for Richard).

When the narrative first enters Peter's mind, it is to register his reaction to Clarissa: "She's grown older, he thought." Then it discloses his irritation at her social life, his memory of her in the moonlight at Bourton, his resentment at her haunting him, his wondering whether to tell her of Daisy, the married woman for whom he has given up his career in India. He does tell Clarissa, bursting into tears as he does so. After Elizabeth interrupts this scene, he leaves. On his subsequent walk to Regent's Park, the narrative becomes a long meditation in his consciousness—again focused largely on Clarissa.

Peter isn't very convincing if he is judged by conventional standards of realism. He seems too preoccupied with Clarissa, who rejected him more than thirty years ago. He never thinks of his work in India or of his wife there, and seldom of Daisy, for whom he is said to have given up both his marriage and career. He seems rather unconcerned with the fact that he is now unemployed and in London to try to make some sort of new beginning.

What, then, is the reality that Peter represents? From a psychological standpoint, he embodies a consuming male desire which has been disarmed and transformed into a lifelong devotion. The narrative can't really get inside that desire: Peter never thinks of Clarissa's body, even when he is said to be thinking of the time when he was "passionately" in love with her (for that matter, he never thinks of Daisy's either—and the name itself may relegate her to some vegetable world beneath the serious notice of the narrative). Instead, desire is translated into lyricism. This first floods the story as Peter falls asleep in Regent's Park and becomes the dreaming "solitary traveller," endowing sky and trees with womanhood. The narrative consciousness itself becomes free to dream, captivated by images typical of visionary moments in Virginia Woolf: sky, trees, breezes stirring the leaves, mermaids riding the waves, the goddess rising from the sea, and so on. "Such are the visions," the narrative insists.

And it is Peter to whom the final visionary moment is assigned at the end of the book:

"I will come," said Peter, but he sat on for a moment. What is this terror? what is this ecstasy? he thought to himself. What is it that fills me with extraordinary excitement?

It is Clarissa, he said.

For there she was.

Terror, ecstasy, excitement: these are abstractions, not the phenomenal realities of the procession at the end of *The Voyage Out* or of the pair of old, empty shoes at the end of *Jacob's Room*. Even the words *he thought*, while they assign these abstractions to Peter's mind, increase the psychological distance between the narrative and that mind. The narrative doesn't render Peter's stream of consciousness directly; it tells us what "he thought." Stylistically, Peter's epiphany remains in the realm of assertion—though the accretion of detail about Clarissa throughout the book does create a rich background for this final vision. But in the final scene Peter seems less convincing as a separate character than as a reflection of Clarissa.

Peter also expresses an important aspect of the narrative consciousness itself: the passionate, awkward outsider with no background and only a very shadowy identity, "a failure," at once envious and contemptuous of everything that Clarissa's class represents. Peter has no family, comes from nowhere. The narrative can't imagine any background for him; the earliest thing it knows is that he was "sent down" from Oxford—for being a Socialist, apparently. He is more alienated from Clarissa's world than Septimus is, for Septimus was never really close to it. Peter expresses the alienation of the narrative consciousness itself from that world.

The distance of Septimus from Clarissa's world is qualitatively different. The narrative discovers him on Bond Street; the quality which it first recognizes in him is "apprehension." In its next look at him it becomes immersed in the terrors of his paranoia: "And there the motor car stood, with drawn blinds, and upon them a curious pattern like a tree, Septimus thought, and this gradual drawing together of everything to one centre before his eyes, as if some horror had come to the surface and was about to burst into flames, terrified him. The world wavered and quivered and threatened to burst into flames. It is I who am blocking the way, he thought. Was he not being looked at and pointed at; was he not weighted there, rooted to the pavement, for a purpose? But for what purpose?" His perception of the pattern of the tree on the blind draws everything together in his vision, and overwhelms his consciousness. These same feelings have haunted the earlier novels. The "immitigable tree" has been there from the beginning (see page 35, note 8), and the other terrors had been present in Rachel's imagination too: things suddenly bursting to the surface from the depths, the fires of sexuality, the anxieties about "blocking the way," about being "rooted" to one place, unable to move. To some extent Peter in *Mrs. Dalloway* also shares such fears— as in the dreams (also "triggered" by trees) in Regent's Park, from which he awakes with a sudden awareness of "the death of the soul." But Septimus can't awake from his terrors. He lives in a constant state of apprehension. And as we learn in this first evocation of his consciousness, those terrors manifest themselves—as they did for Rachel too—through distortions of perspective.

Aside from Clarissa herself, Septimus is the first of the major characters whose consciousness is evoked. In some ways he represents, as Virginia Woolf wrote in her introduction to the Modern Library edition of *Mrs. Dalloway*, Clarissa's "double." But unlike her, he becomes wholly dominated by an inner reality. And that becomes so limited that all he can think to do when Dr. Holmes intrudes upon it is to jump out the window.

Septimus is given a history: he came to London from Stroud, where he lived with his mother, who "lied" and who criticized him for coming to tea "with his hands unwashed"; he confided in his little sister and moved to London, "leaving an absurd note behind him, such as great men have written, and the world has read later." Thus the narrative seems not to be entirely serious about this background, especially his "ethereal and insubstantial" infatuation with Miss Isabel Pole. His volunteering for the war is also viewed as naïve, and his devotion to his superior officer, Evans, is described almost cynically.

The turning point comes after Evans is killed and after the armistice, when Septimus suddenly discovers that "he could not feel." Trying to escape from his ensuing panic, he becomes engaged to Lucrezia. But though she does what she can for him, his condition deteriorates. He rediscovers his literary idols: Shakespeare, Dante, Aeschylus—and their secret message of "loathing, hatred, despair." His wife's desire for a child intensifies that despair, and

At last, with a *melodramatic gesture* which he *assumed mechanically* and with *complete consciousness of its insincerity*, he dropped his head on his hands. Now *he had surrendered*; now other people must help him. People must be sent for. *He gave in*. [italics added]

Thus the narrative insists that Septimus himself is responsible for this crucial step in his descent into madness. It speaks of the mechanical, melodramatic insincerity of his *gesture*, and discovers the climactic fact that *He gave in*.

The consequences of that surrender are explored in the rest of his story, much more fully than the account of his background. The "world" of Septimus becomes progressively more self-centered, until at last nothing is real to him except his own suffering. Dr. Holmes, with all his hearty advice, seems especially repulsive. Septimus has all the sensitivity of Clarissa and none of her empathy: whatever else she may be guilty of, it is not a lack of feeling, as we see in her reaction to the suicide of Septimus, whom she never knew.

In Septimus, then, the narrative explores the fate of the personality that withdraws from the touch of other people into the abstractions of pure vision. It finds a great deal of self-indulgence in such a personality, and discovers that *giving in* to such a temptation is fatal. The need to "prove" this is so strong the Septimus' story often becomes an essay, an expository "telling" rather than a dramatic "showing." But it does enter deeply into his madness, which is evoked with intensity. The causal chain culminating in that madness, however, tends to be told rather than shown—and told from some distance.

The narrative's immersions in the mind of Septimus are not sustained for as long as those in the minds of Clarissa or Peter, but his consciousness is rendered with more depth and immediacy. And it is linked with Clarissa's consciousness through images and motifs suggesting a larger unity in which they both participate and, at times, can recognize. For example, just before Peter arrives on his morning visit, the narrative hovers between the mind of Clarissa and a more impersonal perspective:

So on a summer's day waves collect, overbalance, and fall; collect and fall; and the whole world seems to be saying "that is all" more and more ponderously, until even the heart in the body which lies in the sun on the beach says too, That is all. Fear no more, says the heart. Fear no more, says the heart, committing its burden to some sea, which sighs collectively for all sorrows, and renews, begins, collects, lets fall. And the body alone listens to the passing bee; the wave breaking; the dog barking, far away barking and barking.

This is paralleled by a passage in the mind of Septimus very much later in the book:

Every power poured its treasures on his head, and his hand lay there on the back of the sofa, as he had seen his hand lie when he was bathing, floating, on top of the waves, while far away on shore he heard dogs barking and barking far away. Fear no more, says the heart in the body; fear no more.

The most apparent similarities between the passages have to do with the theme of the "treasures" of experience, the imagery of the waves, the sound of dogs barking, the dirge from *Cymbeline* ("Fear no more the heat o' the sun"), and the phrase "the heart in the body." In the first passage the narrative has been inside Clarissa's consciousness, and whether or not it remains there throughout the passage, it does seem to express the essence of her feelings at this point in the story. But there is also a slight detachment from, and objectification of, that feeling, through a translation of it into a more abstract, figurative language. The quality of the second passage, however, is much more intense and immediate. Septimus, who thinks that he cannot feel, is in reality the victim of his feelings. Clarissa can achieve some distance from her feelings. But when Septimus "gave in," he surrendered to his.

The narrative tries to discover in Septimus' case history some rational explanation for his growing insanity and suicidal impulses. If it can discover the secret of his doom, then perhaps Clarissa can be saved from that same fate. The narrative needs to make Septimus morally responsible for his fate, and it withdraws somewhat from his consciousness at times in order to evaluate it—and also, perhaps, not to become lost in it. To remain immersed in such a consciousness is, as the narrative discovers—and perhaps has known all along—to drown.

The essential dialectical struggle in *Mrs. Dalloway*, then, is between the opposite adaptations to the world which are represented by Clarissa and by Septimus. The configuration of characters in the book gives further definition to these adaptations. Septimus' wife Lucrezia, for instance, is not only a reflector for him but also, in a sense, the symbolic fulfillment of Clarissa's relationship with Peter. Lucrezia submits to a man who demands everything, and to whom she is only an extension of his own personality. He can't relate her feelings to anything real—that is, to anything within his own egocentric reality.

Richard Dalloway remains a rather shadowy figure. The narrative does not enter his consciousness until the second half of the book, and then not in much depth. His thoughts are rather ordinary, except perhaps for his extensive concern with pedigree, with Peter Walsh's love for Clarissa, with his own reticence toward her, and with the "miracle" of their marriage. Elsewhere, Clarissa remembers "Sally Seton saying that Richard would never be in the Cabinet because he had a second-class brain." The limited space given to Richard in the narrative reflects his limited importance in Clarissa's reality, and the curious distance that separates—and, in another way, unites—them. The narrative consciousness sees this distance as essential to a satisfying marriage: Richard gives Clarissa room to be herself.

Their daughter Elizabeth exemplifies that heritage. Caught between the forms of love offered by her mother and by Miss Kilman, Elizabeth instinctively chooses life, and her voyage through the Strand on the omnibus reenacts Clarissa's journey years before (when she told Peter of her theory of immortality). Elizabeth chooses her mother's commitment to life, rather than the commitment to absolutes, and Elizabeth's choice validates her mother's commitment.

Miss Kilman reflects Clarissa in another way: the sexual inhibitions of Clarissa find their grotesque extreme in Miss Kilman. She also reflects Septimus: as his female counterpart, her denial of the flesh is, like his, a denial of life itself.

Sally Seton, whose kiss on the lips had brought Clarissa an ecstasy unequaled thereafter, enters the story in person at the party. The narrative enters into her mind, but primarily to look at the past, and at other people—Clarissa, Peter, Richard. What Sally sees confirms what we already know about them, and adds little to what we know about her. That comes mostly from other perspectives, and isn't very interesting: she is now Lady Rosseter, rich, married to an industrialist in Manchester, the mother of five sons, and so on. Here is still another feminine destiny—and one which the narrative consciousness views from some distance.

Each of these characters, then, reflects the changing aspects of the narrative's struggle toward a final, definitive adaptation to its world. As always, the struggle is reflected through a series of perspectives. And the sequence of perspectives is significant. First, after the evocation of Clarissa's consciousness in her walk to Bond Street, the narrative discovers her antithesis, Septimus, and catches a few frightening but fascinating glimpses of his madness, his withdrawal from the shared reality of Bond Street. Then in Peter's interview with Clarissa, his walk, and his dream, the narrative explores a personality which is opposite to that of Septimus in the sense that it longs not for total transcendence of the need for love, but for total expression of that need. The next major sequence shows Septimus at Sir William Bradshaw's, a confrontation which reveals that their realities too are wholly opposite and irreconcilable. That scene is then succeeded by the luncheon at Lady Bruton's, in which people conscious of their differences act together in reasonable harmony. Then, from his public role at Lady Bruton's, Richard returns to his home and to his private role, his relationship with Clarissa. In that ambiance the previous themes begin to converge, and from it they will radiate. Elizabeth and Miss Kilman, Septimus' female counterpart, leave the house, where Clarissa worries about losing her daughter. But in the next sequence Elizabeth leaves Miss Kilman and, like her mother years before, makes her own pilgrimage through the Strand. This affirmation is in turn succeeded by the sequence in which Peter reminisces and has dinner, and leaves at last for the climactic party. In that final sequence Clarissa survives her experience of Septimus' death, and returns to her primary role as "Mrs. Dalloway": "For there she was." That is the final revelation toward which the dialectical struggle moves, the realization of the nature of Clarissa's existence, a unity emerging at last from this long series of diversities.

Until the very end of the book, and beyond, a fate like that of Septimus seems possible for Clarissa, whose *joie de vivre* seems rather manic and frequently threatened by intimations of despair. In its last penetration into her consciousness, the narrative follows her as she hears of the death of a "young man" from the Bradshaws and as she moves at once into the "little room" where she experiences, in her imagination, the physical sensations of Septimus' death. She feels that she knows, intuitively, why he did it. She knows somehow that Sir William Bradshaw is also responsible. She knows also that "Somehow it was her disaster—her disgrace." She sees the old woman in the house opposite the window going to bed: for a moment the woman stares straight at her—a vision, perhaps of her own old age. And Clarissa feels "glad that he had done it; thrown it away while they went on living. The clock was striking. The leaden circles dissolved in the air. But she must go back. She must assemble. She must find Sally and

Peter. And she came in from the little room."[5] The narrative has followed Clarissa from the noise and confusion of her party into the silence of the "little room" of her innermost awareness. Septimus' final melodramatic gesture of defiance ("I'll give it you!" he cried as he plunged) also turns out to be, when it is perceived by the consciousness of Clarissa, a genuine, generous, even beautiful gift. It redeems and renews her life. Perhaps Peter also becomes aware of that somehow when he feels his final "terror," "ecstasy," and "extraordinary excitement," which he attributes to Clarissa.

The first words of the book announce its subject: "Mrs. Dalloway." It develops like a fugue. The various narrative perspectives constitute the thematic elements which evolve toward a resolution, reached at last in the dominant chord at the end: "For there she was." Clarissa's meaning is completed, as she recognizes in her "transcendental theory," by the people—and even the places—that she has touched. The party at the end brings together the people who complete her. Even the dead are suddenly and unexpectedly present: the mother whose reappearance in the garden of Clarissa's childhood moves her to tears; an unknown young man whose final "gift" suddenly forces her to confront her own innermost nature and sweeps her on to epiphany. As these manifold meanings converge, they confirm the richness of her life. And yet, a poignant distance remains between her and the people she loves.

The fullest and the final embodiment of this distance is Peter Walsh. Like the lover in Keats's "Grecian Urn," he exists only in his perpetual pursuit of his beloved: the essence of Peter Walsh is his eternal love for, and eternal rejection by, Clarissa. In the larger context of the *oeuvre*, he continues the line of final visionaries which had begun with St. John Hirst of *The Voyage Out* and which will end with Miss La Trobe of *Between the Acts*—characters whose origins and backgrounds are obscure, whose existence is on the fringes of the established social order, whose relations with other people are inhib-

---

5 The American edition changes this quotation to "glad that he had done it; thrown it away. The clock was striking. The leaden circles dissolved in the air. He made her feel the beauty; made her feel the fun. But she must go back," etc.

ited, whose sexual nature is troubled, yet whose distance from all of the conventional norms provides a special perspective on them.

The emergence of this perspective into dominance at the end of *Mrs. Dalloway* consigns Clarissa's life to the realm of the past: "For there she was." From the very beginning of her story there has been a feeling, first expressed by Clarissa herself and then confirmed by Peter's perspective, that the most meaningful time in her life has been the time at Bourton, especially the summer when she refused Peter and accepted Richard. The need to justify that choice recurs again and again in the present. Although she courageously accepts the present, she remains haunted by the past. This inescapable past-ness of Clarissa's innermost reality gives *Mrs. Dalloway* its nostalgic, almost elegiac tone, as if her present existence were a posthumous life.

This sense of the relentless flow of time, and of the longing for the past, is like that of Quentin's section of Faulkner's *The Sound and the Fury*. Like Septimus and Clarissa, Quentin is dominated by the past and tempted toward suicide. Like Septimus, he finally gives in—though another part of his schizophrenic awareness knows that giving in is futile too. Quentin knows what his father would say about the inescapable past: "was the saddest word of all there is nothing else in the world its not despair until time its not even time until it was." The last word of *Mrs. Dalloway* reverberates with a similar sadness.

As we have seen, several antiphonal voices of time are present in the book. The one which remains dominant is the voice of Big Ben, which bears Clarissa, Peter, and the narrative consciousness as well, ceaselessly into the past. Its voice is heard for the last time as Clarissa contemplates the suicide of "the young man" whom we have known as Septimus. As Big Ben strikes, Clarissa stops counting the hours after the third stroke. As she continues to think of the young man's death she is aware only that "The clock was striking. The leaden circles dissolved in the air." If the "leaden circles" are a reminder of mortality, the fact that they dissolve in the air may imply that a single human life and death never really ends, but is absorbed instead into a larger, more timeless and universal form of life. Clarissa knows the meaning of the young man's final gesture, though she had not known Septimus himself: "Death was an attempt to communicate. . . ."

As the book begins, the narrative consciousness searches for the secret of Clarissa's commitment to life. What it eventually learns is that her commitment is much more fragile than anyone else knows. No one else knows of her ordeal in the little room after she learns of the young man's suicide. But Peter, Richard, and others do seem to know that there are depths in Clarissa's soul which they themselves have only glimpsed. Clarissa is the identity in which the narrative consciousness first becomes incarnate in the book, and which it tries not only to understand more deeply, but also to escape from and to transcend. Although there are other identities in the opening part of the book, these are only nominal: such characters as Scrope Purvis and Miss Pym have no reality of their own; they merely reflect Clarissa. But after Peter Walsh's morning visit, the narrative consciousness stays with him during his walk toward Regent's Park, his dream there, and his subsequent memories of Bourton and his traumatic parting there from Clarissa. This turns out to be the longest sustained incarnation of the narrative consciousness in one character during the book. In Peter the narrative seems to have found an identity which is an alternative for its identification with Clarissa. In a way, he represents a complementary personality for Clarissa: a masculinity to balance her femininity, an intellectual orientation to contrast with her social one, an exile to offset her English domesticity.

But Peter turns out to have no real life of his own, only a contrasting reflection of Clarissa's life. And so the narrative discovers Septimus, whose inner life is all too authentic—and compelling, so much so that the narrative consciousness must then withdraw to an impersonal perspective in its search for the meaning of Septimus' reality. In Sir William Bradshaw it finds a social villain whom it attempts to blame for the fate of Septimus. But it also discovers that Septimus was doomed long before he met Dr. Bradshaw. At a deeper level the narrative consciousness needs to believe that Septimus is responsible for his own fate. And it needs to see Clarissa's struggle against a similar despair as the essential meaning of her life. Unlike Septimus, she does not give in.

Thus the narrative turns away from its growing preoccupation with Septimus and from its own impassioned attack on Bradshaw, toward life and toward the supportive kinds of awareness which make survival possible. After the attack on Dr. Bradshaw, the next sustained incarnation of the narrative consciousness is in Richard Dalloway— the antidote to what Bradshaw represents. Then, after returning to the mind of Clarissa, the narrative consciousness is sustained for the first time within Elizabeth Dalloway—a confirmation of the victory of the values of Richard and Clarissa over those of Miss Kilman.

Then, immediately after the suicide of Septimus, the narrative returns once more to the mind of Peter Walsh. His view is the only sustained perspective until the final evocation of Clarissa herself, in her confrontation with the death of Septimus. Peter, of course, is the character to whom the final epiphany is assigned: "for there she was."

Formally, the book is now complete. Clarissa's promise at the beginning has been fulfilled: she has not only bought the flowers herself but has also created, out of them and all her social skills, her "gift" of the party. Her husband has enhanced all that by bringing her roses; he has also praised Elizabeth (in fact, he has been as unable to resist praising her as he has been unable to tell Clarissa of his love). Peter's final perspective—now that his skepticism, like Clarissa's coldness, is all warmed through—makes her seem complete. And in withdrawing into that perspective at the end, the narrative achieves a formal finality, as well as a final distance.

But beyond the aesthetic pleasure of the ending, and the technical virtuosity of the book as a whole, some doubts may linger. Clarissa's social achievement is more alleged than illustrated. The social dynamics of her party are alluded to rather than realized. It is seen through various perspectives, including Clarissa's, in which the sense of alienation is much stronger than the sense of community. That could be true, of course, of many, or even most, of the people there. But the fact remains that the characters are not very deeply differentiated or, except for Septimus and for Clarissa herself, very deeply imagined. Nominally the narrative enters more than two dozen characters in the course of the book. But the reality which they reflect is largely predetermined: the narrative often uses them to illustrate its preconceptions rather than to discover anything new. This is especially true with characters of the lower classes, whom the narrative evokes only to patronize or to laugh at. But it is true to a large extent even of such major characters as Richard Dalloway and Peter Walsh. They exist primarily as aspects of Clarissa rather than as multidimensional characters in a larger "world." If *Mrs. Dalloway* is a moving book, its poignance arises partly from the sense of the limitations of that world and of the consciousness which created it, and of the distance between that consciousness and the story which it is able to tell.

CHAPTER V

TO THE LIGHTHOUSE

As the fifth in the sequence of nine novels by Virginia Woolf, *To the Lighthouse* is at the center of the *oeuvre*. It is central thematically too. In it the narrative consciousness once again explores the exciting and perilous voyage out into maturity. But it seeks a more primal meaning here than in *The Voyage Out* or the next three novels. It searches for the secrets of family dynamics: the currents of feeling between children and parents, husband and wife. And it also examines the possibilities of art and of the role of the artist in expressing, analyzing, interpreting, and cherishing these deepest and most universal of all human feelings. In doing so, *To the Lighthouse* moves further into the realm of myth than any of the earlier novels. In both method and meaning it represents a major evolution of the symbolic language of the lifework.

"Yes, of course, if it's fine to-morrow," said Mrs. Ramsay. "But you'll have to be up with the lark," she added.

To her son these words conveyed an extraordinary joy, as if it were settled, the expedition were bound to take place, and the wonder to which he had looked forward, for years and years it seemed, was, after a night's darkness and a day's sail, within touch. Since he belonged, even at the age of six, to that great clan which cannot keep this feeling separate from that, but must let future prospects, with their joys and sorrows, cloud what is actually at hand, since to such people even in earliest childhood any turn in the wheel of sensation has the power to crystallise and transfix the moment upon which its gloom or radiance rests, James Ramsay, sitting on the floor cutting out pictures from the illustrated catalogue of the Army and Navy Stores, endowed the picture of a refrigerator, as his mother spoke, with heavenly bliss. It was fringed with joy. The wheelbarrow, the lawn-mower, the sound of poplar trees, leaves whitening before rain, rooks cawing, brooms knocking, dresses rustling—all these were so coloured and distinguished in his mind that he had already his private code, his secret language, though he appeared the image of stark and uncompromising severity, with his high forehead and his fierce blue eyes, impeccably candid and pure, frowning slightly at the sight of human frailty, so that his mother, watching him guide his scissors neatly round the refrigerator, imagined him all red and ermine on the Bench or directing a stern and momentous enterprise in some crisis of public affairs.

"But," said his father, stopping in front of the drawing-room window, "it won't be fine."

Had there been an axe handy, or a poker, any weapon that would have gashed a hole in his father's breast and killed him, there and then, James would have seized it. Such were the extremes of emotion that Mr. Ramsay excited in his children's breasts by his mere presence; standing, as now, lean as a knife, narrow as the blade of one, grinning sarcastically, not only with the pleasure of disillusioning his son and casting ridicule upon his wife, who was ten thousand times better in every way than he was (James thought), but also with some secret conceit at his own accuracy of judgement. What he said was true. It was always true. He was incapable of untruth; never tampered with a fact; never altered a disagreeable word to suit the pleasure or convenience of any mortal being, least of all of his own children, who, sprung from his loins, should be aware from childhood that life is difficult; facts uncompromising; and the passage to that fabled land where our brightest hopes are extinguished, our frail barks founder in darkness (here Mr. Ramsay would straighten his back and narrow his little blue eyes upon the horizon), one that needs, above all, courage, truth, and the power to endure.

"But it may be fine—I expect it will be fine," said Mrs. Ramsay, making some little twist of the reddish brown stocking she was knitting, impatiently. If she finished it tonight, if they did go to the Lighthouse after all, it was to be given to the Lighthouse keeper for his little boy, who was threatened with a tuberculous hip; together with a pile of old magazines, and some tobacco, indeed whatever she could find lying about, not really wanted, but only littering the room, to give those poor fellows who must be bored to death sitting all day with nothing to do but polish the lamp and trim the wick and rake about on their scrap of garden, something to amuse them. For how would you like to be shut up for a whole month at a time, and possibly more in stormy weather, upon a rock the size of a tennis lawn? she would ask; and to have no letters or newspapers, and to see nobody; if you were married, not to see your wife, not to know how your children were,—if they were ill, if they had fallen down and broken their legs or arms; to see the same dreary waves breaking week after week, and then a dreadful storm coming, and the windows covered with spray, and birds dashed against the lamp, and the whole place rocking, and not be able to put your nose out of doors for fear of being swept into the sea? How would you like that? she asked, addressing herself particularly to her daughters. So she added, rather differently, one must take them whatever comforts one can.[1]

Thus this world begins, with the mother's promise to her son. She is aware, of course that the weather isn't likely to be fine tomorrow. But she is also aware of her son's feelings, and knows that "children never forget." What he will remember, as Part III will show, is not his parents' words, but their attitudes. And so when Mr. Ramsay intervenes with his blunt pronouncement, "But it won't be fine," the essential attitudes of the parents have been announced. The mother is positive, enthusiastic, expansive, supportive; the father negative, narrow, discouraging. While she would allow James to discover for himself that the weather will not allow the voyage, her husband's approach is more authoritarian. Of course Mr. Ramsay is "right," but he doesn't bother to explain, or to invite James to share in his thinking.

Of all the human aspects of a child's world, the parents are the most inescapably *given*. From its very beginning, *To the Lighthouse* explores the mystery of this influence. The exploration must begin with this primal scene, electric with the tensions between mother and father which are puzzling and mysterious to their children—and even, as we see later, to outsiders like Lily Briscoe.

As the book begins, the narrative consciousness is at some distance from the scene it describes, or from the feelings of its characters toward these events. It listens to the promise of Mrs. Ramsay to her son, and it speaks of the "joy" which her words "conveyed" (*i.e.*, inspired) in him. But it also remains somewhat outside of this alleged "joy," generalizing instead about "that great clan" to which "he be-

1 My quotations throughout this chapter are from the first English edition of *To the Lighthouse* (London: Hogarth, 1925).

longed," and imagining that he "endowed the picture of a refrigerator
. . . with heavenly bliss." A more cautious narrative would refrain
from endowing a refrigerator with heavenly bliss. But the hyperbolic
language here expresses the truth of the narrative's feeling for the
Ramsays: theirs is a primordial world of Titans.

Latent in its beginning are indications of its end. Mr. Ramsay
wants his children to know that the voyage out requires "courage,
truth, and the power to endure." And of course he is right. But the
narrative is impatient, from the very beginning, with his passion for
"truth," that is, with his obsession with the darkness of man's final
end, and, especially, with his continual self-dramatization as the only
one heroic enough to gaze into that darkness, or to endure the voyage
into it. And yet, though the narrative satirizes his posturing, it also
admires and may even come to respect him. If his actions seem somewhat larger than life, they also contribute toward a family drama
which is enacted on a much larger than average scale—and which
therefore expands the dimensions of consciousness of the drama itself.
To grow up in such a family is to become aware of a wider range of
possibilities—in certain directions. And Mr. Ramsay's insistence on
the nature of the passage to "that fabled land" is rewarded by the end
of the book.

But while Mr. Ramsay insists upon the dark imperatives of the
voyage out, his wife is preparing her offering, the stocking she is knitting for the "little boy" of the "Lighthouse keeper." Whether the
stocking ever reaches the boy is not specified; after Part I it is not seen
again, except in Lily's memory. (Everything we see of Mrs. Ramsay's
charity, industry, and powers of organization, however, suggests that
she would have finished the stocking and arranged to have it delivered.) But it is only one emblem of Mrs. Ramsay's commitment to
other people, and her sense of duty. Her world, like her husband's, is
highly dramatic, though her sense of drama takes a different direction.
In the opening passage we see this in her view of her six-year-old son
as a distinguished jurist, and then in her imaginative dramatization of
life at the lighthouse. And already in the opening scene she is thinking
about what to take there—a question which must be asked again before the actual voyage in Part III. The answer there, implied rather

than directly stated, is that the voyage itself is what matters—not what one finds to take, but one's commitment to giving. But constant giving, the narrative fears, may be too draining, too exhausting: Lily thinks that "Mrs. Ramsay had given. Giving, giving, giving, she had died."

The first words of Mrs. Ramsay ("Yes") and her husband ("But") announce a dialectic that continues throughout the book, and reaches a final resolution in the synthesis of Lily's "vision." The three parts of the book can be seen as the three phases of this dialectic. Part I, entitled "The Window" because its realm is perception, represents the phase of affirmation. So it is the longest part, is dominated by the consciousness of Mrs. Ramsay, and culminates in her "triumph" over her husband. Part II, "Time Passes," represents the phase of negation. It is the shortest part, is dominated by an impersonal consciousness, and culminates beyond night and chaos in a tentative awakening. Part III, "The Lighthouse," is enacted in a realm of consciousness dominated by the archetypal artist, Lily Briscoe, and culminates in the triumph of her vision, which synthesizes the worlds of Parts I and II.

In Part I consciousness expands each moment of time by filling it with significance. In Part II consciousness is imprisoned by time in a relentless questioning of significance (a dominant motif is of "sleepers" going down to the beach to ask ultimate questions of the sea). These are like the two states of consciousness described by Bergson, in which time is experienced either as durational and leading to freedom or as immutable and leading to necessity.[2] In each part the dominant form of consciousness is opposed by the other form. For example, in Part II the immutable forces of time and necessity are enclosed within a larger frame: a choric consciousness at the beginning, Lily's awakening at the end.

2   The most extensive and valuable discussion of Bergsonian principles in the fiction is by James Hafley, *The Glass Roof: Virginia Woolf as Novelist* (New York: Russell & Russell, 1963). For his discussion of freedom and necessity, see pp. 43–44. Virginia Woolf's sister-in-law Karin Stephen wrote a book on Bergson, and Bergson's ideas were much discussed in Bloomsbury. Although Hafley found no direct evidence that Virginia Woolf had read Bergson, it would be surprising if she had not at least tried to read him, and her work, as Hafley shows, is certainly consistent with those ideas.

Each major part of the book is constituted by a number of sections, whose beginnings are indicated by extra spacing and arabic numbers in the first English edition.[3] As in the previous novels, each section of *To the Lighthouse* represents an avenue of exploration for the narrative consciousness. And again each avenue ends in a moment of heightened awareness which marks the discovery of a significant turning point in the exploration. The narrative consciousness may realize that this avenue can lead no further. Or it may become aware of a new direction to explore. In *To the Lighthouse* more than in the earlier novels these avenues lead toward epiphanies—moments of revelation which could be called religious in their thought and feeling. The search itself is more intense now, and more fully mythic in both its method and its implications.

A dialectical process operates in this aspect of structure too. It is especially evident in the endings of the sections in the first half of each part of the book. In "The Window" the first section concludes by showing that Charles Tansley worships Mrs. Ramsay, the second with the discovery that she despises him. The third section ends with the disclosure of her commitment to Lily, the fourth with the discovery that Mr. Ramsay puts Lily off. The fifth section reveals the richness of Mrs. Ramsay's consciousness, the sixth the melodrama and shallowness of her husband's. The seventh section discovers Mrs. Ramsay's

3   In the American edition, sections are indicated by large roman numerals, except for the first section in part III, "The Lighthouse," where the roman I is omitted. The first English edition skips the number 2 in part III, so that the English Section 3 corresponds to the American Section II, and so on.

J. A. Lavin, "The First Editions of Virginia Woolf's *To the Lighthouse*," *Proof*, II (1972), 185–211, discusses variants between the English and American first editions. He says that there is a difference "in the numbering of subsections in Part III, 'The Lighthouse.' The first English edition divides it into fourteen subsections numbered i–xiv, but with section 2 unnumbered and indicated only by white space. The first American edition closed that spacing to run sections 1 and 2 together as one, and renumbered the sections that followed, thus giving only thirteen subsections in Part III." I have examined the first English edition, and found no evidence in the first section of Part III of the "white space" that Lavin mentions. Furthermore, the subsections in the English edition are numbered not in small roman numbers but in arabic, and page 277 in the first English edition is the page on which Section 7 begins. It seems to me, therefore, that there should be thirteen sections in Part III, as shown in both the English and American first editions.

"demon" (her sexual challenging of every male), the eighth her husband's ("bearing down" on everyone). But as the story evolves toward the status of myth, the dialectical patterns become less significant while the mythic patterns become more so. In the first part of the book Mrs. Ramsay's consciousness becomes so dominant that no other view can really challenge it. And so "The Window" ends with her "triumph."

Grimm's fairy tale of the fisherman and his wife provides a brilliant analogue for the Ramsays. Like the fisherman's wife, Mrs. Ramsay is utterly dominant—and in the excitement of the story we don't anticipate her inevitable fall. She seems omniscient throughout Part I. She alone thinks of the sacred responsibility of raising children: she knows that our lives are lived in the perspective of eternity. Despite her husband's agnosticism, which she has been conditioned to accept intellectually, she knows that "We are in the hands of the Lord." Her real concern for others is greater than her husband's. She is aware, more than anyone else, that human experience is transitory: leaving the dining room after her successful dinner, she knows that it is "already the past." Above all, she has the knowledge of "the other thing," her sexual relationship with her husband which is the primal force of their lives. To the narrative consciousness, sex is always "other," a realm of fire and smoke, distant, awesome, beautiful, bearing within it the seeds not only of life but, as Mrs. Ramsay knows, of death. That is the realm of her final triumph, where the narrative itself can't follow her: it can only see her bedroom as a space of haunted emptiness, inhabited now only by random airs, searched dimly by the beam from the lighthouse.

In Part II the dialectic of the endings becomes more abstract. In the first section the poet resists the darkness; in the second, he ushers in the night. The third evokes the essence of darkness and destruction (Mrs. Ramsay's death), the fourth the essence of "loveliness." The fifth and sixth sections contrast the profane and the poetic. In "Time Passes" the narrative discovers that nature mocks the search for meaning. The narrative turns away from the summer home of the Ramsays, the house of memory and of meaning. But that house must not fall into ruin, and Lily, the artist, arrives to bring it back to life.

Part III shows that transformation. The endings of the sections represent the stages in the artist's progress toward achievement of her final vision. At the end of the first section she commits herself to giving, as the mother, Mrs. Ramsay, had done. In the second she realizes the father's humanity. In the third she finds herself divided (between the voyage and the shore) and begins to perceive the distance and the silence. Thus these first three sections show the deepening commitment and the initiation of the artist.

Another drama of growth in Part III runs parallel to that of the artist. Cam and James, the youngest children of Mr. Ramsay, move from resistance toward acceptance of their father. In a sense, Cam and James represent forms of consciousness which become subsumed in Lily's more comprehensive vision; they are the aspects of that vision which are more specifically filial and sexually differentiated—and less mature. The fourth section ends with the daughter imagining the island from which they sailed as an idyllic place where there is no suffering (the narrative consciousness knows better, of course). This contrasts with the fifth section, in which the artist imagines that "all was miracle" (with overtones of Mrs. Ramsay's "We are in the hands of the Lord," which the narrative knows to be true).

The short sixth section, within brackets, tells how "Macalister's boy" cuts a chunk out of a live fish to bait his hook, then throws the fish back into the sea. The symbolic significance of this epiphany isn't overwhelmingly obvious. But placed as it is within Lily's anguished attempt to evoke Mrs. Ramsay, it seems to suggest the sudden wounding of the artist's consciousness which stimulates creativity. In the next section, the seventh (and the central one of Part III), the artist's concern with technique leads to the realization that the voyage has reached the halfway point.

The eighth section ends with the son suspending his hatred of the father, and beginning to recognize mystery. The ninth is a parenthetical section, enacted in the mind of Lily, in which the artist sees that individual human lives become immersed in the larger wholeness of nature. Then the tenth section ends with the daughter suspending her resentment of the father, and beginning to echo his poetry. In this triad, then, the narrative moves toward acceptance of the father, whom it had viewed with awe, scorn, and above all, fear, in Part I, and toward a more comprehensive perspective on its world. This is confirmed and extended by section eleven, in which the artist recognizes her own love for her art, envisions the mother at last, and instinctively goes on to search for the father.

In the last two sections of the book the Ramsay children and Lily complete their voyages. At the end of the twelfth section the children forgive the father, who renews his youth as they all reach the lighthouse. And at the end of the book Lily finishes her painting, and is satisfied.

In its search for meaning, the narrative enters the minds of various characters. The patterns of these entries are similar to those of the earlier novels: the narrative is more comfortable with women than with men, and very uncomfortable with sexuality. This latter problem is evident in the evocations of Mrs. Ramsay's mind when she thinks of sex as "the thing she had with her husband" or some similar euphemism, and in Lily's when she thinks of smoke or flames or some other appropriate images. These two women become the central characters of Parts I and III, respectively, the primary characters through which the narrative consciousness perceives its world. Their centrality is natural and never really in doubt. The struggle of the narrative consciousness with its world is no longer a struggle to discover characters within whom it can find an authentic existence.

And so it is not surprising to find that the narrative maintains some critical distance from Mr. Ramsay, even when it is nominally located within his mind. Here is its first entrance into that mind: "He shivered; he quivered. All his vanity, all his satisfaction in his own splendour, riding fell as a thunderbolt, fierce as a hawk at the head of his men through the valley of death, had been shattered, destroyed. Stormed at by shot and shell, boldly we rode and well, flashed through the valley of death, volleyed and thundered—straight into Lily Briscoe and William Bankes. He quivered; he shivered." The narrative is clearly "privileged" to know what Mr. Ramsay is thinking. The prose, of course, echoes the rhythms and many of the words of "The Charge of the Light Brigade," which Mr. Ramsay has been chanting as he has marched up and down the terrace. This in itself constitutes an implicit criticism of his character. But here and elsewhere (as in his meditation on marching through the alphabet of knowledge all the way to Q) the effect goes beyond characterization into caricature. Not satisfied with implicit criticism, the narrative must distance itself further to comment on his *vanity, all his satisfaction in his own splendour*—not words that he, however embarrassed, would apply to himself. Thus at the same time that the narrative renders the content and even the rhythms of his thoughts, it maintains a satirical distance, criticizing explicitly what it is also showing implicitly. Almost everything that he thinks and does is shown to arise from his self-consciousness and his desire for power over other people. Even in Part III, when he is seventy-one and his wife is no longer living, his innermost feelings are still almost wholly concerned with forcing others to give him "sympathy." It is true that the other characters whom the narrative enters in Part III—Lily, James, and Cam—do come to see him somewhat more sympathetically by the end of the voyage than they had viewed him at the beginning. But the narrative itself can discover nothing further in him, nothing beyond the self-consciousness and selfishness that it has despised from the beginning.

The narrative is much more comfortable in the mind of Mrs. Ramsay. But there too it creates a certain distance in its idealization of her: beautiful, loving, loyal, patient, generous, gracious, helpful, she is the ideal wife and mother. There is also some critical distance in the narrative's impatience with her submissiveness, as it realizes that her continual efforts at peacemaking are draining her energies and must eventually take her life. Yet it also finds in her a very deep, comprehensive, and subtle awareness, an intuitive feeling for what is true and important that makes her husband's academic interests seem crudely shallow and selfish. Within the first few pages, her perspective emerges as the norm against which all others are implicitly judged, and provides a stability, for one long passage after another, in which the world of "The Window" seems secure.

Part I culminates in the "triumph" of Mrs. Ramsay, after a kind of fugue in which her husband's consciousness has been struggling against hers for dominance. He has finished a chapter in Scott with, strangely enough, a feeling of triumph: "He felt that he had been arguing with somebody, and had got the better of him." Thus even his literary tastes are inseparable from his own egotism: if young men don't like Scott, he thinks, they don't like him either. He resists "his desire to complain to his wife that young men did not admire him," as well as his desire to "bother her again": "The whole of life did not consist in going to bed with a woman, he thought, returning to Scott and Balzac, to the English novel and the French novel." In this passage Mr. Ramsay's critical interest in "the novel" is exposed as a sublimation of his sexual desire—something that he never consciously realizes, and that the narrative itself confronts only indirectly. But his literary tastes are revealing. As we have seen, he is carried away by Tennyson's charge. And while he reads Scott, his wife reads Shakespeare's sonnets. The difference in how they read is as dramatic as in what they read. While he uses Scott to indulge his own sentimentality and his own ego, she loses herself in the music of the sonnets. Because her awareness is so much more comprehensive and powerful than her husband's, her "triumph" is inevitable.

In Part II a more "impersonal" narrative stance becomes dominant. But the impersonality, emerging as it does against the background of Part I, expresses a feeling which is not impersonal at all. The account of Mrs. Ramsay's death, for instance, becomes even more powerful because it is understated: how can the center of meaning for almost two hundred pages suddenly just vanish, in a single sentence? To encounter, within brackets, this offhand reference to her death seems too outrageous. It catches us unprepared, it stuns us.[4] A similar

4 In "A Sketch of the Past," written in 1939, Virginia Woolf recalls her mother's death in the early morning of May 5, 1895: "George took us down to say goodbye. My father staggered from the bedroom as we came. I stretched out my arms to stop him, but he brushed past me, crying out something I could not catch, distraught. . . . I remember very clearly how even as I was taken to the bedside I noticed that one nurse was sobbing, and a desire to laugh came over me, and I said to myself as I have often done at moments of crisis since, 'I feel nothing whatever.'" (*Moments of Being*, 91–92.)

This trauma is relived again and again in the novels: in the death scene in *The Voyage Out*, in the epilogue to *Jacob's Room*, in the discovery of Septimus' inability to feel in *Mrs. Dalloway*, in the death of Mrs. Ramsay in *To the Lighthouse*, in the death of Percival and especially the feelings of Rhoda and the reactions to her suicide in *The Waves*, and, perhaps most explicitly, in the scene of the death of Mrs. Rose Pargiter in *The Years*. What seems most traumatic in these accounts are the sudden, wholly unex-

feeling, though less extreme, surrounds the deaths of Prue and Andrew. And the aching emptiness of the house is felt precisely because it has been so full of noisy life in Part I.

In Part II the narrative moves in the realm of archetype: "*the* house," "*the* shawl," "*the* bed itself," and so on. Because "Time Passes" emerges against the background of "The Window," however, these archetypal images have concrete referents in the lives of the Ramsays: the house is their summer home, the shawl is the one which Mrs. Ramsay draped over the skull in the nursery, the bed is the one she shared with her husband. The impersonal narrative reports what happens. Causality and significance are not confronted directly, but implied symbolically.

For example, there is the motif of the shawl. At the end of Section 3 of Part II Mrs. Ramsay's death is announced in brackets; at the end of Section 4 "one fold of the shawl loosened and swung to and fro." No connection between the two events is stated. But we may recall that when Mrs. Ramsay said goodnight to her children in the nursery, "she quickly took her own shawl off and wound it round the skull" and invented a whole new mythology for it to lull Cam to sleep (the skull frightened Cam, but James wanted it left on the wall). Thus this skull in "Time Passes" is already linked subliminally with death and fear and with a mother's sensitivity and sheltering love, so that Mrs. Ramsay's death and the loosening of the shawl naturally coalesce. In the paragraph after Prue's death is announced, "another fold of the shawl loosened" and "the long streamer waved gently, swayed aimlessly" like a banner of the powers of death and chaos. Then in a muted reference to the guns of August, 1914, the narrative says that

---

pected change of perspective, and the horror of the inability to feel. And as "A Sketch of the Past" shows most clearly, the girl is especially shocked by the father's sudden indifference to her. In real life it was Virginia who stretched out her arms, not her father. But, as in the book, the "arms remained empty," and Virginia was left with the memory of Leslie Stephen, one of the most articulate of men, "crying out something I could not catch." (A split between words and feelings runs throughout the *oeuvre*.) And so she approached her mother's deathbed already in a state of shock. Many of the most powerful scenes in her novels attempt to exorcise what she regarded—mistakenly—as her inability to feel.

"there came later in the summer ominous sounds like the measured blows of hammers dulled on felt [and like the ubiquitous sound of the waves], which . . . still further loosened the shawl"; in the next paragraph the death of Andrew is announced. This pattern of deaths and loosenings of the shawl, then, enables the narrative consciousness to explore beyond the realm of conventional language and the restrictions of conventional logic. In these new fields of meaning the narrative transcends the limits of the given and enters into a new creative freedom—even though the world it describes is the world of necessity. Out of the language of necessity the narrative evokes meanings which have no limits because they remain undefined, implied. In that realm, time is not immutable but durational, and consciousness itself no longer bound by the strict rules of conventional language but free to discover what it will. This, of course, is the process of "vision" which Lily is said to experience in Part III.

The artist, then, is like the "sleeper" relentlessly asking the ultimate questions of the sea, the medium of chaos and creation, dissolution and regeneration. The motif of the sleeper first appears in the third section of "Time Passes," when the narrative says that "should any sleeper fancying that he might find on the beach an answer to his doubts, a sharer of his solitude . . . go down by himself to walk on the sand, no image . . . comes readily to hand . . . making the world reflect the compass of the soul. . . . Almost it would appear that it is useless in such confusion to ask the night those questions as to what, and why, and wherefore which tempt the sleeper from his bed to seek an answer." This passage is followed immediately by the announcement, within brackets, of the death of Mrs. Ramsay. The tortuous syntax of the passage reflects the anguish of the quest and the approaching horror which it will discover. Already the quest is envisioned as taking place in the realm of art (painting or writing): "no image . . . comes readily to hand." And from the first the quest is frustrated.

In the next appearance of the motif, in the fifth section, the sleeper has become the "mystic, the visonary," and the "answer" which is sought is linked, by the sequence itself, to the figure of Mrs.

McNab, the cleaning woman, whose efforts, inadequate as they are, still resist the deline of the house into chaos. Imperfect as she is, she is still a force for order.

In the sixth section the quester becomes "the wakeful, the hopeful." After the death of Andrew in France is reported, those who walk by the sea are confronted with phenomena that are "difficult blandly to overlook": mysterious apparitions of "an ashen-coloured ship" and of "a purplish stain" on the sea itself—a warship and an oil slick from a U-boat, perhaps. The "dream" of finding an answer may be merely a "reflection in a mirror." These reflections are too hard to face, and the quest itself must be suspended: "to pace the beach was impossible; contemplation was unendurable; the mirror was broken. [Mr. Carmichael brought out a volume of poems that spring, which had an unexpected success. The war, people said, had revived their interest in poetry.]" Only the poet can look upon the face of chaos.

And so for the next three sections of "Time Passes" the quest for ultimate answers is suspended. But in the final section the cycle begins anew, with "sleepers (the house was full again)" "entreated" by "the voice of the beauty of the world" once again. This "voice" asks softly "why not accept this, be content with this, acquiesce and resign?" But that would be impossible, of course. The quest must be eternal.

Grimm's fairy tale which Mrs. Ramsay reads to James also reflects the motif of the quest on the seashore. There too the questers are insatiable: each time the husband returns with some new "boon" from the Great Flounder, the wife soon becomes dissatisfied with it and sends him back for more, until they must end where they began. Their story symbolizes the endless cycle of the human quest for the ultimate.

The "omniscient" point of view, the stance of the narrative that knows everything, seems important as the book begins, but can't be sustained. It disappears after the assertion, with perhaps one fourth of Part I remaining, that "'each [person] thought, 'The others are feeling this.'. . . Whereas, I feel nothing at all." Its disappearance reflects the increasing skepticism of the narrative consciousness about its own "knowledge" (in the scientific or "realistic" sense) and a growing commitment to Mrs. Ramsay's intuitive view of reality. This leads to the "impersonal" technique in which the narrative is no longer held to such strict rules of truth, but moves instead into a realm of poetic truth which affords more scope, freedom, and flexibility. "Time Passes" sustains a poetic power that Parts I and III achieve less consistently.

Lily's consciousness is the unifying and stabilizing force for Part III, "The Lighthouse," that Mrs. Ramsay's had been for "The Window." The narrative implies that Lily's consciousness has subsumed all the others in the book, that she has reached an epiphany which allows her to paint the final decisive stroke on her canvas—one which unites Mr. and Mrs. Ramsay, the ideal and the real lighthouse, the sea and the shore, life and death. She has recaptured the world of Mrs. Ramsay's consciousness and made it eternal in her painting—or so the narrative would like to believe. Just as it is appropriate that the only entry into the consciousness of Mr. Carmichael takes place in "Time Passes," it is also fitting that "Time Passes" should culminate in Lily's awareness: this foreshadows the ending of the book as a whole. Similarly, it is fitting that her point of view should be the only one which is evoked in every one of the three parts—another sign of her identification with the final, transcendent consciousness.

The narrative's search for meaning moves from a world perceived through a child's perspective to a world viewed—and created—by an artist. The child's world turns on the axis of the mother, but its stability and very existence are threatened by the intrusions of the father. The artist's world, however, has room for both father and mother.

The search is very visual, and the flow of images in *To the Lighthouse* further develops the already cinematic styles of the *oeuvre*. The visual dynamics of the scenes are always important, especially the angles, focus, and distance of the "camera," the narrative perspective. These characteristics express the intentionality of the narrative consciousness. For example, the relationship of Mr. and Mrs. Ramsay throughout Part I is very cinematic. As the book begins, Mrs. Ramsay is seated in a chair near the drawing-room window, with James sitting on the floor; these positions express the natural dominance of mother over son. Then Mr. Ramsay suddenly appears in the window, darkening the scene, asserting dominance over the mother, eclipsing the son. By the end of Part I the positions of dominance have been reversed: Mr. Ramsay sits in the drawing room; his wife rises from her chair and moves to the window for her moment of "triumph."

A more obvious example is the dynamics of Lily's relationship with Mr. Ramsay in Part III. Their discussion of his boots reveals his dominance. But the increasing distance from Mr. Ramsay changes Lily's feeling for him and enables her to bring him within her painting. Her final perspective on the Ramsays is a slight "down angle" with great distance and a rather soft focus, all of which give the scene a feeling of finality. And the painting itself could be compared to the "freeze frame" in cinema, in which some essential moment is abstracted from the flow of time, transcends its immediate context, and becomes an emblem of the work as a whole. In it she captures the essence of both of the parents. They are no longer overshadowing figures (Lily used to sit at Mrs. Ramsay's feet, and could speak to Mr. Ramsay only of his boots), but now "on a level with ordinary experience."

Another important aspect of the dynamic form of *To the Lighthouse* is the transitions from one part of the linguistic structure to the next. These transitions exist at all levels, of course, from the spaces between words to those between the three major parts of the book. At this macrostructural level there are two transitions: from Mrs. Ramsay's "triumph" over her husband to Mr. Bankes's cautious comment that "we must wait for the future to show," and from Lily's tentative awakening in that future to the questioning of its significance: "What does it all mean then, what can it all mean?"

Part II undercuts Mrs. Ramsay's triumph at the end of Part I, or at least radically modifies its meaning: "Time Passes" contains the future which Mr. Bankes says we must wait for—the events, within brackets, which strike at the very foundations of the Ramsays' world. After "Time Passes" the world of "The Window" is irrevocably the past. The narrative can't return again to what no longer exists, except through "flashbacks." And that, of course, is just what Lily does in Part III—and before she makes any progress with her painting. From her memory she evokes Mrs. Ramsay on the beach (like a sleeper gone down to ask questions of the sea in Part II, or a transformation of the fairy tale in Part I). The sea's answers are never satisfying.

The second transition moves in a more positive direction, from the awakening of Lily at the end of "Time Passes" to the searching questions with which she opens "The Lighthouse." The fact that the narrative remains in her consciousness gives this transition a continuity which the earlier one had lacked, and establishes the possibility, at least, of a creation more enduring than Mrs. Ramsay's. Lily's questioning here may seem somewhat rhetorical, but it later takes more concrete form in her painting. In that medium she interrogates nature (again like the fisherman and his wife and the sleepers who go down to the beach), trying one approach after another, asking the most fundamental—naïve, some might call them—questions, and weighing the exchange (not just the "answers" but the questions too) against her own intuitive sense of truth. It is, of course, the archetype of the process of artistic creation, and in the third part of the book it will bring the thesis and antithesis of Parts I and II into synthesis.

At the next level of structure, the transitions between sections are of two general types: they tend either to extend and confirm the meanings of the previous ending, or to deny and qualify them. These types correspond to the "Yes/But" dialectic. Both types provide continuity, however, by linking the sections thematically. Later in the book, discontinuities begin to appear in the transitions. (These two kinds of transitions, using continuity and discontinuity, are analogous to "matched" and "hard" cuts in cinematic editing.) As the book continues, the negative ("But") transitions become more frequent, and in Part III are dominant. But there is also a growing network of association on the symbolic level which works for coherence despite discontinuities and radical changes in perspective. This subliminal coherence reflects the narrative's movement toward transcendence.

To the Lighthouse begins with a promise; it ends with a vision. The promised voyage is delayed, first by the weather, then by the death of Mrs. Ramsay and by the war, until James himself seems to have forgotten why they are sailing to the lighthouse. He no longer wants to go, but regards the voyage as just another of his father's selfish demands. Yet, as Mrs. Ramsay knew, "children never forget." Unconsciously James knows more than he can admit, and he becomes committed to the voyage in spite of himself, steering the boat straight for the lighthouse, earning his father's "Well done!" For James and Cam, this is a voyage toward maturity, toward an acceptance of their father as he is rather than as they wish he would be. As they reach the lighthouse, "they both wanted to say, Ask us anything and we will give it you. But he did not ask them anything." Through his mission to the lighthouse, Mr. Ramsay has transcended his selfish need for sympathy, and in the narrative's final view of him both Cam and James "rose to follow him as he sprang, lightly like a young man, holding his parcel, on to the rock." The voyage fulfills Mrs. Ramsay's promise to James. In making the voyage, her husband fulfills his promise to her and renews his own youth and his commitment to his family. The image of his landing at the lighthouse echoes an earlier "old-fashioned scene" which has become emblematic: he had been boating with the woman he loved and had asked her to marry him; she had said yes as he helped her to step ashore. His final landing at the lighthouse seals his fidelity to that moment and to that woman.

Somehow Lily's vision includes even that sacred moment. Its last appearance in the book is not in Mr. Ramsay's consciousness, but in Lily's when, in Section 2 of Part III, she brings the prewar world of the Ramsays back to life in her imagination, and hears Mr. Ramsay speak his wife's name.[5] Mrs. Ramsay had made a promise to Lily too: to pose for her painting. And this promise is also fulfilled ten years later, when Lily finally succeeds in getting everything into the right perspective: Mrs. Ramsay's shadow, Mr. Ramsay, the lighthouse itself.

The symbolic meanings of the lighthouse grow and change along with their contexts. We first see it in the panoramic view of the bay which Mrs. Ramsay shows to Charles Tansley. There the lighthouse is "hoary . . . distant, austere," and counterbalanced by the sand dunes and grass which lead into "some moon country, uninhabited of men." It is that latter aspect, she says, that her husband loves.

Her own association with the lighthouse is different. Neither dis-

---

5   Late in Part III Lily is thinking of the relationship to Mr. and Mrs. Ramsay: "he would say her name, once only, for all the world like a wolf barking in the snow, but still she held back; and he would say it once more, and this time something in the tone would rouse her, and she would go to him. . . ."

tant nor austere, hers is the dynamic, rescuing lighthouse. Its light first appears in the novel just as she finishes reading the story of "The Fisherman and His Wife" to James:

"And that's the end," she said, and she saw in his eyes, as the interest of the story died away in them, something else take its place; something wondering, pale, like the reflection of a light, which at once made him gaze and marvel. Turning, she looked across the bay, and there, sure enough, coming regularly across the waves first two quick strokes and then one long steady stroke, was the light of the Lighthouse. It had been lit.

The "end" which Mrs. Ramsay reaches in the fairy tale describes the fall of the fisherman's wife from her position of godlike power into the realm of ordinary mortality. In that sense it prophesies the fate of Mrs. Ramsay too, as James will later see it. The fisherman and his wife in their fallen state "are living still at this very time," immortal, as the parents will be in James's feelings. And just as the fairy tale opens his capacity for wonder, so every work of creative imagination can lead the human consciousness to "gaze and marvel"—even Lily's painting, or *To the Lighthouse* itself. Thus the lighting of the light transforms the first lighthouse, distant and austere, into a warm, living reflection of the mother's caring for her son. It comes, "sure enough," "across the waves" which will crash so ominously on the shore, heralds of the return to chaos. The third stroke of the light, Mrs. Ramsay feels, "was her stroke"—and indeed it is: she is the stabilizing, synthesizing power of her world.

As the boat approaches the lighthouse, James remembers it as "a silvery, misty-looking tower with a yellow eye, that opened suddenly, and softly in the evening"—the lighthouse that he associates with his mother. But now its aspect is quite different—"stark and straight" like his father, whose stern view of life ("our frail barks founder in darkness") seems to deny the saving power of the lighthouse. And James realizes that "nothing was simply one thing. The other lighthouse was true too." This realization marks a major step toward his acceptance of his heritage.[6] He has always associated his father with images of

6 Quentin Bell (I, 32) quotes Virginia's "Hyde Park Gate News" for September 12, 1892: "On Saturday morning Master Hilary Hunt and Master Basil Smith came up to Talland House and asked Master Thoby and Miss Virginia Stephen to accompany them

sterility and destruction (a "sharp and arid scimitar," "the fatal sterility of the male") and his mother with images of fertility and nourishment (flowering trees, "this delicious fecundity, this fountain and spray of life"). Now he—and the narrative—can bring the two together in a healing and satisfying synthesis. The lighthouse itself becomes something more than a symbol: a center of attraction for the imagination, in which symbolic meanings can converge and grow.

As Geoffrey Hartman has pointed out, the book is about darkness as well as light.[7] Indeed, the light itself is given definition and meaning only by the darkness which surrounds it. That darkness becomes dominant, as Hartman has shown, in "Time Passes." Here and elsewhere in the fiction of Virginia Woolf, as in Joyce and Lawrence and Faulkner, darkness represents chaos, creation, sensuality, mystery—a realm more fascinating than the light ("darkness shining in the brightness," Joyce calls it in *Ulysses*), which the poetic novel seems especially suited to explore.

Mr. Ramsay, dominant—nominally, at least—in the daytime, experiences the darkness as threatening: in it "he heard people saying— he was a failure—that R was beyond him." His is the daytime world of single-minded intellect, order, distance, austerity, political power, academic reputation. His lighthouse is the stark tower on the barren rock. Mrs. Ramsay, however, thinks of herself as a "core of darkness" as well as the third stroke of the light from the lighthouse. (And beyond Mr. Ramsay's R, the lighthouse signals U[••—].) Lily, the artist, perceives that darkness in Mrs. Ramsay, and in life. Her work explores

---

to the light-house as Freeman the boatman said that there was a perfect tide and wind for going there. Master Adrian Stephen was much disappointed at not being allowed to go." While Adrian, like the six-year-old James in *To the Lighthouse*, was disappointed, it would seem that Thoby and Virginia, like the sixteen-year-old James and his sister Cam, made the voyage. This seems confirmed by "A Sketch of the Past" (p. 115): Perhaps every ten days we would go sailing. Thoby would be allowed to steer. He had to keep the sail filled with wind, and father said, 'Show them you can bring her in, my boy,' and setting his face, flushing with the effort, he sat there, bringing us round the point."

7 Geoffrey Hartmann, "Virginia's Web," *Chicago Review*, XIV (Spring, 1961), 2–32. Reprinted in *Twentieth Century Interpretations of "To the Lighthouse,"* ed. Thomas A. Vogler (Englewood Cliffs, N.J.: Prentice-Hall, 1970), 70–81.

and expresses both the darkness and the light. Both are required for "vision."

Lily seems to know that the most important meanings must be discovered indirectly—that they must be allowed to reveal themselves as they are, rather than be forced to conform to some predetermined pattern, some expectation. The artist, she knows, "got nothing by soliciting urgently." Instead, the artist must be able to confront "a centre of complete emptiness" like the void left by Mrs. Ramsay's death, in the belief that "the space would fill." In her first attempt to paint the world of the Ramsays, "it had flashed upon her that she would move the tree to the middle, and need never marry anybody." Various images in Part I link Mrs. Ramsay with trees, and this tree in the middle may be an emblem for Mrs. Ramsay's place in her world. But when Lily finishes the painting ten years later, its center is no longer the tree, but the lighthouse.

This change has extensive implications. As far as the world of the Ramsays is concerned, it creates a much larger field of meaning. As far as Lily herself is concerned, it reveals that she has moved closer to Mrs. Ramsay—though not to the "unity" which Lily had desired. The rhythms of her painting are described in terms which apply to the lighthouse as well: "as if the pauses were one part of the rhythm and the strokes another, and all were related." And when she loses herself in this creativity, the narrative says, "her mind" is "like a fountain"— another symbolic link with Mrs. Ramsay. Both women share a solemn view of marriage, revealed in Mrs. Ramsay's recognition of the irony of celebrating the engagement of Paul and Minta, which contains the "seeds of death" (which reach fruition for Mrs. Ramsay and her daughter in Part II), and in Lily's resistance to Mrs. Ramsay's match-making. Even the thoughts of Lily which open Part III echo Mrs. Ramsay's bewilderment at the strange interests of the masculine intelligence: "What did it all mean?" In these and other ways Lily is revealed as the heir to Mrs. Ramsay's consciousness.

The book begins in the consciousness of six-year-old James, to whom the voyage to the lighthouse is a "wonder, to which he had looked forward for years and years, it seemed." When he finally does make the voyage, ten years later, his sense of wonder has been suppressed. But Lily's has not. The book ends in her consciousness, as she sees clearly, through her tears, with "a sudden intensity" the central and final line of her painting. More than anyone else since the death of Mrs. Ramsay, Lily remains open to the meanings of the world. Her consciousness is the norm for "The Lighthouse" as Mrs. Ramsay's had been for "The Window." The climactic voyage of the Ramsays is counterpointed with Lily's toward her vision, which at last subsumes everything else.

The Ramsays' voyage ends with the father springing "lightly, like a young man, holding his parcel, on to the rock." And the artist is somehow aware of that, as the final section of the book discloses:

"He must have reached it," said Lily Briscoe aloud, feeling suddenly completely tired out. For the Lighthouse had become almost invisible, had melted away into a blue haze, and the effort of looking at it and the effort of thinking of him landing there, which both seemed to be one and the same effort, had stretched her body and mind to the utmost. Ah, but she was relieved. Whatever she had wanted to give him, when he left her that morning, she had given him at last.

"He has landed," she said aloud. "It is finished." Then, surging up, puffing slightly, old Mr. Carmichael stood beside her, looking like an old pagan God, shaggy, with weeds in his hair and the trident (it was only a French novel) in his hand. He stood by her on the edge of the lawn, swaying a little in his bulk, and said, shading his eyes with his hand: "They will have landed," and she felt that she had been right. They had not needed to speak. They had been thinking the same things and he had answered her without her asking him anything. He stood there spreading his hands over all the weakness and suffering of mankind; she thought he was surveying, tolerantly, compassionately, their final destiny. Now he has crowned the occasion, she thought, when his hand slowly fell, as if she had seen him let fall from his great height a wreath of violets and asphodels which, fluttering slowly, lay at length upon the earth.

Quickly, as if she were recalled by something over there, she turned to her canvas. There it was—her picture. Yes, with all its greens and blues, its lines running up and across, its attempt at something. It would be hung in the attics, she thought; it would be destroyed. But what did that matter? she asked herself, taking up her brush again. She looked at the steps; they were empty; she looked at her canvas; it was blurred. With a sudden intensity, as if she saw it clear for a second, she drew a line there, in the centre. It was done; it was finished. Yes, she thought, laying down her brush in extreme fatigue, I have had my vision.

Thus the Ramsays' voyage is subsumed within the more inclusive voyage of the artist. Her role in the realm of art is analogous to that of Mrs. Ramsay in the realm of "life itself": giving, giving, giving to the point of exhaustion. Her commitment is total. What is the gift she has given to Mr. Ramsay? She has given him the sympathy he asked for, though not in so direct a way as he had wished. Hers has been the more impersonal but no less valuable sympathy of the artist: the effort to see and express the essential meaning of his life. And in her painting she has helped to guard that meaning against the ravages of time, just as *To the Lighthouse* itself confers an immortality upon the Ramsays.

Mr. Carmichael's final gesture confirms Lily's vision. The old poet presides over several important moments in the novel: when Mrs. Ramsay suddenly realizes that she can't tell her husband the truth, when Mr. Ramsay and he chant "Luriana Lurilee" after her dinner and "he bowed to her as if he did her homage," when he falls asleep at the beginning and the end of Part II to begin and end the flow of immutable time, and now, when he shares a silent communion with Lily during her painting and rises to say "They will have landed" and to extend his blessing over all. The trident here identifies him as the god of the sea, a role in which he presides, symbolically, over the voyage to the lighthouse and over such tales as "The Fisherman and His Wife" and *To the Lighthouse*.

His blessing enables Lily to finish her painting. The canvas calls to her, as the authentic work of art always calls to the artist, and she realizes that "There it was—her picture." She *sees* it now in its wholeness and its completion, rather like Peter Walsh had seen Clarissa at the end of *Mrs. Dalloway*: "For there she was." And the painting is "her picture" not only because she has painted it but also in the sense that it expresses the essence of Lily herself: it is a portrait of the artist. "Yes" had been Mrs. Ramsay's word, the first word of the book. Now it is Lily's too, expressing her affirmation of both art and life. She realizes that the voyage itself is what matters, and that realization enables her to finish her picture. The steps are empty, but Lily has "looked" at them. She can accept the absence of Mrs. Ramsay because she has captured her essence, her "core of darkness," in the triangular shadow in the painting: she has made the absence of Mrs. Ramsay meaningful. She has "looked" at the canvas too. It is "blurred" because Lily sees it through her own tears. But her emotional involvement gives her vision a "sudden intensity," and guides her to the "centre" for the final stroke of her brush. Like the final stroke of the lighthouse which Mrs. Ramsay had felt was her own, this too is a stroke of illumination.

In the mythic world of *To the Lighthouse* all actions are seen as archetypal. They lead toward the final archetype of the artist as visionary which becomes a center of meaning for the *oeuvre*. And the archetype of the voyage, which has been at the center of the lifework from the beginning, finds its fullest expression so far. Constantly present in one form or another throughout the book, the promise of the voyage to the lighthouse becomes the mythic meaning of life itself. The human consciousness looks always toward the lighthouse, longing for security, for illumination, for transcendence of its own limitations. The lighthouse itself has many different meanings: it is endowed with meaning by the consciousness which looks toward it, which is intent upon it. The title of the book expresses this central reality, the essence of the intentionality of consciousness.

More intently than anyone else, the artist looks to the lighthouse. Although Lily herself doesn't make the voyage out into marriage, she somehow discovers and expresses the mythic meaning of that voyage. It doesn't matter that her painting will be shut up in someone's attic. What matters is her experience in creating it—which is her own voyage to the lighthouse. In creating the painting, in discovering the authentic expression of her own deepest feelings, she has entered the realm of poetry, where Augustus Carmichael, poet and god of the sea, welcomes her at last.

At the heart of the poetic vision is the mystery of sexual love. It evokes the most awesome and terrible images in the book, this love that both redeems and kills: the stark tower on the barren rock, the arid scimitar that slashes the lush foliage of the mother's lovely garden by the sea. Time can destroy everything but this. For beyond the dialectical opposition of the mother ("Yes") and the father ("But") there is this realm of synthesis, where "nothing was simply one thing" and the limitations—and comforts—of separate existence are transcended, and the human spirit is born again. That is the realm which Mr. Carmichael's poems have explored—and so it is that he knows that the voyage has been made at last and that "they will have landed."

In *To the Lighthouse* the narrative consciousness seems more fatalistic than in the earlier novels. There is never any real possibility that Andrew Ramsay, for example, would not be killed: his death in the Great War is one of the "given" facts of this world. Jacob Flanders had died in that same war, of course, and in retrospect his death can be seen as predestined, yet there always seemed to be a chance that he might become aware of the ominous undertones of his culture and might see beyond the smug world view which he was taught at Cambridge. The narrative consciousness in *Jacob's Room* had been aware of alternatives, and had watched with growing helplessness as they turned out to be impossible. But in *To the Lighthouse* there are no real alternatives: what will be will be. The only alternatives are in how to view it.

Thus the elegiac tone. From the very beginning, the world of "The Window" is an evocation of what the narrative knows is already the past. "Time Passes" transforms that world by viewing it through the perspective of eternity. The new present that emerges in "The Lighthouse" is the more stylized present of art, which subsumes the past and makes it timeless through the perspective of myth. And that perspective too becomes past when it reaches completion: "I have had my vision."

The struggle in *To the Lighthouse* is no longer the struggle of the narrative to become incarnate in a more authentic character or setting, but an effort to come to terms with what is already the past. The narrative can't change that. It can only try, like the poet of *Paradise Lost*, to try to justify God's ways to man. It can't choose the story—only how to tell it. And so it searches, in Part I, for the essence of the world of childhood, for the principles which have governed these primal scenes. The promised voyage becomes the metaphor for that search.

Parts I and III begin with the idea of the voyage, and end with it. "Yes," says Mrs. Ramsay as the book begins, if the weather is fine. . . . "But," says her husband, it won't be fine. This conflict reaches its resolution at the end of Part I with Mrs. Ramsay "thinking to herself, Nothing on earth can equal this happiness," and saying to her husband, "Yes, you were right" about the weather. Thus, says the narrative, "she had triumphed again." This "triumph" comes from her control of the situation and from her success, once again, in avoiding what he wants most of all: telling him that she loves him. The narrative itself also triumphs by imagining her transcendent happiness. Through its brilliant evocations of Mrs. Ramsay's thoughts throughout Part I the narrative creates a space in which such happiness could exist. And the "triumph" also shows that the arrogant male intellect of Mr. Ramsay is not finally dominant, but overwhelmed by Mrs. Ramsay's larger consciousness.

Part III begins with Lily asking herself the ultimate question, "What does it mean, then, what can it all mean?" as Mr. Ramsay, Cam, and James are about to make their long-awaited voyage to the lighthouse. It ends with her completion of the painting which has somehow captured the meaning of the Ramsays and their voyage. Just as the depth and subtlety of the world of Part I had been subsumed within Mrs. Ramsay's awareness, so the essence of that world, reclaimed from the ravages of time, is expressed in the work of art (even though that work may be "skimpy" in comparison with its subject). By recognizing and expressing the essence both of the Ramsays' world and of the yearning to know that world, the artist discovers the center of all illumination—and of the surrounding darkness as well.

The voyage fulfills the promise of Mrs. Ramsay to her children. It also fulfills her promise to Lily, to pose for her painting. She had other plans for Lily too: at the dinner she thinks that Lily and William Bankes are not close enough, but "That could be remedied tomorrow. If it were fine, they should go for a picnic." But as we know, it turned out not to be fine, and presumably the picnic, like the voyage, was postponed. Lily and William remain good friends, and go their own ways. Lily's insight is, in some ways, greater than Mrs. Ramsay's. Lily sees her as a shadow and paints her as one (and we know from Part I that Mrs. Ramsay had been very conscious of shadows and of herself as a shadow). In a sense Lily herself becomes the shadow of Mrs. Ramsay, approaching in art what Mrs. Ramsay had done in life. But the artist doesn't really belong in the family: she is not a daughter, only a guest.

To the Lighthouse is about hope and promises and, especially, love. And as Lily discovers, "Love had a thousand shapes." It is not only the love of man for woman, which the narrative sees as awesome and terrible. It is also the love of parents for children, and of children for their parents, love which also may find expression in puzzling, even outrageous, ways. It is the quiet love of friends, with its shelter of respect and privacy. And it is the love of the artist for art, which allows both intimacy and distance, detachment and desire.

The forms of love are also the forms of conflict—between mother and father, man and woman, parents and children, friends, the artist and the work of art. These tensions reach moments of unexpected horror, as when Mr. Ramsay says, suddenly, to the woman he loves, "Damn you!" Then the promised voyage to the lighthouse suddenly becomes even more necessary: Mr. Ramsay's unspoken guilt will last for more than a decade.

The problem, then, is somehow to come to terms with who and what one inescapably is, not really in the hope of changing it but in the hope of understanding it. The struggle is to comprehend, to express what is, to paint its picture, tell its story. When that story has been told, a kind of immortality is achieved, so that we can say of Mr. and Mrs. Ramsay what the brothers Grimm say of the fisherman and his wife: "there they are living still at this very time," fallen into ordinary mortality, as they must in order for ordinary mortals to recognize them. So their very mortality gives rise to their immortality. When the narrative discovers their authentic place in time, it also endows them with universality—and timelessness.

The light which plays over the empty house in "Time Passes" is the light of consciousness. In a more poetic sense it is the beam from the lighthouse, a faint ray of hope that some glimmer might somehow relieve the darkness and emptiness of this space, this lost home in the lost summer of childhood. When chaos threatens to overwhelm her dinner, Mrs. Ramsay commands her children to "Light the candles." And they do. At her side, the poet becomes "monumental" in the failing light. In that same realm of twilight, as the story of the fisherman and his wife ends, the failing light of day gives way to the first reflection, in the eyes of a child, of the light of love. Toward that light, to the lighthouse, the human spirit must always turn. In that light the most ordinary actions become monumental, archetypal, reflections of a love and a longing which are so deep, so mysterious, that they can never be directly stated, only surrounded, and suggested, by poetry.

CHAPTER VI

ORLANDO

The first major commentator on the fiction of Virginia Woolf closes a rather perfunctory discussion of *Orlando* with the comment that taking the book seriously "is rather like breaking a butterfly on a wheel."[1] Since the author herself didn't take it seriously, so this argument goes, we too should regard it only as a light-hearted holiday between *To the Lighthouse* and *The Waves*. Other generic grounds can be found for avoiding *Orlando*: it is a biography, a fantasy, a private love letter, a parody, a satire—something other than an authentic, "serious" work of art. This kind of objection has been answered by Jean Guiguet: "one must not confound spontaneity with externality. . . . it is a refusal to go deep, which is not the same thing as a rejection of depth. *Orlando* . . . was not the fruit of a deliberate purpose or an idea, but an inevitable gesture, an urgent need of the whole being," and, like the other novels, "it seeks, with apparent casualness but in all sincerity, to grasp the essence of a fluid and complex reality."[2] *Orlando* is a joke. But like all the best jokes, it is also very serious indeed—and very revealing.

1 Bernard Blackstone, *Virginia Woolf: A Commentary* (Harvest ed.; New York: Harcourt, 1972), 138.
2 Jean Guiguet, *Virginia Woolf and Her Works*, trans. Jean Stewart (New York: Harcourt, 1976), 261–62.

The posture of the narrative consciousness in *Orlando* is different from its involvement in the other books. The joking tone and what Guiguet calls the "refusal to go deep" are the major differences. In *Orlando* the narrative consciousness remains aloof from the characters of its story. The mind of Orlando is the only one it enters—primarily to satirize rather than sympathize. It searches not for an authentic incarnation of itself among the characters it imagines, but for ways to comprehend the authenticity of a single character recognized as mythic from the very beginning. It seeks to bring that overwhelming reality within the scope of its own understanding—and its satire—and thus to disarm and control it. In that sense *Orlando* is truly the biography of Victoria Sackville-West by Virginia Woolf.

Because of this difference in the intentionality of the narrative consciousness, the approach to *Orlando* here must be different from the approaches to the other books. Again the object is to show *how* the narrative is conscious. The drama of consciousness, however, is enacted not among characters or places, but in history and literature. The narrative consciousness, by telling the story of the mythic Orlando, evolves into a universal mythic mind in which such a drama can take place. On this level *Orlando* becomes a novel about the development of the English spirit enhanced by the Italian Renaissance. The analysis of intentionality here, then, tries to suggest some of the ways in which this happens—or, at least, is alleged to happen.

Although the narrative does not search for incarnation among the characters, its range in other directions can be impressive. The dimensions of the search include, as Guiguet recognized, both the most intimately personal—for which Vita and Virginia are the only fully qualified readers—and the mythic. Nigel Nicolson has called *Orlando* "the longest and most charming love letter in literature,"[3] and

3 Nigel Nicolson, *Portrait of a Marriage* (New York: Atheneum, 1973), 202. This is the best single source of information about Vita's life up to 1930. In that year her husband Harold, who had left the diplomatic service, began to keep his regular diary (later edited by his son Nigel), and the Nicolsons bought Sissinghurst Castle, near Cranbrook in Kent, and began its restoration and their garden there, which eventually became—and is today—one of the most beautiful gardens in the world. The facts of Vita's life which I cite come primarily from *Portrait of a Marriage*.

his own *Portrait of a Marriage* reveals more about the complex and fascinating prototype for Orlando than any other source. To read Nicolson's book along with *Orlando* offers a much fuller perspective on Virginia Woolf's achievement: she transforms the merely personal into the mythic, the historical into the eternal. She transforms what Vita herself had felt to be the tragic limitations of a painful personal situation into the larger dimensions of universal human comedy.

Beyond the intimate personal relationship of Vita and Virginia, various "sources" for the book can be identified. Virginia Woolf's diary says that *Orlando* "is based on Vita, Violet Trefusis, Lord Lascelles, Knole, etc."[4] Vita, of course, is Orlando. Violet appears as Sasha, the Russian princess with whom Orlando falls madly in love; in real life, as "Lushka," she played a role scarcely less bizarre. Less has been published about Lord Lascelles and his courtship of Vita, but Nigel Nicolson writes enough about this "Harry" to enable us to identify the prototype for the Archduchess Harriet / Archduke Harry whose pursuit of Orlando is equally relentless. Knole, granted by Queen Elizabeth to her cousin Thomas Sackville in 1566, was, at the time *Orlando* was written, "the largest house in England still in private hands."[5] Unfortunately, these could not be the hands of Vita, and with the death of her father in 1928 Knole went to his brother, who gave it to the National Trust in 1946. Thus *Orlando*, as Nigel Nicolson has pointed out, was a priceless gift to Vita: "the novel identified her with Knole for ever. Virginia by her genius had provided Vita with a unique consolation for having been born a girl, for her exclusion from her inheritance, for her father's death earlier that year. The book, for her, was not simply a brilliant masque or pageant. It was a memorial mass."[6]

    In addition to several personal tours of Knole conducted by Vita, the major source for Virginia Woolf's knowledge of the house was a

4 Anne Olivier Bell (ed.), *The Diary of Virginia Woolf* (New York: Harcourt, 1977), October 22, 1927.
5 Nicolson, *Portrait*, 52.
6 *Ibid.*, 208.

lovely book by Vita, *Knole and the Sackvilles* (1922).[7] And, just as Knole itself embodies English history, so *Orlando* becomes the story of English literature, not from the "objective" perspective of literary history, but from the viewpoint of immediate, passionate human involvement. Except in the view of the archetypal critic—later professor—Nick Greene, literature in *Orlando* is never an abstraction. Instead, it is much more ridiculous, messy, and real: Marlowe's drunken brawling, Pope's nastiness and deformity, Shakespeare himself caught in the act of writing. *Orlando* takes great delight in its raids on the various "periods" of English literature.

For the overall conception of the book and its central figure, literary models are not so immediately apparent. The author herself provides a list in her playful Preface: "no one can read or write without being perpetually in the debt of Defoe, Sir Thomas Browne, Sterne, Sir Walter Scott, Lord Macauley, Emily Bronte, De Quincey, and Walter Pater—to name the first that come to mind." James Naremore has suggested that "her immediate inspiration was apparently Harold Nicolson's series of character sketches, *Some People*,"[8] and it is true that her essay "The New Biography," essentially a review of *Some People*, illuminates the method of *Orlando* as well. Some critics have also seen a possible source in *As You Like It*. Joanne Trautmann, whose familiarity with the background of *Orlando* is impressive, accepts "Floris Delattre's theory . . . that Woolf's Orlando is an amalgamation of Shakespeare's Orlando and Rosalind."[9] A more suggestive parallel, however, is alluded to in Guiguet's commentary on some of the "superficial elements" which connect *Orlando* with history: "Sir John Harington, for instance, whom Lytton Strachey sketches in a few pages; a great favorite with the ladies, who welcomed Queen Elizabeth for a day in that vast Somerset manor to which periodically,

7 For the basic relationship between the two books, see Frank Baldanza, "Orlando and the Sackvilles," *PMLA*, LXX (1955), 274–79, and James Naremore, *The World Without a Self: Virginia Woolf and the Novel* (New Haven: Yale University Press, 1973), 202–208.

8 Naremore, *World Without a Self*, 197.

9 Joanne Trautmann, *The Jessamy Brides: The Friendship of Virginia Woolf and V. Sackville-West* (University Park: Pennsylvania State University Press, 1973), 41.

when out of the royal favour, he would retire to seek consolation with his dog and to translate Ariosto's *Orlando Furioso*."[10]

Legend has it that when Harington circulated a translation of the bawdy story of Jocundo, from the 28th canto of *Orlando Furioso*, among the ladies of the court, Queen Elizabeth banished him—until he could return with a translation of the whole poem. This was no small task; Ariosto's final version of 1532 amounted to 38,736 lines. But Harington was undaunted, as his opening stanzas announce:

1

This begin- ning is taken by imitation from Virgil, the I of his Aeneads. Arma vi- rumque cano	Of Dames, of Knights, of armes, of loves delight, Of curtesies, of high attempts I speake, Then when the Moores transported all their might On Affrick seas the force of France to breake, Incited by the youthfull heate and spite Of *Agramant* their king that vowd to wreake The death of king *Trayano* (lately slayne) Upon the Romane Emperour *Charlemaine*.

2

Meaning hereby his mistresse whom he speakes to likewise in the 35 booke, I staffe	I will no lesse *Orlando's* acts declare (A tale in prose ne verse yet song or sayd) Who fell bestraught with love, a hap most rare To one that erst was counted wise and stayd. If my sweet Saint that causeth my like care My slender muse afford some gracious ayd, I make no doubt but I shall have the skill As much as I have promist to fulfill.[11]

10 Guiguet, *Virginia Woolf*, 278.
11 Ludovico Ariosto, *"Orlando Furioso" in English Heroical Verse*, trans. John Haring-ton (1591), ed. Robert McNulty (Oxford: Clarendon, 1972), 19.

Harington's success, as Barbara Reynolds has said, "must in great part be attributed to the qualities of the English language of that period. . . . The material lay to hand, like some gorgeous glittering brocade; it had only to be cut and fashioned to the shape of the original. His rendering of the first stanza, for instance, glows like a tapestry, romance and colour in every word, enhanced by a patina of archaism which lends it for us a particular charm."[12] Her metaphor seems particularly apt: the National Trust guidebook tells us, though *Knole and the Sackvilles* does not, that the tapestries in the Venetian ambassador's bedroom (Vita's favorite among the show rooms, and the "heart" of the house in *Orlando*) illustrate scenes from *Orlando Furioso*.[13]

Largely forgotten today, the Orlando legends were very popular in the Renaissance, and influential in English literature as late as the Romantic era. Robert Greene—perhaps related to the Nick Greene of the novel—wrote *The Historie of Orlando Furioso* (1592) for the stage; it corrects Ariosto by revealing that Angelica,[14] whose infidelity has driven Orlando mad, was faithful after all. Orlando also turns up in Shakespeare's *As You Like It*, and Spenser wrote to Gabriel Harvey that he hoped to "overgo" Ariosto.[15] As Allan Gilbert has said, almost every literate person in the sixteenth century would have been acquainted with some part of the Orlando legends—if not *Orlando Furioso*, then its predecessor *Orlando Inamorato* (left unfinished by Boiardo in 1494) or one of its many imitators. "So far as an age is affected by what it reads, sixteenth-century Italy was formed in the likeness of the *Furioso*," Gilbert says, and "If the spirit of an age is

12 Ludovico Ariosto, *Orlando Furioso*, trans. Barbara Reynolds (Harmondsworth: Penguin, 1975), I, 90.

13 [V. Sackville-West and later editors], *Knole* (Plaistow: The National Trust, 1976), 24.

14 Angelica was also the name of Virginia's niece, Angelica Bell. She posed for the photograph which was chosen for *Orlando* as "The Russian Princess as a Child." Victoria, Vita's Christian name, is the one chosen by Ariosto for the ideal woman. If only the muse had been called Virginia. . . .

15 For a good summary of *Orlando Furioso* in English literature, see the Introduction to the Reynolds translation, I, 74–78. But she does not mention Woolf's *Orlando*, and concludes that "Ariosto is today largely unknown in England" except among specialists in Italian literature.

indicated by the poetry it chooses, that of the Renascence is to be sought in *Orlando Furioso.*[16]

As a literary representation of Vita, Orlando is an inspired choice. In its English etymology the name *Orlando* means something like "the glory of the land"—appropriate as a tribute to the Sackville lineage of which Vita was so proud, and, in another sense, as an acknowledgment of her love for the country and for gardening, as well as a veiled allusion to her long poem *The Land* (1926), for which she was awarded the Hawthornden Prize in a ceremony which Virginia Woolf attended (and satirizes in *Orlando* as the Burdett Coutts Memorial Prize ceremony). As the Italian evolutions of the French "Roland" legends, the "Orlando" poems are especially appropriate for Vita. In May, 1908, she first visited Florence with Rosamund Grosvenor and Violet Keppel, with each of whom she would later have passionate love affairs. But in 1908 her passion was for Italy itself. As she later described it, "It is a sense almost physical, so strong is it, a feeling of desire, saved from vulgarity by its very mysticism, the intoxicating repletion of beauty, in the mode of calm and sumptuous repose; it is the brilliant, mysterious, resplendent soul of the Renaissance, hovering still, infinitely sad beneath its peacock colours, in its unprobed depths."[17] Her immersion in these unprobed depths was total, and throughout her life Italy would stir these kinds of feelings in her. She became fluent in the language, and for a period of five years kept her diary in Italian.[18]

Thematically, the Orlando legends also express the essence of Vita. The adventures of the characters in the poems are larger than life, just as Vita's seemed to Virginia. Eros rules the world of the poems, as it did Vita's life. She had from the beginning been Vita *inamorato*, as the prodigious literary efforts of her youth reveal. In fact, the romantic writings of Woolf's young Orlando seem less re-

16 Ludovico Ariosto, *Orlando Furioso*, trans. Allan Gilbert (New York: S. F. Vanni, 1954), I, xii.
17 Quoted by Nicolson, *Portrait*, 77.
18 Nicolson, *Portrait*, 82. The reason, he says, was to prevent her mother from reading it. If so, Vita was optimistic, since her mother's first language was French—too close for comfort to Italian. Perhaps Vita chose for her diary the language closest to her heart—another motive, possibly, for the selection of Orlando as her mythic counterpart.

markable than the reality which they parody: "between 1906 and 1910, Vita wrote eight full-length novels (one in French) and five plays"; the first of these novels, written when she was fourteen was "'Edward Sackville: The Tale of a Cavalier,' a novel of sixty-five thousand words penned in a clear childish hand as easy to read as print."[19] The simplicity, immediacy, and vitality of these works, and their subjects, are reminiscent of the Orlando poems. The *furioso*, or frenzied, phase of Vita's life may have been latent in these works, but certainly became unmistakable in her love affairs with Rosamund and Violet; again, the parody in *Orlando* seems less bizarre than the biographical facts themselves,[20] whose appropriate literary equivalent is indeed Orlando, the hero driven mad by love.

The poems go backward and forward in time as the poet wishes, so that the dramatic present is always inseparable from the past and the future. This is appropriate for Vita's own life, whose unconventional qualities could always be "explained" in terms of her Sackville heritage. The wilder episodes could be attributed to her gypsy blood, inherited from Pepita, the Spanish dancer, her grandmother. And even her physical appearance often seemed a fascinating combination and incarnation of the Sackville portraits that inhabit the galleries of Knole. In that sense Vita seemed to transcend the limits of her own lifetime. *Knole and the Sackvilles* reveals her at ease among the ghosts of this great house and thus, in a way, already immortal. Similarly, Ariosto's Orlando, though destined to die at Roncevalles, lives forever in the poems themselves, and the mythic significance of his life transcends the limitations of his time. In his timeless present he receives the favor of the King of Heaven, which makes him invulnerable— except in the soles of his feet—and in that sense too, immortal. Above all, it is the heroic scale of his aspirations, the largeness of his spirit, which seems analogous to the spirit of Vita. In the timeless present of her existence, nothing seemed impossible to her. For such a person

19 *Ibid.*, 62–63.
20 Nicolson's *Portrait* is the best single source for the story of the affairs with Rosamund and Violet. For additional details about the latter, see Phillippe Jullian and John Phillips, *The Other Woman: A Life of Violet Trefusis* (Boston: Houghton Mifflin, 1976).

immortality is not a matter of speculations or beliefs, but a simple reality. Such a life unfolds always in the perspective of eternity.

Orlando shares some important literary qualities with the poems. Some of the salient literary features of *Orlando Furioso* are summarized nicely by Barbara Reynolds:

> The apparently random introduction of one story after another, the abrupt transitions, the cliff-hanging ends of stanzas, the leaps from the sublime to the grotesque, from tragic to comic, are all part of the enjoyment. . . . Eros is omnipresent and, if not omnipotent, he inspires feelings that are forceful in the extreme. [The poem is written with] bravura . . . skill and zest. . . . delight, yet at the same time with the detachment of creative power fulfilled. [Ariosto has written something like] an animated cartoon. . . . His poetic world is situated somewhere between high fantasy and reality, and is made visible by the blending of both or the transition from one to the other.[21]

A major similarity between *Orlando Furioso* and Woolf's *Orlando* is in the narrative point of view. In both the narrator is having a wonderful time, showing off to the audience, indulging every literary whim. In *Orlando*, the narrator, the "biographer," must be identified as "he"—a sardonic smile at the male domination of the literary world. The lengthy asides in which "he" pauses to discuss, rather pedantically, the challenges of "his" art add another dimension to the book: part of the fun for the reader is the spectacle of the narrator struggling with the material—rationalizing, moralizing, revealing in one way after another "his" own quirks and limitations. Similarly, the marginal commentary in Harington's Elizabethan translation adds another level of complication and additional possibilities for parody. In the poem itself Ariosto's narrator loves to introduce each canto with homilies, and to interrupt the narrative in order to give directions to his audience. Here, for example, is the rather sententious opening to Canto 37 (in Guido Waldman's 1974 prose translation):

> If those accomplished ladies who have striven night and day with the most diligent application to acquire some gift that Nature bestows only upon the industrious—and some brilliant work will have been the happy product—if

---

21 Reynolds, Introduction to *Orlando Furioso*, I, 24, 31–32, 41, 42, 45.

those ladies, I say, had devoted themselves instead to those studies which confer immortality upon moral virtues, and had been able by themselves to achieve undying reputation without having to beg it from authors, their fame would soar to heights perhaps beyond the reach of any of the male sex. Male writers are so eaten to the heart with malice and envy that they often pass in silence over the good they might have mentioned, while promulgating all the evil they know.

For many men are not satisfied with titivating each other's reputations: they must also take it upon themselves to disclose any blemishes in woman. They—the men of old, I mean—would never allow women the upper hand, but did their utmost to keep them down, as though the fair sex's honour would cloud their own, as mist obscures the sun.[22]

And so on for two dozen stanzas, in the course of which the narrator chooses the exemplar for all women: her name, prophetically, is Victoria.

Although in many passages such as the one just quoted Ariosto's praise of women is comically exaggerated, still the poem as a whole leaves no doubt that they are equal to his males. Some of the comedy, in fact, arises from the indistinguishability of the sexes in certain situations—for example, when the victor in combat, beneath all that armor, turns out to be a delicate female. The warrior Marfisa, for instance, kills more opponents than most of her male counterparts do. And throughout the poem there are many cases of mistaken sexual identity.

Virginia Woolf would have learned of Harington's translation of *Orlando Furioso* through Lytton Strachey if she had not already seen the poem in her own reading or through Vita's interest in the Italian Renaissance. However she may have discovered it, the poem is very close in form and theme to what Virginia felt about Vita. Nominally "about" the campaigns of the Holy Roman Empire against the Moors, Ariosto's poem actually is motivated by much more primal imperatives. These same imperatives govern Woolf's *Orlando*. And the world of the poem was not restricted to the world of the possible, or even of the conventional, but encompassed everything that the

22 Ludovico Ariosto, *Orlando Furioso*, trans. Guido Waldman (Oxford: Oxford University Press, 1974), 441.

poet dreamed of; so too would *Orlando*. Like *Orlando Furioso*, it too would be a self-conscious creation in which the ultimate interest is not so much in the story itself as in the consciousness which creates it: a brilliant, baroque, but also strangely inhibited Renaissance spirit which is, like its subject, "bestraught with love."

In her introduction to chapter 3 of *Knole and the Sackvilles* Vita speaks of the "representativeness" of the Sackvilles. Because each is typical of his era, the history of the family is also a history of England. Virginia Woolf's phantasmagoria is also based on that assumption, and her story of the evolution of Orlando over the centuries follows the pattern established by Vita herself. Vita's book consists of nine chapters: the first two introduce us to "The House" and to "The Garden and the Park"; each of the remaining seven deals with an historical period—in the reigns of Queen Elizabeth, James I, Charles I, Charles II, and in the early eighteenth, late eighteenth, and nineteenth centuries. In her discussion of the "representativeness" of the family, however, Vita singles out five Sackvilles: "the grave Elizabethan," Thomas Sackville, 1st Earl of Dorset (1536–1608); "his grandson . . . the Cavalier," Edward, 4th Earl (1589–1652); "the florid, magnificent Charles," 6th Earl (1637–1706); "the gay and fickle duke," John Frederick, 3rd Duke of Dorset (1745–1799); and "the last direct male," George John Frederick, 4th Duke (1794–1815).

Each of the first five chapters of *Orlando* can be seen to correspond roughly to the life of one of these five figures, with the sixth chapter representing the climactic incarnation of the Sackvilles, Vita herself. In comparison to the first in the line, it is true that as an Elizabethan Orlando is not exactly "grave," except in the sense of being utterly serious. It is that seriousness which wins Queen Elizabeth, who makes him her Lord Treasurer and sends him on important diplomatic missions, such as informing Mary Queen of Scots of her death sentence.[23]

23 In her discussion of "Knole in the Reign of Queen Elizabeth" in *Knole and the Sackvilles* (4th ed.; London: Ernest Benn, 1976), 47, Vita tells us that in 1586 Thomas Sackville "was one of the forty appointed on the commission for the trial of Mary Stuart, and although his name is not amongst those who proceeded to Fotheringay, nor later in the Star Chamber at Westminster when she was condemned to death, yet he was sent to announce the sentence to death, and received from her in recognition of

The second typical figure, "the cavalier," is reflected in the emphasis in the second chapter of *Orlando* upon poetry and philosophy, and in the emphasis on the house, with extensive inventories of its possessions taken and comically distorted from lists in *Knole and the Sackvilles* for 1624. Vita, at the age of fourteen, had written her first novel about this cavalier.

The third typical figure, "the florid, magnificent Charles," was the one Nell Gwynn is supposed to have called her Charles the first—because of his sexual precedence over King Charles II. In *Orlando* the second chapter ends with Nell sighing over Orlando's departure, and throughout Chapter 3 Orlando is abroad—just where Charles II wishes to keep him, no doubt. But rather than allow us to watch this most entertaining of all English courts, Virginia Woolf exiles us to Constantinople, to watch Orlando become a florid, magnificent woman.

The fourth typical figure, "the gay and fickle duke," is the greatest connoisseur, and clearly Vita's favorite. Thus it is fitting that the fourth chapter of *Orlando* should be the most detailed, and that in it the cultural connoisseurship of her life reaches its peak.

The fifth figure, "the last direct male," died in 1815 in a hunting accident at the age of twenty-one. Engaged but not married, he left no heir. Vita says that "very little record remains of that short life: there is his rocking-horse . . . which in due course became my property . . . his brief friendship with Byron as a schoolboy, and his portrait as a tall, fair young man in dark blue academical robes. There is very little else to mark his passage across the stage of Knole." Perhaps his death is alluded to when Orlando, running through the forest in Chapter 5, falls, breaks her ankle, and succumbs to a Romantic death ("'I am nature's bride,' she whispered") only to be rescued from this state ("'I'm dead, Sir!' she replied") by Shelmerdine. In this Romantic resurrection Orlando's womanhood becomes irrevocable, just as Vita's had in her commitment to Harold. *Orlando* could confirm to Vita that

---

his tact and gentleness in conveying this news the triptych and carved group of the Procession to Calvary now on the altar in the chapel at Knole." This is the basis for the comment in *Orlando* that "She [Queen Elizabeth] sent him to Scotland on a sad embassy to the unhappy Queen."

the death of this "last direct male" was necessary in order for a stronger lineage to emerge. At the mythic level the passage marks a new stage in the development of the representative English conscious- ness, as traditional modes of thought and feeling are transformed into newer, more dynamic ones.

Thus the first five chapters of *Orlando* transform the five Sack- villes who especially haunt Vita into precursors. The sixth chapter subsumes all these historical identities into Vita herself, who by bring- ing these centuries of the tradition to life in her book also transcends them, and enters into a new, authentic existence of her own. If this sixth incarnation of Orlando is the most fully evolved, it is also the most complex and ambiguous.

The first edition, and some later ones, of *Orlando* contain eight photographs which playfully illustrate it. Four of these are of Vita herself, all as Orlando, from Elizabethan times to the present. Three are of paintings: of Edward Sackville, son of the 4th Earl ("Orlando as a Boy"), of Mary, 4th Countess ("The Archduchess Harriet"), and a portrait of an unknown young man bought by Vita in the cellar of an embroidery shop in 1913 ("Marmaduke Bonthrop Shelmerdine, Es- quire"). A photograph of Virginia's niece Angelica ("The Russian Princess as a Child") makes the gallery—and the joke—even more pri- vate.

He—for there could be no doubt of his sex, though the fashion of the time did something to disguise it—was in the act of slicing at the head of a Moor which swung from the rafters. It was the colour of an old football, and more or less the shape of one, save for the sunken cheeks and a strand or two of coarse, dry hair, like the hair on a cocoanut. Orlando's father, or perhaps his grandfather, had struck it from the shoulders of a vast Pagan who had started up under the moon in the barbarian fields of Africa; and now it swung, gently, perpetually, in the breeze which never ceased blowing through the attic rooms of the gigantic house of the lord who had slain him.

Orlando's fathers had ridden in fields of asphodel, and stony fields, and fields watered by strange rivers, and they had struck many heads of many colours off many shoulders, and brought them back to hang from the rafters. So too would Orlando, he vowed. But since he was sixteen only, and too young to ride with them in Africa or France, he would steal away from his mother and the peacocks in the garden and go to his attic room and there lunge and plunge and slice the air with his blade. Sometimes he cut the cord so that the skull bumped on the floor and he had to string it up again, fastening it with some chivalry almost out of reach so that his enemy grinned at him through shrunk, black lips triumphantly. The skull swung to and fro, for the house, at the top of which he lived, was so vast that there seemed trapped in it the wind itself, blowing this way, blowing that way, winter or summer. The green arras with the hunters on it moved perpetually. His fathers had been noble since they had been at all. They came out of the northern mists wearing coronets on their heads. Were not the bars of darkness in the room, and the yellow pools which chequered the floor, made by the sun falling through the stained glass of a vast coat of arms in the window? Orlando stood now in the midst of the yellow body of an heraldic leopard. When he put his hand on the window-sill to push the window open, it was instantly coloured red, blue, and yellow like a butterfly's wing. Thus, those who like symbols, and have a turn for the deciphering of them, might observe that though the shapely legs, the handsome body, and the well-set shoulders were all of them decorated with various tints of heraldic light, Orlando's face, as he threw the window open, was lit solely by the sun itself. A more candid, sullen face it would be impossible to find. Happy the mother who bears, happier still the biographer who records the life of such a one! Never need she vex herself, nor he invoke the help of novelist or poet. From deed to deed, from glory to glory, from office to office he must go, his scribe following after, till they reach whatever seat it may be that is the height of their desire. Orlando, to look at, was cut out precisely for some such career. The red of the cheeks was covered with peach down; the down on the lips was only a little thicker than the down on the cheeks. The lips themselves were short and slightly drawn back over teeth of an exquisite and almond whiteness. Nothing disturbed the arrowy nose in its short, tense flight; the hair was dark, the ears small, and fitted closely to the head. But, alas, that these catalogues of youthful beauty cannot end without mentioning forehead and eyes. Alas, that people are seldom born devoid of all three; for directly we glance at Orlando standing by the window, we must admit that he had eyes like drenched violets, so large that the water seemed to have brimmed in them and widened them; and a brow like the swelling of a marble dome pressed between the two blank medallions which were his temples. Directly we glance at eyes and forehead, thus do we rhapsodise. Directly we glance at eyes and forehead, we have to admit a thousand disagreeables which it is the aim of every good biographer to ignore. Sights disturbed him, like that of his mother, a very beautiful lady in green walking out to feed the peacocks with Twitchett, her maid, behind her; sights exalted him—the birds and the trees; and made him in love with death—the evening sky, the homing rooks; and so, mounting up the spiral stairway into his brain—which was a roomy one—all these sights, and the garden sounds too, the hammer beating, the wood chopping, began that riot and confusion of the passions and emotions which every good biographer detests. But to continue—Orlando slowly drew in his head, sat down at the table, and, with the half-conscious air of one doing what they do every day of their lives at this hour, took out a writing book labelled "Æthelbert: A Tragedy in Five Acts", and dipped an old stained goose quill in the ink.[24]

With its very first words, the book announces both its central theme and its attitude toward that theme. "He—for there could be no doubt of his sex": if there could be no doubt, then why is this insistence necessary? At the most personal level, it alludes to Vita's feelings about having been born a female, and her longing for "masculine" forms of achievement. As a child she had been a tomboy. She was fascinated by the male line of her family, as *Knole and the Sackvilles* shows. She became a writer, and longed for the kind of achievement which could place her in the company of her Elizabethan ancestor Thomas Sackville, or among the poets whose portraits she loved in the Poet's Gallery at Knole. She signed her books and poems V. (not Victoria) Sackville-West. And in her homosexual affairs she played the role of the "man." *Orlando* itself, of course, constitutes the ultimate proof of her success in this role: it is a tribute to Vita from the woman who was inspired for the first time to write a book about her lover.

And the opening comment can be read in a slightly different way. There could be no doubt of Vita's sex in the sense that her sexual drive was her essence: it was at the heart of everything she was and did. The book as a whole acknowledges and celebrates that central fact about her.

At a more universal, mythic level, the comment alludes to the system of "masculine" values which has always made wars possible, and which has encouraged such adolescent fantasies of heroism as the one which the young Orlando is enacting here. "He" aspires toward the same kinds of achievements that his father and grandfather did—

24   The text I refer to throughout is the first English edition of *Orlando: A Biography* (London: Hogarth, 1928).

not a very bright prospect for Orlando or "his" culture. In such cultures the male must not allow a shadow of a doubt about his masculinity—and in that sense "there could be no doubt of his sex."

Also present in the opening sentence is the theme of "the fashion of the time," which will be prominent throughout the book. The specific era is not yet identified, but the idea is clear: the milieu exerts an influence—not wholly deterministic, but enough to "disguise" one's true nature. Biographically, this theme is seen in the influence of the artifacts of "the house" (Knole) upon Orlando (Vita). More broadly, it suggests that we all live in the dual perspectives of time and eternity, and that human nature can be slightly disguised but not really changed by fashion.

The bizarre "slicing at the head of a Moor" furthers the theme of the "masculine" fantasies of prowess in the martial arts, victory in holy wars, *morituri* . . . and so on. The "Moor," of course, relates to *Orlando Furioso*, with its legends of wars against the Moors—and to later allusions to *Othello* and the theme of Shakespeare the poet. The symbolism of decapitation would, in psychoanalytical contexts, suggest castration—which the narrative will achieve at the center of the book. Biographically, the action smiles at Vita's tomboyishness, which is also illustrated by this will which she drew up at the age of nine:

To Mama: A quarter of my bank money and my diamond V [a brooch in that shape].
To Dada: A quarter of my bank money. My pony and cart. My cricket set. My football.
To Seery: My *Khaki*. My miniature. My claret jug. My whip.
To Bentie [her governess]: My pearl V. Half my bank money. My ships.
To Ralph Battiscombe [a Sevenoaks boy]: My armour. My swords and guns. My fort. My soldiers. My tools. My bow-and-arrow. My pocket money. My target.[25]

The image of gentle, perpetual swinging is linked subliminally with the perpetual swaying of the arras at the heart of the house, an image which emerges in the second paragraph of the book—and which will eventually reveal the secret of the house itself. The fuller implications

25 Quoted by Nicolson, *Portrait*, 59–60.

of "rafters" here remain latent, and will come closer to explicitness in the "attic rooms" of the final sentence of the paragraph.

"It was the colour of an old football, and more or less the shape of one . . . ": this sentence undercuts the male pride in the martial arts, deflating it like an old football and shrinking it to the size of a dried husk. The technique here has some precedent in *Orlando Furioso*—*e.g.*, when Orlando skewers six opponents simultaneously, and a seventh must die on the ground because there is no more room on his lance. And in the poem there are so many decapitations that the reader might imagine heads flying like the ball in a soccer match: indeed the mad Orlando can take off a head "as easily as one might take an apple from a tree or a lovely flower from a bush" (Canto 24, Stanza 5, Waldman trans.).

The name Orlando ("the glory of the land") and the references to fathers and grandfathers mark the emergence of the important themes of fatherhood, family heritage, and the merging of generations. On the more personal level, Vita is praised as the living embodiment of the Sackville heritage—a theme which reaches its fullest expression at the end of the book when Orlando sits in Queen Elizabeth's armchair and can gaze through the gallery of the past to her family's mysterious origins in the Dark Ages. The conflicts between this theme of family heritage and that of the uncertainty of sexual identity create some of the most poignant passages in the book. Although some irony seems implied in "the barbarian fields of Africa," the narrative can never be fully ironic about nationality and chivalry. (The theme of nationality later reaches a comic apotheosis when Orlando, after a long absence, sees the shores of England once again: " 'Christ Jesus!' she cried.") The "Pagan" and the "barbarian fields of Africa" also suggest *Orlando Furioso*.

The "breeze which never ceased blowing" is the same perpetual breeze which stirs the arras at the heart of the house; the breeze represents the perpetual possibilities of life. Like other images associated with height and with overviews, the rafters and the attic rooms of this first paragraph imply a perspective of spirituality, superiority, and dominance. Biographically, it probably refers to Vita's bedroom above the chapel at Knole. The perspective from these windows seems to be alluded to elsewhere in *Orlando*, and may represent the origin and essence of Vita's world view: to learn to see the world through these windows could easily lead to the conviction that one is at the center of an eternal life.

In "the gigantic house of the lord": the last three words sway ambiguously between those that come before and after. It is with the house, of course, that the personal and mythic levels of *Orlando* come closest to merging. For Vita, Knole always remained the house of the lord in an almost religious sense: it inspired her deepest feelings and her finest writing. For her, to wander through the house was to wander through history—the history of her family and of England as well. But beyond the countless connections with kings and queens, poets and playwrights, there remained for her something ineffable. It comes closest to expression, perhaps, in the lines which she chose to quote from *Orlando* many years later, about all the "Richards, Johns, Annes, Elizabeths, not one of whom has left a token of himself behind him, yet all, working together with their spades and their needles, their love-making and their childbearing, have left this."[26] For Vita the house was the culmination of centuries of human experience, a temple to the most sacred mysteries. As in *Knole and the Sackvilles*, in *Orlando* the house is like a palace in a medieval mnemonic system, containing the whole of experience, requiring a lifetime to explore, and, above all, essentially beneficent. Some of the most poignant passages in *Knole and the Sackvilles* describe Vita's memories of growing up there.

Knole is not haunted, but you require either an unimaginative nerve or else a complete certainty of the house's benevolence before you can wander through the state-rooms after nightfall with a candle, as I used to do when I was little. . . . The light gleamed on the dull gilding of furniture and into the misty depths of mirrors, and started up a sudden face out of the gloom; something creaked and sighed; the tapestry swayed, and the figures on it undulated and seemed to come alive. The recesses of the great beds, deep in shadow, might be inhabited, and you would not know what eyes might watch you, unseen. . . . But I was never frightened at Knole. I loved it; and took it for granted that Knole loved me.[27]

26 V. Sackville-West, *Knole and the Sackvilles*, 215.
27 *Ibid.*, 28–29.

This passage is reflected in the nocturnal wanderings which evoke the final epiphany in *Orlando*, which arises from the image of the tapestry.

The final words of the first paragraph return to the themes of male aggression and the obsession with death and combat. There are also links with the themes of nationality and chivalry, of fatherhood, family, and the merging of generations, and with "the house of the lord."

Although several new themes appear in the second paragraph, it mainly elaborates those which have already emerged. Much longer than the first paragraph, the second expands the earlier motifs and begins to structure them into the topology of the imagined world. The theme of the exotic ("strange rivers," "many heads of many colours") emerges more clearly. The implied analogy, of course, is to the exotic quality of Vita herself.

In the comment that "he would steal away from his mother and the peacocks in the garden," the emphasis shifts away from the masculine toward the feminine world which sometimes surfaces later in the book in the silences surrounding the louder "masculine" themes. Biographically the sentence alludes to Vita's mother, who entranced such different men as the American president Chester A. Arthur and the French sculptor Auguste Rodin, and to the peacocks at Knole.

"Were not the bars of darkness in the room, and the yellow pools which chequered the floor, made by the sun falling through the stained glass of a vast coat of arms in the window? Orlando stood now in the midst of the yellow body of an heraldic leopard." Light has always had a profound significance in the *oeuvre*, from the first explorations of it in *The Voyage Out* to its much more dramatic manifestations in *To the Lighthouse*. The return of light to a darkened world later becomes the starting point of *The Waves*, where the interludes glow with the radiance of Impressionist paintings.[28] The sun in *Orlando* is this kind of sacred light. In this paragraph the "bars of darkness" are the shadows of the leads of the stained glass windows. The

---

28 Virginia Woolf's own fascination with light was greatly intensified by her viewing of an eclipse of the sun while she was composing *Orlando*. The experience is described in her diary for June 30, 1927, in an essay written in that year called "The Sun and the Fish," and again in the final chapter of *The Waves*.

motif of the sun becomes inseparable from the theme of creation. The heraldic leopard, of course, is the symbol of the Sackville family and a major decorative motif at Knole.[29] It later became an emblem for England. Thus Orlando, bathed in this light, becomes the archetypal English hero. And the image connects him symbolically with Queen Elizabeth, who "flashed her yellow hawk's eyes upon him as if she would pierce his soul."

"When he put his hand on the window-sill to push the window open, it was instantly coloured red, blue, and yellow like a butterfly's wing." Throughout the *oeuvre*, windows are the apertures of perception, and often emblems for the process of perception. The theme of creation and the themes associated with the coat of arms are still resonant, and are reinforced by the allusion to the color of a butterfly's wing. In a way, the symbolic context here is a realization of the aesthetic of Lily Briscoe in the previous novel: "Beautiful and bright it should be on the surface, feathery and evanescent, one colour melting into another like the colours on a butterfly's wing; but beneath the fabric must be clamped together with bolts of iron."

"Thus, those who like symbols . . . ": now the theme of literary self-consciousness, latent from the opening sentence, becomes explicit. And, once admitted, it overwhelms everything else, dominating the rest of the paragraph here, and, indeed, much of the rest of the book. "Orlando's face, as he threw the window open, was lit solely by the sun itself." We are now in a proto-Nabokov world where the only reality is that of the printed word, a world of puns ("lit solely by the sun," with a possible overtone of "son") and dessicated echoes of disillusionment ("My mistress' eyes are nothing like the sun"), the dying fall of lyricism into ironic parody.

Now we see "the shapely legs, the handsome body, and the well-

---

29 In *Orlando Furioso*, the leopard is associated not with the Earl of Dorset, whose symbol is said to be a chariot, but with John of Gaunt, Duke of Lancaster, the leader of the English forces, whose ensign is emblazoned with leopards and fleurs-de-lys. Later in the poem, *leopards* is used as a sign for the English forces. Ariosto's knowledge of—and interest in—English heraldry must have been limited, but everyone, apparently, associated the leopard with England. Virginia Woolf, whose knowledge of heraldry was probably limited also, would have made this association too—and might have been further instructed in the heraldry of the Sackvilles by Vita.

set shoulders": the subject of all this self-conscious literary expression is Orlando's physical attractiveness. The book as a whole makes it clear that the theme of physical attraction is inseparable from its literary expression: sex and literature merge. The parodic rhapsody on the theme of Orlando's attractions dominates most of the rest of this second paragraph, until the theme of literature becomes dominant once again.

The themes in the remainder of the paragraph reiterate themes we have already seen. But most importantly, it concludes with Orlando writing. He returns from the window, "and, with the half-conscious air of one doing what he does every day of his life at this hour, took out a writing book labelled 'Æthelbert: A Tragedy in Five Acts,' and dipped an old stained goose quill in the ink." From what the next paragraph tells us, "Æthelbert" sounds rather like *Gorbuduc* or the Induction to the *Mirror for Magistrates*, both written by Thomas Sackville when he was very young, before he had to devote himself so completely to the service of the Queen—as Orlando will also have to do. The "old stained goose quill" may refer ironically to the aspirations of Orlando's (and Vita's) writing: the wild goose represents that ultimate something that Orlando is always trying to capture. It rises again, like the phoenix, at the very end of the book; here at the beginning Orlando possesses only the stained old quill—which may make his quest more absurd, but no less heroic.

The themes of the two opening paragraphs are less clear, and much less distinct, than this discussion has made them seem. Nevertheless, certain patterns are apparent. The theme which recurs most often is that of fatherhood, family history, and the merging of generations. The themes of the masculine obsession with death and with the martial arts and of the house of the lord are also prominent. The themes of nationality and chivalry and of the perpetual possibilities of life are important in this opening passage, as is the theme of the spiritual overview. All of these themes foreshadow later events in the text.

The most sustained theme, however, is that of literary self-consciousness. As soon as it is acknowledged, it takes over the narrative, transforming some of the other themes into an ironic mode. But irony does not diminish their importance: ironic or not, they are there. And in a way the irony makes them more poignant: the narrative can approach certain themes only through an elaborate series of masks and through great distances of ironic detachment.

These distances are achieved and maintained primarily by the tone of the narrative. Its opening words at once announce the major theme of the story and refuse to take that theme seriously. In the second paragraph the narrative speaks of "the biographer" and the happiness that "he" can feel in recording the life of "such a one" as Orlando. Here too the ironies are very complex. Vita's "biographer" is not "really" a male. But that role is conventionally assumed to be a male role, and in playing it, Virginia reverses the situation from real life, in which Vita played the aggressive, dominant male. In the book the biographer transforms "his" subject from man to woman, and in doing so, achieves dominance. Thus the book becomes both an acknowledgment and a sublimation of "that riot and confusion of the passions and emotions which every good biographer detests." "Orlando's" magic powers are brought under the "biographer's" control. And the imaginative range and energy of the "biography," displayed in this opening passage and continuing throughout the book, enable it to achieve the very truth which it constantly refuses to claim.

Like the other novels, *Orlando* opens into a "given" world which the narrative consciousness wishes to transform. It regards Orlando's fantasies of power and prowess as amusing, but immature and imprisoning. Yet the narrative itself is very self-conscious—aware of its audience watching it watching itself. Its attitudes toward every aspect of this literary situation seem ambiguous, and these ambiguities deepen and enrich its story.

Although the "world" of *Orlando* is so complicated and sometimes so private that it seems opaque, its essential structure is in some ways fairly clear. Although unconventional, ironic, distanced, *Orlando* is still a *bildungsroman*, a novel of psychological maturation. Each chapter represents a major stage in that psychological development, and each culminates in a new state of maturity.

The first chapter ends with Orlando "hurling insults after Sasha." In this first stage Orlando has been the lustful pursuer. Biographically, it represents the earliest stage of Vita's psychological development, in which she saw herself in a masculine role, conquering literary and sexual worlds, writing romantic novels, seducing beautiful women and enslaving them in abject worship of her. It must culminate in the loss of Sasha, who, like Violet's "Lushka," is as much a passionate ideal as a real person, and therefore cannot continue to exist indefinitely in this dual role. She must eventually vanish as the lover's consciousness matures. In a sense, the ending is that of the Elizabethan age, which cannot sustain indefinitely its seriousness, its bawdy, adventurous innocence, its lyric power, but must fall into Jacobean knowledge. Yet the Elizabethan age remains alive in the heritage which develops from it, just as in Vita herself there is something of the "grave Elizabethan" Thomas Sackville which remains alive for her, and which she sees in his portrait in the Great Hall at Knole: "you perceive all his severe integrity; you understand the intimidating austerity of the contribution he made to English letters."[30] So the Elizabethan world remains alive for us in Shakespeare. His influence is inescapable for us, just as in *Orlando* he reappears again and again, always writing. By shaping our perceptions and understanding, by giving us words, he makes us who we are.

The second chapter ends with Orlando sailing for Constantinople, fleeing from "Lust the vulture" in the person of the Archduchess Harriet. Though the arena is still sexual, Orlando is now the pursued rather than the pursuer. Biographically, the archduchess is a grotesque exaggeration of "Harry," Lord Lascelles of Harewood, who in 1922 married Princess Mary, the only daughter of King George V (and would thus seem especially impressive to Virginia Woolf, with her awe of the aristocracy), but who in 1913 was very much in love with Vita.[31] Psychologically the role of pursued seems as limiting as that of pursuer; both are caricatures of "Lust," which dehumanizes. In the first two chapters, then, the personality whose biography this is finishes the exploration of these two sexual roles, which are discovered to be equally unsatisfactory—and only superficially different.

The third chapter is the one in which Orlando undergoes the

30   V. Sackville-West, *Knole and the Sackvilles*, 41.
31   Nicolson, *Portrait*, esp. 94.

miraculous sex change and the audience as well as Orlando discovers the transcendent "TRUTH!. . . . he was a woman." The fullest meaning of this truth, of course, is not immediately apparent, but must be explored throughout the rest of the book. Biographically, it seems to have something to do with Vita's gypsy ancestry. Orlando's second "trance," which leads to the change of sex, is the result, apparently, of his marriage to "Rosina Pepita, a dancer," and the discovery of Orlando's womanhood is followed by her sojourn among the gypsies. Vita herself published the story of her grandfather's involvement with the gypsy dancer, the "Star of Andalusia," a decade later than *Orlando* in *Pepita* (1937), but had already been involved in the scandalous trial in 1910 in which Lady Sackville had to prove her right to Knole by swearing in High Court, "openly and emphatically, that she and all her father's other children were bastards."[32] Fascinated by Pepita, Vita liked to attribute her own sensuality to the Spanish gypsy blood on her mother's side. But there was also a deep pride in her male, Sackville heritage, to which she could attribute her tomboyishness and perhaps her later sexual confusion. In the biographical view in *Orlando*, her discovery of the basic truth of her womanhood and then her acceptance of the gypsy in her heritage enable her to come home.

In the mythic story of England, this chapter shows how the appetites for adventure, the exotic, and fortune all lead to experiences which place England itself in a new perspective and inspire a longing for home. In a sense the action of the chapter seems to exist outside of time: we know only that Orlando goes to Constantinople as ambassador from Charles II to the Turks, and that the return to England in the next chapter is in the early eighteenth century. This mythic feeling of moving outside of time and place becomes more acute because of the very Englishness of the previous chapters. The exotic settings now are created largely by references to English landscapes. For example, "Nothing, he reflected, gazing at the view which was now sparkling in the sun, could well be less like the counties of Surrey and Kent or the towns of London and Tunbridge Wells. . . . parsonage there was none, nor manor house, nor cottage, nor oak, elm, violet, ivy, or wild eglantine. . . . That he, who was English root and

32 *Ibid.*, 65–66.

fibre, should yet exult to the depths of his heart in this wild panorama
... surprised him." In a sense, the settings of the third chapter constitute an anti-England in which that heritage is discovered through
the experience of its antithesis.

The fourth chapter returns the action to London in the eighteenth century, the age of the Enlightenment, and of the essay—and
the chapter is an extensive, sometimes tedious, series of essays on various topics: love, sexual identity, poetry, sexual differences, society in
the reign of Queen Anne, the conversation of the salons, genius as a
lighthouse (an immodest allusion, of course, to the author's previous
novel), the revelations of literary styles, and so on. Inevitably, Enlightenment must end in darkness—the dark cloud of the nineteenth century which engulfs all England at midnight on December 31, 1799.
Biographically, the chapter alludes to various facets of Vita's life. Orlando's litany of "Addison, Dryden, Pope" might be the list of major
antecedents for Vita's style, and "the Round Parlour, which she had
hung with their pictures all in a circle, so that Mr. Pope could not say
that Mr. Addison came before him, or the other way about" alludes
to the Poets' Parlour at Knole. The lawsuits in which Orlando is involved, especially the "Rosina Pepita" case, allude to the celebrated
Sackville cases. Archduchess Harriet Griselda (Patient Griselda?) appears once again and dramatically becomes Archduke Harry (even
closer to Harry, Lord Lascelles). Even the comment that Orlando believed "that to travel south is to travel down hill" alludes to one of
Vita's personal foibles.[33] In the mythic sense, the fourth chapter captures the spirit of eighteenth-century England, as Virginia Woolf saw
it: capable, confident, humane, practical, extroverted. The one date
mentioned in the section—"Tuesday, the 16th of June, 1712"—proves
that its action is precisely 192 years in advance of Joyce's *Ulysses*:
Bloomsday in Queen Anne's London, with an all-night ball at Arling-
ton House.

The fifth chapter, less than half as long as the preceding one,
begins in the miasma of the nineteenth century and ends with the
marriage of Orlando to Shelmerdine. Evidently neither Orlando nor

---

33 Nicolson mentions Vita's "ineradicable belief that rivers like the Nile which flow
northwards must run uphill" (*Portrait*, 191).

her author has much interest in the nineteenth century; both find it rather oppressive ("the spirit of the nineteenth century was antipathetic to her in the extreme"). The opening pages of the chapter yield the entire century to the encircling gloom. Its emblem, to Orlando, becomes the wedding ring (which makes an unspoken contrast with the rings given to Orlando by Queen Elizabeth, then by Archduke Harry), and she "was forced at length to consider the most desperate of remedies, which was to yield completely and submissively to the spirit of the age, and take a husband." He arrives literally as a man on horseback, and leaves immediately after their wedding (a ceremony, significantly, at which "no one heard the word Obey spoken"). But Orlando, driven to marry by the imperatives of the nineteenth century, finds her freedom in the acceptance of that commitment: unexpectedly, acceptance of the social convention of marriage lifts the darkness. Biographically, this represents Vita's marriage to Harold Nicolson, which she seems to have entered into for very complex reasons. Although it is hard to imagine Vita imprisoned by Victorian values, it is true that Harold rescued her, symbolically, as Shelmerdine rescues Orlando, from an intolerable situation (her affair with Rosamund Grosvenor, mainly, but from other anxieties and demands as well), and that throughout her life he would fill for her the role of knight and bold sea captain which Virginia Woolf exaggerates in Marmaduke Bonthrop Shelmerdine. His whirlwind departure after the wedding exaggerates too; actually Vita went with him to Italy and Egypt on their honeymoon, and then on to his diplomatic post in Constantinople. Later in his career, however, his foreign assignments required separations which at last became intolerable, and which are parodied in Shelmerdine's ridiculous recurrent voyages around Cape Horn. (There could also be the cruel suggestion of the horns of the cuckold here, which Vita provided for him more than once—with men and women both.) At the historical and mythic levels Virginia Woolf's own bias against the nineteenth century is obvious in this chapter. The satire is not out of keeping with the book as a whole, of course; but the satirist cannot imagine the spirit of this age as she does the others, especially the Elizabethan era and the Enlightenment, from the inside. There are, of course, acknowledgments of some of the more superficial aspects of nineteenth-century life, but its meaning seems obscured by the great dark cloud and the obsession with marriage. Undoubtedly the shallowness of this view is related to Virginia Woolf's own rebellion against Victorian values. In *Orlando*, and in her thinking in general, the nineteenth century seems to remain a kind of Dark Age out of which a modern renaissance emerges rather miraculously. Yet she was, of course, much more a product of the nineteenth century than she could ever consciously admit, much more like Leslie Stephen than she could ever recognize. The fifth chapter of *Orlando*, despite the delightful satirical portrait of the dark age with which it opens, never comes fully to life: the playful but penetrating allusions to Vita's life and to Knole which enhanced the earlier chapters—even though they remain somewhat cryptic and teasing to the uninitiated— are missing here and the rising noise level of the satire cannot conceal the fact that it has less to say.

The final chapter of the book is more important and relatively more successful; in some ways it does work, even though most readers, probably, find it somewhat puzzling. There are six sections in the final chapter, each concluding in a kind of epiphany. The first section begins immediately after Orlando's marriage and ends with the comment that "she was in an extremely happy position; she need neither fight her age, nor submit to it; she was it, yet she remained herself. Now, therefore, she could write, and write she did. She wrote. She wrote. She wrote." Her marriage, then, has given her the freedom to be herself, and to write. And in writing, she enters into her heritage (Vita as a Sackville, latest in a line of poets; Orlando as a mythic poet in whom the English Renaissance finds its perpetual reincarnation). She is the incarnation of her age, and the acceptance of that destiny frees her powers of creativity, which have been dormant since the Elizabethan era, and certainly since the eighteenth century. Marriage for Vita, as for Virginia herself, provided a structure which was protective without being too inhibiting. And so it is with Orlando: for the first time since the Elizabethan era she can be unconscious of the age, and in that sense she *becomes* her age, at one with it, and free to express it.

The second section then explores the problem of expression; first it meditates on fiction and biography, then on the problem of women in relation to both, and finally on the largest problem of all: "what life is"—to which the only honest answer is "Alas, we don't know." This too seems to be a liberating epiphany: freed of the need to search for ultimate answers, we may attend more fully and truly to the immediate realities in which we exist.

The third section shows Orlando doing just that, and discovering that the world has continued even while she was writing. Realizing that she needs human contact, she returns to London with her manuscript of "The Oak Tree," which is now, at the ripe old age of almost three hundred, almost finished. There she meets her old friend, critic, and parasite Nick Greene, the rowdy Elizabethan now turned eminent Victorian, who relieves her of the manuscript with enthusiastic promises to publish it. Realizing that the literary world has become a farce, Orlando turns once more to the real world, and the section ends with her entrance into her house on Curzon Street "where, when the meadowsweet blew there, she could remember curlew calling and one very old man with a gun." The allusion, presumably, is to the Elizabethan era when in her visits to town Orlando lived in her house in Blackfriars—before London had become a vast metropolis. Now she senses the unity of all this—of the London of Elizabeth with the modern London—and can choose for the moment to live in the world of the old man with a gun who will stalk the curlew forever. The Nick Greenes will go on forever too—in the Elizabethan age saying that their contemporaries are worthless in comparison with the Greeks, in the Victorian age saying that their contemporaries are worthless in comparison with the great Elizabethans. But these are not the voices which interest Orlando.

The next section begins with a playful review of Victorian style, continues with some highly self-conscious meditations on the difficulty of telling Orlando's story, modulates into what must surely be a teasing parody of "The Waste Land" (five paragraphs which breathlessly follow "the kingfisher"), and reaches the happiest ending that a fertility legend could have: " 'It's a very fine boy, M'Lady,' said Mrs. Banting, the midwife. In other words Orlando was safely delivered of a son on Thursday, March the 20th, at three o'clock in the morning."

Personally, Virginia congratulates Vita for bearing sons, for continuing the male line—something that the eighteenth-century Sackvilles had not been able to do. More generally, the epiphany shows that it is not the creation of literature—especially Victorian literature—but of human life that matters. In bearing a son Orlando, like Vita herself, achieved that kind of immortality.

The fifth section of the sixth chapter is the one in which *Orlando* reaches its conclusion and its fullest meaning. In the first paragraph Orlando stands once again at the window (emblem of the process of perception) and sees a horseless carriage. Some very curious things are happening: "Park Lane itself has considerably changed," and even the sky is different (the dark clouds of the nineteenth century are gone), King Edward has succeeded Queen Victoria (and is, of course, visiting "a certain lady"), technological changes are everywhere, and "the immensely long tunnel in which she seemed to have been travelling for hundreds of years widened." The tunnel here, as in *The Voyage Out*, expresses the feeling of entrapment and predestination which the spirit resists, but liberation from the tunnel into this new age of "distraction and desperation" brings its own anxieties. Orlando is aware of brightening light, of increasing loudness, of tightening nerves. Suddenly, at the end of this first paragraph, it is the present: 10 A.M., October 11, 1928. This, the narrative goes on to say, is a "terrifying revelation." We can survive it only "because the past shelters us on one side, the future on another." The narrative then immerses itself once more in the phenomena of Orlando's present.

These phenomena unfold on a scale larger than "normal"—and therefore analogous to the style of Vita's own life. Although the narrative sees such a style as rather grotesque, it also admires the confident unself-consciousness with which Orlando moves from past to future, always in the loud, bright tension of the present. In her, as in Mrs. Dalloway and Mrs. Ramsay, the narrative must view with awe—though with misgivings too—the ability to cope so masterfully with the here-and-now.

In the London of the present, Orlando orders "sheets for a double bed." This is "the royal bed. Many kings and queens had slept there, Elizabeth; James, Charles; George; Victoria; Edward"—the rulers of the eras of *Orlando* itself—and further details point toward the king's bedroom at Knole: "a room fitted in a taste which she now thought perhaps a little vulgar—all in silver; but she had furnished it when she had a passion for that metal."[34] Her plans here are fulfilled by the arrival of the queen at the end of the book. Silver, ostentatious and deathly, does not appeal to Orlando; she prefers the faded colors of the ambassador's bedroom and its tapestry. But she will prepare the king's bedroom too. Like the father's and the mother's views of the lighthouse in the previous novel, the two bedrooms here in *Orlando* represent opposite, yet complementary, views of the same essential realm. Both views are true and both are necessary in the journey of the consciousness toward wholeness and fulfillment.

Now thirty-six, Orlando looks as young as she did when she skated on the frozen Thames. (Vita was 36 on March 9, 1928, eight days before Virginia Woolf finished the book.) She recalls Sasha's extravagant compliment then to her beauty; she cries out, "Faithless!" and envisions Sasha now "a fat, furred woman, marvellously well preserved, seductive, diademed, a Grand Duke's mistress" (allusions to Vita's undying passion and to Violet's later evolution into *grand dame*). The narrative also says that "Orlando was a man till the age of thirty; when he became a woman and has remained so ever since." Perhaps this is an immodest allusion to the influence of Virginia herself: Vita was thirty when they met, and may have discovered her own true "self" in the relationship with Virginia, outgrowing her earlier passions and discovering a deeper kind of love. Their sexual relationship was never as consuming as Vita's earlier ones, and evolved, after a year or two, into a deeper friendship in which Vita became almost a daughter and Virginia played a fatherlike role. Thus *Orlando* becomes both a public acknowledgment of, and a private farewell to, their sexual relationship. More importantly, it reveals a deepening understanding of, and affection for, Vita's heritage, personality, and character.

34 Vita wrote that "the King's Bedroom, otherwise sometimes called the Silver Room. . . . is the only vulgar room in the house" (*Knole and the Sackvilles*, 30).

The search for an identity that can live in "the present moment" leads through the various identities that have been "Orlando" to a self mysteriously associated with Shakespeare, who, throughout the book, has been the emblem of creative imagination. Now Orlando realizes that she has always been "Haunted!" by the same vision.

And it was at this moment, when she had ceased to call "Orlando" and was deep in thoughts of something else, that the Orlando whom she had called came of its own accord; as was proved by the change that now came over her as she had passed through the lodge gates and was entering the park.

The whole of her darkened and settled. . . . she was now darkened, stilled, and become, with the addition of this Orlando, . . . a single self, a real self. And she fell silent.

The deepest insights, Proust believed, are those which suddenly well up involuntarily, unconditioned by conscious expectations or restrictions. And so the true Orlando can emerge only when consciousness can no longer command some preconceived Orlando to appear. The "something else" which occupies that consciousness at the moment when the authentic personality appears is the mystery of the quest for meaning—the same mystery which haunts the work of Shakespeare and of every creative artist, even Orlando. As R. D. Laing would later describe it, it is the discovery that "The truth I am trying to grasp is the grasp that is trying to grasp it."[35] This discovery, in turn, allows Orlando to pass through the gates.

In a biographical sense these are the lodge gates at Knole, Vita's paradise soon to be lost. But in a more mythic sense, that paradise is the emblem of England itself, a community of people working and living together. Returning to Knole always had a therapeutic effect on Vita; it made her, like Orlando now, "a single self, a real self." But the tone now is elegiac as she wanders through the great house for the last time: "She fancied that the rooms brightened as she came in; stirred, opened their eyes as if they had been dozing in her absence. . . . They had known each other for close on four centuries now. They had nothing to conceal. She knew their sorrows and joys. . . . They, too,

---

35 R. D. Laing, *The Politics of Experience* (New York: Ballantine, 1968), 190.

knew her in all her moods and changes. She had hidden nothing from them; had come to them as child, as man, crying and dancing, brooding and gay. In this window-seat, she had written her first verses; in that chapel, she had been married. And she would be buried here, she reflected." This passage captures very beautifully the feeling for the house expressed in *Knole and the Sackvilles*: the rooms truly come to life for Vita; her life is in a way a distillation of theirs; her seasons are their seasons. In a mythic sense the passage expresses the English heritage, which welcomes us, comes to life in our presence, and has room for all of our concerns: poetry, love, death, eternity.

With this reminder of mortality, the imagery begins to return to its origins, to seek the dominant tones of the opening passage of the book once again, and to rediscover "the heart of the house":

She, who believed in no immortality, could not help feeling that her soul would come and go forever with the reds on the panels and the greens on the sofa. For the room—she had strolled into the Ambassador's bedroom—shone like a shell that has lain at the bottom of the sea for centuries and has been crusted over and painted a million tints by the water; it was rose and yellow, green and sand-coloured. It was frail as a shell, as iridescent and as empty. No Ambassador would ever sleep there again. Ah, but she knew where the heart of the house still beat. Gently opening a door, she stood on the threshold so that (as she fancied) the room could not see her and watched the tapestry rising and falling on the eternal faint breeze which never failed to move it. Still the hunter rode; still Daphne flew. The heart still beat, she thought, however faintly, however far withdrawn; the frail indomitable heart of the immense building.

Here Orlando begins to recognize her own immortality. In a more personal sense, Virginia leads Vita toward that same recognition, for though neither believed in personal survival after death, both knew that books live forever. Knole and the Sackvilles had made Vita who she was; *Knole and the Sackvilles* had made her, as well as the house, immortal.

This certainty of immortality emanates from one room more than from any other. By discovering that secret *Orlando* pays the deepest tribute to Vita's book. In *Knole and the Sackvilles* this room is described immediately after the king's bedroom (the silver room), "the only vulgar room in the house":

It is almost a relief to go from here to the Venetian Ambassador's Bedroom. Green and gold; Burgundian tapestry, medieval figures walking in a garden; a rosy Persian rug—of all rooms I never saw a room that so had over it a bloom like the bloom on a bowl of grapes and figs. . . . Greens and pinks originally bright, now dusted and tarnished over. It is a very grave, stately room, rather melancholy in spite of its stateliness. It seems to miss its inhabitants more than do any of the other rooms. Perhaps this is because the bed appears to be designed for three: it is of enormous breadth, and there are three pillows in a row. Presumably this is what the Italians call a *letto matrimoniale*.[36]

It is this tapestry which rises and falls eternally, in the rhythm of the heart of the house. The guidebook to Knole tells us more about it: "The tapestries, depicting scenes from *Orlando Furioso*, are Flemish, by Franz Spierincz, of the late sixteenth or early seventeenth century." And what seems to Vita to be most touching about this room is the feeling of its emptiness, which she attributes to the huge "matrimonial bed." At the heart of this space, then, as at the heart of *Orlando Furioso* (and Woolf's *Orlando*), is a sexual mystery. And this mystery is at the heart of the house itself.

The room is compared to a seashell, frail, iridescent, and empty. As we saw in *The Voyage Out*, the imagery of the sea floor signifies the realm of primal, unconscious feelings. Significantly, Shakespeare's vision penetrates this realm: "a man who does not see you? who sees ogres, satyrs, perhaps the depths of the sea instead?" Implied also in the image of the shell is its voice: the voice of the sea, of mystery, of eternity, of the darkness out of which creation (as in *The Waves*) emerges and to which it returns. And the shell symbolizes the space in which the mystery is sought: we perceive an emptiness, frail, iridescent, waiting to be filled. But that realm can be entered, or perceived, only indirectly: direct, conscious intrusion would disturb it, transform it into something else. And so Orlando must stand on the threshold where "(as she fancied) the room could not see her" to find

36 V. Sackville-West, *Knole and the Sackvilles*, 30–31.

the tapestry "rising and falling on the eternal faint breeze which never failed to move it." This is the diastole and systole of the heart of the house, moved eternally, unfailingly, by the infinite possibilities of life—another theme of the opening passage of *Orlando* which echoes in this closing section.

What is the drama which the tapestry enacts? Daphne is mentioned only once in *Orlando Furioso*, in Canto 34 during Astolfo's visit to hell, among a gallery of women who have been condemned for having frustrated their suitors: "Daphne, who now realizes her error in making Apollo run after her so." Apollo is not only the sun god but also the god of poetry, so that the pursuit of Daphne on the tapestry may represent not only a sexual pursuit, but the poet's pursuit of love as well. What matters most is not the consummation, but the eternal excitement of the chase—as we can see on the Grecian urn. Perfect love and perfect art alike remain always just beyond our reach, but the quest goes on forever for that very reason. And that quest is at the "frail indomitable heart" of human life.

Once again the narrative abandons itself to the treasures of the house, re-creating many of the descriptions from *Knole and the Sack-villes*.[37] Orlando realizes that the house "belonged to time now; to history; was past the touch and control of the living." The sense of loss, and of absence, becomes dominant, and "The great wings of silence beat up and down the empty house." This moment then evokes one of the loveliest descriptions in *Orlando*:

So she sat at the end of the gallery with her dogs couched round her, in Queen Elizabeth's hard armchair. The gallery stretched far away to a point where the light almost failed. It was as a tunnel bored deep into the past. As her eyes peered down it, she could see people laughing and talking; the great men she had known; Dryden, Swift, and Pope; and statesmen in colloquy; and lovers dallying in the window-seats; and people eating and drinking at the long tables; and the wood smoke curling round their heads and making them sneeze and cough. Still further down, she saw sets of splendid dancers formed for the quadrille. A fluty, frail, but nevertheless stately music began to play. An organ boomed. A coffin was borne into the chapel. A marriage procession came out of it. Armed men with helmets left for the wars. They

37 *Ibid.*, esp. 25–27, 164–68.

196

brought banners back from Flodden and Poitiers and stuck them on the wall. The long gallery filled itself thus, and still peering further, she thought she could make out at the very end, beyond the Elizabethans and the Tudors, some one older, further, darker, a cowled figure, monastic, severe, a monk, who went with his hands clasped, and a book in them, murmuring—

The technique is cinematic, as if a movie camera with a zoom lens were looking down the gallery of time. First it focuses on the tableau of the eighteenth century (we know from the previous chapter that it can't penetrate the darkness of the nineteenth). Dryden, Pope, Swift (letters by each are at Knole) are there. As the focal plane moves farther into the past, the figures become more archetypal: statesmen, lovers, people. Then there are dancers and a quadrille—Elizabethan, perhaps. Now, over a bridge of music, the camera lingers at the entrance to the chapel, observes the solemn rites of death and marriage (Vita was married here). The transition to war, sadly but not surprisingly, is hardly noticeable. And at last, coming to the limits of magnification and of available light, the camera perceives, dimly, the cowled figure of a monk.[38] There is no exact source for this paragraph in *Knole and the Sackvilles*, but the context is vaguely suggestive of Vita's account of her relationship with her grandfather: "I clasped my knees and stared at him when he told me these stories of an age which already seemed so remote, and his pale blue eyes gazed away into the past, and suddenly his shyness would return to him and the clock in the corner would begin to wheeze in preparation to striking the hour, and he would say that it was time for me to go to bed."[39] The dynamics of the situations are similar: the shyness of the grandfather is paralleled by the distancing of the narrative in *Orlando*, and the pale blue eyes gazing away into the past must have seen something very much like this passage in the novel. And there, as in *Knole and the Sackvilles*, the reverie is interrupted by the striking of the clock.

Recalled into the element of time again, Orlando is now much

---

38 Historically, this alludes to Knole before the Sackvilles, before even Henry VIII (who took Knole from Archbishop Cranmer). The basic design was established by Bourchier, the fifteenth-century Archbishop of Canterbury. According to Vita, the earliest recorded mention of the house dates from 1281 (*Knole and the Sackvilles*, 20).
39 V. Sackville-West, *Knole and the Sackvilles*, 211.

less vulnerable to it: "she was now one and entire, and presented, it may be, a larger surface to the shock of time." Every detail now appears to her with great clarity; she has seen, after all, how the meaning of everything that has ever been is inherent in the present moment, and she is ready to savor it. This is a sure sign, in the *oeuvre*, that the final moment of vision is approaching.

For that final vision Orlando moves "higher and higher to the oak tree," to the commanding height (on the knoll above Knole) where she will be granted her epiphany. There she decides against a ceremonial burial of her poem; that would be too much like the ceremony in which old Professor Greene gave her the Burdett Coutts Memorial Prize[40]—and poetry is really "a secret transaction" rather than a public one. So she loses herself in a contemplation of the landscape, which, in her new mood of unity, becomes all landscapes.

Now night comes, and a climactic vision, which culminates in the imagery of the eternal sea. And that imagery, in turn, leads her vision to her husband, the intrepid mariner, her culmination, always, in her view, heroic, always finally *other* than herself, moreso even than Shakespeare, Sasha, imagination. It is this discovery which lifts her to ecstasy, which always lifts her to ecstasy (for this is a reprise of an

---

40   Perhaps the Burdett Coutts Memorial Prize alludes playfully to that classic novel of country matters, *Lady Chatterley's Lover*, in which the gamekeeper's nasty and sexually threatening wife is called Bertha Coutts. That book is alluded to in another passage early in Chapter 6:

And if we look for a moment at Orlando writing at her table, we must admit that never was there a woman more fitted for that calling. Surely, since she is a woman, and a beautiful woman, and a woman in the prime of life, she will soon give over this pretence of writing and begin to think, at least of a gamekeeper (and as long as she thinks of a man, nobody objects to a woman thinking). And then she will write him a little note (and as long as she writes little notes nobody objects to a woman writing either) and make an assignation for Sunday dusk; and Sunday dusk will come; and the gamekeeper will whistle under the window—all of which is, of course, the very stuff of life and the only possible subject for fiction.

Probably Virginia Woolf had heard of Lawrence's scandalous novel but had not read it (Connie didn't write little notes to Mellors, nor did he whistle under her window). In any case, it would be difficult for a feminist to take *Lady Chatterley's Lover* seriously. Perhaps the prize comments on Vita's pastoralism as well as Lawrence's.

A final question about literary allusions: is Basket, Orlando's butler, named for Gertrude Stein's dog?

earlier culmination, in the third section of the sixth chapter, in which the same progression is experienced: toy boat on the Serpentine, then the Atlantic, then ecstasy).

Orlando calls her husband now, and "He was coming, as he always came, in moments of dead calm," from the ridiculous, heroic world of men to rescue her. In this perfect stillness and certainty Orlando is now granted her final vision:

All was still now. It was near midnight. The moon rose slowly over the weald. Its light raised a phantom castle upon earth. There stood the great house with all its windows robed in silver. Of wall or substance there was none. All was phantom. All was still. All was lit as for the coming of a dead Queen. Gazing below her, Orlando saw dark plumes tossing in the courtyard, and torches flickering and shadows kneeling. A Queen once more stepped from her chariot.

"The house is at your service, Ma'am," she cried, curtseying deeply. "Nothing has been changed. The dead Lord, my father, shall lead you in."

This scene is enacted far above the limitations of "the house" and "the present," in the eternal realm of pure imagination—which does not, of course, make it any less "real." In the raising of the phantom castle, with its windows robed in silver, the ghostly promise of the king's bedroom, the silver bedroom, is fulfilled at last; the sheets which Orlando bought impulsively in London earlier that day turn out to be necessary after all. In a visual sense the queen's arrival echoes, but heightens, Orlando's own arrival earlier in the day, and reinforces our feeling that the two are somehow inseparable. The dead queen is not named: Queen Elizabeth, the Faerie Queene, Mary Queen of Scots, Queen Anne, Queen Victoria, Queen Alexandra—she is the ghost of all the queens who haunt this very English house and book: the queen. In another sense she represents Vita herself, whose spiritual claim to all this is greater than anyone else's. The queen is called into being as Vita had evoked the great figures of English history in her writing. And she too, as writer and as custodian of Knole, might tell the queen that "Nothing has been changed"—and she might have added that much has been enriched. Her final words to the queen, "The dead Lord my father shall lead you in," are her farewell to this beloved house. She is giving it back now to her queen and country, and to time and history. (Because Vita's father died during the writing of *Orlando*, and Knole went to his brother, this passage would have had a special personal poignance.)

Several important themes from the opening of the book reach their closure here. The theme of fatherhood, family history, and the merging of generations, which was so prominent in the opening passage, is crucial here too: secure now in her family heritage, accepting it as a transcendent unity, Orlando has, in a sense, assumed the role of father in her final words to the queen. The masculine obsession with death and the martial arts, also prominent in the opening, has now given way to a more mature perception of death as inevitable in, and inseparable from, life; and the martial arts are seen now as ceremonies bordering on the religious—dark plumes in the torchlight. And of course the theme of the house of the lord reaches transcendent significance here: the great house has become a temple, literally the house of the Lord. The theme of nationality and chivalry reaches its closure in this final scene of the phantom castle. The theme of the perpetual possibilities of life, imaged in the tapestry rising and falling forever at the heart of the house, remains now as an overtone. And the theme of spirituality, associated with the cinematographic "down angle" of the opening passage, becomes dominant once again in the ending: from the oak tree on the knoll Orlando and the narrative look down on the phantom castle, on history, on all the themes, in fact, which seemed so troubling in the opening passages. The perspective now is large enough for the perception—or is it an illusion?—of unity.

Once again the moment of stillness is broken by the intrusion of time: "Immediately, the first stroke of midnight sounded." *Immediately* may suggest a causal connection between Orlando's words to the queen and the first stroke of midnight: as if the promise, "The dead Lord, my father, shall lead you in," *enables* the clock to strike and the story to proceed. Aware once more of the present moment, Orlando feels "its little breath of fear. She looked anxiously into the sky." She seems to know that her rescuer will come from there (three paragraphs earlier, in response to Orlando's call, "The beautiful, glittering name fell out of the sky like a steel-blue feather"). Perhaps there is also the symbolic suggestion of the god and goddess of creation, Uranus and Gea, sky and earth, here. Orlando's mate is both aviator and sea captain, master of the realms of creation, and she calls to him, "baring her breast to the moon . . . so that her pearls glowed like the eggs of some vast moon-spider. . . . like a phosphorescent flare in the darkness." Here again the imagery returns to the mystical stillness between sky and sea, the latent moment of creation, illuminated by moonlight. (The pearls are Vita's, as we see in the photographs in the first—and some subsequent—editions, and probably also have some erotic implications.)

And now the final paragraphs of the book:

And as Shelmerdine, now grown a fine sea captain, hale, fresh-coloured, and alert, leapt to the ground, there sprang up over his head a single wild bird.

"It is the goose!" Orlando cried. "The wild goose. . . ."

And the twelfth stroke of midnight sounded; the twelfth stroke of midnight, Thursday, the eleventh of October, Nineteen hundred and Twenty-eight.

Something seems vaguely wrong with the style here—the string of nanny-like, incongruous, and slightly silly adjectives, the bird which "sprang," the fall into factuality at the end. The hour is late, and perhaps the narrative consciousness is falling asleep. Or perhaps, more cruelly, the passage parodies what Virginia Woolf considered to be Vita's "pen of brass."[41] At any rate, the style itself seems to whirl off into irrelevance—which is fun, and perhaps the most appropriate ending for such a book. In a biographical sense, Virginia gives Vita back to Harold at last, and in such a way that Vita could not have resented it, for the book itself is public and permanent proof that Virginia admired, understood, and loved her.

The public acknowledgment of Virginia's love for Vita makes *Orlando*, in that sense, the most "confessional" of the nine novels. In an era when *The Well of Loneliness* could be considered a sensational book, the sexual implications of *Orlando* must have seemed daring indeed. The photographs of Vita herself would have made a reading

41 Bell, *Virginia Woolf*, II, 119. The wild goose could suggest that Orlando's literary efforts have amounted to a wild goose chase.

as a *roman à clef* irresistible, and many of the book's details, as we have seen, reward such a reading.

But while *Orlando* is a brilliant "biography" of Vita, it is also the story of the life of a culture. It brings five periods of English history to life in the experience of its central character, whose essence is the glory of the land. In that sense it anticipates the final novel, *Between the Acts*, which dramatizes English history—or the history of English literature—in a more complex and very different way. If *Between the Acts* is an elegy for that culture and its literature as they—and the narrative consciousness itself—pass into the ultimate emptiness and silence, *Orlando* remains a romance in celebration of the vitality and the glory of England and its poetry. In it Shakespeare is not an academic influence, but a constant, mysterious, living presence. And the narrative consciousness is Shakespearean in its creative vitality and spontaneity, imaginative scope, technical virtuosity, and tolerant humanity. Even today, the book remains an astonishing imaginative achievement.

The biographical and historical aspects of *Orlando* invite a feminist interpretation of English history and literature. The change of sex in the center of the story represents the crucial transformation of the relatively juvenile masculine values of Orlando's youth into the more feminine values of maturity. The masculine values are not denied or destroyed, but subsumed into a larger value system in which the more feminine traits are dominant. The successive eras of *Orlando* show this feminization as an evolutionary process leading toward higher, more fully and subtly developed, forms of awareness. The boy slicing at the head of the Moor at the beginning of the book is thus revealed as a primitive stage in the evolution of the androgynous woman who is in full command of her own personality and heritage at the end.

As a dramatization of intentionality, however, *Orlando* displays its own control from the very beginning. The narrative consciousness remains aloof from its characters throughout the story, except sometimes for Orlando—and even there it withdraws, when intimacy threatens, into playful lectures on the vicissitudes of "the biographer." In its admission of "his" difficulties, the narrative acknowledges, in a very veiled way, its own inability to achieve the androgynous whole-ness which it envisions for Orlando.

In a sense "he" asserts dominance over everything that Orlando represents: aristocracy, wealth, historical and literary tradition, the glory of the land and its culture. "He" transforms the virile Orlando into a beautiful woman, and then, at last, gives her back to her ridicu-lous husband. In its absolute control over this created world, then, the narrative consciousness appears godlike. Yet in that need for ab-solute transcendence, it poignantly reveals its own deep isolation and uncertainty.

CHAPTER VII

THE WAVES

After the expansive, liberating *jeux d'esprit* of *Orlando*, the lifework turns inward once again, to continue to explore the mysteries of consciousness. *To the Lighthouse* had carried that quest into the heart of the family, confronting the powerful archetypes of the father and the mother which overshadow, and both nourish and threaten, the tender growth of the child's consciousness. Now in *The Waves* the narrative searches for the origins and nature of consciousness itself. In that search the phenomena of the physical world are perceived as elements of the *consciousness of*, the state of intentionality. And there is now an enhanced awareness of language as both the instrument and the medium of the search. The strange, haunting formality of *The Waves* emphasizes the distance between the infinite richness of experience and the finite capacity of language to describe that experience. This distance is the domain of the poet, the archetypal linguistic creator. So *The Waves* begins with a poetic account of the origin of its world. Its biblical parallel is not with Genesis, in which the creation is from nothing, but St. John, in which the beginning was the Word.

The sun had not yet risen. The sea was indistinguishable from the sky, except that the sea was slightly creased as if a cloth had wrinkles in it. Gradually as the sky whitened a dark line lay on the horizon dividing the sea from the sky and the grey cloth became barred with thick strokes moving, one after another, beneath the sur-face, following each other, pursuing each other, perpetually.[1]

As the creation begins, the physical world is still latent, undifferentiated, a mass of potential energy. The sun is hidden; the illumination of the earth is still to come. Yet the world of nature is already perceived in very human terms. The metaphor of the cloth has human associations, and the fact that the sea is seen from a height implies a human perspective. As the paragraph reaches its climax, the waves themselves are perceived: moving, pulsing, perpetually. The language (e.g., *pursuing*) cannot remain entirely impersonal.

In the next paragraph the sea and the sky become more specifically humanized with a series of similes and personifications: the waves sigh *"like a sleeper whose breath comes and goes unconsciously"*; the horizon becomes clear *"as if the sediment in an old wine-bottle had sunk and left the glass green"*; illumination of the sky is *"as if the arm of a woman couched beneath the horizon had raised a lamp"*; and so on. The motifs of sleeping/dreaming and of illumination will later become very important. Now they emerge with the aura of myth, in images of an ancient world in which all phenomena are somehow created by the actions of the gods.

Throughout *The Waves* these italicized descriptive passages, or "interludes,"[2] reverberate with overtones of myth. This first interlude, especially, echoes the account of creation which opens the King James Bible: "In the beginning God created the heaven and the earth. And the earth was without form, and void; and darkness was upon the face of the deep. And the Spirit of God moved upon the face of the waters. And God said, Let there be light, and there was light." The passage in Genesis continues with the creation of Heaven and Earth, and all the riches of the earth, and at last man and woman, and for them a gar-

---

1 The text I refer to here is the first English edition of *The Waves* (London: Hogarth, 1931).

2 Various critics have used various terms to identify the two kinds of narration in *The Waves*. In her diary Virginia Woolf usually calls them *interludes* and *chapters*, and, on the whole, these terms seem as good as any. For the fullest account of the genesis of *The Waves*, see Virginia Woolf, *The Waves: The Two Holograph Drafts Transcribed and Edited by J. W. Graham* (Toronto: University of Toronto Press, 1976). Graham prefers the terms *interludes* and *episodes*.

den, in the midst of which stands the tree of life—and of knowledge of good and evil.

The pattern in the first interlude of *The Waves* is almost identical, except that God does not appear—at least, not in a form that we recognize immediately. In the beginning the earth is dark, formless, void. Then the illumination begins; sea and sky are differentiated. Most of the first interlude describes this illumination. The personifications attribute it to a woman, and the imagery relates it both to sexuality and to consciousness. (We may recall from *To the Lighthouse* that Lily's feeling for Paul Rayley had blazed up like a bonfire, and Minta's aura of sexuality had been a golden haze. Haze, incandescence, and transparency are also associated with the famous "luminous halo" of consciousness.) In *The Waves* the physical world of the interludes is always perceived through the radiance of human consciousness.

In the third and fourth (final) paragraphs of the first interlude the illumination extends to living things (the trees in the garden, the birds) and to human artifacts (the house, the blind, the window). Later interludes expand and modulate these descriptions. But the interludes invariably begin with the sun, the source of all life. In the closing paragraph, the illumination reaches the landscape and the house:

The light struck upon the trees in the garden, making one leaf transparent and then another. One bird chirped high up; there was a pause; another chirped lower down. The sun sharpened the walls of the house, and rested like the tip of a fan upon a white blind and made a blue finger-print of shadow under the leaf by the bedroom window. The blind stirred slightly, but all within was dim and unsubstantial. The birds sang their blank melody outside.

Thus the first interlude closes, with the *blank melody* of the birds. Why *blank*? Because the sound has no significance to the consciousness which perceives it. Yet *melody* implies an expectation of significance.

An expectation of significance, then, bridges the silence between the end of the interlude and the beginning of the chapter. Significance is to be discovered not *outside*, in the predestined patterns and sounds of the world of nature, but inside the house, where meaning may still be latent, though to the searching consciousness it appears *dim and unsubstantial*, opaque and uncertain. And so the quest for inner illumination begins:

"I see a ring," said Bernard, "hanging above me. It quivers and hangs in a loop of light."

"I see a slab of pale yellow," said Susan, "spreading away until it meets a purple stripe."

"I hear a sound," said Rhoda, "cheep, chirp; cheep, chirp; going up and down."

"I see a globe," said Neville, "hanging down in a drop against the enormous flanks of some hill."

"I see a crimson tassel," said Jinny, "twisted with gold threads."

"I hear something stamping," said Louis. "A great beast's foot is chained. It stamps, and stamps, and stamps."

This is the first of a series of speeches which, taken together, could be considered a kind of prologue. The chapter begins with three series of six speeches—one by each voice. Then in the fourth series the voice of Neville is absent. After another "complete" series, the voice of Bernard is absent from the sixth series. This prologue is followed by longer speeches by Louis and Jinny. Then what could be considered a dialogue between Susan and Bernard (eleven speeches) reveals their shared fantasy of "Elvedon." Next, longer speeches begin once again to differentiate several "characters": Rhoda ("All my ships are white"), Neville ("Where is Bernard?"), and Louis ("I will not conjugate the verb until Bernard has said it"). There is then a series of four short speeches concerned with that recitation of words, followed by longer speeches by Rhoda ("Now Miss Hudson") and Louis ("There Rhoda sits"), revealing that he is already attracted to her. Bernard and Jinny are then together briefly as he tells stories once again and she remains fascinated with her own body. After Jinny and then Susan speak about walking, there is a final series of speeches to bring the speakers to fuller revelation: Neville ("Since I am supposed to be too delicate to go with them": his revelation of his horrified discovery of "death among the apple trees"[3]), Susan ("I saw Florrie": her revelation of

3 For the meaning of "death among the apple trees" in Virginia Woolf's own childhood, see page 35 herein, note 8.

her discovery—less traumatic than Neville's, but shocking nonetheless—of sex among the servants), Louis ("Now we all rise": his expression of his awareness of their common fears and their desire to be together), Bernard ("Mrs. Constable, girt in a bath-towel": the much noticed "black arrows of sensation" speech), and finally Rhoda ("As I fold up my frock and chemise": her revelation of her profound fears and anxieties). The chapter ends with the speakers already significantly differentiated, and the dominant final chord is Rhoda's sensation of being out of control, overwhelmed: "Let me pull myself out of these waters. But they heap themselves on me; they sweep me between their great shoulders; I am turned; I am tumbled; I am stretched, among these long lights, these long waves, these endless paths, with people pursuing, pursuing."

This first chapter culminates in feelings of falling, loss of identity, distortion of perception, threatening darkness, drowning, helplessness, paranoia, and pursuit (the waves in the first paragraph of the interlude, too, were "pursuing"). And although Rhoda's consciousness represents the most extreme embodiment of these qualities, the other speakers are threatened by them too; Rhoda brings them to their fullest development in the speech which closes the chapter. If there is one quality which all six speakers share, it is a profound sense of determinism. Their strangely formal speeches record their feelings of awe at the things that *happen to* them, individually and collectively. "I see," "I hear," "I feel," "I burn, I shiver": these are the first realities of this "world"—raw sensations inflicted upon these victims. And even after a sense of community and interdependence develops, the speakers are still very much at the mercy of their destinies; even Bernard, the one who from the beginning seems to have the most promise for gaining some measure of control of his destiny, can report: "We troop upstairs like ponies. . . . We buffet, we tussle, we spring up and down on the hard, white beds. My turn has come. I come now." Despite the self-conscious heroism of Bernard's monologue in the final chapter, this feeling of predestined fatality remains predominant.

Just as the individual waves in the first interlude become visible as the light rises, so the individual personalities in the first chapter slowly become differentiated. The formality and tonal uniformity of the language of the speakers forces the narrative to differentiate them at some deeper level. The individual voices become differentiated through the qualities of their consciousness: what they think about, and how— especially the images which become characteristic of each. In retrospect we can hear these voices separately rather than in their immediate sequential contexts. This retrospective approach imposes a certain order that is false to the text itself, and enables us to discover certain patterns of clarity that are also, strictly speaking, false. The only way to fully know something, D. H. Lawrence said, is to kill it. But phenomenologists insist that we can "bracket" a text for an autopsy, and resurrect it at the end.

"'I see a ring,' said Bernard, 'hanging above me. It quivers and hangs in a loop of light.'" This is the first—and the last—of the six named speakers in *The Waves*. His first perception is of a ring of light, emblematic of the illumination which he will seek throughout his life and which his final summing up seems to achieve. The ring comes to symbolize completeness and wholeness, and thus Bernard's destiny— to bring the vast realms of awareness which are latent at the beginning of the book into illumination at the end—is foreshadowed in this first speech. The book itself becomes a symbolic ring which embodies all of the disparate forms of awareness within it, and all of this is revealed in the final chapter to be Bernard's creation: his consciousness subsumes all others in the work, even that of the interludes. This first perception is itself incorporated within that final luminous halo of awareness, when he recalls the nursery and that first perception: "I saw something brighten—no doubt the brass handle of a cupboard." Thus the inner illumination penetrating what had previously been "dim and unsubstantial," first comes to Bernard, who becomes at last the spokesman for the whole luminous halo of awareness which constitutes the book itself.

The position of the formal identification of the speaker ("said Bernard") within the speech subtly affects the meaning. If the speech had begun with "Bernard said," the emphasis would have been more on Bernard's identity than on the perception which enables us, eventually, to create that identity. Or if the speech had begun with "'I see a ring hanging above me,' said Bernard," the rhythm would be different and the relationship between speaker and speech slightly altered, with somewhat less emphasis on the ring and somewhat more on its position in relation to Bernard. So although the identification of the voices in *The Waves* is formulaic in one sense, that formula itself is modulated subtly throughout the book, in ways which enhance—often without our being conscious of it—our feeling of the tension and the space between what is said and what there is to say. Within this tension and this space, then, the creative consciousness—of reader as well as writer—is free to discover meaning.

"'Look at the spider's web on the corner of the balcony,' said Bernard. 'It has beads of water on it, drops of white light.'" The imagery of this second speech is also concerned with illumination and wholeness, and also implies the theme of *effort* which Virginia Woolf's diary (December 22, 1930) identifies as a major theme of *The Waves*. The image of the spider's web recurs in several later contexts which emphasizes its beauty, complexity, delicacy, and its power to capture. It becomes a metaphor for the organic growth of the personality: as Jinny says, "our senses have widened. Membranes, webs of nerves . . . [capture] faraway sounds unheard before." The latent significance, then, of this second perception of Bernard's reaches its fullest development in his final monologue, where it becomes the ultimate ontological symbol: "the being eviscerated—drawn out, spun like a spider's web and twisted in agony round a thorn." The "drops of water" on the web connote purity, fertility, renewal; and they link this conventional (after "The Waste Land") motif with that of the fulfillment of time, which becomes a major theme at the beginning of the seventh chapter: "'And time,' said Bernard, 'lets fall its drop.'" The "white light," not yet differentiated into colors by the prism of the imagination, echoes the opening theme of creative illumination. The fact that Bernard sees the corner of the balcony suggests that the children may be outside the house now; this seems confirmed by other speeches in this second series. And the fact that his speech begins with "Look" breaks the pattern of "I see, I hear" which marked the first series; perhaps it also foreshadows Bernard's destiny as a writer, who will ask his audience to share his perceptions. At any rate, it is the first speech to reach beyond the boundaries of the self toward the audience which is only implied in "I see, I hear."

" 'Now the cock crows like a spurt of hard, red water in the white tide,' said Bernard." The first word of this third speech came to have an almost mystical significance for Virginia Woolf; it is fitting that Bernard, who becomes her spokesman at last, is the first to announce the present moment in *The Waves*. *Now* is always an intensifier, and usually incantatory, in the book. The first eight interludes begin with "The"; the fact that the ninth begins with "Now" announces, subliminally at least, its transcendent significance. And the ninth chapter also begins with that word: " 'Now to sum up,' said Bernard. 'Now to explain to you the meaning of my life.' " The experience of the language of the book makes us realize, without necessarily being conscious of it, that *now* has these special kinds of significance. And so we are prepared to realize the truth that the ninth interlude subsumes all other interludes, the ninth chapter all other chapters. The rest of this third speech connects, rather obviously, the themes of time, sensuality, and the cycles of life. Bernard's perception of those relationships reveals the comprehensiveness of his insight.

" 'The walls are cracked with gold cracks,' said Bernard, 'and there are blue, finger-shaped shadows of leaves beneath the windows.' " The imagery in this fourth speech is rather familiar in Virginia Woolf's symbolic landscapes, and not too obscure even for readers unacquainted with those other landscapes, though it does have a complexity and indeterminacy which transcend the merely conventional. The "walls" are those of the house; they enclose and shelter as well as exclude. The cracks in them are perceived as "gold"; perhaps this foreshadows Bernard's ability to discover warmth, life, and value in what others might perceive as flaws and discontinuities. The consciousness of light and shadow is another sign of the comprehensiveness of his imagination. Since "leaves" are used rather conventionally in *The Waves* to indicate cycles of the seasons, the passage of time, their shadows here may be significant; Bernard becomes the ultimate lecturer on these themes. The "finger-shaped" shadows further humanize the insight, and link it subliminally with the language of the interlude which speaks of "*a blue finger-print of shadow under the leaf by the bedroom window."* "Windows," as we know from *To the Light-house*—if not from Henry James himself—are the apertures of perception and illumination. Here they seem to locate Bernard's feelings more precisely on the plane of the "walls," and to suggest that those walls are not absolute.

" 'The dining-room window is dark blue now,' said Bernard, 'and the air ripples above the chimneys.' " In this fifth perception attention is even more precisely located: "the windows" have given way to one window. The dining-room becomes simply "the room" in the interludes; the sun illuminates it, constantly modulating the appearance of its furnishings, but the room always remains achingly empty. In the chapters, the two dinners at which the six speakers gather are symbolic communions, like Mrs. Ramsay's climactic dinner in Part I of *To the Lighthouse*. Bernard's awareness of the dining-room window, then, seems significant. The "dark blue" signifies the obscurity and mystery of that space. The word most strongly emphasized positionally, however, is *now*; this word lends immediacy and intensity. The air rippling above the chimneys here, like the air which moves the tapestry in *Orlando*, connotes the ambiance of "now," the infinite, perpetually changing possibilities of what Virginia Woolf so often called "the moment." The air ripples because of the house, yet "above" it, in some realm of vague, potential transcendence.

Bernard's voice is missing from the sixth series of speeches in the first chapter. The reasons—if any—for this are not clear, but the rather rhythmic or musical structure of the sequences of speeches can make us feel this absence. Perhaps this voice has vanished into the mysterious space which its last two speeches had suggested—into the dark blue shadows in which, as in Mrs. Ramsay's wedge-shaped core of darkness or in the world of *The Waves* before sunrise, the deepest sources of creativity are contained. Perhaps this is a subliminal hint that this voice is qualitatively different from the others whose speeches close this prologue, though our discovery that those voices will be contained in that of "Bernard" must be postponed until the very end.

Bernard's five perceptions in the opening prologue are primarily visual; in the third he even translates an initially aural perception into visual terms. The imagery, as we have seen, often follows that of the earlier fiction; thus the reader who approaches *The Waves* from that direction will have some cues for its interpretation. Another dimension of the visual imagery, somewhat more difficult to interpret but cumulatively significant, is its colors. The implications of colors throughout *The Waves*, and throughout the lifework, are rather consistent. To some extent color itself constitutes a universal language: color preferences can be very revealing. In *The Waves*, of course, this process involves the selection of colors and sequences of colors not from a narrowly limited and controlled field, but from an unlimited range of possibilities. The colors of Bernard's consciousness may be interpreted both in the context of Virginia Woolf's novels as a whole and in the light of more "objective," standardized values.[4]

The primary elements of vision, light and darkness, appear in the very first words of the book, and the first interlude as a whole shows that creation begins with illumination. Bernard's first perception, of a ring which "quivers and hangs in a loop of light," connects him with this first principle of creation. It reveals a personality which looks toward the light, toward the future. His second perception, of a spider's web which holds beads of water, "drops of white light," reveals a similar desire: white suggests affirmation and potentiality, and perhaps the pages which Bernard, as writer, has yet to begin. The colors of his other perceptions in the prologue are also coherent and consistent with what the narrative discloses in other ways.

The five opening speeches of Bernard, then, reveal a personality that moves instinctively toward the light and toward completeness. It moves relentlessly, but with an innate sense of the rich beauty and complexity of its environment and a patient faith in its own destiny and in the potentialities of time to bring about its fulfillment. Its insights into the dynamics of the present are deep and comprehensive. It is not paralyzed by the ambiguities of its own awareness, but discovers value in phenomena which less thoughtful personalities might perceive only as anomalies. It regards all phenomena as mysterious—

---

4 For example, see Max Lüscher, *The Lüscher Color Test*, trans. and ed. Ian A. Scott (New York: Random House, 1969). Dr. Lüscher's tests are rather widely used in Europe as diagnostic tools by psychological therapists. My comments on the psychological significance of colors in *The Waves* are indebted to his work.

that is, as manifestations of the immanent mystery. Its perceptions are primarily visual, or find expression, at least, largely in visual terms. Despite the particularity of these insights, their terms are not idiosyncratic, but compatible with the vision of others. Its ultimate fate is inherent in the possibilities of this beginning. It becomes "fate," however, only after these possibilities have been developed, and their governing principles discovered, in the larger structures of their "story."

" 'I see a slab of pale yellow,' said Susan, 'spreading away until it meets a purple stripe.' " In this first speech of the second voice in *The Waves* we also see a personality that turns toward the light—not the more inclusive "light" of Bernard's first perception, but the "pale yellow" which is further limited by "a purple stripe." The word *yellow* is used most often in the book to denote that specific color; in those contexts where it is used in a broader, connotative way it is associated with the sun and sunshine, lamps, "fiery" words, and warmth. In describing the experience which seems to represent her traumatic discovery of the world, Susan later says that "The yellow warmth in my side turned to stone when I saw Jinny kiss Louis"; this makes more explicit the latent frustration implied in her first speech, and foreshadows a life whose deliberate choices (marriage to a farmer in Lincolnshire, commitment to domesticity, child-bearing, etc.) can be seen as defiant responses to this sense of frustration. The latent meaning of the "purple stripe" also becomes explicit in a later speech: "I shall be sullen, storm-tinted and all one purple. I shall be debased and hide-bound by the bestial and beautiful passion of maternity." Susan's first perception seems to have great autobiographical significance for Virginia Woolf herself; its language is almost identical to that of the "most important of all my memories" in "A Sketch of the Past."[5]

5 "If life has a base that it stands upon, if it is a bowl that one fills and fills and fills— then my bowl without a doubt stands upon this memory. It is of lying half asleep, half awake, in bed in the nursery at St. Ives. It is of hearing the waves breaking, one, two, one, two, and sending a splash of water over the beach; and then breaking, one, two, one, two, behind a yellow blind. . . . hearing this splash and seeing this light, and feeling, it is almost impossible that I should be here; of feeling the purest ecstasy I can conceive" (*Moments of Being*, 64–65). The reader of *The Waves* will recognize in "A Sketch of the Past," written in April, 1939, many of the central images and motifs of the novel—and the *oeuvre*. The first chapter of the novel explores the same memories which

"'The leaves are gathered round the window like pointed ears,' said Susan." This second speech anticipates Bernard's fourth speech in its perception of the leaves around the window; the implications of those two images are present here too. Susan's perception of the leaves as "pointed ears" reveals her affinity with the world of nature, and perhaps a feeling that nature somehow listens to human consciousness—or even that it may stalk that consciousness (the reflexive possibilities seem unlimited, and are heightened by "gathered").

"'A caterpillar is curled in a green ring,' said Susan, 'notched with blunt feet.'" Positionally, the green ring is emphasized in Susan's third speech. Although the ring is primarily Bernard's symbol, the other voices speak of rings too, and in the process differentiate themselves. Susan's ring, obviously, is that of nature. In the psychology of color, green is chosen by the passive, defensive personality; this seems consistent with most of the uses of the word in *The Waves*. Bernard is the only other voice in the book to mention a caterpillar—on Jinny's neck. We might allow this caterpillar to escape if we didn't know that it could metamorphose into one of those creatures which haunt the dark center of Virginia Woolf's imagination (the other title which she seriously considered for this book was, in fact, *The Moths*). Nature's mysterious transformations, then, and the beautiful, fascinating, and self-destructive potentialities of natural creatures may be implied here.

"'Birds are singing up and down and in and out all round us,' said Susan." Positionally, "all around us" is emphasized—an awareness of the environment and of community. This is what is missing from the perception which this seems to echo most closely: Rhoda's first speech. The motif of birds, also important in connection with Rhoda, reappears in Susan's final speech in the book: "Still I gape, like a young bird, unsatisfied, for something that has escaped me." This final speech seems to solidify the feeling of frustration which had been present in her personality from the first.

"'Now Mrs. Constable pulls up her thick, black stockings,' said

---

the essay recalls, and the six voices begin speaking about those memories in such a way that each voice explores a particular facet—perhaps a destiny—of the possibilities awakened in that nursery at St. Ives. The final chapter, spoken by Bernard, integrates—or claims to—all of those diverse possibilities into one transcendent whole.

Susan." Positionally, the black stockings are emphasized, and make the perception seem even more cryptic. Later contexts make it reflexively more meaningful. Susan herself reveals one meaning of blackness in her meditation on her own polarization between the extremes of love and hate: "'It is hate, it is love,' said Susan." "That is the furious coal-black stream that makes us dizzy if we look down into it," and we begin to understand why Susan could not say this earlier. Mrs. Constable, an old woman, wears black stockings—not the gaudy colors which Jinny will choose, or the green which will, in a sense, be chosen for Susan, yet Mrs. Constable's stockings clothe the same mortal reality. And it is she who, raising her sponge in the bath, initiates those "black arrows of sensation" in what Bernard remembers as his most formative experience.

"'A swallow is perched on the lightning-conductor,' said Susan. 'And Biddy has smacked down the bucket on the kitchen flags.'" This is Susan's sixth and final speech of the "prologue." Positionally, the emphasis is on the lightning-conductor, where the ambient electrical field is "grounded" in the earth—an appropriate, as well as highly imaginative, metaphor for Susan herself. The swallow provides another subliminal link with Rhoda, the only other voice to mention swallows: Rhoda's are always feminine, and always envisioned as dipping their wings in "midnight pools" on "the other side of the world"; Susan's are less fully realized, and always local: typically they "skim the grass." This final perception of the prologue, then, suggests that Susan "sees" the swallow too, but refuses to follow its flight; she turns, instead, to the almost violently mundane perception which ends up her speech.

The personality disclosed by the voice of Susan in this "prologue" seems more confined than that of Bernard. Like him, she is drawn toward the light, but toward a narrower spectrum of illumination, delimited by threatening realms of darkness. In that darkness things exist which she is aware of but refuses to recognize, and rejects violently in favor of the earthy and the domestic. Her attention is focused instead on environmental and communal values and a kind of vegetative completion which, predictably, will leave her unsatisfied. She represents a personality rather foreign in most ways to Virginia

Woolf herself; perhaps that is why her voice seems, for many readers, less interesting than the others.

Yet Susan moves to the forefront in this prologue. In the first two series of speeches her voice follows that of Bernard, the first speaker. But in the remaining four series her voice is heard first. Of the six speakers she comes closest to becoming a spokesman for society, and of the six she conforms most fully to the social role assigned to her: Woman, thou shalt marry and bear children, cook and keep house, obey thy master. . . . In that sense Susan's voice becomes antiphonal to those of the other personalities, and of course, to that of Virginia Woolf herself.

"'I hear a sound,' said Rhoda, 'cheep, chirp; cheep, chirp; going up and down.'" It is significant that Rhoda's first perception is aural, and the position of "sound" in her speech emphasizes that. This aural emphasis also suggests her affinity with Louis, the only other character to "hear" in this first series.

Rhoda's mysterious affinity with the birds of the interludes is also apparent from this moment—though what the birds may "mean" in *The Waves* is more obscure. The narrative sees them in many different ways, from its first perceptions of them in the first interlude, with its enigmatic closing sentence (*"The birds sang their blank melody outside"*) to its final straining after a dying sound in the ninth interlude (*"There was no sound save the cry of a bird seeking some lonelier tree"*). It is especially fascinated by their eyes, golden and penetrating, which at times seem to gaze directly into the sun and to be *"intensely conscious of one object in particular."* The birds behave mysteriously: at one moment *"lovelily they came descending, delicately declining,"* and at the next they *"spiked the soft, monstrous body of the defenseless worm"* and dig in the *"purulence"* of the rotting subsoil. And though the narrative consciousness listens intently to their songs, they remain finally a *"blank melody."* The birds seem to represent an entirely instinctive form of life which moves quickly, *"lovelily,"* and brutally in accordance with sudden imperatives, at once beautiful and terrifying. And in Bernard's final summing up, the birds of the interludes become identified with the females of the chapters: "with what a whirr the birds rise! You know the rush of wings, that exclamation, carol, and confusion; the riot and babble of voices; and all the drops are sparkling, trembling . . . and a bird sings close to the window. I heard those songs. I followed those phantoms. . . . And from among them rise one or two distinct figures, birds who sang with the rapt egotism of youth by the window; broke their snails on stones, dipped their beaks in sticky, viscous matter ; hard, avid, remorseless; Jinny, Susan, Rhoda." It is Rhoda's fate, apparently, to be born with this awareness. And her own conduct, both as she describes it and as others see it, seems often to merge with the mysterious actions of the birds which the narrative describes in the interludes.

" 'Islands of light are swimming on the grass,' said Rhoda. 'They have fallen through the trees.' " Her second perception moves more toward metaphor than the second speeches of any of the other personalities, and it reveals an awareness of causality which is also unique for this stage of development. The light is the same as that perceived by Bernard, except that Rhoda's perception is not of a "ring," but of fragmented light. This foreshadows her lifelong inability to unify her "world," and may foreshadow her suicide (as the word *fallen* forecasts her method). Trees become symbolic, in Bernard's final speech, of the organic growth of being: "The mind grows rings; the identity becomes robust." The metaphoric swimming links Rhoda's perception here with the complex imagery of the waves and with the pastoral implications of "grass" (the word becomes almost an emblem for nature in its purest stage) throughout the book.

This second perception is deepened in the third: " 'The grey-shelled snail draws across the path and flattens the blades behind him,' said Rhoda." Grey, in color preference tests, is often chosen by a personality that does not wish to be stimulated or involved. Furthermore, Rhoda sees not only "the grass" but its individual blades as well; this kind of vision is, in *The Waves*, a feminine trait, exemplified by Jinny and Susan and by the birds of the interludes.[6] The snail is the

6 See my quotation from Bernard on page 217. It is as if the narrative consciousness sees the behavior of the birds, which it has watched with such fascination throughout the interludes, as an analog in the world of "insensitive nature" for the essence of the female in the human world.

first of many which fascinate the narrative consciousness: in the interludes the beautiful birds smash the snails' shells "furiously" and probe the "purulence" gracefully. There also seems to be a subtle, subliminal linking of this process of preying in general, and of the snail in particular, with Rhoda and Louis: Louis speaks of "Rhoda, with her intense abstraction, with her unseeing eyes the colour of snail's flesh"; Susan says that "Louis regards the wall opposite with snail-green eyes."

" 'Cold water begins to run from the scullery tap,' said Rhoda, 'over the mackerel in the bowl.' " This fourth perception seems mysterious. Like the mackerel which is cut into bait while still alive in Part III of *To the Lighthouse*, this one may be perceived as another reminder of man's atavistic cruelty; at least, a sensitive child might perceive it in this way (which seems reinforced by Neville's perception that "Now Biddy scrapes the fish scales with a jagged knife on to a wooden board"). Many of the other references to fish in *The Waves* seem to focus on their timeless role as prey (*e.g.*, in Bernard's vision of a naked man spearing fish in blue waters, or Rhoda's of fishermen on the verge of the world) and their helplessness (*e.g.*, in several references to fish stranded in tidal pools).

" 'The birds sang in chorus first,' said Rhoda. 'Now the scullery door is unbarred. Off they fly. Off they fly like a fling of seed. But one sings by the bedroom window alone.' " In her fifth speech Rhoda again perceives the birds: at first they sing in chorus, then fly off "like a fling of seed," and she notices that "one sings by the bedroom window alone." Bernard's comment, much later in the book, that "I may have children, may cast a fling of seed," shows that Rhoda's speech here does indeed have a latent sexual meaning. Her later feelings of being "flung far" by her emotional instability are also foreshadowed in this perception. The bird singing by the bedroom window expands this perception into the aural realm as well as the visual, and links this moment with the illumination of the house in the interlude ("*The sun ... made a blue finger-print of shadow under the leaf by the bedroom window*") as well as with Rhoda's own first perception. It also connects the moment with the extraordinary second paragraph of the fourth interlude, in which the narrative describes how "*the birds sang in the sunshine, each alone. One sang under the bedroom window . . . "* and goes on to report how each *"sang stridently, with passion, with vehemence . . . no matter if it shattered the song of another bird with harsh discord."* And with increasing fascination the narrative sees the birds picking through garbage, smashing snails "furiously," soaring "sharply" to high vantage points where their gleaming eyes watch the life below; their songs blend and separate, inexplicably. Later in the book Bernard draws an analogy between the individual personality and the bird which " perched solitary outside some bedroom window and sang of love, of fame and other single experiences so dear to the callow bird with a yellow tuft in its beak." The reflexive implication for Rhoda's fifth perception may be that it signals her isolation and her helpless fixations upon "single" things; unlike Bernard, she will never have a real chance for the luminous ring of completion and fulfillment.

"'Look at the table-cloth, flying white along the table,' said Rhoda. 'Now there are rounds of white china, and silver streaks beside each plate.'" Positionally, the word emphasized in Rhoda's final speech of the prologue is *table*. In *The Waves* tables become rather important because of their human associations: at tables the lady in the garden at Elvedon writes, the six speakers dine (first in London with Percival, then at Hampton Court without him), Jinny secretly touches her lovers, Susan kneads bread, and so on. Tables become sacramental. The table Rhoda sees here is empty, like the one throughout the interludes, prepared for a communion which never comes. The tablecloth seems important too: later contexts associate tablecloths with feelings of blankness and expectancy, and they become reflectors of personality—as when Jinny's fingers dance along a tablecloth or touch someone else's fingers beneath it, or when Susan hides her hardened hands beneath it, or when Rhoda focuses her attention on the yellow stains on it lest she "fall alone through this thin sheet into gulfs of fire." The feeling of blankness and expectancy is best exemplified, however, in Neville's perception of the tablecloth in the earlier dinner: "Things quiver as if not yet in being. The blankness of the white tablecloth glares." Whiteness, of course, is associated with Rhoda early in the book, especially with the white petals which are the ships she sails in her lonely fantasies. In connection with Bernard's perceptions we have already noted white as the color of the page on which the story has yet to be written. In other significant contexts in *The Waves* white becomes associated with the waves themselves (especially their dissolution), with death, with emptiness, with renewal, with purity, and with unprotectedness. All of these qualities make it an appropriate color for Rhoda. In this last perception of hers in the prologue, the white tablecloth and white china give way to the silver which is the final color of the perception. In all of the contexts where silver seems to have some meaning beyond the merely literal, that meaning is death.[7] One other aspect of this final perception seems especially striking: the description of the tablecloth as "flying." This is an early indication that reality will not hold still for Rhoda, that situations and even artifacts which we regard as solid or stable may, for her, dissolve into terrifying instability. Her consciousness is haunted by fears of falling, the other side of which is a transcendent dream of flying. Both sides reach their consummation in her suicide.

The personality revealed by the opening speeches of Rhoda may be the most fascinating in *The Waves*—partly because Rhoda, like Septimus in *Mrs. Dalloway*, is so obviously related to Virginia Woolf's own insanity and eventual suicide, but also because of the nature of Rhoda's consciousness: a strangely beautiful but deeply frightening realm which at some points touches the more familiar worlds of awareness which the other personalities inhabit, but which essentially lies far beyond them, in an unknown region from which no traveler may really return. From the moment that we discover her world— actually recognize it—we know she is lost. Her mysterious affinity with the instinctive life of the birds, her sudden, intense, and helpless

7 Neville's discovery of "death among the apple trees" provides him with a memory of "the implacable tree with its greaved silver bark," and several chapters later he thinks of the "apple tree with its silver leaves held stiff" (for the origin of "death among the apple trees" see page 35, note 8.) Susan says, "I also make wreaths of white flowers, twisting silver-leaved plants among them for the dead," and she later speaks of a "silver-grey flickering moth-wing" (throughout the *oeuvre* the moth is an emblem for the irresistible impulses which lead to self destruction). And in his summing up, Bernard speaks of all their personalities as "a seven-sided flower, many petalled, red, puce, purple-shaded, stiff with silver-tinted leaves" (associated subliminally with "death among the apple trees," these leaves foreshadow Percival's death in the next chapter).

fixations upon random phenomena, the compulsive, fragmented quality of her vision, her seemingly absolute sensitivity and susceptibility, her premature sexual awareness and anxieties, her longing for some transcendent communion, and for death—all of this discloses a personality incompatible with survival in the worlds which Susan or the others inhabit. Rhoda seems even less free than the others to choose her world; rather, her world seems to inflict itself upon her.

"'I see a globe,' said Neville, 'hanging down in a drop against the enormous flanks of some hill.'" Neville's first perception reveals—at least in retrospect—his penchant for order and for completion. Here as elsewhere in Virginia Woolf's writing, the image of the globe is used as a symbol for human experience; it is like the ring, but three-dimensional, complete in itself. The ring can be penetrated in one dimension, and it often has an aura which suffuses its surroundings or its beholders; the globe is something primarily to be contemplated, turned and studied from many different perspectives. This analytical detachment is characteristic of Neville; he is not less sensitive than the others, but he is never lost in his sensations, however powerful they may be. He always sees things, as he does here, against a background, in a context. His perceptions are more colorless than those of the other personalities. The background in this first perception seems rather vague, and perhaps overwhelming: "the enormous flanks of some hill." Perhaps this vaguely menacing, vaguely sexual phrase reveals something of the origins of Neville's drive for success, which Louis later summarizes succinctly: "Neville mounts rapidly to the conspicuous heights." Neville's compulsive climbing, then, may be foreshadowed in this vaguely menacing hill which forms the background of his first perception. Exactly what he literally sees here is never revealed. If we assume that the children are inside the nursery during their first perceptions, then he would be looking out of the window here; perhaps the drop he sees may be like the dewdrop of Bernard's third perception. The word *drop* is used later in the book to suggest the gathering and passage of time: "'And time,' said Bernard, 'lets fall its drop'" is the sentence which opens the seventh chapter; it announces a theme which becomes very important as the book reaches its climax. Perhaps that theme too is suggested in Neville's first perception, and motivates his drive toward achievement.

"'The birds' eyes are bright in the tunnels between the leaves,' said Neville." Rhoda, of course, is the personality most closely associated with the birds of the interludes; Neville's awareness of the bright eyes of the birds links him with her: it shows that he is sensitive to the instincts which the birds embody—their sudden perceptions, their automatic actions. The tunnels between the leaves may remind us of the tunnels which haunted Virginia Woolf's first heroine, Rachel Vinrace: they seem to represent the narrowing corridors of her destiny. And so the tunnels here disclose a perception of the natural world ("between the leaves") in which bright-eyed predators lurk menacingly. Tunnels in *The Waves* too are darkly deterministic. During Rhoda's identity crisis, when she suddenly finds herself unable to step over a puddle, she says that "I was wafted down tunnels." The most important instance of this imagery in the book, however, is in Jinny's consciousness. During her ride to the North out of London the train enters a tunnel, and she notices the man sitting opposite her smiling at her reflection in the darkened window. It seems to be a revelation to her of life's essential sexuality and of her own destiny: swept along in the tunnel of dark passion and unspoken needs, smiling bravely into the darkened glass. The train leaves the tunnel before Jinny's discovery reaches the ultimate horrors of Rachel's nightmares: the oozing walls, the bestial, deformed, "gibbering" man who lurks in the "vault" at the end. But the experience is traumatic enough for Jinny to recall it at least twice later in the book.

"'Stones are cold to my feet,' said Neville. 'I feel each one, round or pointed, separately.'" This speech reinforces the link with Rhoda's extreme sensitivity: both she and Neville share, to some extent, the kind of vision that the birds have—the ability, or perhaps the compulsion, to see "the single object." In this third perception, of course, the emphasis is on *feeling*; Neville feels single sensations. Stone in *The Waves* has many of its traditional symbolic connotations: heaviness, enduringness, lifelessness, emotionlessness. The birds break snails against stone, and the waves break on the stone of the shore; in one instance stone breaks on rock, revealing Rhoda's compounded anguish: "I want publicity and violence and to be dashed like a stone on the rocks."

Neville's voice is absent from the fourth series of speeches. Why? The three preceding series have established a pattern in which each of the six voices is heard. Is there something in Neville's personality which requires that his voice be the first of the six to be absent, suppressed, or for some other reason, unheard? The sequence of speeches teases too. In the first two series, Neville's voice has followed Rhoda's; in the third Louis's voice comes between them. In the first three series Neville's voice has come just before Jinny's. If these sequences "mean" anything, then, it is that Neville's fourth speech would be expected just before the voice of Jinny. But what does that slight expectation—and its frustration—mean? Is Neville already hiding from us, and from the others? Here, as in the discontinuity between the interlude and the first series of speeches, the form itself invites the silence to speak.

"'Now Biddy scrapes the fish-scales with a jagged knife on to a wooden board,' said Neville." His voice returns in the fifth series of speeches, now just after Jinny's. We have already seen, in the discussion of Rhoda's perceptions, that the fish here and elsewhere are emblems of helplessness. The jagged knife too is probably related to similar instruments elsewhere, from the one used in grisly decapitation of chickens in *The Voyage Out* to the "arid scimitar" of the male which James somehow knows is killing his mother in *To the Lighthouse*. Neville, of course, discloses in his first long speech the traumatic experience of "death among the apple trees" which he feels has marked him for life. Biddy and her jagged knife, then, do seem to signal a profound psychic conflict which is already latent in Neville—and which, indeed, he himself will never fully recognize despite the many ways in which his speeches reveal it. His fear of women and his homosexuality both seem, in retrospect, to be implied in this speech.

"'Suddenly a bee booms in my ear,' said Neville. 'It is here; it is past.'" The first word of Neville's final speech of the "prologue" seems important: the suddenness of the perception is what he finds exciting and disturbing. This is related, no doubt, to his preoccupation with time and with achievement. The idea of intrusion is also disturbing to him; he will guard his privacy and his emotions fiercely. In *The Waves* the bee as intruder is seen in one other important context: at the graduation ceremony at the boys' school, where it is seen through the consciousness of Bernard as a reminder of real life, the present moment, etc. These implications are present in Neville's perception too. Positionally, the word *ear* is emphasized; the aural nature of the perception associates Neville with Rhoda and Louis, who seem more sensitive to sound.

The opening speeches of Neville reveal a personality aspiring to order and completion, viewing its experiences with analytical detachment, and deeply motivated toward success and independence, escape from dominance. He is in touch with very deep instincts in the natural world and in other personalities, but his own deep-seated fears inhibit his own behavior. Thus his extreme sensitivity is guarded by an unrelenting coldness and sometimes by total withdrawal. His sexual fears, especially of women, are very deep, but above all he fears helplessness. Despite his guardedness, however, he is constantly vulnerable to sudden sensations, and to the intrusion of inescapable realities.

" 'I see a crimson tassel,' said Jinny, 'twisted with gold threads.' " The colors of Jinny's first perception are vivid. Crimson suggests sensuality, blood, aggression, optimism, immediacy. And gold, in Virginia Woolf's palette, seems more "autonomous"—more capable of being chosen by the personality, rather than imposed from outside—than yellow; gold tends to appear in contexts where it implies value—not just monetary value but value which can be endowed by human consciousness. For instance, in the dawn of the first interlude "the sea blazed gold" not because "gold" describes light of a certain wavelength but because it describes the qualities which the creative consciousness perceives in the light. The tassel, beautiful and decorative rather than merely functional, is the kind of thing that Jinny will always be drawn toward. The word *twisted* has interesting ironic possibilities. Does the speech imply that sensuality is twisted by the values which the consciousness assigns to it? Is Jinny herself ever aware of this?

" 'The stalks are covered with harsh, short hairs,' said Jinny, 'and drops of water have stuck to them.' " This second speech may foreshadow her involvement with Louis, who thinks of himself as a stalk: "I am the stalk. My roots go down to the depths of the world." He has cut a flower stalk, and is peering through it when Jinny discovers him and, perceiving him as dead, impulsively kisses him. This is the kiss that Susan sees; it remains as traumatic for her as, apparently, for Louis and Jinny. The drops of water that Jinny sees on the stalks reflect her personality; just as Neville sees a drop of water as a globe against the "enormous" background of a hill, and Bernard notices the drops of water on a spider's web, so Jinny finds hers on "stalks" which seem, if not phallic, at least vaguely masculine.

"'The back of my hand burns,' said Jinny, 'but the palm is clammy and damp with dew.'" Hands in *The Waves* can be important signs of psychological states. Jinny's hands usually seem to indicate her sensuality. In her first waking moments in the morning, she says, "My hands pass over my legs and body" as if to confirm, for another day, the central reality of her existence. In her third speech here the almost schizoid quality of that sensuality is foreshadowed. She is sensitive both to the heat of the sun and the chill of the dew, and she feels both at once, and is unable to reconcile them. Positionally, *burns* is emphasized, and this burning sexuality is, of course, her dominant trait. The image is ubiquitous: sex "burns" throughout the *oeuvre*.

"'Look at the house,' said Jinny, 'with all its windows white with blinds.'" Jinny's fourth speech seems more obscure than her third. Although the house receives positional emphasis, the perception culminates in the "windows white with blinds." When we think of the meanings of windows in other works, especially in *To the Lighthouse*, the fact that they are perceived here as opaque and white (*i.e.*, latent with meaning but not yet "readable") may imply that they have something to do with Jinny's inability to discover any "final" meaning. Perhaps the blinds also suggest her inability to get in touch with anyone else except in a purely physical sense. She will never fully enter the house of life, but will remain outside, gazing at windows which will always remain opaque for her.

"'Bubbles form on the floor of the saucepan,' said Jinny. 'Then they rise, quicker and quicker, in a silver chain to the top.'" This fifth speech repeats, in a rather indirect way, the motifs of fire and water of her second and third (and possibly first, also) speeches. The bubbles, like the effervescence of her personality, are "formed" by the fire and become a "silver chain" in the medium of water, rising to the top and escaping into the ambiance. The "silver," as we saw earlier, is linked subliminally with death—though that can be seen only in retrospect. This fifth speech then becomes more intensely personal in the sixth: "'I burn, I shiver,' said Jinny, 'out of this sun, into this shadow.'" The "prologue" as a whole closes with this sixth speech of Jinny's. The word "shiver" is emphasized positionally, and the direction of the speech is away from heat and sunshine toward cold and shadow: symbolically, toward the eternal night to which the whole book returns after Bernard's triumphant final monologue. Thus the direction of the prologue foreshadows the course of the book as a whole.

The speech also deepens our awareness of the very deep conflict within Jinny's personality. She both burns and shivers; her sensuality emerges as a denial of the ever-present reality of death. Her primal gesture is her kiss of Louis, and it enacts her defiance of death: "'Is he dead?' I thought, and kissed you." But Jinny's final turning, here in the "prologue," is toward the shadow.

Her opening speeches, then, reveal a personality that manifests itself primarily in sensual terms. Her immediate desire for sensual stimulation may be potentially "twisted"; in any case she is exceptionally aware of the males in the world. Her personality is effervescent, driven by the fire of passion toward dispersion in the ambient atmosphere, but tempted also by the shadows. Despite her desperate reaching out, society, home, and the family remain essentially closed to her, and opaque. From her primal longing for the crimson-and-gold tassel, she is drawn at last toward the shadow.

"'I hear something stamping,' said Louis. 'A great beast's foot is chained. It stamps, and stamps, and stamps.'" Like Rhoda's first perception, Louis's is aural; perhaps this signals their latent closeness. Positionally, *stamping* is emphasized; apparently the relentless repetition of the sound impresses Louis here, and several of his later speeches about the "great beast" emphasize that repetition. Later contexts reveal that the beast is death.[8] The crash of the waves on the shore becomes inseparable from this idea, and thus the final sentence of the book, *"The waves broke on the shore,"* moves Bernard's peroration against death into a final ironic silence.

"'A shadow falls on the path,' said Louis, 'like an elbow bent.'" Louis' second speech suggests the unhappiness—even fatality—which shadows the path of life. This is consistent, of course, with the uses of shadow and light we have noted in connection with the other voices. Positional emphasis on "the path" foreshadows Louis' later sense of duty. The "elbow bent"—hard for the American reader to dissociate from barroom jokes—probably speaks more subtly of tentativeness, the potentiality of human gestures, the changing shapes and planes of living sculpture, etc.

"'And burning lights from the window-panes flash in and out of the grasses,' said Louis." This third speech continues the theme of illumination. He sees the same windows as Jinny, apparently, but not in the same way; while to her they are rendered opaque by the blinds, to him they flash "burning lights" on the grass. The quality of this light seems threatening: "burning." And it seems surprising or unpredictable in its flashing in and out. Louis, like Jinny, is aware of the house, and can no more enter it than she can. To him it is the source of flashing, burning energy which now illuminates, now shadows, the leaves of grass.

"'The beast stamps; the elephant with its foot chained; the great brute on the beach stamps,' said Louis." His fourth speech returns to the theme of his first. Now the beast is specifically an elephant—which provides a further link with death, in the story which Bernard tells Jinny, set "in a malarial jungle. There is an elephant white with maggots, killed by an arrow shot dead in its eye."[9] The repetition, the

---

8 The links between death and the "great beast stamping" build throughout the book, but are revealed most dramatically in the unspoken bridge between the fifth interlude and the fifth chapter:

The waves fell; withdrew and fell again, like the thud of a great beast stamping.

"He is dead," said Neville. "He fell. His horse tripped. He was thrown."

9 From a biographical standpoint, the elephant strengthens the association of Louis with Leonard Woolf, who served for seven years in the Colonial Service in Ceylon, and

heavy sound, and the positional emphasis on *stamps* in the speech reinforce its depressing effect, and together with the thematic return, help to confirm the obsessional nature of Louis' personality.

"'When the smoke rises, sleep curls off the roof like a mist,' said Louis." This fifth speech reveals Louis' insight into a realm which seems almost mystical in *The Waves*. Sleep first appears in the first interlude: each wave, the narrative says, sweeps over the sand and then withdraws, "sighing like a sleeper whose breath comes and goes unconsciously." Subsequently Susan becomes the personality most closely identified with this unconscious realm of sleep, which becomes the subject of her long speech in the sixth chapter. For Louis, sleep is the realm of unconscious and the eternal, where he sees the women with red pitchers on the banks of the Nile, and from which he is awakened by Jinny's kiss. His perception of the smoke rising and sleep curling off the roof like a mist seems to represent this awakening. "Mist," positionally emphasized here, and haze, throughout Virginia Woolf's fiction, stand for the luminous halo, the ambiance, which unites one consciousness with all others—a metaphor for our mode of spiritual being. Louis seems to have a special sense of the spiritual oneness of the personalities in *The Waves*—perhaps because he is always conscious of his own differences from the others.

"'That is the first stroke of the church bell,' said Louis. 'Then the others follow; one, two; one, two; one, two.'" The final speech of Louis in the "prologue," like his first and third speeches, announces an aural perception—and is a sign, perhaps, of his fuller intellectual development. Bells in *The Waves* seem to be most often associated with the idea of summons: here the summons to church, elsewhere to school, to class, to service in the drawing room, to funerals. The idea of the passage of time is important in some of these contexts, and all of them are concerned in some way with collective action, and with

wrote about that experience in his novel *The Village in the Jungle* (1913) and in *Growing*, the second volume of his autobiography. Louis' fascination with death seems to be a factor in his attraction toward Rhoda. White, of course, is her color ("All my ships are white"). And the "eye" of the elephant may link this gruesome image with the strangely terrible eyes of the birds in the interludes. Whatever the private or pathological implications of all this, its overtones of morbidity and hostility emerge clearly enough from the text alone.

duty. Of all these personalities, Louis seems especially aware of their mutual social interdependence, their inescapable commitment to each other, despite their many—and even painful—differences. It is Louis who hears the beast of death stamping on the beach, and Louis who hears the rhythm of the church bells, whose insistent "one, two; one, two" may speak subliminally of the conflict, but also the harmony, between our perceptions of the duality, the polarity, of everything and our desire—or perhaps even our duty—to shape it all into some transcendent unity. Certainly no one is more sensitive to this than Louis. Fittingly, the first extended speech is given to him; it emerges from his loneliness; "Now they have all gone. I am alone. . . ."

The personality revealed by the first six speeches of Louis is obsessed by death, the great beast stamping, whose presence is announced in the first and fourth speeches. Louis *hears* to a greater extent than any of the other personalities, and his speeches disclose a sensitivity and an intellectual awareness which are also greater. Already he feels excluded from others at the same time that he is keenly aware of a transcendent unity which they all share. And he hears the call to duty, to responsibility, more keenly than they. His insights come to him surprisingly, unpredictably, even burningly—insights into the unconscious, the eternal, and above all, into mortality. Perhaps it is this strange affinity with death which draws him toward Rhoda, just as it prompts Jinny to kiss him.

Each of these six voices, then, represents a potential identity, even a destiny, envisioned by the narrative consciousness. Each represents a developing mode of being in the world. Each struggles toward a fuller expression, toward fulfillment. Each becomes more differentiated from the others. Yet each longs for communion with the others. And as the voices expand, the silence surrounding them also becomes more complex: its latent meanings multiply.

In a sense, the figure of Percival later comes to embody that silence: he somehow represents the promise of wholeness. Perhaps his name suggests the Grail Knight who may bring renewal to this wasteland of unfulfilled identities. In the music of *The Waves* he represents a latent theme which might bring the six voices together in harmony.

But just as the sun of this archetypal day reaches its zenith, Percival suddenly dies. A world which had appeared to be open and infinite is suddenly revealed to be tragically limited. The six voices must then confront the mortality and temporality which shadow the afternoon of their lives.

Just as the formal speeches of the six voices suggest characters that are archetypal, so the formal language of the interludes creates an archetypal landscape: *the* garden, *the* house, and so on. In the seventh interlude the perspective begins to expand to include, for example, "a whole village." This expansion continues through the eighth and ninth interludes, so that the final perspective becomes universal, or nearly so—alluding, for example, to girls on verandahs looking up at snow-covered peaks. The first interlude begins before dawn, and each subsequent one advances the sun further in the course of this archetypal day, until the ninth interlude, which announces that "Now the sun had sunk," returns the world of nature to the eternal night from which it had originally emerged. The seasons advance too, from early spring in the second interlude to late autumn in the eighth; the first and last interlude seem to exist outside this seasonal pattern.[10]

These patterns in the interludes seem important because of their implicit parallels with the events described by the six voices. The chronology of the lives in the nine chapters is analogous to the chronology of the day in the interludes. The speeches of the first chapter show the

10   In the first interlude the rising light makes "*one leaf transparent and then another,*" and the birds are singing; these phenomena seem compatible with any season except winter. The phenomena of the second interlude are more profuse, and the fact that "*a bud here and there split asunder and shook out flowers*" seems most typical of spring. Details of successive interludes provide a growing correlation between the development of the day and that of the year, so that the interludes become the account of the cycle of nature and of all life: this day is every day, and as it advances, the year advances. In the interlude before the final chapter, the description of the garden at the beginning seems to suggest early winter, but the perspective later expands to include "*the mountains where the snow lodges for ever . . . and girls, sitting on verandahs, look up at the snow, shading their faces with their fans*"—an evocation, perhaps, of Spain, where Rhoda has wandered at the end of the seventh chapter. This interlude before the final chapter ends in a darkness which envelops everything: all times, places, people, seasons.

231

emergence of consciousness in the nursery and early childhood. Each successive chapter continues the lives which the voices represent. But the final chapter subsumes the whole story into the consciousness of Bernard, the writer. In one sense this represents the ultimate triumph of consciousness. But in another sense it shows the fading of consciousness, paralleling the spread of darkness in the final interlude. Virginia Woolf seems to have intended Bernard's monologue as an apotheosis, but in some ways it turned out to reveal the dissolution of consciousness instead.

As the voices in the chapters speak, of what they see, hear, and feel, they define their own uniqueness. At the same time, however, they also become increasingly aware of what they have in common. The voice most capable of expressing the sense of commonality becomes the dominant—or at least final—voice. At the end Bernard becomes a whole personality by subsuming all other voices within his own. But in becoming everyman he has also experienced the death of the self.

The thematic action rises toward the central chapter, and falls away from it. In the morning of their lives the six personalities become increasingly differentiated, but in such a way that their identities remain largely potential. Then, in the central chapter, at noon, death strikes Percival down. Destiny moves from potentiality to fatality, and in Chapter 6 the separate identities become established (except, significantly, for Bernard and Rhoda). In Chapter 7 the identities are solidified, or "frozen"; each character speaks once (Bernard and Rhoda do speak here, because their identities have been frozen even though they aren't established in the same sense that the identities of the other characters are: Bernard and Rhoda are locked into their roles, polar opposites, of writer and suicide).

In the eighth chapter the six voices enter into communion at Hampton Court. In the opening movement of the chapter all six characters speak, with Bernard and Rhoda, the opposites, speaking twice. There is then a moment of communion, announced by Bernard ("Drop upon drop, silence falls") in which the six voices merge in a hymn to the silence, each voice in turn sustaining the melodic line without breaking the continuity. Then there is an almost ceremonial procession down the avenue toward the river, a procession preceded and succeeded by speeches between Rhoda and Louis, who stop by a stone urn. The four others return, led by Bernard, who becomes aware that "We have destroyed something by our presence"; each of the four speaks once; then Bernard closes the chapter with a meditation on "Must, must, must. . . . How we worship that sound. . . ."

One important aspect of the structure, then, as Bernard's speech discloses, is a growing awareness of necessity. This is already latent, of course, as we have seen, in the first speeches of these six personalities, in their compulsive perceptions and in their curiously distanced reports of the things that happen to them. It becomes most overwhelming at the noontime of their lives, when Percival is suddenly struck down. He represents, to them, some kind of wholeness which their own disparate personalities have never achieved. And the destruction of that wholeness is something from which none of them ever fully recovers. It seems to be a door which slams shut, closing off their vision of the possibilities of life, which had hitherto seemed infinite. It brings on the afternoon of their lives, in which they become more or less reconciled to their fates, the congealing of their identities, their limitations. Perhaps Rhoda and Bernard transcend those limitations, or perhaps they merely escape.

Subtle rhythms operate throughout the book, at various levels. There are the rhythms of the prose itself, which seems to vary not so much from one voice to another as it does from one phase of life to another. And most importantly, there is the counterpoint formed by the six voices. These rhythms seem analogous to those of the waves in the interludes. At the beginning of the book the voices emerge like the waves—very regular but so low in amplitude as to be almost imperceptible: the six series of speeches with which the first chapter begins. Then come the longer speeches by Louis and Jinny, then a "dialogue" by Bernard and Susan, and so on, in the pattern we have seen in the analysis of the opening chapter. In the second chapter the duration of the speeches becomes somewhat longer, their recurrence somewhat more regular, until the speech of Neville which closes that chapter lasts for just over three pages. These longer speeches, which correspond, perhaps, to more fully developed individual waves, become the dominant pattern until about midway in the fourth chapter when, with the arrival of Percival, the individual voices seem like spray breaking on the rock of his central existence. But that existence suddenly ceases; longer speeches return to comment on it, and dominate the book once again. This pattern of long speeches persists until the "communion" at Hampton Court, where the voices merge into each other once again, and the voice of Bernard rises at the end of the eighth chapter to claim the "story" once and for all—until the voice of insensitive nature returns in the final sentence.

Thus it seems that the narrative may explore its story in either of two directions: in breadth, with the various voices complementing each other to create a panoramic field of awareness, or in depth, with one voice exploring a particular aspect of that larger reality. If the narrative chooses the panoramic view, the exploration in depth must be suspended, and vice versa. The final chapter of the book, then, attempts to merge these two directions: the single voice of Bernard subsumes all of the other voices (even, eventually, the voice of the interludes) and enunciates a panoramic view. But that view also, at the very end, dissolves.

The music of *The Waves* arises not only from what its voices say and from their duration in time, but from the sequences in which they are arranged. If the duration of the voices is analogous to the duration of the notes in this six- (or is it seven?) tone scale, then the sequential order of the voices is analogous to the melodic line—and perhaps, because of the persistence of their sounds, to the formation of chords.

The relationships between the voices become very complex. Certain voices have affinities for each other. Bernard, for example, speaks next to Susan almost three times as often as he does next to Jinny. And within such pairs the orders of speaking may be patterned as well. Bernard's speeches, for example, precede Susan's more often than they succeed them. Pairs which are adjacent significantly often are Louis and Rhoda, Bernard and Susan, Bernard and Neville; significantly seldom, Bernard and Jinny, Susan and Neville, Louis and Susan. Why?

The sequences reflect the essences which the voices represent. Let us consider the voices which are seldom paired: first, Bernard and

Jinny. His is the literary personality; hers is sensuality incarnate.[11] Although they are said to have been sexually intimate, that is revealed only in retrospect, in a curious passage in Bernard's "summing up": "It was a tree; there was the river; it was afternoon; here we were; I in my serge suit; she in green. There was no past, no future; merely the moment in its ring of light, and our bodies; and the inevitable climax, the ecstasy." *It was a tree*: Jinny's common-sense view of the willow which for Bernard has an almost mystical significance. And the sexual encounter, if that is what it was, must be translated into that realm of consciousness (*the moment in its ring of light*—Bernard's primal perception) in order to come into existence. The scene, with the river and the willow trees, suggests Cambridge, yet there is no mention in the third ("college") chapter—or anywhere else—of this sexual passage between Bernard and Jinny. It can only be recollected in tranquillity, in the safety of pure consciousness; during the first eight chapters Bernard and Jinny must keep their distance.

The distance between Susan and Neville is the natural one between earth mother and male homosexual, and is addressed most directly by Neville himself at Hampton Court ("I want to diminish your hostility, your green eyes fixed on mine"). The distance between Louis and Susan is less extreme, but again seems essentially sexual. Louis could not play the male next to Susan's archetypal female. Jinny kisses him because she senses that he is essentially dead—she wants to restore him to life; Rhoda has an affair with him because they are both lonely, and she leaves him.

The relative dominance between adjacent personalities often seems to be implied in the sequence of voices. Within a given segment of text, the sequence seems generally to be one of diminishing power,

11   With this character too the autobiographical implications are interesting. Virginia's father called her Jinny. He would have been sexually attracted toward, and morally disapproving of, a woman like the Jinny of *The Waves*. Whether or not the name there carries overtones of an Electra complex, the character does represent a troubled, if not pathological, sexual nature. Bernard, on the other hand, represents someone of whom Leslie Stephen, as a literary critic who studied novels and novelists, might approve. The etymology of the name in Virginia Woolf's imagination, however, remains puzzling to me. Roger Fry, whose biography she later wrote, lived in Bernard Street. In earlier versions of the manuscript, Bernard was called John, Johnnie, Archie, and Roger, according to J. W. Graham, *The Holograph Drafts*, 67.

a series of dying falls, in which each successive voice evokes a less powerful one. This is clearly evident in the endings of the chapters. Chapters 1, 3, 5, and 7 end with the voice of Rhoda, Chapters 2, 4, and 6 with the voice of Neville, and Chapters 8 and 9 with the voice of Bernard, whose final "triumph" becomes deeply ironic. "Dominance" and "power," of course, aren't simple, and though a personality may be impotent in some ways, it may be very powerful in others: Rhoda's imagination, for example, is more powerful than Bernard's—though much less controlled. Nevertheless, in the macrostructure of the book the general sequence is one of diminishing power.

The reasons for the closeness of certain pairs are also interesting. Louis and Rhoda are the most obviously close; for a time they are lovers, until, as she says, "I left Louis; I feared embraces." Louis is a perfectionist, serious, single-minded, materialistic, ambitious, prim, suspicious, "too cold, too universal" Neville says, a formidable intellect, energetic, always ill at ease, incapable of small talk or even, Bernard says, of "those simple attachments by which one is connected with another." Touches like these displace Louis from character to caricature. It is no wonder that Rhoda would wish to leave such a joyless creature. Louis then takes a mistress, whose cockney accent comforts him but makes the servants laugh behind his back. But the parting of Louis and Rhoda is only sexual, and they become much more intimate after their sexual relationship is over. Both, of course, are outsiders—he because of his self-consciousness about his origins, she because of her fears about her mental instability—and their affinity is one of need: they complement each other—though not enough to form one whole personality.

The alliance of Bernard and Susan is also ambiguous. In a way they represent what the outsiders both desire and despise: complacent normality. Essentially, Susan represents the traditional destiny which society approves for the woman: fulfillment through her family and by nature. It isn't a very convincing destiny, even to Susan herself. Poets will love her, Bernard says, and Percival loves her; but she refuses Percival, longs for Bernard, and marries a farmer. Her passions are elemental and deep ("I hate, I love"), and her life becomes a long effort to escape from them. Bernard, on the other hand, represents a literary destiny. This too seems frustrating, an endless struggle with a story which has no real end. Yet the struggle is, apparently, a real alternative for the awful self-consciousness which afflicts all the other personalities: in his obsession with phrases and stories Bernard can actually forget himself. He is alleged to have a wife and sons, but they have no real place in his consciousness, which is almost purely literary (the other voices complain, too, that he turns everything into a story). Thus while the narrative consciousness of *The Waves* favors Bernard from the beginning, and at last seems to embody itself in him entirely, it nevertheless remains highly self-conscious, and aware of the falsity of its own chosen absolute truth. In the closing sentence the book itself breaks on the shore of that awareness. Like Louis and Rhoda, Bernard and Susan together can forestall that awareness.

Bernard also has an affinity with Neville, who represents the world of Cambridge. Neville feels that Bernard's stories are amusing, even at times uplifting, but on the whole irrelevant. Yet he views him with some jealousy, and realizes that Bernard is "shaded with innumerable perplexities." Neville's own vision is more penetrating, narrower, and more sharply focused; he says that Bernard "half knows everybody; he knows nobody (I compare him with Percival)." Neville's tentative advances (mainly through his poems) toward Bernard are no more successful than those toward Percival, whom he idolizes. Between Bernard and Neville the primal scene is the one in which Bernard goes to comfort Susan, leaving Neville in the tool shed with their toy boats—and even taking with him Neville's knife (the emblem, like Peter Walsh's knife in *Mrs. Dalloway* or Mr. Ramsay's "arid scimitar" in *To the Lighthouse*, of his maleness); the trauma remains vivid for Neville years later. The affinity between these potential worlds of Cambridge and of literature remains close but uneasy throughout, with claims of superiority and feelings of inferiority on both sides. Though the narrative consciousness of *The Waves* is attracted toward both worlds, it can become more authentically incarnate in the world of Bernard. In the end literature triumphs, as it must, and Neville takes his predestined place in Bernard's story.

The narrative also creates what could be called "dialogues" between the characters—passages in which two voices speak alternately, with no others intervening. If a "dialogue" is defined as a series in which each of the two voices speaks at least twice, then there are six such dialogues in *The Waves*: two between Louis and Rhoda, and one between Bernard and each of the others except Rhoda. There are also eight passages in which one voice is enclosed by two speeches of another voice; this pattern too is interesting: the voices which are enclosed and do not "answer" are those of Neville (once with Jinny and twice with Louis), Rhoda (with Bernard and Neville), Louis (with Neville and Rhoda), and Bernard (with Neville). This subliminal pattern confirms that the voice of Bernard is the one most interrelated with the others; the most isolated are Neville, Rhoda, and Louis—the voices of sexual maladjustment. As in a complex chemical chain, certain elements have certain affinities and form certain characteristic bonds, and other affinities and bonds are less likely, or even impossible. Louis and Rhoda have such an affinity for each other, but not for the other elements, or voices. Among those others, it is the voice of Bernard that holds the complex chain together—and so it is not surprising that his voice emerges at the end as the dominant one.

The process of differentiation and definition goes on at many levels and in many ways. At the microstructural level the personalities become differentiated by the phenomenology of their consciousness, as we have seen in the opening speeches of the book. As this process goes on, it creates a field of meaning whose constituent elements are these phenomena—words, ideas, images—in a dynamic, increasingly complex context. In whatever ways it comes into existence, that whole field of meaning must be "deconstructed" to some extent in order to be analyzed.

At the level of words and images, analysis can then begin to "reconstruct" essential patterns of evolving meaning. For example, we could look at the theme of fear in the book. With the help of a concordance, we can identify passages in which the words *fear*, *afraid*, *dread*, or close cognates appear.[12] There are twelve such passages

12   My analysis of the text of *The Waves* would not have been possible without the excellent concordance prepared by Deborah E. Swain as Appendix A to her "Feeling and Form in Virginia Woolf's *The Waves*" (M.A. thesis, University of North Carolina at Chapel Hill, 1975). She first established a definitive text: after collating the first En-

which refer to Rhoda and five which refer to Louis; Neville and Jinny are each referred to in two passages, Bernard and Susan in only one. This first step, of course, only verifies what most readers already know: that Rhoda is the most fearful of the six voices, and that Louis is the most fearful of the male voices. But as the reconstruction moves into its second step—examination of additional contexts suggested by other words in the original contexts of "fear"—it becomes more complex and interesting. For instance, we can look at the additional contexts suggested by words in the original passages concerned with Rhoda's fears. Such words include *dream* (often a response to fear), *tiger* (a recurrent sign of Rhoda's fear), *fling* (with its overtones of abandonment—sexual and otherwise—scattering, and even suicide), *hid* (whose contexts almost always express paranoia), *depths* (always signifying emotional, as well as physical depth), and *figure* (whose contexts usually involve depersonalization). Examination of these contexts in turn can disclose more key words, and still other patterns. The word *tiger*, for instance, is spoken eight times in the book: seven times by Rhoda (in contexts expressing the beauty, the power, and the ferocity of her fears), and once by Louis, who speaks of himself as a "caged tiger" (which invites still other speculations about their relationship).

A more complicated and interesting example is the word *dream*, which with its cognates appears twenty-seven times in *The Waves*. It is spoken by Rhoda ten times, by Bernard eight, by Louis four, by Jinny three and by Susan one time. Two of the mentions by Bernard, one by Louis, and the one by Susan all refer to Rhoda. Thus it seems clear that Rhoda is the one most concerned with dreams. At the other extreme, Neville, whose mind is oriented toward logic and order, never mentions dreams at all, and Susan, who is oriented toward domesticity, mentions them only once—and in regard to Rhoda. Bernard also mentions dreams significantly often, and his awareness of Rhoda as dreamer prepares us subliminally, perhaps, to accept the

---

glish and first American editions and evaluating the several hundred variants, she determined that the English edition was the better text. She then entered the corrected final text into a computer program which indexed each word in the novel and printed it in context. The result is an exceptionally accurate and valuable concordance.

incorporation of her consciousness into his at the end. Perhaps Rhoda and Bernard exemplify dreams run amok and dreams turned toward more "constructive" purposes.

Several other aspects of these direct references to fear in *The Waves* are interesting. First, they are distributed throughout the book rather than clustered in a few passages. Thus the theme seems pervasive, and may come from a deeper level of the narrative consciousness than some of the more clustered words. Second, the fears attributed to each character by the other voices are very accurate. In the manifestations of the theme of fear, as in other themes, there seems to be very little dramatic irony in *The Waves*: the six voices seem almost entirely aware of each other's deepest feelings, and the narrative consciousness as a whole seldom reveals more about them—explicitly—than they know themselves.

Third, the fears themselves seem very central to the characters which the voices reveal. Rhoda is a classical case of what R. D. Laing calls "ontological insecurity"[13]—unsure of every aspect of her being, she is afraid in ways which would never occur to most of us. Louis is most afraid of being ridiculed as an outsider. Neville, who longs for success and intellectual status, fears the future—and fear itself: in poetry, he says, "Nothing is to be rejected in fear or horror." Jinny, the sensualist, is afraid of growing old. Susan, the country girl, is afraid of social rituals. Bernard is the least afraid; his phrase-making, the others complain—and he admits—allows him to escape. The creation of fiction, then, emerges in *The Waves* as the most effective answer to ontological insecurity: when Bernard says he "evoked to serve as opposite to myself the figure of Rhoda . . . always with fear in her eyes" he is revealing that he has created this figure called Rhoda in order to give a name to his own fears and to give them an existence apart from and "opposite to" himself.

13 R. D. Laing, *The Divided Self* (New York: Random House, 1969), 40–64. The ontologically insecure person, according to Laing, suffers from three forms of anxiety: "engulfment" (losing one's sense of autonomous identity), "implosion" (the sudden crushing of one's identity, which is vacuous but still separate, by the impingement of the world), and petrification and depersonalization. Obviously, the three forms are not entirely separable. Laing's description of them could serve almost as a case history of Rhoda.

There are many other ways in which the voices are differentiated, despite the superficial sameness of their language. All of these differences have to do with what the voices are conscious of, and how. Certain personalities are predisposed toward certain colors, as we saw in the analysis of the opening speeches, or toward certain imagery. The different personalities think of the same image in different ways: Bernard's "ring," for example, is a ring of light, but Louis speaks several times of forging a ring of steel—out of "poetry." That word, incidentally, belongs to males: it is spoken thirteen times in the book, never by a woman; *poem(s)* is spoken nineteen times by males, three by females. The uses of *novel(s)* and *story(ies)* are even more overwhelmingly male: the former word is spoken five times, always by males; the latter fifty-two times, once by a female. All of this confirms the reader's intuition that the realm of literature in *The Waves*, as in earlier books (even in the androgynous *Orlando*) is the province of males. The grouping of voices in *The Waves*, as well as many aspects of what those voices say, reveals that the differences between the sexes are usually greater than the differences between individuals within the same sex.

In *The Waves* each chapter depicts a phase in the development of its voices. Each phase constitutes a search for significance as well as a period of time in these lives, and the direction and duration of the actions are governed not so much by chronology as by the search for significance. Each chapter ends when that search, within its particular phase, can go no further.

The nine chapter endings reveal many similarities and, above all, a remarkable uniformity of tone: desperation. Most emphasize the imagery of the waves, with their contextual suggestions of helplessness, drowning, endless repetition, uproar, breaking, fragmentation, dissolution, death. The search for significance invariably ends in a sense of loss or anguish. This may not be immediately apparent in the endings of Chapters 8 and 9. Indeed, many readers, as well as Virginia Woolf herself, have regarded Bernard's final soliloquy as a victory. In a sense it is, but in a very ambiguous sense.

The antagonist in that final victory is death, and in the largest sense *The Waves* is about the struggle between life and death. Frightening but also fascinating, death offers a dark, seductive promise of silence and relief. Throughout the *oeuvre* death surprises in the midst of life: it breaks Rachel's engagement, reduces Jacob's existence to relics in an empty room, intrudes into Clarissa's party, and without warning causes Mr. Ramsay to stumble along a dark hallway one morning with outstretched, empty arms. And so in *The Waves*, when the sun has risen to its full height in this archetypal day, the presence of Percival suddenly becomes an absence.

This mysterious figure first appears in the second chapter: "Look now, how everybody follows Percival," says Bernard. "His magnificence is that of some medieval commander. A wake of light seems to lie on the grass behind him." *Look now*: both of these are words of incantation in *The Waves*, invoking the mysteries of "vision" and of "the moment," and when Percival enters the book he trails a cloud of glory, a wake of light. From the beginning he is a hero to the boys. Neville perceives him as "remote from us all in a pagan universe," falls in love with him, and, waiting for him at the dinner in London, feels that "without Percival there is no solidity." Louis resents his power, but idolizes him too: "it is Percival who inspires poetry." And the voice of the final soliloquy achieves such transcendent heroism that Bernard becomes Percival ("I ride with . . . my hair flying back like a young man's, like Percival's"), the knight of the Holy Grail who will redeem the wasteland. He is much less important to the female voices: Susan, we learn from Bernard, refused Percival; Jinny seems to recognize that he is largely a symbol: "we shall perhaps never make this moment out of one man again"; his death releases in Rhoda the "desire to be spent, to be consumed," and she commemorates it by throwing her bunch of violets into the waves.

Death, of course, is a presence in *The Waves* from the beginning. It is there in the first perceptions of Rhoda and of Louis. Jinny somehow senses it in Louis, and kisses him—one of the primal events to which the voices return again and again. Neville's personality is somehow deeply scarred by his discovery of "death among the apple trees." When Susan sees Jinny kiss Louis, she says "I shall eat grass and die in a ditch in the brown water where dead leaves have rotted"—a strange reaction, we might think, to the sight of one child kissing

242

another. But Bernard senses her despair, follows her, and attempts to comfort her with his "words, moving darkly, in the depths of your mind": he creates for her their private world, known to none of the others, of Elvedon.

Death means different things to the different personalities which the different voices represent. Susan, for example, never speaks of "death," but uses the word *dead* eight times in the book. This is in keeping with the concrete quality of Susan's speech: to her, "dead" is just an attribute of nature—"dead leaves," "the dead shepherd," etc. She never speaks of the abstraction "death." Of the six personal voices in *The Waves*, hers is closest to the impersonal world represented in the interludes, where organisms can be "dead" but where "death" has no place. For Rhoda, however, death is always a real presence; she speaks the word six times, but says *dead* only once. Louis is also very much aware of death as an abstraction; he says *death* nine times, *dead* only three times. Thus the affinity of Louis and Rhoda, as well as their distance from Susan, is reflected in their uses of these two words. (The other three voices use both words with equal, or almost equal, frequency.)

Death disrupts the narrative pattern of the book itself. We have already noticed the disruption of the long speeches into the "spray" which surrounds Percival at the dinner in London. There is also a disruption of the pattern which opens and closes the chapters. Up until the beginning of the fifth chapter, when Percival's death is announced, every chapter had been opened by the voice of Bernard. Thus by the time of the opening of the fifth chapter, "'He is dead,' said Neville," we may have become so conditioned to expect the voice of Bernard that we only slowly become aware that Neville is speaking not of him, but of Percival. This opening speech also changes the narrative pattern in another way: Rhoda's voice had closed the first and third chapters, Neville's the second and fourth, so that his opening of the fifth chapter now bridges the silence between the fourth and fifth chapters. The fourth chapter ends with his lament that "Percival is gone"; the fifth begins by transforming that lament into the most extreme of its possible forms: "He is dead."

Between these two statements is the "objective" prose of the fifth

243

interlude which now, from the perspective of our afternoon knowledge, seems much more sinister than it had as the climax of the
morning:

*The sun had risen to its full height. It was no longer half seen and guessed at, from
hints and gleams, as if a girl couched on her green-sea mattress tired her brows with
water-globed jewels that sent lances of opal-tinted light falling and flashing in the
uncertain air like the flanks of a dolphin leaping, or the flash of a falling blade.
Now the sun burnt uncompromising, undeniable.*

No longer a manifestation of the feminine principle of mystery and
fecundity, the sun is now *uncompromising, undeniable*. The narrative
consciousness seems reluctant to admit this, and lingers lovingly over
the description of the *"girl."* But the truth is suddenly there, in *"the
flash of a falling blade,"* announcing the presence of the threatening
male principle at the same time that it celebrates the female. And in
the next paragraph faint echoes of a leitmotif in *Mrs. Dalloway*—the
dirge from *Cymbeline*: "Fear no more the heat o' the sun" are com-
bined with this motif of masculine destruction. The sun is described
in terms of violence—it "beat," "glared," "struck," etc.—and we see its
effects throughout the symbolic landscape of the interlude. Within the
house, however, there is still "a zone of shadow in which might be a
further shape to be disencumbered of shadow or still denser depths of
darkness." The heat of the sun, presumably, still cannot disturb the
innermost mysteries. The final paragraph of the interlude returns first
to the waves themselves (the subject of Louis's very first speech), and
then to the silence which ends with the fifth chapter and its stark
announcement of death.

The Waves opens with the dawn of an archetypal day, followed by
the dawning of archetypal forms of consciousness. The two forms of
creation are analogous to the Old and New Testament creations of the
world and the word. Within both forms, and especially in the darkness and silence surrounding them, the creative power is immanent:
between the interludes and the chapters, and between the soliloquies
themselves, the narrative energizes a field of potential meaning. Although this field continues to expand throughout the book, its subject
is always the phenomenology of consciousness—the mystery of the

differentiation and development of personality. "Bernard" is now the consciousness of "a ring hanging above me. It quivers and hangs in a loop of light"; now the awareness of "the spider's web on the corner of the balcony" with "beads of water on it, drops of white light"; and so on. Consciousness must always be consciousness *of* something.

The formal structure of *The Waves* implies a dialectic relationship between the kinds of creation in the interludes and in the chapters. In the interludes the sun moves inexorably across the sky, and the world of nature moves in accordance with its own laws. The birds, especially, seem to exemplify the mysteries of nature. Yet these mysteries exist not in nature alone, but in the perception of it. This perceiving consciousness is the ultimate, inescapable *presence* of the interludes. Objectivity is exposed as a pretense, and the interludes are revealed to exist—indeed, always to have existed—in a pre-Copernican universe in which not only the earth, but above all the perceiving consciousness, is at the center of all things.

In the other realm of creation there is a more complicated action. Six possible personalities struggle toward knowledge, toward unification, perhaps toward dominance, at least toward control. The narrative consciousness tests these six possible adaptations as it goes along. It knows intuitively before the struggle really begins which of the six must prevail. And it also knows which of the six must die. The mind of the narrative consciousness is with Bernard and the creation of the word. But its heart is with Rhoda, who must die so that the word can become dominant. And while the story demonstrates that Rhoda's death and Bernard's ascendancy are inevitable and "right," it also reveals that Rhoda's consciousness is the more beautiful and exciting, and that the ascendancy of Bernard is the price that must be paid for survival.

The others play their roles too, rather schematically. Bernard's feminine complement is Susan, the archetypal mother to play opposite his own role as archetypal father. And for Rhoda, in love with the ultimate absolute of death, there must be Louis, whose dedication to other absolutes makes him an ally in the resistance to homogenization. The sensualists, Neville and Jinny, exemplify the other major alternative: her seductions in London and his in Cambridge attempt to suspend the ravages of time; success in academe and in society sustain an illusion of immortality.

We could think of this configuration of characters as the embodiment of Freud's famous components of the psyche: Neville and Jinny seem governed primarily by the id and the pleasure principle, Louis and Rhoda by the superego and the morality principle (though Rhoda's necessities seem more extreme than this), Bernard and Susan by the ego and the reality principle. In each of these three realms there must be both a male and a female exemplar; here, as in the view of Freud himself, there are profound differences in the masculine and feminine ways of being in the world. Freud felt, of course, that the goal of the healthy person should be to maximize the growth of the ego, to bring within the scope of that individual's "reality principle" ever increasing areas of experience. Perhaps the emergence of Bernard as spokesman could be justified on that ground.

Such schematic diagrams of the "characters" in *The Waves* are too reductive, of course, but the highly stylized narrative technique seems to invite them. And the book itself can be seen as a process of "eidetic reduction," in the phenomenological sense of the term: the search for essence through the "testing" of various predicates, whose subject is consciousness itself. The narrative explores the various possibilities until their potentialities, in its own view, seem exhausted. These potentialities are there from the beginning, of course, in the creative consciousness itself. What is being tested are the possible modes in which that consciousness may become incarnate. And so the various voices emerge, each to speak of its own reality. The larger narrative consciousness allows them to speak, listens to them, and to some extent orchestrates them. It auditions them, in the hope of discovering the authentic, definitive voice of its own reality. The narrative omits everything that is not essential, all the details of "realism" and the conventional novel; it renders only essences.

The Waves begins with a view of the creation in nature. The narrative consciousness itself, though never directly acknowledged, is the ultimate presence in this world. The narrative describes the phenomena of nature in such a way as to suggest that they foreshadow the human drama to be enacted within "the house." And there, the first voice to speak announces its vision of wholeness: "I see a ring. . . ." That voice is counterpointed, and then diminished, by others which rise, speaking of alternatives. More and more, the voices learn to speak of the mundane, and the rest is silence.

Still, that silence contains the meaning which the voices seek so relentlessly. In the first half of the book it seems identified with Percival, around whom the others form their "six-sided flower." But this center does not hold: Percival suddenly becomes an aching absence. At last the narrative suspends the search among the modes of consciousness which the voices represent: it brings them all within the mode which it has favored from the beginning.

But the narrative can't suspend its own disbelief indefinitely, and "Bernard" too is exposed as an illusion, a dream. The final words of the eighth chapter ("even now, even sleeping") suggest that Bernard has fallen asleep on the train back to London; if so, the ninth chapter, spoken entirely by him, may represent his dream. Indeed, it does function very much like a wish-fulfillment dream for Bernard, as well as for the larger narrative consciousness:[14] at last all doubts can be answered; at last transcendence seems within reach; at last suppressed and fragmented feelings can be transformed into a coherent, definitive, even triumphant expression. The final chapter, Bernard's long monologue, fulfulls every author's dream. It represents the narrative's

14   The "plot" of *The Waves* is essentially a later version, more artful and sophisticated, of the story of *The Voyage Out*: the ontologically insecure young woman must die so that the transcendent consciousness of the artist may take control. From an autobiographical standpoint, *The Waves* may be about the realization that the grail knight (Percival in the book, Thoby Stephen in life), with his potential for wholeness, perfection, and unification, cannot survive in an imperfect world, but that the artist (Bernard in the book, the writer in Virginia Woolf) can realize at least some of that potential through craftsmanship, a growing command of the medium of artistic experience and expression. And the artist's achievement can then subsume other, more limited, roles and identities—especially Rhoda, the writer's "opposite" because she really has no role or identity, only her terrifying sensitivity. For Virginia Woolf personally, the book became a means of exploring various possibilities of her own personality and of her relationships with the world, without the risks that such explorations would entail in "real life"—but perhaps with other, special risks that only the artist can know.

transcendence of its own story, the transformation of that story into a realm no longer threatened by interruption, distraction, or contradiction. And so the search for an authentic, satisfying mode of consciousness turns again, at last, to the same conclusion as the search in *To the Lighthouse*: that the essence of life can be discovered and expressed by the questing consciousness of the artist.

Death, the antagonist in this final transcendent victory, has, as we have seen, captured the center of the book and displaced Bernard from his accustomed position as opening narrator. Although all of the voices react then to Percival's death, and though all their personalities are shown to have been shaped to some extent by traumatic discoveries of death in their childhoods, Bernard and Rhoda objectify the polar extremes. She finally embraces death; he finally defies it. His speech ends with that defiance, but the book itself ends with an acknowledgment of death: "*The waves broke on the shore.*" Neither cancels the other; both remain in eternal suspension. The book announces its own literary artifice at the same time that it lays claim to universal truth. Such an ending seems closer to the dying falls of Beckett than to the art of its own time.

The "plot" of *The Waves*, then, is the drama of the intentionality of the narrative consciousness. As one voice succeeds another there is always the hope—though it constantly diminishes—that the narrative will discover its own authentic voice. Its last desperate hope is the voice of Bernard, which from the beginning has been the most comprehensive and stable. Indeed, in retrospect Bernard's assumption of authority seems inevitable: it is latent in his first speech, announcing the ring of light. But his final authority also comes about by default—because none of the other voices, except for Rhoda, proves capable of enlarging the realm of awareness which the voice of Bernard already encompasses. And although Bernard finally claims authority for every voice in the book, the most profound aspects of Rhoda's awareness are never really incorporated within his imagination. The image of "the square upon the oblong," for example, stands in her mind for "our dwelling-place. The structure is now visible. Very little is left outside." But Bernard never thinks of the square upon the oblong, nor do any of the others; the eight appearances of the image are confined to Rhoda's awareness alone. And so Bernard enters into his final ride against death, a spiritual Charge of the Light Brigade, insisting that his fantasy of heroism is a real victory, but aware of being haunted by "those old half-articulate ghosts who . . . put out their phantom fingers and clutch at me as I try to escape—shadows of people one might have been; unborn selves." Precisely: selves that have struggled toward incarnation, but failed—and fade once again into the realm of silence.

As the "summing up" continues, the absence of these other voices becomes more painful. Bernard announces that "I was the inheritor; I, the continuer; I, the person miraculously appointed to carry on." Perhaps this is really a political appointment, made not "miraculously" but expediently by the narrative. Yet it does seem right in the sense that it fits the world we have seen throughout the book, in which the six voices report, with a strangely chilling sameness of tone, what is happening to them, what is being done to them or inflicted upon them. They almost never speak of what they choose to do, but almost always of what life has chosen for them. They move through their lives like figures in a mechanical clock in a Gothic cathedral. Their speeches describe, at a very great distance, and with great formality, abstraction, precision, and elegance, human experiences which are almost entirely painful. Perhaps the voice of Bernard becomes dominant at the end because it can achieve the greatest distance from that pain. But that voice too must dissolve, and perhaps the power of the book comes from the postponement of that dissolution for so long, as well as from its withholding of the "background" which we know is there—and which the technique forces us to supply.

The pattern for the ending of *The Waves* was first discovered in the ending of *The Voyage Out*. In the novels after that, the same kind of conclusion was reached again and again in various forms, each of which resolves its preceding dialectical conflicts by translating them into some more inclusive field of consciousness where their final synthesis could be discovered. In the first novel, this final act of consciousness is attributed to St. John Hirst. Although he is not an artist, he may be a writer: how else could he have become a fellow of King's and, by his own admission, one of the three or five most distinguished young men in England? Among the final visionaries of the early novels, the unnamed narrator of *Jacob's Room* is the first who could be called a creative writer. But she is so self-effacing that she seems almost to have vanished by the time the final scene is reached: although her presence there is theoretically important, it remains implied. The importance of the artist becomes crucial, of course, in *To the Lighthouse*, where the final form of awareness is first called "vision." In *Orlando* the playful biographer remains anonymous, but "his" presence, constantly implied by the style itself, is central—and allows the narrative to transcend the conventional limitations of time and mortality. And now in *The Waves* the final transcendence is given to the voice which represents the personality of a writer.

A tendency toward mindscape had been present from the very beginning of the *oeuvre*. In *The Voyage Out*, on the surface a rather conventional novel, the most crucial moments suddenly open into a dimension which is almost exclusively mental. Subdued somewhat in *Night and Day*, this tendency becomes dominant in *Jacob's Room* and in the other novels of the 1920s. *The Waves* represents the furthest development in this direction, the most cerebral reality in the lifework. All physical impurities are removed, or translated to a purely mental realm. Places in the physical world acquire an almost talismanic significance: the house by the sea, the garden where the lady writes, the avenue at Hampton Court—each of these becomes an emblem for a larger field of meaning. Certain actions become emblematic too: Louis hears tramplings, Jinny finds him still and kisses him, Susan sees what is close to the ground, Bernard comforts her with words, Rhoda sails her white ships over the waves to reach the islands, Neville is left alone with his fear of disorder. The book expands the implications of these actions, creates other actions, expands their implications, and so on. Eventually, however, they all constitute the web of words for which Bernard claims final responsibility.

Words are all that Bernard has—all that the narrative itself has—to oppose death. Near the end of his "summing up" Bernard claims to discover "a sense of the break of day. I will not call it dawn." Dawn, of course, is what it had been called in the beginning, and Bernard's speech suggests at least a tentative new beginning. This sense of "eternal renewal" then enables him to recognize death as the enemy, and to defy it. But when, at the very end, *"The waves broke on the shore,"* echoing the sound of death which had been the essence of Louis' first awareness, the narrative shows that death is still the final reality. Yet the italics also show that this too belongs within the domain of words, and so this mysterious interpenetration of words and silence, life and death, meaning and nothingness, is the ultimate reality which the narrative can discover in *The Waves*. The drama of intentionality must end with this moment, when the ultimate antitheses appear, in their most stark, essential form, either suspended indefinitely or merging in a final synthesis, according to our consciousness of them.

CHAPTER VIII

THE YEARS

After the stylized soliloquies of *The Waves*, which evolved toward the creative vision expressed by and in Bernard, the archetypal writer, the lifework turns toward the public world once again. The narrative consciousness does not reject the interior world of the previous novel. It tries instead, in *The Years*, to synthesize that inner, poetic realm and a more outward, prosaic scene, to merge poetry and "realism." It also tries, as it had much more lightly in *Orlando*, to explore the history out of which the present moment emerges.

"1880": the very title of the first chapter seems to announce an objective style. And the chapter then proceeds to illustrate the lives of a middle-class family of that era. That is followed by vignettes of various lengths which illustrate life in 1891, 1907, 1908, 1910, 1911, 1913, 1914, 1917, and 1918. Then a long final chapter entitled "Present Day" describes an existential present no longer confined by the historical years. (Though none of the topical references is precise in time, they clearly point to the mid-1930s, the time of the book's composition.)

Like *The Waves*, *The Years* uses descriptive passages as prologues to each chapter, and concludes the final chapter with a descriptive sentence set off by itself. But these passages in *The Years* are not italicized, are less formal and formulaic than those of *The Waves*, and sometimes extend beyond the world of "impersonal nature" into the lives and minds of the characters themselves. Strict differentiation between the personal and the impersonal is no longer possible for the narrative in *The Years*.

The characters are revealed by a series of dramatic scenes. In keeping with the more objective style, the presence of the narrative consciousness in these scenes is implied rather than directly stated. It seems much more concerned with what happens than with what the characters are thinking, and it remains more on the surface of events than in the earlier novels. But it does enter into the minds of various characters, where its "privilege" ranges from rather tentative guesses about their thoughts and feelings to full disclosure. The narrative perspective tends again to identify more with some of these personalities than with others, and the pattern here is similar to previous ones. As in earlier novels, this drama of shifting perspectives constitutes the world of *The Years*, which represents the "trace" of the struggle to find authentic correlatives for the feelings of the creative consciousness.

"It was an uncertain spring."[1] The narrative begins its search in the world of nature. Spring is the season of the renewal of natural life. But the word *uncertain* reveals the subjectivity of the search: objective description is infected from the very beginning with the need for value judgment. And the value which the narrative longs for is certainty: stability, order, assurance. But certainty, as Heisenberg demonstrated, involves movement through time. And, indeed, *The Years* illustrates the Uncertainty Principle: in search of absolute knowledge, the narrative discovers instead the limits of its own ability to know. The opening sentence, then, reveals a consciousness which is haunted by uncertainty and which seeks its antithesis in the world of nature.

The rest of the opening descriptive passage expands that initial feeling and confirms the direction of the search. "The weather, perpetually changing," becomes a source of anxiety and apprehension for the narrative consciousness. The natural world seems mutable and meaningless. Here, as in the opening scene of *The Voyage Out*, it is

1 The text I refer to here is the first English edition of *The Years* (London: Hogarth, 1937).

better not to think. Otherwise, the narrative only becomes aware of "interminable processions" of people "perpetually marching," of traffic moving in an "incessant" stream. Even the sounds of pigeons are perceived as a "lullaby that was always interrupted." City life is perceived by the narrative as an endless round of meaningless activity which fades at last into the dusk as "the moon rose and . . . shone out with serenity, with severity, or perhaps with complete indifference. Slowly wheeling, like the rays of a searchlight, the days, the weeks, the years passed one after another across the sky."

The reference to the searchlight seems incongruous here, as well as anachronistic for "1880." It is an omen of the future, of the searchlight which appears in the descriptive prologue to "1917." But that meaning is still latent here, as the search begins. Like "the sky of the mind" at the end of *Between the Acts*, the sky of *The Years* is the realm into which the insubstantial human pageant fades and vanishes. Serenity, severity, indifference: the adjectives grow more depressing. What they describe is the feeling of the search for meaning, which finally must end in silence. The indifference of nature, which had emerged so clearly in *The Waves*, now extends into the realm of human history as the narrative perceives the years "one after another" continuing their meaningless procession. The years themselves are indifferent to the narrative consciousness, opaque to its longing for certainty.

As in *The Waves*, the opening descriptive passages of *The Years* give way to chapters which explore human life. But while the first soliloquies of *The Waves* were concerned with the inner realities of six personalities, the first scene of *The Years* focuses on one character: Colonel Abel Pargiter. In this Genesis of the book, he is the archetypal father—and the wrathful god. Although he bears some resemblance to his predecessors, such as Willoughby Vinrace and Ridley Ambrose (the successive fathers of the first novel) and Mr. Ramsay (the definitive father in the lifework), the Colonel is more brutal. Although he is said to have gone to Oxford, he has no discernible intellectual interests and very little social assurance. The fact that he was once stationed in Scarborough may remind us of another retired military officer, Captain Barfoot, who also had an invalid wife and who became a sort of substitute father in *Jacob's Room*. When he is at home he seems interested mainly in bullying his children and avoiding his wife. He is impatient for her to die so that he can be—he imagines—free.

The narrative first discovers him at his club in Piccadilly. But it is not privileged to enter immediately into his thoughts, or even to hear what he hears. Rather, it watches him and his friends from some distance, and strains to hear what they are saying. Its reference to him as "Colonel Abel" is revealing: only a woman or a servant would call him that. The narrative perspective is that of an outsider, observing him and speculating about his thoughts—or about whether he is thinking at all ("Suddenly a thought struck him"). At last it seems to enter his thoughts as he gazes down on Piccadilly: "People were coming back to London; they were settling in for the season. But for him there would be no season; for him there was nothing to do. His wife was dying; but she did not die. . . . One of these days—that was his euphemism for the time when his wife was dead—he would give up London, he thought." The perspective here is very complicated. The narrative seems to know what the Colonel is thinking, and it claims to enter into his thoughts. But the use of "him" maintains a certain distance from the character, or could even hint at a certain alienation of the character from himself. Yet the explicit identification of the "euphemism" is surely the narrative's rather than the character's. And there may be a sardonic judgment by the narrative in the Colonel's thought that "he would give up London."

In the meantime, he consoles himself with Mira, his mistress, who is less attractive—and attracted—than he would like to believe. Because she needs his money she tolerates the fumbling caresses of his "hand that had lost two fingers." (With this hand also, presumably, he examines the ears of her dog for eczema.) As the scene closes, the Colonel realizes that her room is a "dingy little hole," and around her house, so close to other houses, dusk falls quickly. He begins, "impatiently," his lovemaking, "and then the hand that had lost two fingers began to fumble rather lower down where the neck joins the shoulders." The strange impersonality of it all—"the hand . . . the neck"—seems more descriptive of the compulsive gropings of organisms than the caresses of lovers. And in retrospect this distaste is intensified as the narrative discloses the suffering and death of the Colonel's wife, Rose. His insensitivity to her and to the feelings of his daughters can't be forgiven, and this opening sequence at the club and then with Mira becomes, in retrospect, even more damning.

The narrative reveals his personality as pathological from the very beginning. It emphasizes his clawlike hand, suggesting that his touch in general is impaired; the sordidness that he sees in Mira's surroundings reveals his own world view; and so on. He is only what he sees, or what he is said to see—since the narrative does not create for him a convincing inner being. And without that, he remains a bogey-man (his nickname is Bogy), more a projection of the narrative's fears than a character in whom those fears are really explored.

But that is the figure which dominates the given world of *The Years*—i.e., the world which the book opens into and which the narrative tries to break out of. Colonel Pargiter represents the authoritarianism, the pettiness, the insensitivity, the contempt for women (yet the sexual susceptibility) of Mr. Ramsay—but carried to a more corrupt extreme. The Colonel is the darkest incarnation of the father in the *oeuvre*. Like Mr. Ramsay, he is unreasonably demanding, but his wife, unlike the Mrs. Ramsay of "The Window," is unable to shelter the children from these demands. She is an invalid as "1880" begins, and her death closes that chapter. Here, as in *To the Lighthouse*, the psychological implication is that the father's demands have drained the mother's vitality, and eventually take her life. And in both books the relationship is seen from a very complicated, even ambiguous, perspective which is not entirely stable or predictable but which is, on the whole, always closer to the feminine than to the masculine viewpoint, and ultimately closer to the perspectives of the children than those of the parents.

After the opening sequence in the club and at Mira's rooms, the narrative remains outside of Colonel Pargiter's mind, observing him through the perceptions of his daughters: Milly, Delia, Rose, and Eleanor. His sons Martin, Morris, and Edward also enter the story of "1880," but the narrative enters the mind only of Edward, who is at Oxford. In all of the scenes at the Pargiter home, the perspective is associated with one of the daughters even when Martin or Morris is present. It enters the minds of the daughters easily and naturally, and renders their thoughts directly—and without the simultaneous creation of an ironic background to comment on their perceptions. Such a double perspective is necessary, as we have seen, for the Colonel. And it is also used with Edward: at Oxford he is revealed not only through his own thoughts but also through those of his admirer, Ashley, and once through the almost incongruous suggestion of a feminine perspective: Edward "brushed his crest up with the half-conscious gesture that irritated his sister."

The narrative in "1880" also enters the mind of Kitty Malone, the daughter of the master of an Oxford college, to show her encounter with a visiting American couple; her thoughts about herself; her history lesson with her tutor Miss Craddock; tea with a lower-class professor and his family, the Robsons; and dinner at the college, after which the Malones learn that their cousin, Rose Pargiter, is dead. All of this attention to Kitty seems disproportionate to her eventual role in the novel as Lady Lasswade. Perhaps her function here is to exemplify an alternative to the environment of the girls in the Pargiter household. Her father seems more like Ridley Ambrose of *The Voyage Out* than the Colonel; he is a benign, if remote, figure rather than a powerful, negative presence in his daughter's life. He sits up in his study "writing another chapter in his monumental history of the college."

After twenty-five pages devoted to Kitty, the narrative closes the "1880" chapter with the funeral of Mrs. Pargiter, seen entirely through the consciousness of Delia. Just as the season at the beginning of the chapter had been designated as "an uncertain spring," so now the funeral takes place on "an uncertain day." Delia is self-conscious and acutely aware of her surroundings and of the "pose" taken by this person or that during the funeral. She is aware—and ashamed—of her own detachment from it all. She resents the "damnable lie" of the minister, that her mother has been delivered "out of the miseries of this sinful world." He has cheated her, Delia feels, "of the one feeling that was genuine," of the perception of the unity of all life and death. Then "She looked up. She saw Morris and Eleanor side by side; their faces were blurred; their noses were red; the tears were running down them. As for her father he was so stiff and so rigid that she had a convulsive desire to laugh aloud. Nobody can feel like that, she thought. He's overdoing it. None of us feel anything at all, she thought: we're all pretending." It all ends rather anticlimactically, as funerals must, with a return to the world of the living. An inquisitive woman "was stooping down to read the names on the cards. The ceremony was over; rain was falling."

Under slightly different circumstances but with strikingly similar feelings—and even details—in *The Voyage Out*, *To the Lighthouse*, and *The Years*, a woman's death suddenly intrudes. But although it is sudden in its emotional impact, it is revealed, in retrospect, to be inevitable—and sexually inflicted. That death is then followed by a process of total depersonalization and detachment, and an emotional numbness that is more frightening than the death itself, an inability to feel (like the numbness after the death of Evans that Septimus sees as the beginning of his troubles in *Mrs. Dalloway*). In *The Years* the narrative approaches this primal scene more openly and directly than in the earlier works, and much sooner in the story. Still, it has that same quality of ultimate experience which the narrative can't get past. For Delia, and for the feminine perspective as a whole, this is the final outcome of marriage, and it is to escape this fate that Delia, Eleanor, Rose, and Milly must each launch her voyage out.

The structural pattern of *The Years* is, once again, the familiar one of the search for a way out of a confining and unsatisfying situation. That situation is objectified here in "1880" primarily as the world dominated by Colonel Pargiter. The fraudulence of his claim to that domination does not make it any less real, only more sad and bitter. This unfair masculine domination is also exemplified, less crudely but no less powerfully, in the world of Oxford, where Edward Pargiter is studying classics. Edward's thoughts are represented to some extent in that world, but the major perspective on Oxford is that of Kitty Malone, the young woman who is trapped there as the Pargiter girls are in Abercorn Terrace. Together, these settings constitute the given world which the narrative consciousness tries to escape from, or transcend. That world is seen largely through a feminine perspective. In this first chapter, perspectives which can be identified with female

258

characters are used more than four times as often as perspectives identified with males. Another, impersonal perspective is used about as often as the male perspective. This impersonal perspective usually seems somewhat closer to the feminine point of view, however.

The world opens, as we have seen, on the presence of the father, Colonel Pargiter, but his consciousness is entered on only about five pages of this first chapter. His mind, troubled and confused from the very beginning, soon becomes a dead end for the narrative. The only male consciousness which is explored at much length in the chapter is that of Edward. Here as elsewhere in the lifework of Virginia Woolf, the narrative consciousness finds it easier to enter the mind of the intellectual male than that of the sensual male. But it does discover in Edward a sensuality which he does not admit to himself: he is in love with Kitty Malone, but can't acknowledge that feeling, and he eventually ends up as an Oxford don, sheltered in the world of books and abstractions. The narrative also enters briefly the minds of two of Edward's classmates: Gibbs, the country squire type who talks to him about hunting and girls; and Ashley, the aesthete who admires Edward for his Greek beauty and his "perfect figure." Neither of these minds is taken entirely seriously by the narrative. It is more fascinated with Jo, the sensual son of the tutor Mr. Robson, but enters his consciousness only very tentatively and briefly on a couple of pages. There is also a brief glimpse into the mind of Morris Pargiter, the Colonel's son who has become a lawyer.

Most of the intrusions of the narrative into the minds of the Pargiters, of course, are into the thoughts of the daughters. Milly, whose mind is the first to be entered, is revealed only very briefly, and remains a rather vague figure throughout the rest of the book. Delia, the most self-conscious of the sisters, is preoccupied with her mother's dying, and it is through her consciousness, at the end of the chapter, that we see Mrs. Pargiter's funeral. Delia's is an isolated personality, unable to relate to the feelings of the other people around her. She sees the family's unhappiness and their responses to her mother's death as dramatizations, as play-acting that she herself can't enter into. When the narrative enters the mind of Eleanor, the responsible one, it finds bewilderment, loneliness, but above all, a feeling of duty: "She seemed to be alone in the midst of nothingness; yet must descend, must carry her burden." Rose, the youngest sister, is entered by the narrative in this first chapter primarily to reveal her traumatic encounter with a sexual exhibitionist and its aftermath. The allusions to this throughout the book suggest that the narrative regards it as a crucial experience, but the experience itself, as it is registered in Rose's consciousness, seems much less traumatic than the narrative later implies that it has been.

In defining its given world of "1880," the narrative has shown slices of middle-class life in London and Oxford. As its story begins, the narrative is preoccupied with the meaninglessness of time—the empty succession of days, months, seasons, years. The story begins as a search for meaning. But the given world is totally dominated by an archetypal father who is either deformed (like Colonel Pargiter) or remote (like Doctor Malone). The possibilities of consciousness in such a world are painfully limited. This depressing world view culminates in a numbed perception of the empty ceremonies mourning the mother's death, and a horrified recognition of the inability to feel. Whether the narrative consciousness can ever believe in the possibility of meaning, whether it can feel again (or allow itself to feel again), whether it can discover an authentic embodiment for its own inner longings—all of these questions remain open at the end of the first chapter of *The Years*.

The longest chapters in the book are the first, "1880," and the last, "Present Day." In between, a series of vignettes links that past to this present. In them the narrative searches, as always, for meaning. But most of them end in the revelation of some loss. As a whole, they illustrate the law of entropy: the created world degenerates toward disorder, enervation, and death.

At the end of "1891" Colonel Pargiter is visiting his brother. Sir Digby Pargiter, his wife Eugénie, and their daughters, Maggie and Sara, represent an alternative to the way of life—or death—of Abercorn Terrace. The Colonel has always admired Eugénie and wishes that he could talk to her alone, but she and Digby are dining out, and the Colonel leaves "depressed and disappointed." "He envied Digby his house, his wife, his children. He was getting old, he felt." And he senses that "the autumn was drawing in" with all its signs of dissolution. This scene represents the narrative's most extensive penetration into the Colonel's consciousness, an entry which is possible because he is no longer the virile, dominant male. Whether or not the narrative takes pleasure in his decline and his loneliness, it is certainly fascinated by them, and it now regards him with some pity.

As "1907" ends, Maggie stops in the hallway to listen to her parents talking downstairs. They are discussing a lock which Eugénie had promised to have put on the kitchen door, but had forgotten. Then there is the sound of a drink being made, and the lights go out downstairs. It all seems very inconsequential. And that may be its point, for we learn in the next chapter that Digby and Eugénie are dead. In retrospect, then, this overheard conversation acquires a special poignance.

As "1908" closes, Eleanor is thinking how terrible old age is, and how much better it is to die in the prime of life, like Digby and Eugénie. We never really know anyone or anything in our lives, she thinks. Then the wind gusts, and there is the sound of crashing glass: "Miss Pym's conservatory?" Martin asks. "Miss Pym?" Eleanor replies, "She's been dead these twenty years!" Miss Pym is very remote indeed: in "1880" there is a reference to Martin's "shooting Miss Pym's cats next door." For him, apparently, that had been an important experience, and for him the breaking glass must be from her conservatory (perhaps he had shot at her greenhouse as well[2]). The gusting wind, too, suggests the randomness and fatality of experience. We are locked into who we are, and never really outgrow our primal experiences.

The "1910" vignette ends with the cry of a man in the street, "The King's dead!" This moment, perceived through the consciousness of Maggie, marks the end of the Edwardian era.

At the close of "1911" Eleanor goes to bed in the home of the Chinnerys, Morris' in-laws whom she visits each summer in Dorset.

2 This guess is confirmed by a passage in *The Pargiters*, ed. Mitchell A. Leaska (New York: New York Public Library, 1977), 48, where the boy is called Bobby. *The Pargiters* is the first version of what later became "1880."

"She felt as if things were moving past her. . . . people's lives, their changing lives." William Whatney, to whom she had been vaguely attracted and attractive, is going to bed alone in the next room. Moths enter her open window. Desultorily she reads Dante, and "Brushed lightly by her mind that was watching the moths on the ceiling, and listening to the call of the owl . . . the words did not give out their full meaning. . . . Again the sense came to her. . . . Things can't go on for ever, she thought. Things pass, things change. . . . And where are we going? Where? Where? The moths were dashing round the ceiling; the book slipped on to the floor. . . . Darkness reigned." Now in her mid-fifties, Eleanor has the feeling that her life is just beginning, whereas Whatney's is over. Moths, here as elsewhere in the *oeuvre*, are perceived as being governed entirely by instinct, and relentlessly driven toward sex and death. Moths can't resist the lure of the flame. Drawn into Eleanor's room by her candle, they symbolize the intrusion of the instinctual into the customarily intellectual "room" of awareness, so that the mind relaxes its grip, and the whole consciousness lapses into the realm of darkness. For the moment Eleanor's relentless abstract questioning ceases, and she simply *is*: existence displaces the search for essence. The darkness here is like that of "Time Passes" in *To the Lighthouse*: both the lapse into chaos and exhaustion, and the possibility of regeneration.

At the end of "1913" Martin has told Crosby that "I must be off." But it is a lie, intended merely to free him from the discomfort of having to talk to the family's old servant. He thinks of his father's mistress, whom the family had learned about only after the Colonel's death, and of the atmosphere of the house at Abercorn Terrace, where "all those different people had lived, boxed up together, telling lies." And as Crosby disappears into the winter afternoon, "He turned away." This vignette creates an implied contrast with Eleanor, whose goodbye to Crosby opened this chapter: Eleanor showed much more feeling for her than Martin does. But it is his perspective in which the chapter must culminate. He, after all, is the man, the inheritor and exemplar of the system which exploits both Crosby and Eleanor. His concern about "lies" is real enough, but so is his insensitivity to

Crosby's suffering and to women in general. "What was the harm of keeping a mistress," he thinks; what he disapproves of is that his father "lied" about it. He prefers to turn away from the realities involved there, just as he turns away from Crosby when he sees that she is "like a frightened little animal." This vignette reveals that men's insensitivity never changes: it is one of the principles of the world which the narrative consciousness detests, but which it rediscovers in each generation.

As the events of "1914" come to an end, Kitty takes the train north, and then her new motorcar, to the great house which now is hers, temporarily ("Nothing of this belonged to her; her son would inherit"), as the wife of Lord Lasswade. Like Eleanor at the end of "1911," Kitty feels that "All passes, all changes." And, like Orlando in her final return to her great house, Kitty climbs to the top of a hill, where she can see everything in a dominant perspective: she "looked out over the billowing land. . . . as she watched, light moved and dark moved; light and shadow went travelling. . . . A deep murmur sang in her ears—the land itself, singing to itself, a chorus, alone. She lay there listening. She was happy, completely. Time had ceased." Here she enters into a mysterious appreciation of nature which enables her to stop time, suddenly to transcend the relentless sweep of the seasons and the years. Suddenly she knows that light and shadow are inseparable aspects of the same transcendent whole, that they move together, are experienced together, in a rhythm which she can suddenly become aware of, and which can lead to deeper insights. The imagery is related to that of the eclipse of the sun.[3] In her moment of epiphany she realizes that she is part of the land itself, that its rhythms are hers, in a universal and timeless whole. It is the same longing for symbiosis with the earth that Vita expresses in her poem *The Land* (quoted as "The Oak Tree" in *Orlando*) and which she tried to express in her design of the gardens at Sissinghurst Castle. Kitty's epiphany illustrates that same longing for transcendence through a merging into the timeless energy of the earth itself—even though that is not an

3   See page 181 herein, note 28.

outcome in which the narrative consciousness can be finally satisfied. And there is the additional irony that this is the last season of peace before the Great War.

At the end of "1917" Eleanor is in an omnibus on her way home from a visit to Renny and Maggie in Westminster, where they have been through an air raid. There she learns that her friend Nicholas is a homosexual—and discovers that this doesn't change her feeling for him. On the bus she finds herself staring at an old man who "was eating something out of a paper bag." He catches her staring at him and, with a sardonic "Like to see what I've got for supper, Lady?" he "held out for her inspection a hunk of bread on which was laid a slice of cold meat or sausage." Throughout "1917" the range of Eleanor's awareness is expanded. Confronted with one thing after another which she had felt to be disgusting, she emerges from each experience with greater tolerance, and a larger awareness. Nevertheless, the revelations themselves are depressing: although Eleanor can become more tolerant of the sordid, she still sees it as essentially sordid—and that is mostly what she sees.

The brief vignette of "1918" takes place in Crosby's consciousness, and ends with her learning of the armistice. She is angry because she has to clean the bathtub after another roomer, the "Count,"[4] has used it. She hears the guns booming again, and someone tells her that the war is over. As the scene ends, "The guns went on booming and the sirens wailed." This too is a poignant moment because of what is not said, and Crosby herself is a poignant figure because of what we know of her many years of service to the Pargiters and its pathetic rewards. Her bad temper now is more understandable to us than to her. The narrative emphasizes the limitations of Crosby's consciousness. The fact that peace has come at last means absolutely nothing to her. In that sense this ending is an ironic anticipation of the ending of the book as a whole, where first Eleanor and then the narrative itself discover a more all-encompassing peace.

---

4   The "Count" and his greasy bathtub foreshadow a later scene, in the "Present Day," when North Pargiter visits Sara and is disgusted, even "sickened," by what she tells him of a Jew who shares her bathroom: "Damn the Jew!" North exclaims. The implications are very complicated, both for the book and for the author, whose husband was a Jew.

Thus the drama of intentionality returns inexorably toward the present. In "1880" it had looked at life in London and in Oxford, entered the minds of at least sixteen different people, continued for over eighty-five pages in its effort to define a world. But despite the scope of the exploration, "1880" remains a series of fragments. Perhaps another decade would serve better. And so the story shifts to 1891. But there too there can be only "orts, scraps, and fragments" (to borrow a phrase from the future, from *Between the Acts*). And so the search continues, into the twentieth century. But again and again the vignettes reveal only death, loss, bewilderment. Old Miss Pym, Digby and Eugénie, the King himself: no one is immune. Eleanor realizes that people's lives are moving past her like landscape seen from a train, and "Darkness reigned"; Martin turns away from Crosby's fear and loneliness; Kitty escapes into a vision in which "Time has ceased." But time does not cease. Instead it brings the Great War and the subsequent "peace"—both of which are greeted with equal incomprehension. And so the scene shifts at last from "1918" to what can only be called "Present Day"—an admission that the search for meaning in history has failed. There is no history other than the present moment. Although we may think we are looking at "1880," "1891," or some other point in history, we are really looking only at ourselves, in the here-and-now. The past is a perspective.

In its long exploration of the existential present, the narrative is more limited, more stable, and less ambitious than it had been in "1880." It enters only half as many minds now, and even the range of its physical settings reflects the narrative's falling levels of energy and motion, of thought and feeling. The narrative consciousness now identifies almost exclusively with three characters: North, Eleanor, and Peggy. Eleanor, whom we have known since "1880," emerges now as the visionary character, the one who transcends the merely personal, sexual, social, and political domains to enter into a new realm of knowledge, to perceive the unity and necessity of all things.

There are forms of consciousness from "1880" that have no real place in the present. That first chapter had culminated in the mother's funeral. There the narrative was aware primarily of a lack of feeling, of a great distance from other people, and a suspicion of their sincerity. It assigned these feelings to Delia. But in its later search for their antithesis it turns away from her. Through the rest of the story she remains in the background, occasionally alluded to by the other characters, but not reappearing until the final chapter. When Eleanor hears of Parnell's death in 1891 she knows at once that she must go to Delia, who had left home, apparently, to fight for his "Cause," and for "Justice." We learn in "1910" that she has married an Irishman. And in the final chapter she gives the party at her house in Westminster. It is a complete transformation, from the alienated girl of "1880" to the social hostess of the "Present Day." But the only stage of her development which is revealed from the inside is her alienation. The subsequent stages are only reported from the outside, except for a few brief glimpses into her mind in the final chapter, where we learn that "That had always been her aim; to mix people; to do away with the absurd conventions of English life." While such an "aim" could follow from the state of her mind as it is shown in "1880," the change itself is too great to be consistent with the structure of the story which we have seen. Instead, Delia's transformation remains an assertion by the narrative, not a truth which is revealed by it. The creative consciousness wishes to believe that such a transformation is possible, that a self-centered, alienated girl like Delia could become a Mrs. Dalloway. But it can't imagine how that could happen; it can't see how it could happen. It can only claim that it has happened. The assertion remains an assertion.

Rose, for whom the encounter with the sexual exhibitionist is so traumatic in "1880," devotes her life to feminism. Although she is present at Delia's party in the final chapter, the narrative no longer enters into her mind; it only reports what she says. In her case, as in Delia's, the narrative tells about, rather than shows, the development of the personality. And Edward, whose thoughts are known to the narrative in "1880," is treated in the same way. Although he too is at Delia's party, the narrative is no longer interested in his thoughts. He has become a stereotypical Oxford don: proud, pedantic, cautious, mannered, inhibited, dull.

Kitty, whose mind the narrative enters on more pages than any other in "1880," has by 1891 become Lady Lasswade and entered into a way of life which the narrative can only catch glimpses of—most notably in 1910 when she attends a meeting where she sees Eleanor and then goes to the opera, and in 1914 when she travels to her great country house and has her climactic vision in which "Time had ceased." In the "Present Day" the few glimpses of her consciousness show that she still "wanted something." In that feeling she is very much like Eleanor. But Kitty's feelings are seen too infrequently to create a very convincing picture of her development. Her character too remains largely in the realm of assertion.

The emergence of North and Peggy into prominence is unexpected. They are brother and sister, but seem more aware of their enmity for each other than their love. Their father, Morris, is Eleanor's brother. In her youth he had been a promising barrister, but is now thought of as a failure—by his son, at least. The mother, Celia, is dead—a repetition of the same pattern as in the previous generation, where the Colonel's wife died many years before he died, and Eugénie some months before Digby.[5]

North has just returned to London after many years in Africa, where he had owned a sheep farm. The only previous extended mention of him had been in "1917," where Sara reports his visit to her on the eve of his departure to join his regiment (which she refers to as contemptuously as the "Royal Rat-catchers") and Eleanor can only remember him as "a nice cricketing boy smoking a cigar on a terrace." Although we never learn about his experience in the war, we might guess that it was a factor in his exile to Africa. And his fondness for Sara may have something to do with her status, similar to his own, as a sort of outcast. Mildly deformed by a childhood accident, she has never married (North hasn't either), and she has chosen to live in not-very-genteel poverty. Like him, she has a tendency to mock hallowed institutions.

North's consciousness, then, is that of the sensitive man of his

5   The early death of a woman and the subsequent trauma for the survivors are recurring motifs in the *oeuvre*. In *The Voyage Out* there are Rachel's mother and Rachel herself, in *To the Lighthouse* Mrs. Ramsay and her daughter Prue. In these cases too, successive generations—mother and daughter —are stricken.

generation, now middle-aged and disillusioned by experience, but unable to find anything else to believe in. He is very much aware of being "an outsider. After all these years, he thought, everyone was paired off; settled down; busy with their own affairs." But he had been an outsider in Africa too, "and very lonely." His extreme self-consciousness reflects his ontological insecurity. At Delia's party he dances with a girl who invites him to meet her tomorrow. The narrative does not describe this moment of invitation directly, but describes North's remembering it and "feeling effusive." His sexual feelings can be acknowledged, it seems, only in the realm of memory. And one of these memories, which emerges during his visit to his cousin Sara, makes his sexual nature seem even more ambiguous. Sara remembers the "wonderful letters" he used to write her, and recalls one in particular:

"And then you had a day off," she went on, "and jolted along a rough white road in a springless cart to the next town—"

"Sixty miles away," he said.

"And went to a bar; and met a man from the next—ranch?" She hesitated as if the word might be the wrong one.

"Ranch, yes, ranch," he confirmed her. "I went to the town and had a drink at the bar—"

"And then?" she said. He laughed. There were some things he had not told her. He was silent.

"Then you stopped writing," she said.

The narrative point of view throughout this scene is consistent with North's perspective. It sees what he sees rather than what Sara sees (*e.g.*, "A thimblefull of wine always made her tipsy, he remembered. Her eyes shone; her cheeks glowed"), and has access to his mind, not hers. Yet it doesn't think of the specific "things he had not told her"; it represses them. They must remain unspoken, in the heart of darkness, like Marlow's fevered imaginings of Kurtz's orgies with the natives. Is it significant that the man at the bar is mentioned by Sara and not by North? Although this reticence with Sara may indicate nothing more than a social convention, his reticence with himself is more revealing. And so is the narrative's reluctance to explore his inner nature. He goes on to tell Sara that he stopped writing because "I forgot what you were like." But this too, like the reference to meeting a man from the next ranch, is surrounded by silence. Why did North suddenly forget what Sara was like? Whatever he has or has not told her, the narrative seems to imply that he has some secret knowledge of "the horror, the horror." Whatever that is, it seems to be incompatible with writing—and with thinking. So while the narrative consciousness enters into the mind of North more frequently than it does into the mind of any other character in this chapter, what it reveals is likely to be what he is not thinking.

Except for a brief glance into the mind of Martin as he admires Delia, North's is the only male consciousness which the narrative enters in the "Present Day." On the whole, the various representatives of the female consciousness are more prominent in this final chapter, though not so overwhelmingly as in "1880." The narrative gives equal attention to the perspectives of Eleanor, whom we have known ever since 1880, and Peggy, North's sister, who is a doctor. Kitty, Lady Lasswade, has some significance as a "reflector" character here, but the narrative isn't nearly as interested in her mind now as it was in "1880." And Delia, through whose eyes we saw the funeral then, has also married money. Now she seems trapped, like Mrs. Dalloway, in the role of perfect hostess, saying over and over again, with as much sincerity as possible, "How very nice of you to come!" But when the narrative does enter her mind again at last, it discovers there a sense of irony rather than complacency. Although the other two Pargiter sisters of her generation are at her party, the narrative does not enter their minds. Milly, who in 1880 had thought of herself as "a mousy, down-trodden, inefficient little chit . . . always snubbed by Papa," is now grossly fat and, North imagines, mindless; she is the wife of Hugh Gibbs, Edward's rich country-squire classmate at Oxford. Little Rose is now a stout old woman and, says Martin, in an unconscious allusion to the fantasy which had brought her to her traumatic encounter with the grey-faced pervert at the pillar-box in 1880, "the very spit and image . . . of old Uncle Pargiter of Pargiter's Horse." She had become a militant feminist, and had been jailed for it. She never married. But the narrative, once so fascinated with her reaction to the exhibitionist, no longer wishes to know what she is thinking.

Peggy Pargiter is the female representative of the next generation. Professionally the range of possibilities is wider now than it was for the women of that earlier generation; Peggy is a doctor. But in her personal life she seems even less satisfied than her aunts. In the passages that evoke her consciousness, there is one glimpse after another of distress and anxiety. In their cumulative effect, they constitute a view of the world and of the self which comes as close to despair as anything in Virginia Woolf's novels.

Peggy, marooned when the dance started, over by the bookcase, stood as close to it as she could. In order to cover her loneliness she took down a book. It was bound in green leather; and had, she noted as she turned it in her hands, little gilt stars tooled upon it. Which is all to the good, she thought, turning it over, because then it'll seem as if I were admiring the binding. . . . But I can't stand here admiring the binding, she thought. She opened it. He'll say what I'm thinking, she thought as she did so. Books opened at random always did.

"*La médiocrité de l'univers m'étonne et me révolte,*" she read. That was it. Precisely. She read on. ". . . *la petitesse de toutes choses m'emplit de dégoût.* . . ." They were treading on her toes. ". . . *la pauvreté des êtres humains m'anéantit.*" She shut the book and put it back on the shelf.

Precisely, she said.

This scene discloses, as well as any, the psychological reality of Peggy in the "Present Day." The word *marooned* links her with other spinsters in Virginia Woolf's work. Alone and very self-conscious on an island of rationality—or of rationalization—in a chaotic sea of emotion, she is like Lily Briscoe, who feels "moored to the shore" and destined to watch others make their climactic voyages out, to the lighthouse. They feel their isolation not as shelter, but as exposure, nakedness, and feel compelled to "cover" it. That is where books and art come in: they can objectify our existential anguish, can transform it from the merely personal to the universal, make it more fully meaningful. Peggy is aware of only the cover and the binding of the book, not the author's name or the title.[6] Driven further by self-consciousness, she opens it, knowing that it will say just what she is thinking; "Books opened at random always did." But as the scene has just

6 But somehow she knows that it was written by a man—which may show that she knows more than she is conscious of here.

shown us, books are not really opened at random: they are there to say just what we wish them to say. And so Peggy reads that the insignificance of human beings in general makes her own being insignificant too.

She is very conscious of her heritage, but of being trapped rather than freed by it. She knows that she looks like her grandmother (in the painting which keeps reappearing in *The Years*) even though she doesn't want to. And she is conscious of how other people, too, seem locked into their destinies: "Each person had a certain line laid down in their minds, she thought, and along it came the same old sayings." She feels a nostalgia for an older, simpler world that she herself never really knew, but which has become identical, in her mind, with Eleanor the believer and with the vanished era of the 1880s, "so beautiful in its unreality."

Peggy is trapped in another way, a way which she doesn't recognize so consciously: "And what's this? she asked, for the sight of her father in his rather worn shoes had given her a direct spontaneous feeling. This sudden warm spurt? she asked, examining it. She watched him cross the room. His shoes always affected her strangely. Part sex; part pity, she thought. Can one call it 'love'? But she forced herself to move." One could call it "love." Or one could call it an unresolved Electra complex. And one might also think of the final scene in *Jacob's Room*, where the old shoes become the emblem of Jacob's absence, the final image of him, shared by his mother and his *bon ami*. Lily's excessive admiration of Mr. Ramsay's boots may also come to mind: the woman who is not quite a daughter deflecting the advances of the man who is not quite her father. And there are the memorable tennis shoes of Giles in *Between the Acts*, bloodied in a moment of compulsive violence that expresses his inner sexual nature, and which his wife finds so repulsive and so irresistibly fascinating. In *The Years* Peggy does try to understand her feelings. But her rationalizations do not reach the depth of the feelings themselves: the "warm spurt," the sudden paralysis from which "she forced herself to move."

A similar moment recurs later, when she overhears Delia praising her to her father: "There, said Peggy, that's pleasure. The nerve down her spine seemed to tingle as the praise reached her father. Each emotion touched a different nerve. A sneer rasped the thigh; pleasure thrilled the spine; and also affected the sight. The stars had softened; they quivered. Her father brushed her shoulder as he dropped his hand; but neither of them spoke." Here she is more analytically aware of her feelings and of their causes. But she is still very much at their mercy. Suddenly her world must be seen through tears, which aren't really recognized. Rather, the world itself suddenly changes: *The stars had softened. They quivered.* It is a frequent feeling in the world of Virginia Woolf, beginning with the first scene of the first novel: the sudden moment when familiar perspectives dissolve and a new and frightening reality overwhelms the established order.

Thus Peggy, who prides herself on her honesty and her grasp of scientific, objective reality, is always at the mercy of her emotions, the sudden thrill in the thigh or the spine. She is very much afraid of love, and feels awe for those who can become involved: "How do they manage it—love, childbirth? The people who touch each other and go up in a cloud of smoke: red smoke? . . . Pain must outbalance pleasure by two parts to one, she thought, in all social relations. Or am I the exception, the peculiar person? she continued, for the others seemed happy enough. Yes. . . . I'm the exception; hard; cold; in a groove already; merely a doctor." Again this is reminiscent of the mental imagery of Lily Briscoe, whose feelings about Paul Rayley, ten years after she had seen him, could blaze up like a bonfire. To become involved in physical love is to burn, to go up in smoke, to experience twice as much pain as pleasure. Peggy is aware that she must continue in her hard, cold, lonely destiny. And she is aware that "I do not love my kind." Her recognition is not too distant from that of Septimus in *Mrs. Dalloway*, who discovers that he could not feel.

Unable to love, Peggy represses her own ego. She is afraid of the development of an "I" that would be visible to the world. And she resents the emergence of the "I" in others. At Delia's party she talks with a young man: "I, I, I—he went on. . . . with that nerve-drawn egotist's face. . . . He had to expose, had to exhibit. But why let him? . . . For what do I care about his 'I, I, I'?" Yet she also resents the attempt to repress emotion—when she detects it in other people: "All her patients said that, she thought. Rest—rest—let me rest. How to deaden; how to cease to feel . . . to cease to be."

Only once during the "Present Day" does Peggy seem to be lifted from her depression. She sees Renny laughing, and "Her muscles began to twitch involuntarily. She could not help laughing too." For a moment she experiences a new "state of being in which there was real laughter, real happiness, and this fractured world was whole; whole, vast, and free." Although the laughter is welcome, it comes *involuntarily*—indeed, against her will. And the "state of being" which she enters so briefly here—"whole, vast, and free"—is the antithesis of her usual state. She seems fated to perceive her world as "fractured," narrow, confining.

Peggy's aunt Eleanor becomes the final visionary figure in the book. She is the one character whose consciousness is evoked to a significant extent in both the first and last chapters. The narrative enters her mind in every year except "1907," "1914," and "1918," and it gives her its final transcendent perspective. In a sense, that represents a transformation too, from the Eleanor of "1880," conscious primarily of "carrying her burden" of responsibilities, to the elderly visionary of the "Present Day," conscious that life is a "miracle." In her case, unlike the others, the narrative does emphasize the inner reality of both the first and final stages of development, as well as a number of stages in between. Her expectancy at the end—"And now?"—shows that she is still capable of growth and looking toward the future.

Her transcendent vision comes not long after she has wakened from her nap at the party. It is as if she had been reborn: "Here she was; alive; in this room, with living people. . . . At first they were without identity. Then she recognized them." Her consciousness endows them with identity. And as the conversation continues around her, Eleanor is swept on to epiphany:

There must be another life, she thought, sinking back into her chair, exasperated. Not in dreams; but here and now, in this room, with living people. She felt as if she were standing on the edge of a precipice with her hair blown back; she was about to grasp something that just evaded her. There must be another life, here and now, she repeated. This is too short, too broken. We know nothing, even about ourselves. We're only just beginning, she thought, to understand, here and there. She hollowed her hands in her lap, just as Rose had hollowed hers round her ears. She held her hands hollowed; she felt that she wanted to enclose the present moment; to make it stay; to fill it fuller and fuller, with the past, the present and the future, until it shone, whole, bright, deep with understanding.

This passage can be interpreted as evidence of a visionary victory over the powers of darkness and chaos. And certainly it does confirm Eleanor's capacity for belief, which is the quality in her that Peggy admires so much. But Eleanor's consciousness also reveals a capacity for doubt. The biblical equivalent of her feeling could be "Lord, I believe; help my unbelief." Her desire is for transcendence, "another life," but in the "here and now," and in the space of her present consciousness, "in this room." Her vision of herself as standing on the edge of a precipice with her hair blown back combines several familiar Woolfian motifs: the sudden overview of a promised land (of order, peace, stability, the wholeness of all things), the terror—and temptation—of plunging to one's death in transcendent knowledge (like Rhoda does in *The Waves*, and Clarissa doesn't in *Mrs. Dalloway*), the threatening but exhilarating winds of chaos, and of sexuality. Rose hollowed her hands round her ears because she couldn't hear; Eleanor hollows hers in her lap because her lap is empty. She wishes to fill the present moment because she senses that it is not full. She wishes it to shine because it does not, to make it "whole, bright, deep with understanding" because it is none of these things.

Eleanor herself recognizes her vision as wishful thinking, and "It's useless, she thought, opening her hands. It must drop. It must fall. And then? she thought. For her too there would be the endless night, the endless dark. She looked ahead of her as though she saw opening in front of her a very long dark tunnel. But, thinking of the dark, something baffled her; in fact, it was growing light. The blinds were white." It is, of course, the dawn. The tunnel, which throughout the *oeuvre* has been symbolic of restriction and predestination, dissolves into illumination. Nature here, and in the closing passages of the book, is perceived as benevolent: it intervenes to bring about what the human consciousness alone could not. And now Eleanor is given her final vision: she sees a young couple get out of a taxi and enter a house:

He fitted his latch-key to the door. "There," Eleanor murmured, as he opened the door and they stood for a moment on the threshold. "There!" she repeated as the door shut with a little thud behind them.

Then she turned round into the room. "And now?" she said, looking at Morris, who was drinking the last drops of a glass of wine. "And now?" she asked, holding out her hands to him.

The sun had risen, and the sky above the houses wore an air of extraordinary beauty, simplicity and peace.

In this final passage of *The Years* Eleanor reaches the transcendent perspective which had been implied earlier. Her choric—though cryptic—comment, "There!" invites us to see more in the young couple than we do. In that sense she becomes both the creator and the medium of the final vision. She reconciles the longing for what should be with the knowledge of what is. And so she joins the others whose visions closed the previous chapters of the *oeuvre*, from Hirst of *The Voyage Out* to Bernard of *The Waves*.

In the final sentence of the book the narrative consciousness withdraws from Eleanor to a more impersonal position. But what it sees is what she has just seen, and in the merging of the two perspectives, the world of human consciousness and the world of impersonal nature are revealed as one world. It is as if nature itself reflects Eleanor's consciousness, and confirms her perceptions.

Her view of the young couple getting out of a cab two doors down the square echoes, rather vaguely, a moment in 1880 when Delia and Milly had stood at a window in Abercorn Terrace to watch a young man get out of a cab "two doors lower down" and Eleanor had warned them, "Don't be caught looking." Now Eleanor herself is looking, and that act of perception moves her to a mysterious sense of completion: "There!" The words which describe this taxi at the end, "gliding slowly round the square" in the morning twilight are the same ones which described the taxi which brought Eleanor and Peggy to the party in the evening twilight. That cab had taken "the long way round" the square, but Eleanor, though she is aware that the meter is running and the bill mounting, says simply, "He'll find his way in time." In a slightly different sense, that is what everyone in the book must try to do. Circling the square may also have broader implications. The circle encompassing a square is a traditional symbol of wholeness and completion, and Eleanor's final vision is undoubtedly intended, by the narrative consciousness, to square the circle—in the sense of justifying the whole cycle of life shown in the story.

Is that vision more than an assertion of wholeness and meaning? That is, does it emerge authentically out of Eleanor's experiences as the narrative has described them? Or is it only a fantasy of transcendence? In one sense, the apparent confirmation of Eleanor's feelings by the natural world may seem no more than another instance of the "pathetic fallacy," the attribution of human feelings to inanimate nature. Or it may be seen as another attempt by the narrative to tell what it cannot show, or to translate the psychological drama here into some new mystical dimension where the former rules no longer apply, and where a conclusion need only be proclaimed rather than achieved.

When *The Years* is seen as a drama of intentionality, the meanings of the ending are revealed in a different way. Throughout the drama the narrative consciousness has been searching for an embodiment which will be fully satisfying, and therefore final. The last sentence of the book does reach a satisfying perspective, a view of a promised land of "extraordinary beauty, simplicity, and peace." That perspective arises out of the story itself. But it is not really all that the narrative had hoped for—a final synthesis and resolution of contrapuntal themes, like Lily's "vision" at the end of *To the Lighthouse*, or even Bernard's "summing up" in *The Waves*. It represents, instead, the antithesis of what the narrative has learned throughout the story. The dominant perspective of the existential present in *The Years* is the reality of North and Peggy: an almost unrelieved experience of alienation, skepticism, insecurity, repression, entrapment, longing for escape, psychosexual compulsions.

Eleanor's life is said to have been different from that. She has lived for others: "My life's been other people's lives, Eleanor thought—my father's; Morris's; my friends' lives; Nicholas's." Yet none of these people loom very large in her consciousness when the narrative reveals it. Similarly, although the narrative says that Eleanor has just returned from India, she never thinks of India. Her mind is more likely to be focused on abstractions: "is there a pattern; a theme, recurring, like music; half remembered, half foreseen? . . . a gigantic pattern, momentarily perceptible? The thought gave her extreme pleasure: that there was a pattern. But who makes it? Who thinks it? She could not finish her thought. 'Nicholas . . . ' she said. She wanted him to finish it; to take her thought and carry it out into the open unbroken; to make it whole, beautiful, entire." Once again the theme of the frustrated search for unity and wholeness emerges into dominance. The "gigantic pattern" which is longed for remains always just beyond reach. "Who thinks it?": Virginia Woolf had written those very words in her diary (September 25, 1929) as she was wrestling with the original version of *The Waves*. And in that diary entry those words are followed by two sentences which seem relevant to *The Years* as well: "And am I outside the thinker? One wants some device which is not a trick." In *The Years* a hint of the "device," the "trick," remains, perhaps, in the evocation of Eleanor by the consciousness that really "thinks" the story. Longing for a gigantic pattern, the narrative consciousness can't really see one. It wishes to believe that Eleanor could, and implies that she does. But what it actually shows is that she remains at the mercy of her desire for transcendent patterns, just as North and Peggy remain the victims of their emotions. Eleanor remains convinced that "it's been a perpetual discovery, my life. A miracle." Her discoveries, however, are more alleged than shown. And her optimistic convictions are sometimes undercut. For example, just after this realization that her life has been a perpetual discovery, a miracle, she sees Peggy "reading a book," and is reassured by this perception of "something solid." But when the narrative consciousness itself shifts to Peggy's mind, it reveals that Eleanor's view of her is quite mistaken: Peggy has picked up the book in an agony of insecurity, and her reading is confirming her feeling of the insignificance of everything.

In a sense, Eleanor's final perspective is posthumous. Having already given her own life to others, she can only wait to see what happens: "And now?" The existential present belongs to North and Peggy. But Eleanor's final gesture should not be overlooked. She turns to Morris, "holding out her hands to him." This gesture acknowledging the love of brother and sister contrasts with the present alienation of North and Peggy—which we know, however, to be opposed by their love and concern for each other. And Eleanor's gesture may also suggest a final reconciliation with the father. We know little about Morris, really. We may recall that at Abercorn Terrace he was irritable at being "cooped up with all these women in an atmosphere of unreal emotion" and that even then he had already taken over some of the father's family responsibilities from the Colonel, or that his son North thinks that Morris is a failure, or that when his daughter Peggy sees him cross a room she is overcome with emotion, or that his wife is dead. In the world of the "Present Day" he is the father, as the Colonel had been in the world of "1880." And if the obscurity of Morris represents a repudiation of the father, then Eleanor's welcome at the end may suggest a final reconciliation, a potential return of the forgotten father into the wasteland of the present.

In the search for a more authentic existence in *The Years*, the narrative ranges from "1880" to the "Present Day." But the present turns out to be the inescapable reality against which the earlier years can be seen only as background. All of those earlier events are necessitated, as it turns out, by the inescapable presence of the here-and-now, which can't be fixed in history (as, say, "1936"), but only experienced, existentially, as an immediate present. It has no real place in history, only that disquieting immediacy which Eleanor's final words acknowledge: "And now?" In whatever terms we may try to write the story of the past, we find that we can write it only through the perspective of this existential present. So "1880," "1891," etc., are meaningful only in relation to the present.

As *The Years* opens, the narrative consciousness seems preoccupied with the meaninglessness of the succession of days, months, seasons, years. The story begins, like its predecessors, as a search for meaning. The long first chapter locates the origin of this story in "1880." Then, after a rather long look at "1891," the narrative skips to

"1907." Now it has discovered its era, apparently. Events from that era form a series of vignettes as England moves toward, and at last out of, the war. In one sense, time slows down: the intervals between the years now become shorter. But in another sense it speeds up: the text of "1907" is less than half as long as that of "1891." Perhaps these tendencies illustrate the more fragmentary quality of modern life. The narrative also modulates the intervals between these years, returning always to one: 1, 2, 1, 2, 1, 3, 1. It is almost as if the narrative were illustrating an uncertainty principle: we can know either the present moment or the vector of history, but not both together. And after the war, the narrative ceases to search in history. It chooses instead to explore the "Present Day." History has been unmasked as a form of nostalgia.

In "1880" the narrative turns away from the death of the Colonel's wife in London. It turns first toward a world which seems antithetical: Oxford. There, perhaps, Edward could become a better man than his father. There, perhaps, a girl like Kitty could be free of the limitations which face the Pargiter girls. Or perhaps education is its own reward, an enrichment of life. But that turns out to be a false hope. The Colonel himself had gone to Oxford, we are told, and his son turns out to be just as limited in his own way as his father had been. And Oxford is even more oppressive for women in some ways than London. They aren't taken seriously, intellectually, in the university. A woman might aspire to become a Lucy Craddock, a tutor of the daughters of the dons. Or if she were exceptionally lucky, she might be invited to join the faculty of one of the new women's colleges. If Oxford does anything for Kitty, perhaps it gives her the social opportunity to marry a title and money. When the narrative enters her consciousness in the years after her marriage, however, it never catches her thinking about her husband. And there is no reason for the narrative to return to Oxford in the "Present Day." The existential present belongs, instead, to North and Peggy, who are so self-conscious, alienated, skeptical, repressed, insecure, and lonely. Peggy, an educated person, perceives her fellow men as emotionally atrophied, desiring only their physical comfort and an emotional invulnerability. They wish, she thinks, to be emotionally dead.

In the structure of the *oeuvre*, *The Years* could be seen as an expansion of the "Time Passes" section of *To the Lighthouse*, the heart of darkness which links the mother's edenic domain of "The Window" with the father's promised land of "The Lighthouse." In "Time Passes" the mother suddenly vanishes into the long night, and the paradisal childhood world of "The Window" becomes a memory. The displaced artist must then struggle to recapture that world, and to bring it within the perspective of the voyage to the lighthouse. The childhood paradise had been the "given" world of *To the Lighthouse*. "Time Passes" was its antithesis, the fall or expulsion from paradise. "The Lighthouse" was the artist's attempt to regain that paradise. But the given world of *The Years* is the terrible world of the mother's death. What had seemed like an aberration, a nightmare in *To the Lighthouse*—and had to be expressed in the dreamlike narrative of "Time Passes"—is now the given reality of *The Years*.[7]

In the structure of the lifework, *The Years* also attempts to extend the insights of *The Waves* into the larger "world" of society as a whole, and especially to relate it to the dominant middle-class culture of that society. Yet the social dimension of *The Years* is much more shallow than its psychological dimension. The narrative isn't really familiar enough with that culture to make it come alive convincingly, from the inside. In *The Waves* the focus had been upon types more familiar in Virginia Woolf's own experience—and upon the inner lives of these characters. *The Years* strains after social relevance and social consciousness. Despite the naming of some realistic details, it does not evoke realistically the feeling of life in that time and place. The book remains a mindscape.

In that dimension, however, it tells the whole truth. It tells the

---

7 The actual death of Mrs. Pargiter was not included in the first version of what became "1880," published forty-five years later as *The Pargiters*. There she is said to be "a confirmed invalid—and indeed has not many months to live." Her illness is identified as Bright's disease. And there is no hint of her husband's infidelity. *The Pargiters* was begun as an attempt to illustrate a feminist speech. In it vignettes of the Pargiter family are interspersed with essay commentaries. *The Years* presents a darker view of this same fictional material. And while it is not as crudely didactic as *The Pargiters*, it is still more of a tract than any of the other novels, and more deductive in its method. It tends toward the illustration of ideas rather than the embodiment of feelings. Still, it has vivid moments of deep feeling.

story of the increasing depersonalization of modern life. In the final chapter, Eleanor's relentless optimism is admired—or envied—but exposed as unrealistic. As her successors, North and Peggy emerge as modern man and woman, cut off from everyone and everything, longing for meaning and commitment but unable to reach them. Once again, the narrative suggests that the phenomena which contain the essential meanings, and require the essential commitments, are sexual. That is what Eleanor seems to recognize in her final epiphany. The narrative itself shares Eleanor's longing for meaning, endorses it, proclaims it fulfilled at the end. But the world which the narrative has described has always frustrated that longing. That world began with the mother's death, and with an essentially feminist account of the father's crime against her.[8] That perspective changes significantly as the narrative discovers that the father is a victim too. In the final chapter both North and Peggy, man and woman, emerge as victims. The end of *The Years* is, in that sense, even bleaker than its beginning. The world is now essentially fatherless despite the longing for reconciliation. The story has reached its own heart of darkness, an achingly empty place despite the final gestures toward belief. The long night remains the essence of this world, despite the narrative's announcement of dawn.

8 This primal crime is at the heart of the lifework, and is enacted over and over again: destruction of the paradisal garden of the female by the arid scimitar of the male. Mrs. Ramsay is the most memorable victim, but there are many others.

CHAPTER IX

BETWEEN THE ACTS

After the struggle with *The Years*, the search for significance once again turns away from the political, sociological, and ideological toward the more instinctive, psychological, and poetic realities which had always been at the heart of the fiction of Virginia Woolf. In this more natural, relaxed, even playful mood, the narrative once again becomes more fully open to the possibilities of its created world. And that world becomes more fully archetypal. *Between the Acts* becomes the mythic drama of the twilight of a culture, and of the dramatist whose destiny it is to try, in the deepening shadows, to reveal that culture to itself. In her lonely exile, the dramatist is seldom satisfied with her work. Yet it moves her and her audience in mysterious ways, as they all merge together in the gathering darkness. At last the form of the narrative comes to reflect the form of its discovered truth, and that final aesthetic achievement enables the voice of the creative consciousness to enter into a final silence.

Because the *oeuvre* is an organic whole, this final novel emerges against the background of all of the earlier work, and achieves its fullest meaning against that background. Its poetic language subsumes and fulfills the languages of the earlier works. Like the cut-outs of Matisse, or his designs in the chapel at Vence, it distills the essence of a lifework. And so, as Jean Guiguet has said, "Perhaps *Between the*

Acts is fully intelligible only to a reader prepared by long familiarity with Virginia Woolf's writings. He alone can recognize her characteristic themes under the faint outlines, and amplify a mere allusion with a full context from elsewhere."[1] Such a reading does not deny the autonomy of the text of *Between the Acts*. Rather, it emphasizes the richness of the text as the culmination of the lifework. The quiet poetry of this final novel is consistent with the languages of the earlier books. But it also represents a further—and final—transformation of those languages.

It was a summer's night and they were talking, in the big room with the windows open to the garden, about the cesspool. The county council had promised to bring water to the village, but they hadn't.

Mrs. Haines, the wife of the gentleman farmer, a goose-faced woman with eyes protruding as if they saw something to gobble in the gutter, said affectedly: "What a subject to talk about on a night like this!"

Then there was silence; and a cow coughed; and that led her to say how odd it was, as a child, she had never feared cows, only horses. But, then, as a small child in a perambulator, a great cart-horse had brushed within an inch of her face. Her family, she told the old man in the arm-chair, had lived near Liskeard for many centuries. There were the graves in the churchyard to prove it.

A bird chuckled outside. "A nightingale?" asked Mrs. Haines. No, nightingales didn't come so far north. It was a daylight bird, chuckling over the substance and succulence of the day, over worms, snails, grit, even in sleep.

The old man in the arm-chair—Mr. Oliver, of the Indian Civil Service, retired—said that the site they had chosen for the cesspool was, if he had heard aright, on the Roman road. From an aeroplane, he said, you could still see, plainly marked, the scars made by the Britons; by the Romans; by the Elizabethan manor house; and by the plough, when they ploughed the hill to grow wheat in the Napoleonic wars.

"But you don't remember . . ." Mrs. Haines began. No, not that. Still he did remember——and he was about to tell them what, when there was a sound outside, and Isa, his son's wife, came in with her hair in pigtails; she was wearing a dressing-gown with faded peacocks on it. She came in like a swan swimming its way; then was checked and stopped; was surprised to find

1 Guiguet, *Virginia Woolf*, 324.

people there; and lights burning. She had been sitting with her little boy who wasn't well, she apologized. What had they been saying?

"Discussing the cesspool," said Mr. Oliver.

"What a subject to talk about on a night like this!" Mrs. Haines exclaimed again.

What had *he* said about the cesspool; or indeed about anything? Isa wondered, inclining her head towards the gentleman farmer, Rupert Haines. She had met him at a Bazaar; and at a tennis party. He had handed her a cup and a racquet—that was all. But in his ravaged face she always felt mystery; and in his silence, passion. At the tennis party she had felt this, and at the Bazaar. Now a third time, if anything more strongly, she felt it again.

"I remember," the old man interrupted, "my mother. . . ." Of his mother he remembered that she was very stout; kept her tea-caddy locked; yet had given him in that very room a copy of Byron. It was over sixty years ago, he told them, that his mother had given him the works of Byron in that very room. He paused.

"She walks in beauty like the night," he quoted. Then again:

"So we'll go no more a-roving by the light of the moon."

Isa raised her head. The words made two rings, perfect rings, that floated them, herself and Haines, like two swans down stream. But his snow-white breast was circled with a tangle of dirty duckweed; and she too, in her webbed feet was entangled, by her husband, the stockbroker. Sitting on her three-cornered chair she swayed, with her dark pigtails hanging, and her body like a bolster in its faded dressing-gown.

Mrs. Haines was aware of the emotion circling them, excluding her. She waited, as one waits for the strain of an organ to die out before leaving church. In the car going home to the red villa in the cornfields, she would destroy it, as a thrush pecks the wings off a butterfly. Allowing ten seconds to intervene, she rose, paused; and then, as if she had heard the last strain die out, offered Mrs. Giles Oliver her hand.

But Isa, though she should have risen at the same moment that Mrs. Haines rose, sat on. Mrs. Haines glared at her out of goose-like eyes, gobbling, "Please, Mrs. Giles Oliver, do me the kindness to recognize my existence. . . ." which she was forced to do, rising at last from her chair, in her faded dressing-gown, with the pigtails falling over each shoulder.[2]

This opening section of *Between the Acts* reflects the richness and subtlety of the language which creates it. Its poetic power subsumes

2 The text I refer to here is the first English edition of *Between the Acts* (London: Hogarth, 1941).

the symbolism of the earlier books, and the narrative consciousness finds expression with an ease, economy, and mastery which transforms that earlier symbolism into a new dimension of style. Emerging against the background of the earlier works, this style represents the fullest, most economical, and most elegant expression of the language of the *oeuvre*. It is as if the social and historical perspectives of *The Years* could now be embodied in the disparate personalities and the biological imperatives of *The Waves*—and expressed with the wit and easy grace of *Orlando*.

"It was a summer's night": *Between the Acts* opens into a realm when familiar daylight shapes appear "dim and unsubstantial"—as in the morning twilight of *The Waves* when the creation begins and everything within the house is still in shadow, between night and day. Throughout the *oeuvre* night and day represent primary modes of awareness: unconscious and conscious, intuition and reason—whatever antithetical terms we choose for them. The characters in the novels often drift uncertainly between those two sides of their own personalities, like Katharine in *Night and Day*, where the conflict gives the title to the book itself, or like Mrs. Ramsay in *To the Lighthouse*, who becomes both the long stroke of light from the lighthouse and a wedge-shaped core of darkness. *Between the Acts*, and the lifework which it concludes, reach their culmination in that realm of twilight, as Giles and Isa become unsubstantial in the fading light, and the coming night merges into eternity.

The fullest description of this symbolic twilight, however, is not in the novels but in "The Moment: Summer's Night," the title piece for the posthumous volume *The Moment and Other Essays*. This essay—or meditation or prose poem—touches both the themes and the language of *Between the Acts* in so many ways that it can be read as an introduction to the novel. It speaks of the "visual and . . . sense impressions" of the moment, and then of a growing sense that "we are spectators and also passive participants in a pageant. And as nothing can interfere with the order, we have nothing to do but accept, and watch."[3] The "pageant" (the word itself was one of the working titles

---

3 *Collected Essays* (New York: Harcourt, 1967), II, 293. My two later quotations from this piece are from pp. 294 and 296–97.

for *Between the Acts*) referred to here is the succession of changes in light and color as the day is transformed into night; the changes "seem to make an order evident." And so it is within the book, which discloses pageant within pageant within pageant—the many layers of significance in the complex drama of human life. The "passive participants" and "spectators" mentioned in the essay suggest the feeling not only of this final novel but of the others as well—especially *The Waves*, with its strange chorus of disembodied, lamenting voices—which seem less like active participants than like spectators, who "have nothing to do but accept, and watch." That description is especially apt for the characters in *Between the Acts*.

The setting of "The Moment" is very much like that of the opening of *Between the Acts*: a summer evening, surrounding fields in which cows are grazing, the garden with its trees and table, and finally the house itself and its final shelter. And this setting evokes a climax which is somewhat more specific than that of the novel: first, "the vibrations that rise red," then the climactic, "terror . . . exultation . . . to be consumed; to be swept away . . . to feel the glory run molten up the spine, down the limbs," then the discovery that " 'Everything's sopping wet,' " and at last the return to the familiar patterns of perception. What seems so exciting and frightening is the power of the experience, and especially the loss of control and identity. The consciousness must then seek familiar forms in which identity may be enclosed once more; it must become "boxed and housed." Thus "The Moment: Summer's Night" provides a fascinating glimpse into a dimension which, in *Between the Acts* itself, is present and important, but not so directly stated: the dimension of sexual experience.

Finally, the "summer's night" of this opening passage prepares the way for the eternal night into which the book itself disappears at the end. And together with that final night it constitutes a frame for the events between. The two nights are significantly different; in the first scene the silence is filled with talk which we hear and which we recognize as merely social; in the final scene we do not hear "the first words," which are familiar anyway to all men and women, and which may be too sacred for the book itself to pronounce. In the first scene the man of the house is absent; in the final one he is present. So perhaps the book itself has no beginning and no ending. Only the pageant seems to give it historical order—but "history" is the product of the creative imagination.

"Talking," a form of communion, is somewhat more meaningful than "talk." That Mrs. Haines doesn't understand this is made evident by her comment in the second paragraph. Talking is a way of filling the threatening silence; the "subject" doesn't really matter, as we see in a number of moments of communion later in the book; what matters is the feeling that people have for each other. As the book opens, the "talking" adds to the magic of the occasion; Mrs. Haines's insensitivity to that is typical.

Rooms, throughout the *oeuvre*, represent the existential spaces of consciousness. Thus the fact that this one is "big" seems promising; that promise is fulfilled at the end of the book, when the family retires to this same "big room" for the final scene. The opening to the garden had been important also in the sitting-room in *To the Lighthouse* and the empty dining-room in the interludes of *The Waves*. The open windows are also a good sign; they are the apertures of potential perception and communication. Already they link this interior space, filled with "talking," with the exterior space of "the garden" and the world of nature.

The "subject" of which Mrs. Haines disapproves (the cesspool) brings the conversation back to earth. "The county council had promised to bring water to the village, but they hadn't" continues the deflationary movement; the paragraph begins in the realm of magic and ends in the mundane, with the drab and empty protest against depersonalized authority: "but they hadn't." But in another sense, this sentence introduces, in an ironic way, what will become an important theme in the book as a whole: what might be called the wasteland motif. Miss La Trobe's pageant eventually brings the rain which the land and the village need, but which the villagers, at least, would prefer to receive in the more manageable form that the council promised.

Thus the first paragraph of *Between the Acts* opens on a world which is described almost entirely indirectly, through motifs used in a disarmingly offhand—indeed, almost shorthand—way. The range of the narrative is larger than it may seem at first, and its seriousness is achieved without the tinges of solemnity which mark the earlier novels.

Although we need not examine the remainder of this first section in this kind of detail, there are some other aspects of the opening which seem important. First, there is the matter of the narrative point of view. Where is the narrative consciousness located, and what is its nature? The question first arises, perhaps, in the second paragraph: "Mrs. Haines, the wife of the gentleman farmer, a goosefaced woman with eyes protruding as if they saw something to gobble in the gutter, said affectedly: 'What a subject to talk about on a night like this!'" The narrative's observation of Mrs. Haines seems too bitchy to be impersonal; it is more like something that Isa might think about her. But Isa isn't on the scene yet, and the reference to old Bart in the third paragraph as "the old man in the arm-chair" is not one that would come to Isa's mind. Then comes the fourth paragraph: "A bird chuckled outside." It is as if the bird were responding to Mrs. Haines's inadvertently profound comment about her family, that they had lived near Liskeard for many centuries—and had the graves to prove it.

The narrative consciousness seems to remain outside of all three of the characters present at the beginning: Mrs. Haines, her husband, and Mr. Oliver. At times it quotes what Mrs. Haines says; in the third paragraph it seems merely to summarize her speech, unless it is then actually inside her train of thought—which seems unlikely, in view of the reference to her goose face. The comment that "No, the nightingales didn't come so far north" may summarize the response(s) to her question, or it may not. Perhaps the question doesn't deserve a response: perhaps everything else in the paragraph may represent the meditation of the narrative itself; certainly the final sentence does. In the fifth paragraph the narrative identifies old Mr. Oliver for us, and in the sixth it observes the entrance of "Isa, his son's wife." Three paragraphs later, however, the narrative is privileged to know what "Isa wondered," then "felt," about Rupert Haines. And so, after hovering indeterminately over the scene, the narrative consciousness rather easily becomes incarnate in Isa when she enters. As the book continues, the distance from which each character is observed and the extent to which the narrative penetrates the mind of each one vary rather significantly. In *Between the Acts* as in much of the earlier work, tension arises from the uncertainty of the narrative point of view, from the efforts of the narrative to discover the right perspective for its story.

With regard to Isa, the narrative seems comfortable from the beginning, and when she is physically present in a scene the narrative is likely to share her point of view. For example, as the first section of the book nears its end, Isa thinks of herself and Haines as two swans that are "entangled" by their respective mates. At first glance we might think that the point of view has shifted to Mrs. Haines, or to narrative omniscience. But the perspective actually remains with Isa who, in a sense, now takes over the narrative. "Mrs. Haines" is the name she gives to her antagonist, rather than the name that Mrs. Haines would give to herself. The "Mrs. Giles Oliver" at the end of the paragraph is Isa's ironic title for herself ("entangled," by "her husband, the stockbroker" in the previous paragraph) as well as a representation of the stiff formality which Isa senses in the occasion: she feels that Mrs. Haines is addressing her as "Mrs. Giles Oliver." When the narrative says that "Mrs. Haines was aware," it means that Isa feels that Mrs. Haines is aware. Why doesn't it say so, then? Because such a statement would render a different feeling—less immediately incarnate in Isa herself, more distant and detached. That would take the narrative further toward abstraction, away from showing toward more impersonal telling. The "red villa in the cornfields" also renders Isa's, not Mrs. Haines's, feeling about the Haineses' house. The analogies between Mrs. Haines and a churchgoer and the thrush pecking wings off a butterfly also belong to Isa's consciousness—and do more to characterize her than to define Mrs. Haines. The analogies remain assertions—interesting mainly for the questions they raise about Isa; why does she feel such animosity toward this woman? Why do her feelings find these particular expressions (we recognize the second analogy, especially, as an expression of sexual fear[4])? Such questions lead toward the essence of her character and personality. The narra-

---

4 At the end of the thirteenth chapter of *The Voyage Out* Rachel sees a butterfly moving its wings involuntarily and asks herself "What is it to be in love?" "Hypnotised by the wings of the butterfly and awed by the discovery of a terrible possibility in life," she suddenly has a premonition that sex is lethal. From that moment forth, throughout the work, butterflies—and moths—become emblems for compulsive, self-destructive behavior, driven by sexual imperatives.

tive, moving toward the discovery of these essences, imagines the phenomena of consciousness which will lead in that direction.

This first section of the book is only one of a series of fragments which, taken together, define the space—largely empty, it seems—in which the drama of *Between the Acts* begins. The setting seems strangely vacant and unrealized, far from the London or the variations on St. Ives which provide the landscapes in which all the other novels except *Orlando* originate. The essence of the house itself is emptiness and silence, unrelieved by any wandering airs or momentary gleam from some distant lighthouse. Pointz Hall is located in "the very heart of England." The "heart of the house" is the library, but within this heart of hearts is emptiness and silence:

Empty, empty, empty; silent, silent, silent. The room was a shell, singing of what was before time was; a vase stood in the heart of the house, alabaster, smooth, cold, holding the still, distilled essence of emptiness, silence.

Books line the walls of the library, but Isa finds no help there: "Book-shy she was, like the rest of her generation; and gun-shy too." In the face of the imminent apocalypse, it seems that books have become irrelevant. It is the fate not only of Isa, but of a whole "generation"— and perhaps of a whole culture; the emptiness and silence at the heart of Pointz Hall are not local phenomena.

The emptiness and silence of the house are reflected in the people who live there, and in the people who don't. *Between the Acts* opens on what is largely a woman's world, and the world of an unfulfilled woman at that. The essential situation never really changes, despite the exploration of various alternatives to it. As the book begins Giles, the man of the house, isn't there—only old Bartholomew, whose masculinity has largely faded (but not entirely: he can still frighten children and intimidate women); the boy George, already in training for manhood, being frightened by his grandfather; and, for a moment, the gentleman farmer, who exists almost exclusively in Isa's imagination. The presiding spirit of the house is sainted Lucy Swithin, the fate that the younger women can look forward to: "Old Batty" in her post-sexual ridiculousness. The woman whose destiny is still open— or at first seems to be—is Isabella. The changes rung on her name are interesting: it is a diminutive of "beautiful," and her beauty is very diminished indeed (her body is "thick," her personality "abortive"). As the book goes on she becomes merely Isa, a linking verb which drifts between an unnamed, and perhaps unnamable, subject and predicate.

Described in such a summary fashion, the "world" of the opening of *Between the Acts* sounds bleaker than it really is. That world, of course, is constituted not by these abstractions about it, but by its own phenomena, whose richness transcends the limitations of abstractions. This novel, like every truly literary work, is larger than its "ideas," its "philosophy," its "world view." Its size is in its style—in the ways in which the language "works" to create a field of meaning which is rich, beautiful, and moving. Like most late works of major artists, *Between the Acts* exhibits a style that has emerged from, but also developed far beyond, the styles of the earlier works. It subsumes those earlier styles and brings them to fuller expression.

Another factor which mitigates the bleakness of *Between the Acts* is its tendency toward comedy. This is largely a matter of its underlying assumptions about the human condition, and a matter of emphasis—on celebration rather than criticism, on abundance rather than limitation, on generation and renewal rather than death and decay. It assumes that people can achieve some control over the quality of their lives, and that those lives, though obviously limited in many ways, are still important, and can be made more meaningful. "Old Batty," "Old Flimsy," however she may be mocked at the moment, still achieves transcendent meaning: her life is, in the truest sense, holy. And Isa too has that potentiality.

Between the Acts consists of perhaps thirty-three sections,[5] arranged chronologically and observing the classical "unity of time": the book

---

5 Breaks between sections are indicated by extra spacing in the text. But some of these divisions are not clear, especially where the pageant is intercalated with the action of the characters. It may be that neither the first English nor the first American edition reflects precisely the author's intentions with regard to the structural divisions of the book; five of the breaks in the English first edition do not appear in the American. Because Virginia Woolf died before she finished her final revisions for the printer, there may be some ambiguities even in the surviving manuscripts.

opens on a "summer's night" (*i.e.*, at dusk) in June, 1939, and closes at dusk of the next day. The two longest breaks in the continuity of this time occur after the first section of the book and before the last section. In a sense this first section functions as a prologue and the final one as an epilogue: together they constitute a perspective, withheld until the end, through which the entire "drama" must then be seen. Within these outward forms of order, however, chaos constantly threatens. What we see instead of a fairly well defined point of origin in the book is a series of fragments. The opening situation, then, is defined not only by these fragments themselves but by the distances between them—distances of various kinds: formal, thematic, psychological, tonal. The meanings of the book are constituted as much by its discontinuities as by its continuities.

As in the earlier novels, each section of *Between the Acts* represents an exploration, by the narrative consciousness, of a certain avenue of possibilities inherent in the created world. And again, most of these explorations end not in discovery but in exhaustion, not in new vistas but in cul de sacs. This is especially evident in what we might call the opening movement of the book—the fragments which culminate, at the end of the ninth section, in "the still, distilled essence of emptiness, silence." Typically, each section ends with the eye of the narrative pulling back from the scene, very much like the return to a "master shot" after a series of close-ups in cinema, and with much the same feeling.

This repeated pulling back expresses the intentionality of the narrative consciousness: the nature of its presence in, and its relation to, the phenomena with which it constitutes its world. The "plot" of *Between the Acts* is concerned not so much with what happens as with how what happens is perceived: the plot is the drama of intentionality, the dynamics of the "consciousness of" as it constitutes its story. If we compare this intentionality at the end of its story with that at its beginning, we could argue that it moves from withdrawal to commitment. Yet that final commitment seems ambiguous, and most of the sections of the book seem to end in perspectives which express the narrative's detachment or withdrawal from the scenes it describes, and which emphasize its awareness of necessity, uncertainty, ambiguity, dispersion.

The configuration of characters in *Between the Acts* is reminiscent of that in *The Waves*. In the earlier book there are six speaking voices that interact with each other, and a seventh silent character, Percival, set somewhat apart from them; in the final novel there are six main characters that interact, and a seventh, Miss La Trobe, somewhat apart from them. In both books the six main characters are three males and three females. In *Between the Acts* they are more obviously paired: Bartholomew Oliver and his sister Lucy Swithin, Giles Oliver and his wife Isabella, Mrs. Manresa and her companion William Dodge. Whereas the characters in *The Waves* are of roughly the same age, those in the final novel represent the "old" generation at Pointz Hall (Bart and Lucy) and the present generation there (Giles and Isa) and outside (Mrs. Manresa and Dodge). There is also a new generation, represented by Isa's children George and "Caro" (Caroline?); the little girl is only glimpsed, and George seems to exist primarily to be frightened by his grandfather. Still, the presence of three generations of this family at Pointz Hall seems to be significant; it suggests the same kind of continuity in English daily life that the pageant suggests in English literature. Isabella thinks of herself as "the age of the century, thirtynine"; to that extent she is conscious of being the embodiment of the twentieth century. Mrs. Manresa is forty-five and a more conscious rebel against her Victorian heritage. In the age distribution of its characters *Between the Acts* subtly merges the family chronicle of *The Years* with the triangle of pairs of *The Waves*.

Pairs and triangles, always shifting, define and constantly redefine the psychological force fields of *Between the Acts*, the space in which these characters have their existence. These kinds of tensions are evident from the very beginning, in Isa's feeling that "Mrs. Haines was aware of the emotion circling them, excluding her." This first triangle probably exists only in Isa's awareness; the narrative never enters into the minds of Mr. or Mrs. Haines, and there is no "objective" confirmation of any interest in Isa by Mr. Haines.

During the day several triangles develop. Mrs. Manresa and her companion, William Dodge, focus and intensify the conflict already present between Isa and Giles. At forty-five Mrs. Manresa has lost none of her influence upon the men who encounter her; even old Bart, for whom sex is now a memory, is electrified. Giles, of course, is her primary target, and the Manresa-Giles-Isa triangle energizes him for the encounter which the ending of the book predicts.

Because William Dodge is a homosexual, women can open their feelings to him in ways which would be impossible for them with heterosexual males. With him they can return to a somewhat childlike state of sexual innocence. Isa recognizes this almost immediately, and soon they are talking "as if they had known each other all their lives"—a rather new experience for her, but not for him. In a sense both he and Giles are competing for Isa. But there is another important triangle in which Giles, rather than Isa, is at the center. As she and William are talking during tea in the barn, he watches Giles approaching: "here he was; and the muscular, the hirsute, the virile plunged him [William] into emotions in which the mind had no share. He forgot how she would have looked against vine leaf in a greenhouse. Only at Giles he looked; and looked and looked." This may also be a source of Giles's energy that evening: a recognition of this attraction, and the denial of it by proving his masculinity. He seems, certainly, to feel threatened by William. Yet the narrative deals with all of this only indirectly.

It seems that William may deflect Isa somewhat from her infatuation with the gentleman farmer (with whom, after all, she has exchanged only a few words—none of which are ever recalled) and may help to return her to her husband at the end. After the pageant is over she sees "Dodge the lip reader, her semblable, her conspirator, a seeker like her after hidden faces. He was hurrying to rejoin Mrs. Manresa who had gone in front with Giles—'the father of my children,' she muttered. The flesh poured over her, the hot, nerve wired, now lit up, now dark as the grave physical body. By way of healing the rusty fester of the poisoned dart she sought the face that all day long she had been seeking." Although she does not yet realize it, her quest now is for her husband, and in her intensity she "swept past" William without really seeing him, intent upon breaking up Giles's tête-à-tête with Mrs. Manresa. She finds them talking together. "Did they perceive the arrows about to strike them?" she thinks. These are the arrows of Eros himself, left in Isa's imagination by the pageant, in which they had wounded Sir Spaniel Lilyliver so comically in Miss La Trobe's Restoration comedy, "Where There's a Will There's a Way." Isa certainly has her will, and later will have her way. She is still thinking consciously of the gentleman farmer, "had we met before the salmon leapt like a bar of silver," and imagining what it would be like if George were the son of Haines rather than of Giles. But the imagery itself suggests that at the deepest level of her imagination, it is only Giles who matters: "They had first met in Scotland, fishing—she from one rock, he from another. Her line had got tangled; she had given over, and had watched him with the stream rushing between his legs, casting, casting—until, like a thick ingot of silver bent in the middle, the salmon had leapt, had been caught, and she had loved him." The overtones of Isa's memories here may matter more than the obvious sexual meaning—her feelings of excitement, admiration, even awe, toward this man who, whatever he might have done and become since that magic moment, will always exist at the heart of that moment. Even now, seven years later, the thought of it fills her with vivid sensations. The suddenness and inevitability of "she had loved him" are consistent with the ways in which women are stricken by sexual love in the *oeuvre*, and the silver tint may imply that this love could be lethal.[6]

The two visitors—or intruders—Mrs. Manresa and William Dodge, create the most conspicuous triangles. But others, more important because they are less transitory, already exist within the family itself. Old Bart, for example, seems possessive of his son Giles, and unconsciously resentful of Isa. When he tells her that her son George is a crybaby, all kinds of unspoken conflicts are implied: Bart's disappointment at his own inability to get in touch with the boy, his shame at having frightened him, his hostility (and attraction) toward Isa; her fierce love for the boy, her maternal protectiveness, her anger at Bart's

6 The archetype of the woman *stricken* by sexual love is, of course, Rachel of *The Voyage Out*. For the lethal implications of silver in the oeuvre, see page 221 herein, note 7.

bullying, at Giles's absence, at the unfairness of male dominance and the shallowness of "masculine" values. All of this is largely unspoken, but still rendered very effectively. The relationship between Bart and Lucy is also disclosed with great power and economy.

The distances which exist between the six main characters and the author of the pageant are among the most poignant in the book. Not much is known about Miss La Trobe, who is not even mentioned until more than a fourth of the book has gone by. With a name like that, the narrative suggests, rather snobbishly, "she wasn't presumably pure English," yet she is English enough, of course, to write a pageant which parodies the history of English literature. There are a few rumors about her, but all that we can be certain about—aside from her total dedication to her art—comes from a brief glimpse into her consciousness very near the end of the book: "Since the row with the actress who had shared her bed and her purse the need of drink had grown on her. And the horror and the terror of being alone. . . . She was an outcast. Nature had somehow set her apart from her kind. Yet she had scribbled in the margin of her manuscript: 'I am the slave of my audience.'" In her essential isolation, attributed here to an almost biological determinism, she is the familiar visionary figure who emerges at the end of every one of the major novels of Virginia Woolf.

In an important sense, *Between the Acts* is more the story of this woman than it is of Giles and Isa and the rest, whose relationships are so complex, so seemingly uncertain yet in the final analysis so totally predictable, even predestined, perhaps. Miss La Trobe seems to realize, to accept and believe, that her art can exist only on the edge of failure. She has failed, and it has failed, again and again. Yet it may be that authentic art can exist only in this region, where the artist struggles to create out of his own anguish, and from his unique perspective as an "outcast," some totally new thing.

The pageant at the center of *Between the Acts* serves both as a framework for potential meaning and as an ironic commentary on its own limitations—of the impossibility of capturing more than scraps and fragments of the richness of "life itself" within the generic limitations of a work of art. Yet it affirms the necessity and the value of art despite its limitations. Any work of art must "parody" its historical period in the sense that it must limit itself to certain phenomena in that period and develop or magnify them out of proportion to the "field" in which they exist. An Absurdist play, for example, may seem to be a grotesque caricature of contemporary life, yet may reveal inner meanings of that life very effectively. The dramas within the pageant in *Between the Acts* parody the historical eras which they represent, and also parody the "present moment," which is both the product of those eras and a synchronic entity apart from them.

The pageant consists of a Prologue, three dramas written in imitation of Elizabethan, Restoration, and Victorian styles, and a final "act" without words in which the spectators are confronted with their own reflections in mirrors. Sometimes this last act has been called an "epilogue," but the fact that it is separated from the Victorian drama by an interval seems to show that it is just as important as the other dramas (the Prologue is not separated from the first drama by an interval). At any rate, the final confrontation with mirrors represents both the diachronic culmination of this grotesque literary history and the synchronic chaos of "the moment."

Miss La Trobe seems aware that her pageant parodies, but also interacts with, the infinitely larger drama in which it must be enacted. Perhaps she recognizes the regressiveness of the literary game she is playing: her pageant parodies earlier plays that derive from still earlier pageantry, etc., in a long chain that extends to the most ancient origins of drama and of man himself, to the days which Lucy reads about—and imagines—before there was history, before there was an English Channel, before man became self-conscious. But Miss La Trobe seems less concerned with the theory of what she is doing than with the immediacy of it, the *life* of it. When the irreverent voice interrupts, the audience is somewhat shocked and embarrassed, but Miss La Trobe rejoices in this spontaneous excitement. When Lucy says that she has made her feel like she could have played Cleopatra, the people who overhear take it as confirmation that the old lady is indeed "Batty," but Miss La Trobe knows exactly what she means: "You've stirred me in my unacted part." Whatever the ultimate dimensions of her talent, Miss La Trobe is an authentic creator: "One who seethes wandering bodies and floating voices in a cauldron, and makes rise up from its amorphous mass a re-created world." It is not so much what is said, but whether it is brought to life, that matters. And Miss La Trobe does bring something to life during her pageant—not alone, for no author can do it alone, but with the full cooperation, participation, of her audience and of nature itself. Magically, the audience and nature do enter into the pageant, and for that its author, despite her rather violent opposition to the forms and dogmas of religion, must "Thank Heaven!"

Miss La Trobe's work isn't especially memorable as literature: no great lines remain emblazoned in "the sky of the mind" as the pageant drifts into the background. The pageant is very "modern": its values are there to be discovered between the acts—"acts" in the broadest sense of "actions" or "events," down to the smallest identifiable unit of expression. It requires the active participation of its audience in the creation of its meaning. The most significant dimensions of that meaning seem to be expressed indirectly, experientially.

The view of English history and literature which emerges from it seems deeply ironic. At the beginning the little girl who is England forgets her lines (just as Lucy later will lose her place in the Outline of History); the destiny of England, which in the hindsight of history can be made to seem so awesome, may actually come into existence as a series of accidents. Chaucer's pilgrims wander among the trees; the words of their hymn are lost in the wind. Queen Elizabeth is upstaged by the village idiot. Drama in the age of Shakespeare is revealed as a pastiche of stolen and distorted lines. But now it is time for tea, and history must be interrupted.

Our experience of English history and literature in the pageant, in its whirlwind progress from the beginning through the Elizabethan Age, has been fragmentary and confusing. In the interval which follows that age, Giles angrily crushes the "monstrous inversion," Mrs. Manresa plays her chosen role as wild child, Isa murmurs her poetry and thinks of suicide, William Dodge observes everything, Lucy ponders the mysteries of the swallows and the prehistoric world, Bartholomew loses track of his son and retires to his room. These experiences too seem fragmentary and confusing, but they merge to some extent, as the audience begins to assemble again, in a kind of collective consciousness: "Music wakes us. Music makes us see the hidden, join the broken. Look and listen." Significantly, we hear this as Miss La Trobe hears it, and we discover the dynamics of her inspiration: she is somehow in touch with this collective consciousness, this "voice" which arises out of, but transcends, the individual consciousnesses which constitute it. Many passages in *Between the Acts* can be attributed neither to an individual character's awareness nor to an "omniscient" awareness which controls the scene; instead, such passages seem to render a collective consciousness as it experiences the "given" phenomena of the scene. These passages seem to shape themselves through internal rhymes and rather pronounced rhythms, almost as if the narrative consciousness lapses into a state between sleep and waking, and floats free of its ties to specific characters.

The next act of the pageant depicts the Age of Reason, which turns out to be rather unreasonable: it is represented only by a parody of Restoration comedy ("saved" between the acts by the cows). In the interval which follows it, the audience too acts on impulse: Giles ponders the meaning of the title "Where There's a Will There's a Way," and abruptly invites Mrs. Manresa to see the greenhouse; Miss La Trobe improvises rather frantically, while watching the audience with her "bird's eye"; Lucy Swithin offers lavish but somewhat incoherent praise; Isa muses on her own wandering, and then, unseen, follows Giles and Mrs. Manresa back to the opening of the nineteenth century.

That act is narrated, appropriately, by a policeman, and dramatized by a family picnic which mocks the complacency of the Victorians—and their belief in religion, altruism, prosperity, imperialism. The interval after the Victorian Age is occupied with speculations—and complaints—about the meaning of the drama and with the undercurrents of various personal antagonisms. The interval is "saved" by rain, which once more unifies the audience's wandering and dispersing consciousness.

The final act is entitled "The Present Time. Ourselves." It is dramatized effectively—and offensively—by mirrors which are held up to the audience, catching scraps and fragments of them; by various voices of the pageant, shouting, all at once, characteristic lines from their roles; and finally by the anonymous, amplified voice of the author herself, sermonizing. It epitomizes every "present time" in history and literature, when it seems that all we can see are fragments of ourselves and others, and all we can hear are conflicting speeches from the voices of the past, along with the sententiousness of some contemporary author or other.

The pageant discovers the essences of English literary history through its parodies: the childlike enthusiasm of the Elizabethans, the belief in reason which provides the norms for Restoration comedy, the public commitment to morality which moved the Victorians, the fragmented inwardness of the moderns. Like most literary history, it is second-rate because it is second-hand, an imitation of an imitation. Yet the audience can become engaged with it, and that engagement seems most meaningful when it is indirect. We see things in their true shapes when we allow them to be what they are, rather than demand that they conform to what we expect. Despite its flaws and lapses, Miss La Trobe's pageant creates a large space in which true and important things can come into existence. And that is only part of the greater space of the book as a whole.

The significance of *Between the Acts* reaches its culmination in the final section of the book. Like the earlier novels, it does not reach a neat "conclusion" in which all loose ends are tied up, or the great complexity of the created world is simplified into a single dominant tone, theme, or "message." Nevertheless, because of the almost shorthand density of the style, the ending probably is more "conclusive" than we may recognize at first. The final section, of course, emerges from the context of the whole book. And though we can't consider all of that in detail, we can at least look at the immediate context out of which the final section emerges. That penultimate section is focused on Miss La Trobe, as she comes out of her hiding place behind the tree after the audience has dispersed.

"Glory possessed her—for one moment. But what had she given? A cloud that melted into the other clouds on the horizon. It was in the giving that the triumph was. And the triumph faded." Her view of her creation as an ephemeral "cloud" associates this passage with a number of others in which clouds and wind symbolize the fading, transitory quality of individual human achievements. This imagery will recur in the final section, with somewhat more positive connotations. And now Miss La Trobe's feeling that her pageant has been a failure seems to be suddenly contradicted, as it had been twice before during the performance itself (when she had experienced "death, death, death . . . when illusion fails"). Now nature intervenes: suddenly "her" tree is "attacked" by starlings, so that it becomes "a rhapsody, a quivering cacophony, a whizz and vibrant rapture, branches, leaves, birds syllabling discordantly life, life, life." Here the triple rhythm transforms any resonant echoes of the earlier "death, death, death"—not only through the climactic "life, life, life," but also through the more subtle echoes of triads throughout the book (*e.g.*, love, hate, peace) which disclose over and over again the dialectical process through which the questing consciousness moves toward fulfillment. The birds are augurs and omens here, as they are elsewhere in the book and the *oeuvre*. At this moment, however, Miss La Trobe seems not to be aware of that; her consciousness is focused on her work. And her awareness always lags behind that of the narrative itself—until the very end of the book, where the final scene is revealed, reflexively, as her creation.

At this moment she is aware only of the sudden flight of the birds from the tree, and she attributes the "interruption" to "old Mrs. Chambers, creeping through the grass with a bunch of flowers . . . to fill the vase that stood on her husband's grave." The vase on the grave modulates the motif of the vase at "the heart of the house" which holds "the still, distilled essence of emptiness, silence." The implication is that Mrs. Chambers' love, not just the flowers themselves, fills the vase on her husband's grave. And love, or the potentiality of love, can fill the empty vase at the heart of the house as well.

Miss La Trobe walks away from the scene of the pageant. Now it is dusk, the magical time in which the book began, when daylight realities begin to lose their familiar shapes as they merge into the archetypal night:

It was growing dark. Since there were no clouds to trouble the sky, the blue was bluer, the green greener. There was no longer a view—no Folly, no spire of Bolney Minster. It was land merely, no land in particular. She put down her case and stood looking at the land. Then something rose to the surface.

"I should group them," she murmured, "here." It would be midnight; there would be two figures, half concealed by a rock. The curtain would rise. What would the first words be? The words escaped her.

The comment that "something rose to the surface" links this passage subliminally with the motifs of the lily pool, its mysterious great carp, and the "words" which originate somehow in the fertile mud. The vanishing of the clouds seems significant too: the sign of the emergence of a timeless present, or eternity. And the scene which Miss La Trobe envisions here turns out to be the final scene of the novel: the "two figures" there are Giles and Isa, who become simply man and woman, reenacting their timeless drama in this landscape, which also loses its specificity, and becomes mythic. But for the moment "The words escaped" Miss La Trobe, and so she must take her inevitable voyage out, in search of the Word: "She took her voyage away from the shore. . . . She was an outcast. Nature had somehow set her apart from her kind."

In this ultimate isolation the artist can only look and listen, and fall into a renewing sleep:

Words of one syllable sank down into the mud. She drowsed; she nodded. The mud became fertile. Words rose above the intolerably laden dumb oxen plodding through the mud. Words without meaning—wonderful words.

. . .There was the high ground at midnight; there the rock; and two scarcely perceptible figures. Suddenly the tree was pelted with starlings. She set down her glass. She heard the first words.

She puts down her glass, presumably, because she is ready to write—or at least to listen, more intently, to these *first words*. The mud is the medium from which they emerge. The imagery connects this moment with the complex imagery of the lily pool and with the iterative image of the patient donkey which haunts Isa during the *entr'actes*. The artist must be patient, receptive, and persevering for the mud to become fertile.

This, then, is the immediate context out of which the final section of *Between the Acts* arises. The sequence itself implies a causal connection. Although various kinds of connections may be implied, the last two sections can be joined most closely by the assumption that "the first words" that Miss La Trobe hears in her imagination are what Giles and Isa, man and woman, are said to say as the curtain rises, and the book closes. The first words of the final section also help to bridge the emptiness and the silence. They are the first words we read after we read that Miss La Trobe "heard the first words":

Down in the hollow, at Pointz Hall, beneath the trees, the table was cleared in the dining room. Candish, with his curved brush had swept the crumbs; had spared the petals and finally left the family to dessert. The play was over, the strangers gone, and they were alone—the family.

This final section opens with a narrative perspective which seems objective. *Down in the hollow* contrasts implicitly with *the high ground* of the setting in which Miss La Trobe "heard the first words." Thus the narrative consciousness imagines the relationship between the two scenes as a cinematographic down angle: the vision of the artist (Miss La Trobe) encompasses the final scene. The fact that the house is called Pointz Hall once again (rather than "the house") also indicates a greater distance, and takes us back, in a sense, to the end of the book's opening section and the beginning of the second: "Pointz Hall was seen in the light of an early summer morning to be a middle-sized house." The narrative's movement is equivalent, in cinematographic terms, to the camera pulling back—one of the standard techniques for closure. The trees here seem to connote shelter, as they do throughout the book. They also provide a place for Miss La Trobe to hide from her audience; they serve as the columns in the pilgrims' "cathedral," and so on. And the dining-room table here, as elsewhere in the life-work, is the setting for a communion.

303

Candish the butler also seems to symbolize some unspoken depth: the family doesn't pay much attention to him, but at the beginning of the ninth section the narrative observes him alone in this dining room, arranging the flowers: "Queerly, he loved them, considering his gambling and drinking"—"Queerly" because the family regards him less as a person than as a problem, with his gambling and drinking, and so they are rather shocked at Mrs. Manresa, "ogling Candish, as if he were a real man, not a stuffed man." Thus in the opening paragraph of the final section the narrative sees Candish from the perspective of "the family," impatient with him for lingering so long over the table and sparing the flower petals that have fallen on the tablecloth. Yet, because of what it has said before, the narrative consciousness is sympathetic toward Candish—and critical of the family's impatience with him. The paragraph culminates in another triad: "The play was over, the strangers gone, and they were alone— the family." The effect seems analogous to the deepening twilight of the previous section: specific identities fade into general archetypes, and at last the essence is reached—"the family."

Yet the narrative resists the twilight; instinctively it returns to the first element of the dialectical triad: "Still the play hung in the sky of the mind—moving, diminishing, but still there." The pervasive imagery of wind and clouds throughout the novel often suggests the beauty and ephemerality of the artist's creations, as it does in Prospero's moving farewell to his art in *The Tempest*.[7] Mrs. Swithin (not

7   Our revels now are ended. These our actors,
        As I foretold you, were all spirits, and
        Are melted into air, into thin air.
        And, like the baseless fabric of this vision,
        The cloud-capped towers, the gorgeous palaces,
        The solemn temples, the great globe itself—
        Yea, all which it inherit—shall dissolve
        And, like this insubstantial pageant faded,
        Leave not a rack behind. We are such stuff
        As dreams are made on, and our little life
        Is rounded with a sleep. . . .
Although "the great globe itself" may allude to Shakespeare's Globe Theatre, in a larger sense it becomes an emblem of wholeness, perfection, completion, transparence, illumination—and in that sense a favorite symbol in Virginia Woolf. The ambiguity of "all which it inherit" expresses beautifully the paradox of the artist's achievement and of his

Lucy now—another sign of the increased distance of the narrative) asks the others what the play meant, and "Each of course saw something different," but the narrative quotes only one, old Bart, now called Mr. Oliver once again. In the time that it takes him to light his cheroot, he dismisses the play as too ambitious. Although the narrative perspective isn't very sharply defined here, it is clearly closer to that of Miss La Trobe than to either Mr. Oliver or Mrs. Swithin.

In the next paragraph, however, it seems to become incarnate in Isa: "It was drifting away to join the other clouds: becoming invisible. Through the smoke Isa saw not the play but the audience dispersing. Some drove; others cycled. A gate swung open. A car swept up the drive to the red villa in the cornfields. Low hanging boughs of acacia brushed the roof. Acacia petalled the car arrived." Thus Isa sees the dispersion not of the play but of the audience, and especially Haines, the gentleman farmer, who during the pageant becomes "the man in grey." The red villa in the cornfields is his house, and the allusion to it returns the narrative to the beginning. A dialectic is implied here too, between Giles (the name means *aegis*, shield or protection) and Haines (*haine* = hatred). This has its counterpart in the dialectic of love and hate which preoccupies Isa during the pageant, where the death of the beldame suddenly reveals to her the synthesis to which this dialectic leads: "Peace was the third emotion. Love. Hate. Peace. Three emotions made the ply of human life. Now the priest, whose cotton wool moustache confused his utterance, stepped forward and pronounced benediction." This helps to shape the horizon against which the final passage of the book emerges—Giles and Isa as dog fox and vixen: they must fight before they embrace, but from that embrace another life may be born. Although she has imagined herself "in love" with Haines, that feeling is really the complement of her feeling for Giles: she thinks of Haines at just those moments when she is feeling for Giles. And her husband *is*, ultimately, her shield and pro-

---

relations to his "worlds"—both the "real" world in which he is incarnate and the imagined world which he brings into incarnation.

Like *The Tempest*, *Between the Acts* is a drama of reconciliation—of human life with the forces of nature, of the generations with each other, of the individual with his heritage and his destiny—and, perhaps, of the artist with the inevitable final silence of art itself.

tector, just as Haines is the embodiment of her hatred—a means, entirely in fantasy, of escape from the sometimes overwhelming presence
of Giles. Her husband evokes both her love and her hatred, and, at
least potentially, her peace. "Acacia petalled the car arrived": the phantom bridegroom cometh, in the romantic poetry of her imagination.

After a further, perfunctory gesture toward a discussion of the
pageant's meaning, the subject is closed. The familiar dialectic of love
and hate is then dramatized in a blatant parody of Freudian imagery:
"Here, with its sheaf sliced in four, exposing a white cone, Giles offered his wife a banana. She refused it. He stubbed his match on the
plate. Out it went with a little fizz in the raspberry juice." Mrs.
Swithin, never at a loss for something to fill the silence, remarks on
the "weather, which was perfect, save for one shower." Ironically, the
shower had saved the pageant by bridging the second of the two crises
of silence ("death" when the "illusion failed"); in that sense it had
reclaimed the wastelands of failing imagination.

The family continues to resist the deepening twilight: "They
never pulled the curtains till it was too dark to see, nor shut the windows till it was too cold. Why shut out the day before it was over?"
But Mrs. Swithin turns toward the shadows of another work of art,
"the great picture of Venice—school of Canaletto. Possibly in the
hood of the gondola there was a little figure—a woman veiled; or a
man?" There seem to be two kinds of paintings in *Between the Acts*:
historical portraits of ancestors, which lead the viewers into talk; and
more mysterious pictures, which lead the viewers into silence. The
two types are exemplified by the paintings which hang opposite the
window in the dining room: "The lady was a picture, bought by
Oliver because he liked the picture; the man was an ancestor. He had
a name. . . . He was a talk producer, that ancestor. But the lady was a
picture. In her yellow robe . . . she led the eye up, down, from the
curve to the straight, through glades of greenery and shades of silver,
dun and rose into silence. The room was empty." William Dodge,
whom Mrs. Manresa calls an artist but who insists that he is a clerk in
an office (which may mean that he is an artist in need of money), likes
the picture. And indeed its lady seems to preside over the dining
room: "They all looked at the lady. But she looked over their heads,

looking at nothing. She led them down green glades into the heart of silence." This is the heart of darkness at the center of all of Virginia Woolf's works, from *The Voyage Out* to *Between the Acts*, which the characters are drawn toward, but from which they cannot return: like Rachel and Rhoda, they die there. (And that is another meaning of the "peace" that they seek.) And so the company is glad to escape from the dining room, in the wake of the hearty Mrs. Manresa, who can't be bothered with these inner mysteries: "now they could follow in her wake and leave the silver and dun shades that led to the heart of silence." There is another lady, in another picture, who presides over the stairs to the bedrooms. Dodge and Mrs. Swithin pass her on their tour of the house. She too is mysterious: "'Not an ancestress. . . . But we claim her because we've known her—O, ever so many years. Who was she?' she gazed. 'Who painted her?' She shook her head. 'But I like her best in the moonlight.'" The dining room and the bedrooms, sacramental spaces, are almost always empty—and silent. Art leads us into, or at least invites us to enter, that emptiness and silence at the heart of every house.

The picture of Venice by the school of Canaletto is in a room whose function is not even named; it is called only "the big room," and is across the hall from the dining room. After dessert the family enters that room, ladies first—the occasion of Mrs. Swithin's stopping by the picture, whose hooded gondola prefigures the "great hooded chairs" of the room itself, in which Giles and Isa, in the gathering dusk, will reach the hugeness and indistinctness of archetypes. Here "the school of Canaletto" probably alludes to a work of one of the imitators of Canaletto, whose paintings of Venice were very popular in eighteenth-century England. Original Canalettos, though not likely to be found in places like Pointz Hall, are still well represented in England—at Windsor Castle, Woburn Abbey, Goodwood, the National Gallery, and the British Museum. Many of the paintings of Venice contain hooded gondolas in which seated figures can be glimpsed. Almost all of the exteriors of these scenes are bright, sunny, and full of activity; the allusion here seems to suggest that Lucy penetrates beyond that, into the mysteries of the quiet shadows. That is confirmed in other ways, of course: in her sensitivity to her brother's unspoken thoughts, or in her tactful withdrawal from the room so that Giles and Isa may revert to their roles of dog fox and vixen.

Now the two women settle into the "big room": "Isa . . . sank . . . into the chair by the window. Within the shell of the room she overlooked the summer night. Lucy returned from her voyage into the picture and stood silent. The sun made each pane of her glasses shine red. Silver sparkled on her black shawl. For a moment she looked like a tragic figure from another play." Mrs. Swithin is now Lucy once again—an indication that the narrative is now closer to her, and perhaps that it is more at ease when the men are not present. The suggestions of water imagery evoke the fluidity always characteristic of "the summer night" in the lifework. The "room," the existential space of the moment, is said to be a "shell"—an image which returns, subliminally, to the "heart of the house": "The room was a shell, singing of what was before time was; a vase stood in the heart of the house, alabaster, smooth, cold, holding the still, distilled essence of emptiness, silence." Lucy's experience with the picture is called a voyage, rather like Miss La Trobe's "voyage away from the shore" and the familiar voyage out of the visionary into the realm of silence throughout the *oeuvre*, so that it is fitting that Lucy, after her return, "stood silent." The illumination in the next two sentences seems more mysterious, but not entirely obscure, since it too, symbolically, is connected with many other phenomena in the book, and in the other books. The sun, important symbolically throughout those books, reached its fullest significance as a complex symbol in *The Waves*: there it makes possible the emergence and differentiation of all life, but it is also indifferent toward that life; at noon the sun is perceived as "uncompromising, undeniable," and Percival suddenly dies. Even now, at twilight in *Between the Acts*, the sun has that kind of power: Isa's "hand burnt in the sun on the window sill." The sun on Lucy's glasses, then, has something of that quality too—as if her vision were, for that moment, as searching and undeniable as the sun itself at noon in *The Waves*. The narrative sees not her eyes but her glasses, which "shine red"—implying that her vision is radiant with life, sexuality, vitality. The silver sparkling on her black shawl defines Lucy's "moment" on the scale of color (*i.e.*, light) called "brilliance"[8]; it also links this moment with Lucy's moment of epiphany by the lily pool, when "she had a glimpse of silver—the great carp himself, who came to the surface so very seldom," but is suddenly manifest now in "her private vision; of beauty which is goodness; the sea on which we float." Now, in the dusk, "For a moment she looked like a tragic figure from another play"; again the narrative begins to lose its specificity, to merge into the immanent realm of archetype: the reference is not to some specific drama, but to all drama, and especially, to the inevitable recurrence of drama—in a foreshadowing of the epiphany with which the book, and the lifework, will end.

Lucy makes the effort to come back from that realm, and raises the subject of the pageant once again, trying to anchor her feelings in the mundane: "Then she spoke in her usual voice. 'We made more this year than last, he said. But then last year it rained.'" But Isa is now on her own voyage out: "'This year, last year, next year, never . . .' Isa murmured." Lucy continues to try to explore the mystery, asking whether Isa felt that, as the Reverend Mr. Streatfield had said, in interpreting the pageant in his closing remarks, "we act different parts but are the same?"

"Yes," Isa answered. "No," she added. It was Yes, No, Yes, yes, yes, the tide rushed out embracing. No, no, no, it contracted. The old boot appeared on the shingle.

"Orts, scraps and fragments," she quoted what she remembered of the vanishing play.

Again the narrative moves toward patterns of triads and opposing polarities: the dialectic of opposing forces, opposing emotions, whose synthesis is life itself. The imagery is like that of *The Waves*, even to the old boot on the shingle—left over, perhaps, from Interludes 5 and 8, where it seemed to symbolize the way in which nature reclaims all

8 Brilliance is the dimension of color which goes from black to white. The other two dimensions are hue (the angular position on the "color wheel") and saturation (the relative distance from neutral gray toward "pure" color). Silver, as I mentioned in note 6, implies death—here for England too, perhaps, as well as for Lucy herself.

human efforts and artifacts. Here it leads naturally into the lines of the pageant which Isa is recalling, in which the final voice, "megaphonic, anonymous, loud-speaking," asks how what we *"call, perhaps miscall, civilization"* is *"to be built by* (here the mirrors flicked and flashed) *orts, scraps and fragments like ourselves?"* That profound pessimism speaks to something very deep within Isa, the despair against which Giles is no shield at all. Of all the lines of the play which has, like every insubstantial pageant, faded into the cultural unconscious, these are the ones that she remembers. Somehow Lucy senses Isa's despair, and wishes to comfort her, but is interrupted: "Lucy had just opened her lips to reply, and had laid her hand on her cross caressingly, when the gentlemen came in. She made her little chirruping sound of welcome. She shuffled her feet to clear a space. But in fact there was more space than was needed, and great hooded chairs." Her instinctive caressing of her cross is a characteristic gesture; from the first time that she appears in the narrative her gold cross is seen as the climactic emblem of her identity, and she reaches for it as she does for the resources of her faith. Her other actions here are instinctive too: her sound of welcome, her symbolic clearing of a space. For although the "big room" contains more physical space than is needed, Lucy's gesture opens the necessary existential space. The "great hooded chairs" recall her "voyage" into the "picture of Venice" in which she searched "the hood of the gondola" and links it with the final epiphany, when "The great hooded chairs had become enormous."

In the next paragraph the men sit down, "ennobled both of them by the setting sun. Both had changed." This is the sun that had ennobled Lucy and displayed her visionary quality; now it begins to touch Bart and Giles with its mysterious light and to transform them from specific, limited men into archetypes: grandfather and father. Isa looks at Giles' feet, which are now in "patent leather pumps" rather than the white sneakers which he had bloodied in his angry crushing of the "monstrous inversion" during the first interval of the pageant. The fact that "Both had changed" refers not only to their clothes, but to their transformation into archetypes by the setting sun of the narrative perspective. Isa senses this transformation, surely, as she thinks, "'The father of my children, whom I love and hate.' Love and hate—

how they tore her asunder! Surely it was time someone invented a new plot, or that the author came out from the bushes." Thus the dialectic of love-hate-peace emerges once again, even though Isa isn't yet conscious of the third term, but only of her anguish. Yet the exasperated humor of the final sentence suggests that the process is continuing, and that the synthesis isn't out of reach. The sentence also indirectly identifies "the author" as Miss La Trobe, and even more indirectly raises the question of "plot." All stories are essentially the same, it seems to imply, because there is only one story—and all that an author can do is to confront that fact, and express it with whatever skill is at hand.

Once again everyday "reality" intrudes, reasserting itself against the gathering darkness. Candish brings in the "second post": "letters; bills; and the morning paper—the paper that had obliterated the day before. Like a fish rising to a crumb of biscuit, Bartholomew snapped at the paper," confirming the vague identification of him with the great carp ("It was always 'my brother . . . my brother' who rose from the depths of her lily pool"). The paper, with its ordering and explanation of the random phenomena of national and international experience, nevertheless "obliterates" our sense of continuity by its focus on the immediate. The events which it describes are no more meaningful now than they were in the morning, when Bart had read that M. Daladier had stabilized the franc and Isa had read about the horse guards enticing a girl into their barracks in Whitehall. The franc may be stable, but Europe is not, and the terror of the girl in the barracks persists in Isa's imagination because she too knows the sudden, irrational violence of men, even though the "case" at Whitehall may be closed. It is she, more than any of the others, who now embodies the narrative consciousness: "Sitting in the shell of the room she watched the pageant fade"—not only Miss La Trobe's pageant, but the insubstantial pageant of life itself, here in this room. In her eyes Bart, Giles, and Lucy become fabulous: "the grasshopper, the ant, and the beetle, rolling pebbles of sun-baked earth through the glistening stubble."[9]

9   These three insects appear in fables from the time of Aesop on, but not, so far as I have found, all together in the same fable. By the time of La Fontaine in the seventeenth century, some animals had become emblematic of human traits (the fox is sly, the ass

One by one the members of the family relax their grips on consciousness. Bart drops his newspaper, Giles retrieves it. The house itself seems to alter: "The clock ticked. The house gave little cracks as if it were very brittle, very dry. Isa's hand on the window felt suddenly cold. Shadow had obliterated the garden. Roses had withdrawn for the night." This is the eternal night, an undifferentiated darkness from which all emerges and to which all returns, as in *The Waves*. Lucy, as if she were aware that the roses have withdrawn for the night, must replace them with the paper roses in the nursery:

> Mrs. Swithin folding her letter murmured to Isa: "I looked in and saw the babies, sound asleep, under the paper roses."
> "Left over from the coronation," Bartholomew muttered, half asleep.
> "But we needn't have been to all that trouble with the decorations," Lucy added, "for it didn't rain this year."
> "This year, last year, next year, never," Isa murmured.
> "Tinker, tailor, soldier, sailor," Bartholomew echoed. He was talking in his sleep.

Several themes return for the last time in this passage, uttered thoughtlessly, almost unconsciously, by the characters. The coronation is that of George VI (May 12, 1937); the fact that decorations left over from it are used for the pageant is mentioned early in the book and several times thereafter; other villages have done the same thing. Such references are only one way in which the book reveals the love which the people in it—all of them, without exception—have for their country, which will very shortly have to lay a heavy claim upon them.

---

patient, etc.). The grasshopper and the ant, in the first fable in La Fontaine's first book, embody the opposite philosophies of immediate gratification and of foresighted industry; like the *gracehoper* and the *ondt* in Joyce's final fabulation, they represent the essential human ambivalence. In another fable of La Fontaine derived from Aesop, a beetle achieves an ingenious victory over an eagle by dropping dung on the robe of Jove. And in another of Aesop's fables about an ant and a beetle, the latter scorns the ant's patient industry. The rather crude characterizations in these fables aren't inconsistent with what we know of Bart, Giles, and Lucy—and can provide an extra dimension of comic resonance. But the paragraph really characterizes Isa, in whose consciousness these three persons are transformed into grasshopper, ant, and beetle. Her mind often seems to lapse into the mode of fable—in her spontaneous verses she and the people around her are often transformed into something like the creatures of fable: *e.g.*, "On, little donkey. . . ."

Lucy's comment that "it didn't rain this year" isn't strictly correct, but the fact that she doesn't remember the rain shows that she accepted it as part of the pageant. Isa's nonsense refrain which arises from Lucy's remark echoes an earlier moment, where the refrain revealed that for Isa this time is merging into all time. And Bart's "talking in his sleep" "echoed" Isa's refrain. This motif first appeared when Mrs. Manresa, at lunch, started the game of counting the cherry stones and old Bart responded by "chaffing" her. The stones are consulted for the destinies of the diners; it is nonsense, of course, but fun—and the point, if there is one, may be that all destinies are the same, or, perhaps, that "destinies" are irrelevant. In its final appearance the refrain seems more important just as sound—like the refrain ("Sinbad the Sailor and Tinbad the Tailor and Whinbad the Whaler . . . ") echoing in the mind of Bloom as he falls asleep at the end of the Ithaca episode of *Ulysses*. And so it is here too: not only Bart, but the narrative consciousness too, is approaching the rhythms of sleep.

Now that consciousness shifts toward Lucy: "It was time to read now, her Outline of History. But she had lost her place." She isn't alone: everyone in *Between the Acts* has lost his place in history. The emphasis on English literary history in the pageant attempts to re-cover and celebrate the meaning of English history in the face of the coming apocalypse. The book that Lucy turns to, presumably, is H. G. Wells's *The Outline of History*. Perhaps its use too is ironic: his "rational" explanation of history doesn't seem to fit the irrationality into which Europe was falling in 1939. On the other hand, Wells's longer view was pessimistic, although his deepest pessimism came after the war. Or perhaps Lucy's volume itself is mythical: it is like a child's picture-book history in which she finds her place by searching through the pictures. And when she finds it, nature itself seems to become darker and colder: "The darkness increased. The breeze swept round the room. With a little shiver Mrs. Swithin drew her sequin shawl about her shoulders. She was too deep in the story to ask for the window to be shut. 'England,' she was reading, 'was then a swamp. Thick forests covered the land. On top of their matted branches birds sang.'" The existential space of the story itself has become dark and drafty. Lucy is seen more impersonally, as Mrs.

Swithin, but also as part of "the story" and merging with the dark, cold space that is not only this "room," but England itself on the eve of its nightmare. The words she is reading come not from any actual history book but from the realm of poetry, and sustain a vaguely elegiac tone: it is all in the past, lost beyond recall, and the progression from England to swamp to forests to branches and birds seems a fading and a diminishing, the feeling of Shakespeare's Sonnet 73, with its "Bare ruined choirs where late the sweet birds sang."

This kind of imagery is intensified in the next paragraph: "The great square of the open window showed only sky now. It was drained of light, severe, stone cold. Shadows fell. Shadows crept over Bartholomew's high forehead; over his great nose. He looked leafless, spectral, and his chair monumental. As a dog shudders its skin, his skin shuddered. He rose, shook himself, glared at nothing, and stalked from the room. They heard the dog's paws padding on the carpet behind him." The window now shows only sky: the illumination is gone, and the outside world has become entropic, undifferentiated. The description of old Bart as "leafless" enhances the Sonnet 73 feeling. The words *spectral* and *monumental* further soften the focus as the scene continues to fade into archetype. Bart's rising anticipates what Lucy will read about prehistoric man: his actions are described at an animal level. The fact that "They heard" the dog, rather than saw him, intensifies that feeling—as if the perceiving consciousness were in a darkness where it can only hear the movements of possible predators (*shook*, *glared*, and *stalked* contribute to this too). And the closeness of the family is implied: there is no need to look for the dog because they all know that it is there.

Now the narrative renders the unspoken intimacy between Bart and Lucy:

Lucy turned the page, quickly, guiltily, like a child who will be told to go to bed before the end of the chapter.

"Prehistoric man," she read, "half-human, half-ape, roused himself from his semi-crouching position and raised great stones."

She slipped the letter from Scarborough between the pages to mark the end of the chapter, rose, smiled, and tiptoed silently out of the room.

Her response to Bart's leaving here is reminiscent of an earlier moment, at the end of the first interval of the pageant: Bart "knocked the ash off his cheroot and rose. 'So we must,' said Lucy; as if he had said aloud, 'It's time to go.'"

Lucy's reading about "prehistoric man" comments ironically on Bart's departure from the room, as he "rose, shook himself, glared at nothing, and stalked from the room." Modern man is not so far removed from the first ancestor who stood upright as we would wish to believe. The allusion to Stonehenge makes the implication specifically English, and prepares for the opening out into the "fields of night" at the end, where Giles and Isa will enact their "prehistoric" roles. The "criss-cross from an old friend at Scarborough" is more opaque. Perhaps we should listen for an echo of the original *Christ's cross*, the symbol which Lucy is always caressing. In *Jacob's Room* the Roman ruins at Scarborough are rather important; perhaps the "great stones" of Stonehenge naturally lead the narrative consciousness to Scarborough. Lucy's departure from the room is in a rather marked contrast to her brother's, and that contrast, in a way, prepares for the final antithesis—and synthesis—which ends the book.

The old people had gone up to bed. Giles crumpled the newspaper and turned out the light. Left alone for the first time that day, they were silent. Alone, enmity was bared; also love. Before they slept, they must fight; after they had fought, they would embrace. From that embrace another life might be born. But first they must fight, as the dog fox fights the vixen, in the heart of darkness, in the fields of night.

Bart and Lucy are now *the old people*, and the narrative sees them from the perspective of Giles and Isa, even though the narrative consciousness maintains some distance from the younger couple too. Giles's treatment of the newspaper and the light seem to comment, indirectly, on the values of "civilization" as opposed to the imperatives of the impending night. Now the narrative observes the couple and their silence, and comments rather directly on their relationship. Earlier it might have entered into Isa's consciousness, but it has now begun the withdrawal which will place the drama in its final perspective. Its conscious concern is still with the dialectic of love and hate, and it states, more directly than usual, the possible outcome of that dialectic. Then, as if to soften its own explicitness, it withdraws into metaphor: dog fox and vixen—not too extreme a way to summarize the animal feelings that have seethed all afternoon between Giles and Isa, it conveys something of their natural grace too. The "heart of darkness" is reminiscent of Conrad, and of *The Voyage Out*, in which the phrase appears several times. In "the fields of night" the feeling of darkness opens out, like the feeling of Whitman, and perhaps the *Rubaiyat*.[10] Night is now dominant. The imagery of atavism and of night foreshadows the fate of Europe in the fall of 1939.

The perspective becomes increasingly archetypal: "Isa let her sewing drop. The great hooded chairs had become enormous. And Giles too. And Isa too against the window. The window was all sky without colour. The house had lost its shelter. It was night before roads were made, or houses. It was the night that dwellers in caves had watched from some high place among rocks." Just as Giles's crumpling the newspaper and turning out the light had initiated the events of the previous paragraph, so Isa's letting her sewing drop enables the process to continue here. The scene dissolves. And there is another cinematographic shift in perspective: the eternal night itself is said to be seen "from some high place." It is the same perspective from which *The Waves* emerges at the beginning, and to which it returns at the end. And it is also the perspective, of course, from which Miss La Trobe had envisioned this very scene.

Within the paragraph there are other interesting effects, all related to the phenomenology of the narrative consciousness. "The great hooded chairs," as we saw earlier, seem related to the hooded

10   The final edition of Fitzgerald's *The Rubáiyát of Omar Khayyám* opens with this famous quatrain:

Wake! For the Sun who scatter'd into flight
The Stars before him from the Field of night,
Drives Night along with them from Heav'n and strikes
The Sultan's Turret with a Shaft of Light.

The phrase does not appear in Whitman. Still, the feeling of "the fields of night" is one of ultimacy, of a world of final archetypes in which the most primal instincts find their expression. That is the world of poetry.

gondola which Lucy had inspected in the "great picture of Venice," looking in its shadows for a human "figure—a woman, veiled; or a man?" Now the chairs themselves will not stay in their proper (*i.e.,* daylight) perspective, but become "enormous"—as objects sometimes do when consciousness enters that mysterious realm between sleep and waking, or during a fever; the shift is also appropriate, of course, as a sign of the significance of this man and this woman. Isa is seen against the window—the setting for the most womanly of all of Virginia Woolf's women, Mrs. Ramsay, and a sign of Isa's confirmation as a woman. The ancient mythic personification of sky and earth as male and female may also be operating here; Isa must be seen "against" the window and the sky, yet the window, the narrative has reminded us earlier, is open—always a sign, in the lifework, of an openness in consciousness too, in awareness and in relation to the ambient environment. The fact that the sky is "without colour" shows that differentiation has faded entirely. "The house had lost its shelter" also reveals that this transformation is in consciousness: the house is seen as no longer sheltering. One of the first things we learn about Pointz Hall is that it is a comfortable house, built in a hollow—in other words, built for shelter rather than for a view. So the implication now is that not even this most sheltering of houses can prevent the merging of this man and this woman into the eternal night. The last two sentences of the book seek the essence of that night.

Then the curtain rose. They spoke.

The last words of the book complete the process of the opening out and the dissolution of perspective. Nothing specific remains except the eternal drama of consciousness itself. In a sense, these lines reveal that everything in the final section of *Between the Acts* is the drama that Miss La Trobe had envisioned when "She heard the first words" at the end of the penultimate section. In another sense, the ending is about a larger creative process: a creative consciousness envisioning a consciousness envisioning a dramatic action—the infinitely regressive "subject" of modern art.

In this final section the narrative consciousness sees the personalities largely from the outside. It reports what they do, and what they say to each other. Yet it is closer to some than to others, more "privileged" with respect to some than to others—and these distances help to constitute the story: they are an important part of what it is about. In the final section Mrs. Manresa and William Dodge have left, and the focus is now on the permanent residents of Pointz Hall: Bartholomew Oliver and Lucy Swithin, Giles Oliver and Isabella, the older and the younger "couples" in the story. Throughout the final section the men are seen entirely from the outside, and at some distance. The "camera" of the narrative is much closer to the two women, and at times becomes incarnate in Isa's consciousness. This is first apparent in Isa's thoughts about Haines and his arrival at the villa in his "acacia petalled" car.

Momentarily it seems to share Lucy's speculation about the picture of Venice, but essentially it still observes, rather than enters, her personality: it describes what "she looked like" and what she says. The subsequent penetrations into Isa's mind are deeper and more extensive. But the narrative point of view is not entirely stable within this final section: its distances from each character vary as the narrative explores the scene.

Toward the end of the section the narrative seems to enter Lucy's mind once again as she reads "her Outline of History." Yet the words quoted are not from *The Outline of History* by H. G. Wells, which presumably is what she is reading (with its pictures of "mammoths, mastodons, prehistoric birds"). Nor are the narrative's observations of her always compatible with what she herself might be aware of: *e.g.*, "She was too deep in the story to ask for the window to be shut," or she "turned the page quickly, guiltily, like a child." Such things are, instead, compatible with what Isa might notice. And the words quoted from the *Outline of History* seem to express what Isa might imagine that work to say (Wells wrote it, he says, "plainly for the general reader," but not quite so plainly as this passage in *Between the Acts* imagines it).

The closing paragraphs, too, are largely compatible with Isa's point of view. She would see Lucy slip the letter from Scarborough into the book (Isa would know where it was from, since her bills were on the same silver salver), rise, smile, and tiptoe from the room. She would feel then that "The old people had gone up to bed." She would see Giles crumple the newspaper and turn out the light. She would feel the emotional currents between her husband and herself which the narrative then describes. She would then "let her sewing drop" and could become aware of the perspective which is described thereafter—though "And Isa too against the window" does seem to show that the narrative has now withdrawn from her as well. That too would be fitting, since the narrative could not possibly remain with Isa for the encounter between dog fox and vixen. But throughout the scene, the narrative has been closer to her than to any of the other characters, and the fact that it must take refuge in these abstractions at the end shows, paradoxically perhaps, how deeply it is involved with her.

In the end, then, the narrative consciousness can't discover for itself a wholly authentic human existence. There is no Molly Bloom whose voice could fill the darkness on which the final curtain rises. Isa herself goes too gently into that good night, despite the rhetorical allusion to dog fox and vixen.

Miss La Trobe (the name itself seems cognate with trouble, and perhaps troubadour, the itinerant artist) is the rather grotesque figure in whom insight into this realm of darkness is said to be embodied. We see only scraps and fragments of that vision, through the medium of the pageant itself, and partly, perhaps, in the reflexive final revelation that her vision encompasses the realms of existence of the characters in residence in Pointz Hall. She is the last in a long line of visionaries—from St. John Hirst at the end of *The Voyage Out* through Eleanor Pargiter at the end of *The Years*—who emerge in the final stillness of Virginia Woolf's novels to announce, never altogether convincingly, that they have had their visions. And of all these characters Miss La Trobe is probably the one whose authenticity is most in doubt. What little we know about her we know almost entirely at second hand.

The mysteriousness of her origins suggests a kind of wonder with which the narrative consciousness regards her appearance. Where does she come from? What are the conditions which call her forth? How should other personalities "relate to" the artist? Miss La Trobe first shows up rather late (in the fifteenth section of the book), and we don't learn much about her until the next-to-last section. There we discover that she is a lesbian, that she drinks too much, that she is an "outcast," or that she feels that she is, and so on. We don't really see her interacting with any of the other major characters except Lucy, whose praise moves her: "Glory possessed her." Yet that seems rather abstract: the narrative doesn't render Miss La Trobe's feeling, but tells about it instead. That too is typical of the curious distance that the narrative maintains from her throughout the book. It removes her from the final scene while implying that the scene itself *is* her consciousness.

Between the Acts can be seen as the drama of six characters in search of a seventh, who enters the drama late, or is discovered late—and is revealed by the drama itself as its author. From another point of view the book can be seen as the search of that author for her story. These views are only seemingly opposite, of course—different perspectives on the same drama of intentionality. The six characters—Bart and Lucy, Giles and Isa, William Dodge and Mrs. Manresa—are in search of the seventh, Miss La Trobe, who is also in a sense searching for them. In the end she creates a scene in which the extraneous (the social world, Dodge and Manresa) has been bracketed, suspended, and the essential world of the family emerges at last. This too is then reduced to its essence: Giles and Isa, man and woman, dog fox and vixen, in the heart of darkness, in the fields of night. The relationship of the seventh character to all of this remains unspoken, as does the relationship of all that to the larger creative consciousness whose drama this is.

At last the book itself, like the pageant within it, must merge into its horizons. And its final words, "they spoke," open into that realm of the unspoken: the book and the lifework close on that threshold between language and silence. The narrative consciousness of the lifework completes its archetypal journey, classically defined by Stephen Dedalus: "The personality of the artist, at first a cry or a cadence or a mood and then a fluid and lambent narrative, finally refines itself out of existence, impersonalizes itself, so to speak." From the lyric cry of

The Voyage Out to the impersonal drama of *Between the Acts* the narrative consciousness has come very far indeed. In this last book it discovers once again the impossibility of transcendence through literary creation, but once again reveals the compelling necessity and the strange beauty of the effort itself, a necessity and a beauty which we recognize as transcendent despite everything we know.

Between the Acts: the title itself implies an awareness of the essence of art: a dramatization of the search for the ineffable. Its meanings are discovered between the acts of the dramatist, the actors, and the audience, in the dynamics of intentionality, the "consciousness of." Merleau-Ponty has described this process in his essay on Husserl: "To think is not to possess the objects of thought; it is to use them to mark out a realm to think about which we therefore are not yet thinking about. Just as the perceived world endures only through the reflections, shadows, levels, and horizons between things . . . so the works and thought of a philosopher are also made of certain articulations between things said. . . . we can be faithful to and find them only by thinking again."[11] Modern fiction, too, records the struggle to make the silence speak. And that speech can be heard only by "thinking again," along with the questing *consciousness of* which is the narrative itself. Beginning as the dramatization of the twilight of a way of life, *Between the Acts* explores the complex relationships between the acts of individuals in that culture and the pageantry which is both cause and effect of their civilization, and ends as the revelation of the intentionality of the dramatization itself. That is the fullest revelation in the lifework. And it is therefore final.

11 Maurice Merleau-Ponty, "The Philosopher and His Shadow," in *Signs*, trans. Richard C. McCleary (Evanston, Ill.: Northwestern University Press, 1964), 160.

SOURCES CITED

For more comprehensive bibliographies, see the annual *MLA International Bibliography*; Barbara Weiser, "Criticism of Virginia Woolf from 1956 to the Present," *Modern Fiction Studies*, XVIII (1972), 477–86; and Robin Majumdar, *Virginia Woolf: An Annotated Bibliography of Criticism, 1915–1974* (New York: Garland, 1976).

Ariosto, Ludovico. *Orlando Furioso*. Translated by Allan Gilbert. New York: S. F. Vanni, 1954.

———. *"Orlando Furioso" in English Heroical Verse*. Translated by John Harington (1591). Edited by Robert McNulty. Oxford: Clarendon, 1972.

———. *Orlando Furioso*. Translated by Barbara Reynolds. Harmondsworth: Penguin, 1975. Vol. I.

———. *Orlando Furioso*. Translated by Guido Waldman. Oxford: Oxford University Press, 1974.

Bachelard, Gaston. *The Poetics of Reverie*. Translated by Daniel Russell. Originally published in 1960. Boston: Beacon Press, 1971.

Baldanza, Frank. "Orlando and the Sackvilles." *PMLA*, LXX (1955), 274–79.

Beckett, Samuel. *Proust*. Originally published in 1931. New York:

Grove Press, 1958.

Bell, Quentin. *Virginia Woolf: A Biography*. New York: Harcourt, 1972.

Blackstone, Bernard. *Virginia Woolf: A Commentary*. Originally published in 1949. New York: Harcourt, 1972.

Booth, Wayne C. *The Rhetoric of Fiction*. Chicago: University of Chicago Press, 1961.

Dupee, F. W. *Henry James*. New York: William Sloane, 1951.

Fleishman, Avrom. *Virginia Woolf: A Critical Reading*. Baltimore: Johns Hopkins University Press, 1975.

Guiguet, Jean. *Virginia Woolf and Her Works*. Translated by Jean Stewart. Originally published in 1963. New York: Harcourt, 1976.

Hafley, James. *The Glass Roof: Virginia Woolf as Novelist*. Originally published in 1954. New York: Russell & Russell, 1963.

Harper, Howard M., Jr. "Mrs. Woolf and Mrs. Dalloway," in *The Classic British Novel*. Edited by Howard M. Harper, Jr., and Charles Edge. Athens: University of Georgia Press, 1972.

Hartmann, Geoffrey. "Virginia's Web." *Chicago Review*, XIV (Spring, 1961), 2–32. Reprinted in *Twentieth Century Interpretations of "To the Lighthouse."* Edited by Thomas A. Vogler. Englewood Cliffs, N.J.: Prentice-Hall, 1970.

Jullian, Phillippe, and John Phillips. *The Other Woman: A Life of Violet Trefusis*. Boston: Houghton Mifflin, 1976.

Laing, R. D. *The Divided Self*. New York: Random House, 1969.

———. *The Politics of Experience*. New York: Ballantine, 1968.

Lavin, J. A. "The First Editions of Virginia Woolf's *To the Lighthouse*." *Proof*, II (1972), 185–211.

Lawrence, D. H. *Studies in Classic American Literature*. Originally published in 1923. New York: Viking, 1964.

Leaska, Mitchell A. "Virginia Woolf's *The Voyage Out*: Character Deduction and the Function of Ambiguity." *Virginia Woolf Quarterly*, I (Winter, 1973), 18–41.

Lévi-Strauss, Claude. *The Raw and the Cooked: Introduction to a Science of Mythology*. Translated by John and Doreen Weightman. Originally published in 1964. New York: Harper, 1969.

Lüscher, Max. *The Lüscher Color Test*. Translated and edited by Ian A.

Scott. Originally published in 1948. New York: Random House, 1969.

Merleau-Ponty, Maurice. *The Prose of the World*. Edited by Claude Lefort. Translated by John O'Neill. Originally published in 1969. Evanston: Northwestern University Press, 1973.

———. *Signs*. Translated by Richard C. McCleary. Originally published in 1959. Evanston, Ill.: Northwestern University Press, 1964.

Naremore, James. *The World Without a Self: Virginia Woolf and the Novel*. New Haven: Yale University Press, 1973.

Nicolson, Nigel. *Portrait of a Marriage*. New York: Atheneum, 1973.

Novak, Jane. *The Razor Edge of Balance: A Study of Virginia Woolf*. Coral Gables: University of Miami Press, 1974.

Richter, Harvena. *Virginia Woolf: The Inward Voyage*. Princeton: Princeton University Press, 1970.

de Rougemont, Denis. *Love in the Western World*. Translated by Montgomery Belgion. Originally published in 1940. Revised ed. New York: Fawcett, 1966.

Sackville-West, V. *Knole and the Sackvilles*. Originally published in 1922. 4th ed. London: Ernest Benn, 1976.

[Sackville-West, V., and later editors]. *Knole*. Plaistow: The National Trust, 1976.

Schorer, Mark. "Technique as Discovery." *Hudson Review*, I (1948), 67–87.

Swain, Deborah E. "Feeling and Form in Virginia Woolf's *The Waves*." M.A. thesis, University of North Carolina at Chapel Hill, 1975.

Trautmann, Joanne. *The Jessamy Brides: The Friendship of Virginia Woolf and V. Sackville-West*. University Park: Pennsylvania State University Press, 1973.

Woolf, Virginia. *Between the Acts*. London: Hogarth, 1941.

———. *Books and Portraits: Some Further Selections from the Literary and Biographical Writings of Virginia Woolf*. Edited by Mary Lyon. London: Hogarth, 1977.

———. *Collected Essays*. 4 vols. New York: Harcourt, 1967.

———. *The Diary of Virginia Woolf.* Edited by Anne Olivier Bell. Introduction by Quentin Bell. 5 vols. New York: Harcourt, 1977--.

———. *A Haunted House and Other Short Stories.* London: Hogarth, 1943.

———. *Jacob's Room.* London: Hogarth, 1922.

———. *Moments of Being: Unpublished Autobiographical Writings.* Edited by Jeanne Schulkind. New York: Harcourt, 1976.

———. *Mrs. Dalloway.* London: Hogarth, 1925.

———. *Mrs. Dalloway's Party.* Edited by Stella McNichol. London: Hogarth, 1973.

———. *Night and Day.* London: Duckworth, 1919.

———. *Orlando.* London: Hogarth, 1928.

———. *The Pargiters.* Edited by Mitchell A. Leaska. New York: New York Public Library, 1977.

———. *To the Lighthouse.* London: Hogarth, 1927.

———. *The Voyage Out.* London: Duckworth, 1915.

———. *The Waves.* London: Hogarth, 1931.

———. *The Waves: The Two Holograph Drafts Transcribed and Edited by J. W. Graham.* Toronto: University of Toronto Press, 1976.

———. *The Years.* London: Hogarth, 1937.